LAW, POLITICS, AND LOCAL DEMOCRACY

# Law, Politics, and Local Democracy

IAN LEIGH

OXFORD
UNIVERSITY PRESS

*This book has been printed digitally and produced in a standard specification in order to ensure its continuing availability*

OXFORD
UNIVERSITY PRESS

Great Clarendon Street, Oxford OX2 6DP

Oxford University Press is a department of the University of Oxford.
It furthers the University's objective of excellence in research, scholarship, and education by publishing worldwide in

Oxford New York

Auckland Bangkok Buenos Aires Cape Town Chennai
Dar es Salaam Delhi Hong Kong Istanbul Karachi Kolkata
Kuala Lumpur Madrid Melbourne Mexico City Mumbai Nairobi
São Paulo Shanghai Taipei Tokyo Toronto



Published in the United States
by Oxford University Press Inc., New York



Reprinted 2004



ISBN 0-19-825698-1

Cover illustration: © David K. Harris

*For Sue*

# *Preface*

The purpose of this book is to consider how local authorities function as political institutions within a legal framework. The book should therefore be relevant to students and teachers of public law, public administration, and politics at undergraduate level and beyond. Although it is not intended as a practitioner work, I hope it will nevertheless be of interest to local government officers and councillors working at the interface of law and politics. The book is not concerned with the substantive law of the specialist fields within local governmnent, such as planning, highways, or social work; with the sole exception of education, to which some reference is made for illustrative purposes in Chapter 5, it is not concerned with the functions of councils at all. Rather, it discusses the procedural and political framework within which decisions affecting them are made by councillors and officers, courts, and other outside sources of control. Nor is it intended as a book on central–local relations. Although fascinating, that is terrain which has been well covered, especially by lawyers.[1] Indeed, part of my objective is to redress the balance, since modern academic lawyers often seem only to be interested in local government in terms of legal conflict with the centre.

More than any other area of the constitution, local government has undergone constant change over the past two decades. The Conservative legislation introducing compulsory competitive tendering, replacing rates with first the community charge and then the council tax, the structural reorganization of local councils (first with the abolition of the GLC and metropolitan counties and then with the creation of unitary authorities), the outlawing of political propaganda and restricting the rights of officers, and the increasing emphasis on rights for users of local services, have all left an enduring legacy. Meanwhile, the actions of some local authorities on the municipal left and the new right have tested the legal limits of local democracy to the full. Over the same period the courts have been preoccupied with numerous conflicts arising directly from party politics in local government, for instance the GLC ('fares fair') case, the disqualification of the Liverpool and Lambeth councillors, the 'interest rates swaps' case, and the litigation from the 'homes for votes' scandal in Westminster. The Labour Government has initiated further changes with the 'best value' regime, the creation of a new strategic authority for London, the reform of executive structures, by introducing elected mayors and cabinets in local authorities, and new powers for councils to become 'community leaders',

[1] See M. Loughlin, *Legality and Locality: The Role of Law in Central–Local Government* (Oxford, 1996).

working in partnership with other public, private, and voluntary bodies within their areas. Moreover, other aspects of the constitutional reform programme, especially devolution, regionalism, and freedom of information, have substantial implications for local government.

This study assesses these and other developments in terms of the underlying questions they raise about the nature of local democracy and its legal recognition. It considers the competing and legally interlocking claims of local representative democracy, financial accountability, and consumerism and their implications for the governing structures of local authorities and for local electors, councillors, taxpayers, users of local services, and council employees. Finally, it asks whether the legal shape and powers of local government fit it for the changing role it is now asked to play.

The book is divided into four parts. Part I deals with the consititutional context in which councils operate. Chapter 1 is introductory in nature: it tries to identify the main sense in which councils are local democratic institutions and to assess their place in the broader constitutional order, especally in relation to regional and devolved authorities. It discusses the case for constitutional recognition of local government. The important topic of the position of councils as regards the courts is taken up in Chapter 2. This explores the significance of the distinctive legal form which local authorities take (corporate personality) and the implications of the ultra vires rule, together with proposals for its reform.

Part II considers the relationship between local authorities and the public. The legal regime for three patterns of accountability is explored here: the representative model, accountability to consumers of local services, and financial accountability to taxpayers. Chapter 3 is concerned with matters that necessarily underlie local representative democracy: the provision of information to the electorate. Freedom of information is an important aspect of this but it is only a part. The chapter therefore also considers public rights of observation in local government business and the legal regime for consultation and participation of the public in decision-making, including the use of such novel devices as local referendums, citizens' juries, and focus groups. Moreover, communication with the public is a two-way process, if only because local politicians hope to be re-elected. Broader controls on freedom of expression, especially those which prohibit the use of council resources in political advertising, are therefore discussed. Chapter 4 deals with financial accountability. This includes treatment of the local contribution to local government finance, rates, the community charge, and the council tax, the interaction of financial and democratic accountability, the common law trustee concept, and statutory accountability processes (powers to obtain information, to object to the accounts, the auditor and the surcharge). In Chapter 5 consumer accountability is addressed. The development of consumerist devices is perhaps the most important legacy to democratic practice of the past two decades, although consumerism is best seen as a difference of emphasis, and not as a wide-scale theory of government. The chapter examines the implications for local government of the Citizen's Charter and the statutory recognition of consumer choice, both individually and collectively, especially in the field of education (for example, in parental ballots and 'opt-outs' and in choice of school). Mechanisms for complaining about local services, both internal to local authorities and to the Local Ombudsman are placed within a democratic context.

In Part III the positions of party groups, of officers, and of the decision-making structures within the legal framework are examined. Chapter 6 considers the position of the party group, as regards the council as a whole, individual councillors (focusing especially on the issue of group discipline), and relationships between groups (a factor of some importance in 'hung' councils'). In Chapter 7 an overview of the legal framework for decision-making through delegation to committees and officers is presented. The strains on this framework in the position of 'backbench' councillors and 'hung' councils and from the introduction of compulsory competitive tendering are then considered. Finally, the chapter discusses the question of political leadership and current reform of executive structures, including the introduction of cabinets and of directly elected mayors. The (ostensibly) non-political role of officers is discussed in Chapter 8; after an examination of legal position as regards officer neutrality, special attention is given to the question of how officers may act as a safeguard against political and other abuse through 'whistle-blowing'.

Part IV discusses the 'external relations' of local authorities, by which I mean their relations with the local community, with business, with other public bodies, and with the voluntary sector. In Chapter 9 the contractual powers of local authorities are discussed. It evaluates the courts' attitude to the interaction of politics and contract, 'contract compliance', and the statutory exclusion of non-commercial criteria from contractual decision-making. Underlying these is a limited legal model of the role of local authorities, which sees their role purely as the effective or economical delivery of services. This is quite at variance with aspects of the new vision of councils as community leaders. Chapter 10 addresses this as a development of the concept of 'enabling authority'. It therefore examines the narrow version of enabling, involving the introduction of competitive tendering before looking to the more recent broader aspects, such as partnership with voluntary and private bodies and local quangos. The Conclusion reviews the three strands of the present government's democratic renewal programme: the 'best value' regime to replace compulsory competitive tendering; the reform of executive structures (including the introduction of cabinets and directly elected mayors); and new powers for councils to become 'community leaders', working in partnership with other public, private, and voluntary bodies, both under a new power to promote community well-being and under the 'Beacon' council scheme. It examines the tensions between these initiatives and the extent to which they amount to a coherent vision for local democracy within the changing UK constitution.

I have endeavoured to state the law up to the end of July 2000. While it has been possible to include reference to the Local Government Act 2000, the future of the Freedom of Information Bill 2000 was unclear at that time—all references are to the version of the Bill then published.

# *Acknowledgements*

This book would never have been written without the interest and enthusiasm for local government and politics first engendered during the years that I spent, before returning to academic life, working as a lawyer at Portsmouth City Council. I remain grateful to all those who gave me encouragement and wise counsel in the early stages of my career, and especially to Ronald Tweed, my principal. That was a different era. Much has changed in the intervening decade and a half, and nothing of my personal experience is recognizable in what follows. Nevertheless, perhaps the book may atone in some way for my desertion of the cause of local democracy.

I began work on this project during a period of research leave at Osgoode Hall Law School, at York University, Ontario—perhaps not an obvious place to reflect on the law of English municipalities. I am grateful to the faculty there for making my stay a valuable and stimulating one. Many people working in and around local government have responded helpfully to my inquiries, especially at the Local Government Information Unit, the Local Government Association, the Department of Environment Transport and Regions, Unison, the Commission for Local Administration, the Audit Commission, Public Concern at Work, and the Campaign for Freedom of Information. I have also trespassed on the hospitality of a number of academic colleagues with my requests, especially John Alder, Patrick Birkinshaw, Colin Crawford, Alison Dunn, Carl Emery, Barry Fitzpatrick, Tim Frazer, Joanna Gray, Reuben Hasson, Peter Hogg, Martin Loughlin, Laurence Lustgarten, Paul Meredith, Michael Purdue, Paula Stirling, Bob Sullivan, Colin Warbrick, and Robin Widdison. None of these, however, has seen the final text or is in any way responsible for it.

Some of the ideas here have been presented as papers at conferences on 'The Voluntary Sector and the State' at the University of York and 'Local Government and the Rule of Law' at the University of Bristol, and at meetings held under the auspices of the Society of Public Teachers of Law Public Law Group, the Local Government Information Unit, and the Socio-Legal Studies Association. I am grateful to all who commented or contributed. Some paragraphs from the text have appeared in *Public Law* and in the *Journal of Local Government Law*, and in my chapter 'The Legal Framework for Community Involvement' in A. Dunn (ed.), *The Voluntary Sector, the State and the Law* (Oxford, Hart, 2000). I am grateful for permission to reproduce them.

I am grateful also to Eilidh Gardner, Adrian Hoggarth, and James Watson for helping to locate many technical and obscure pieces of information, and to Newcastle Law School for the funding which made it possible to employ them under its summer research assistants scheme during my time there. At Durham, Nick Goodwin and Elena Martin-Salgado prepared the bibliography, table of cases, and table of statutes cheerfully and to a tight schedule. Generations of secretaries have skilfully manipulated my labyrinthine textual amendments, but I would particularly like to thank Alma Sotelo-Lewis at Osgoode Hall, Jo Milne at Newcastle, and Joanne Gillespie, Pauline Morris, Helen Hewitson, and Sheila Jobling at Durham. All these people have probably absorbed by osmosis more about local government law than they could have ever dreamed (or wished).

Apart from the emotional support and encouragement without which I would have abandoned hope of completing this project long ago, my wife, Sue, also gave much practical assistance in checking the text and preparing the tables. It is to her that I gratefully dedicate the end result.

# Contents

# *Abbreviations*

| | |
|---|---|
| CLA | Commission for Local Administration in England |
| CLD | Commission for Local Democracy |
| EAT | Employment Appeal Tribunal |
| GLA | Greater London Authority |
| GLA Act | Greater London Authority Act 1999 |
| GWA | Government of Wales Act |
| LCA | Local Commissioner for Administration |
| LGA | Local Government Act |
| LGHA | Local Government and Housing Act 1989 |
| RDA | Regional Development Agency |
| RDA Act | Regional Development Agencies Act 1998 |
| Widdicombe Report | *The Conduct of Local Authority Business*, Cmnd. 9797 (1986) |

# *Table of Cases*

**The United Kingdom**

**European Cases**

**ECJ**



**ECHR**



**Other Jurisdictions**

# *Table of Statutes*

**United Kingdom Acts**

Part I

# Legal and Political Foundations

# 1

# *Local Democracy in Its Constitutional Setting*

## INTRODUCTION

Constant experimentation and change are the enduring features of the local state. Whereas the essential structure of central government in the United Kingdom had (until devolution) remained remarkably stable in the last 150 years, local government has undergone a regular series of transformations.[1] These range from the single-purpose public authorities created by Victorian entrepreneurs and philanthropists to provide the essential social, health, educational, and transport infrastructure for the new industrial conurbations to the systematic division of the country into elected multi-purpose authorities, and to their decline and partial replacement over the past two decades by the ever-increasing range of quangos and appointed bodies.

Every feature of local government has proved contentious, from the range of the functions it undertakes to the form of body most appropriate for those functions, the most appropriate size and geographical domain, and the division of functions between different layers of authorities and the central state itself. In the last thirty years alone the structure of local government has been systematically reformed three times: with the partition of the country into metropolitan and non-metropolitan areas (with a different split of functions between the two tiers of councils in each case) in 1972, with the abolition of the Metropolitan Counties in 1986, and, most recently, with the review undertaken by the Local Government Commission and brought into effect from 1996.[2] The latter body

[1] An extended discussion of the development of local government is not appropriate here. The classic work is: S. Webb and B. Webb, *English Local Government* (London, 1922); for accounts by lawyers see: M. Loughlin, *Legality and Locality* (Oxford, 1996), ch. 1, and Sir I. Jennings, *Principles of Local Government Law* (4th ed., 1960, by J. Griffith), chs. 3 and 4 (a dazzling account which sets the developments against social history).

[2] Following this review, many urban areas in England, and the whole of Scotland and Wales, now have only one layer of local government. In England, most of these authorities have the appellation district, borough, or city council. In Wales there are some county unitary authorities, and district councils can also be called borough or city councils. These unitary authorities are responsible for all the local authority services within their area. However, in rural areas of England it is still common to find two layers (a district and a county council). The more important (and more expensive) functions are exercised by the counties (such as education and social services) whereas the districts are responsible for more localized services (e.g. housing, development control, and environmental health). The London boroughs exercise many of the powers of unitary authorities elsewhere in the country, but there is in addition a new, strategic, regional authority, the Greater London Authority.

epitomizes the point, since its statutory function is to review not merely the boundaries of local authorities at regular intervals but also the very structure itself.[3]

Change on this scale should not be a matter of surprise if it is remembered that one of the key arguments in favour of local government is to encourage experimentation. However, few of these changes can be explained as part of the pattern of organic growth: many have been imposed from above. Local government enjoys no constitutionally privileged position—there is nothing except the practical counter-arguments to prevent the abolition not merely of individual authorities or layers but of the very concept itself. This goes a long way to explain why it has been regularly changed to reflect the prevailing social and political mood of the nation, whereas the central state has proved more resistant.

While many people are broadly familiar with what local government is and what it does, identifying its essential characteristics is more difficult. One comparative survey considers and rejects criteria based on the geographical size and area of the authority (since these are meaningful only within the national system in question), on subordination to a higher authority (since this is contingent upon a country's prevailing constitutional arrangements), or on the need for direct elections, for the authority to be multi-purpose, or for it to have powers of taxation.[4] International and historical variations rule out the last three as universal characteristics of local government. However, they are commonly asserted to be fundamental characteristics of the British system, together with a degree of discretion for councils to execute their functions according to local needs.

Why do definitions matter anyway? One use in this context is to distinguish local government from other bodies exercising power delegated from Parliament or central government at the regional or local levels. Recent political history in the UK suggests that this is a necessary endeavour: the Blair government has created an intermediate and variegated layer of regional chambers and administrations in Scotland, Northern Ireland, Wales, London, and the English regions,[5] whereas its Conservative predecessors conferred extensive local functions not on elected councils but on a range of local appointed bodies.[6] It would be helpful to be able to distinguish local authorities from devolved bodies and local quangos. Interesting light is shed on the problem by what amounts to an international legal aside, a declaration entered by the United Kingdom when it ratified the European Charter of Local Self-Government: 'it is the understanding of the United Kingdom that the term "local authority" in the

[3] See pp. 16–22 below.

[4] M. Cole and G. Boyne, 'So You Think You Know What Local Government Is?', (1995) 21 LGS 191.

[5] See pp. 22–9 below.

[6] See pp. 331–5 below.

Charter does not include local or regional bodies such as police authorities which, by reason of the specialist functions for which they are responsible, are composed of both elected and appointed members.'[7] Officially, then, it would seem that it is the elected nature of local government which distinguishes it from other public bodies operating at the same level.

This will not suffice, however, as a historical explanation for the development or survival of local institutions. Local government based upon parishes, boroughs, and the functions of the Justices of the Peace existed for hundreds of years before the idea of democratically elected authorities emerged in the nineteenth century. In the same way as with central government, the gradual introduction of universal suffrage was by pragmatic accretions to existing and evolving institutions. The Poor Law Amendment Act of 1834 created the first elected local bodies, local boards of guardians, but on a considerably restricted franchise. It was followed shortly by another piece of reforming Whig legislation, the Municipal Corporations Act 1835, which provided for councils elected by burgesses (subject to a property qualification) in the towns. Elected county councils did not follow until the Local Government Act 1888, and elected rural district councils were introduced in the Local Government Act 1894.

As a matter of history, therefore, there is no question of local government taking its *raison d'être* from the elected character of local democracy. The notion of local government also involves more than simply elections: the ability to raise local taxation and a measure of discretion in the performance of its functions are other important attributes which distinguish it from local administration, although each of these was severely curtailed under the Conservative administrations in the period 1979–97. Nevertheless, arguments about the desirability of local democracy have been synonymous with discussion of the role of local government for the last 150 years.

The point can be made vividly by briefly reviewing the justifications offered for local government in four official reports spanning the last thirty years. In 1969 a Royal Commission stated the purpose of local government to be the efficient provision of services, the focusing of national attention on local problems, and a viable system of local democracy which retained people's interest.[8]

In 1986 the Widdicombe Committee argued:

the value of local government stems from its three attributes of:
(a) pluralism, through which it contributes to the national political system;

[7] Declarations contained in a letter from the Secretary of State for Foreign and Commonwealth Affairs, dated 14 Apr. 1998 , handed to the Secretary-General (of the Council of Europe) at the time of deposit of the instrument of ratification, on 24 Apr. 1998. On the Charter, see p. 30 below.

[8] *Report of the Royal Commission on Local Government in England*, Cmnd. 4040 (1969), 10–11.

(b) participation, through which it contributes to local democracy;
(c) responsiveness, through which it contributes to the provision of local needs through the delivery of services.[9]

The committee recognized that to some extent these were competing virtues, and that differing emphases given to the mix of them accounted for much of the controversy about the place of local government. The concepts of responsiveness, representation, and accountability for effective delivery of local services were still central to the Conservative government's thinking in proposing reorganization of local government in 1991, although it argued for these in a new climate: 'Local authorities are undergoing a fundamental transformation from being the main providers of services to having responsibility for securing their provision. The task of setting standards, specifying the work to be done and monitoring performance is done better if it is fully separated from the job of providing the services.'[10]

In a 1998 White Paper announcing a ten-year programme for the renewal of local democracy, the Labour government indicated that there would be no going back to councils as the sole or main providers of local services. However, in place of the Conservative vision it offered a broader, community leadership role:

> Among all our public institutions councils have a special status and authority as local, directly-elected bodies. They are uniquely placed to provide vision and leadership to their local communities. They are able to make things happen on the ground—where it really matters. People need councils which serve them well. Councils need to listen to, lead and build up their local communities. We want to see councils working in partnership with others, making their contribution to the achievement of our aims for improving people's quality of life.[11]

The concept of democracy is elusive. The quotations just cited suggest that local democracy implies much more than the simple election of local politicians as councillors by the electorate at regular intervals: so-called 'representative democracy'. Few commentators would now restrict it in that way. Theoretical debate apart, there are strong pragmatic reasons for not doing so: public participation in local elections in the United Kingdom has declined steadily in recent decades. The devalued legitimacy of local government from the point of view of representative democracy does much to explain the interest in alternative models. One typology published at the height of the Thatcher era proposed the three additional

[9] *The Conduct of Local Authority Business: Report of the Committee of Inquiry Into the Conduct of Local Authority Business*, Cmnd. 9797 (1986), para. 3.11 and ch. 3.

[10] DoE, *The Structure of Local Government: A Consultation Paper* (London, 1991), para. 19.

[11] Department of the Environment, Transport and the Regions, *Modern Local Government: In Touch with the People*, Cm. 4014 (July 1998), foreword and introduction by John Prescott.

categories of 'delegate democracy', 'participatory democracy', and 'market democracy'.[12] A more recent analysis suggests two complementary additional types: 'direct' democracy involving, for example, use of referendums, and 'deliberative' democracy, where an attempt is made to engage with the public or a section of it in formulating policy on specific matters (involving the transformation of public attitudes rather than the simple aggregation of their preferences).[13] What these alternatives to representative democracy have in common is an attempt to stress the qualities of responsiveness, transparency, and openness as valuable democratic attributes.[14]

It may be helpful to begin by showing how the reasons which have been offered as justifications for local democracy constrain the form chosen, how it is arranged, and the functions granted to local authorities.

## ARGUMENTS FOR LOCAL DEMOCRACY

It is not my intention to engage in this chapter in an extended theoretical discussion of local democracy.[15] However, the influence of one theorist has been so pervasive and enduring that his presence cannot be ignored. The classical theoretical arguments for local democracy were those advanced by the nineteenth-century liberal John Stuart Mill.[16] Mill believed that local democracy allowed for experimentation, with the advantage of only limited adverse consequences if the result was failure, while successes could be copied elsewhere. Local government could also be justified on pluralist grounds: it divides power and provides an alternative source of authority to the central state. Most important for Mill was the argument that local government provided an education in democracy, for both the electorate and the local politician.

[12] J. Gyford, S. Leach, and C. Game, *The Changing Politics of Local Government* (London, 1989), ch. 9. In delegate democracy the councillors were seen as having responsibility for implementing a political programme approved by the electorate in a manifesto, and some caucus (typically members of the local constituency party) took on the task of monitoring progress. Participatory democracy, on the other hand, made direct attempts to discover the wishes of the local community or sections of it. Market democracy sought to replicate the idealized 'democracy of the market', where suppliers respond to the wishes of consumers within a competitive atmosphere.

[13] L. Pratchett, 'Introduction: Defining Democratic Renewal', (1999) 25 LGS 1, 9–12.

[14] C. Copus, 'The Party Group: A Barrier to Democratic Renewal', (1999) 25 LGS 76, 78.

[15] See H. Wolman, 'Local Government Institutions and Democratic Governance', in D. Judge, G. Stoker, and H. Wolman (eds.), *Theories of Urban Politics* (London, 1995); J. Sharpe, 'Theories and Values of Local Government' (1970) 18(2) Political Studies 153–74; D. Hill, *Democratic Theory and Local Government* (London, 1974).

[16] J. S. Mill, 'Representative Government', ch. 15 in J. S. Mill, *Three Essays* (Oxford, 1975), esp. 365ff.

Mill argues for elected popular organs (or, as he describes them, 'sub-Parliaments') both locally and regionally with the task of controlling local officers. The franchise should be co-terminous with liability to local tax, neither more nor less.[17] He provides justifications for unitary authorities,[18] first, by way of a parallel with the Westminster system, where a unified legislature supervises divergent ministries, and, secondly, because if supervision of functions is too fragmented it will be difficult to attract people of quality into government to exercise control.[19] In the same passage there is a statement which would not be out of place either in a modern report on local administration or as a vision of the 'enabling authority': 'the business of the elective body is not to do the work, but to see that it is properly done . . . .'[20]

Mill's views on the allocation of functions between organs of the local and central state have a timeless relevance.[21] After arguing that business which is purely local should devolve to local authorities (for example, street lighting and paving), he recognizes that there is a second category where there is a justifiable national interest because of the national consequences of non- or poor performance (the police, for example) or where there is no good reason for local variations in service. Even if there is a pragmatic case for local management, national standards can be maintained through central inspectorates in the latter cases. A third category of functions (sanitation, for example), while of national importance, must be managed locally. For these, 'the question arises, how far the local authorities ought to be trusted with discretionary power, free from any superintendence or control of the State'.[22] On the one side, Mill places what he sees to be the poor quality of local officers and local representatives, and the weakness of the local press and local electorate in calling them to account.[23] On the other, the parochialism of the subject matter provides little incentive for central scrutiny, which may also be hampered by lack of local knowledge and remoteness.

[17] J. S. Mill, 'Representative Government', ch. 15 in J. S. Mill, *Three Essays* (Oxford, 1975), 366; cf. the discussion of the Community Charge in Ch. 4.

[18] See p. 19 below.

[19] Ibid. 369–70.

[20] Ibid. 369.

[21] Ibid. 373–80. The growing acceptance in the nineteenth century of central powers over local authorities has been attributed to Mill's influence: W. Holdsworth, *History of English Law*, vol. xiv (Aberdeen, 1964), 253. Bentham had earlier espoused the idea of elected local sub-legislatures operating under the supervision and inspection of central government: see F. Rosen, *Jeremy Bentham and Representative Democracy: A Study of the Constitutional Code* (Oxford, 1983), 163–7. Bentham's thought is said to have directly influenced the Whig government's local government reforms of 1834 and 1835: see Jennings, op. cit., 43–5; Holdsworth, op. cit., 220–1; see further Loughlin, op. cit., 29.

[22] Ibid. 365.

[23] This is not merely a question of quality; he recognizes also that the comparatively minor questions involved in local government are also unlikely to attract close attention.

Mill's solution is that principles of management of local government ought to be decided centrally, because of the superior resources available to central government to determine such questions, whereas the power of detailed implementation should be left to local authorities. Central government should act as a clearing-house of ideas on local management from all local authorities, since it will have access to comparative experience in a way that a single local authority will not. Powers of central intervention may be necessary to protect minorities, for example, from unequal imposition of local taxes. General principles of local taxation and of welfare should be prescribed nationally. In extreme cases Mill envisaged that central interference might extend to suspension or dissolution of a local representative council. He explicitly recognizes the tension between powers of central intervention of this kind and his general argument for local democracy based on the education of citizens, but argues that 'the education of citizens is not the only thing to be considered: government and administration do not exist for that alone, great as its importance is.'[24] Much of this discussion is indistinguishable from the current debate (140 years later) concerning 'best value', performance indicators, and central intervention in 'failing' local services.[25]

Whatever the theoretical attractions of Mill's arguments, in practice contemporary local government falls far short of fulfilling his aspirations. Political education is a minor function for the electorate in view of the low turnout in and the imperfect nature of local elections (discussed below). The educative role of local government is also in decline for political actors, councillors, and political activists. Historically, major political figures have made the transition from leadership in local politics to national prominence, like Joseph Chamberlain in the nineteenth century and Herbert Morrison in the twentieth. In recent years, however, it has become less important than business or the professions as a breeding-ground for those seeking national political recognition. In contrast to other countries, in Britain even those few politicians who graduate from pre-eminence in local politics to national politics only step on to 'the bottom rung of the national government ladder'.[26] It is too early to say whether the creation of posts of national significance (for example, the Mayor of London) will change this.

Mill's pragmatic arguments for local democracy based on the need for local knowledge and expertise to meet varying circumstances with different responses are also questionable in modern conditions. The ability of local government to provide experimental solutions to local problems has been severely constrained by the growing centralization and standardization

[24] Ibid. 379. [25] See pp. 339–43 below.

[26] I. Loveland , 'Local Authorities', in R. Blackburn and R. Plant (eds.), *Constitutional Reform: the Labour Government's Constitutional Reform Agenda* (London, 1999), 311.

which has been a feature of recent legislation. Experimentation has been further inhibited by financial grant allocations by central government, whose starting assumption is some notional level of standard service provision across the local government system as a whole. Although this does not of itself prevent a different allocation of spending where legislation otherwise permits, since the starting-point is not a generous allocation of funding, expenditure to fund new initiatives has to be at the cost of other services which are themselves under constant strain. Increasingly also, grants from central government are earmarked for particular purposes and cannot be used freely by the recipient authorities.[27]

These same centrifugal tendencies cast doubt on the arguments about pluralism. Local government may have been responsible (along with the House of Lords and the European Union) for preserving the collective memory of alternative political custodianship during the longest period of same-party rule that Britain has known in the twentieth century. However, the subservient constitutional position of local government makes it a feeble alternative power base. It has the capacity to annoy and delay central government through non-cooperation, but not ultimately to resist central policies.

Moreover, these justifications may also conflict among themselves. The two-tier approach to local government which is still common even after 1996 illustrates how these theoretical justifications may conflict at the practical level. The division of functions between district and county authorities may be supported on grounds of pluralism since it can and does produce authorities of different political persuasions at different levels, especially where an urban borough is located in a mainly rural or mixed county. However, as the Conservative government argued in proposing reform based on unitary authorities, the division of functions can also undermine the representative quality of local democracy if the electorate is unclear where political responsibility lies. The potential for confusion is exacerbated by the current arrangement where the bulk of local taxation is raised for services provided by county councils, but is collected by district councils.[28]

Nor do the arguments from political education or pluralism suggest which functions should be left to local government,[29] except that in either case there should be enough real decisions and powers to make the exercise viable. Herbert Morrison stated this clearly when, in a 1945 cabinet paper about the removal of municipal hospitals from local government, he argued:

[27] See further Ch. 4.

[28] DoE, op. cit., paras. 21–3.

[29] Ganz has argued that the UK lacks discernible principles for allocation of administrative functions between layers of government: G. Ganz, 'The Allocations of Functions Part I and II', [1972] PL 215 and 299, 308.

It is possible to argue that almost every local government function, taken by itself, could be administered more efficiently in a technical sense under a national system, but if we wish local government to thrive—as a school of political and democratic education as well as of administration—we must consider the effect on local government of each particular proposal. It would be disastrous if we allowed local government to languish by whittling away its most constructive and interesting functions.[30]

If there are no governmental functions which *must* be done locally then the essence of contemporary local government can be said to lie in its 'multi-functionality'. If this is accepted, the further step taken by Morrison then follows: that local authorities need a minimum number of tasks in order to make them viable units of government. The pragmatic arguments based on local experimentation suggest that there is an optimum level of local government appropriate to certain governmental functions. This notional point is presumably as local as possible, but far enough away from the people for variations in local circumstances to be apparent. If an optimum of this kind exists there may be a further complication, namely, that this point may vary according to the function in question—the optimum size or level of council may be different for road maintenance than for education. If the British model of multi-purpose authorities is followed this last factor either leads to multi-tier authorities or to compromise on the optimum size of the authority.

The history of local government is one of a movement from single-function local boards in the nineteenth century towards the familiar multi-functional authorities of today. However, in recent years, as many commentators have noted, there has been a substantial trend back towards single-purpose authorities exercising governmental functions at a local level, frequently run by unelected ministerially appointed members. The creation of Urban Development Corporations, NHS Trusts, and Training Enterprise Councils[31] fits within this pattern. Debate rages among political scientists over whether these bodies are correctly labelled as part of local *government*.[32] In the light of this, it is worth briefly examining the supposed virtues of 'multi-functionality' as an attribute of local government in its own right.

Several advantages of multi-functional authorities can be identified. They provide a common and identifiable reference point for local accountability, especially for the local citizen. Rhodes has argued that citizens increasingly face a 'differentiated polity' in which even a simple transaction requires

[30] Quoted in P. Hennessy, *Never Again: Britain 1945–1951* (London, 1992), 139.

[31] See pp. 331–5 below.

[32] For an extensive discussion of this whole area and the networks between the various institutions and of layers of government: R. Rhodes, *Beyond Westminster and Whitehall* (London, 1988).

them to deal with a multiplicity of local agencies. This is essentially an argument derived from transparency. A further advantage lies in the ability of multi-functional authorities to coordinate policies in relation to different services, and to shift resources flexibility between them. The latter is more difficult where institutional boundaries have to be crossed. However, the ability of multi-functional authorities to do so depends to a considerable degree on the extent to which they are given budgetary freedom: heavily prescribed statutory levels of service and specifically earmarked central grants leave little freedom for virement in practice. A third justification is the administrative economies of scale which 'multi-functionality' allows, with shared staff (especially for core tasks like legal and financial advice), shared premises, and so on.

We have so far taken it for granted that representative democracy is a strength of local government although its claim to be the defining feature of it is debatable. In the next section we shall examine its weaknesses.

## THE IMPERFECTIONS OF LOCAL REPRESENTATIVE DEMOCRACY

All councils are divided into smaller areas for the purpose of electing representatives: these are called wards in the case of district councils (normally three councillors will represent each ward) and divisions in the case of the county councils (represented by a single councillor). With the sole exception of the Greater London Authority (where the mayor is elected by the Supplementary Vote system and the authority by the Additional Member system[33]), elections take place under first past the post. Councillors serve a four-year term of office and elections take place over a four-year cycle, but the pattern varies according to the type of local authority, and at no time do all local authorities elections occur simultaneously. The simplest arrangements are in the county councils, the London boroughs, the Greater London Authority, and the Welsh unitary authorities, where the whole council is elected together once every four years. In metropolitan districts one-third of the seats are up for election in each of three years, and in the fourth year no elections are held. Other district councils can choose to follow this system (in which case in the fourth year the county council elections will be held) or to opt for a four-yearly election of the whole council. No power exists for a council to dissolve itself and to trigger an election (although individual councillors can resign, resulting in by-elections); consequently, power-sharing administrations are common since local politicians have no option but to play the hand that the electorate deals to them. These electoral arrangements are

[33] See pp. 242–3 below.

convoluted, so much so that commentators have argued that their labyrinthine nature is a real bar to public accountability.[34]

Many commentators have pointed to the low participation rates in local elections (since the 1950s turnout has typically hovered around 40 per cent of the electorate but has recently fallen below 30 per cent). Equally, the irrelevance of local issues in determining local election results can be seen as undermining the representative nature of local democracy. Support for these views can be found in an extensive survey of voter attitudes undertaken in 1985/6 by Miller.[35] About two-thirds of Miller's respondents professed little or no interest in local politics and at best 50 per cent estimated that a local issue would influence their voting in a local election.[36] More significantly, even at the time of a local election only 8 per cent felt strongly about an issue which was the exclusive responsibility of the local council—the majority of issues of concern were the responsibility of central government.[37] In practice, 84 per cent of those questioned voted in local elections in accordance with their voting in national general elections.[38] This would not itself be a decisive argument against local democracy: if, for instance, it produced local authorities based on geographical differences in political control, it could be an argument for pluralism. However, in practice it was combined with a tendency to use a local vote as a mid-term protest vote against central government.[39] The local electorate do not connect local elections with local issues—they may become referendums on central government policy on local government as a whole, or popularity contests for central government (a kind of substitute by-election). More recent research done for the Commission on Local Democracy points to a higher turnout in local elections as a general election becomes imminent.[40] The same study found that where wards were marginal or the local parties active, interest among the electorate increased.

Interest is much lower than interest in national politics. Fewer than half of the respondents could name a ward councillor, and they were (slightly) more likely to believe that contacting their MP or signing a petition would be a more effective way of opposing a council decision than contacting a councillor. Voting was seen to be a less effective way of controlling the

[34] M. Thrasher and C. Rallings, 'An Audit of Local Democracy in Britain: the Evidence from Local Elections', (1999) 52 (1) Parl. Affs. 58.

[35] W. Miller, *Irrelevant Elections? The Quality of Local Democracy in Britain* (Oxford, 1988).

[36] Ibid. 15–16.

[37] Ibid. 17.

[38] Ibid. 236. The minority of cases where respondents voted differently in national and local elections were accounted for by a preparedness to vote Alliance (as it then was) locally despite national political preferences.

[39] Leading to Miller's suggested antidote that councils should either be elected at and for the same term as governments or that a one-third election rule should be imposed universally (rather than by choice as at present): ibid. 237–8.

[40] C. Rallings, M. Temple, and M. Thrasher, *Community Identity and Participation in Local Democracy* (London, 1994).

local council than contacting the press, going to the council offices or contacting the local Member of Parliament.[41] Nevertheless, and paradoxically, those questioned seemed attached to the idea of local autonomy, to increased functions for local government, to local elections, and a substantial proportion wanted less central control of local government.[42]

### Reform of the Electoral Process

Although dated, these findings are damning. Worse still, the average rate of participation has declined substantially since this study, by about 25 per cent. Paradoxically, the most obvious form of response to the crisis of local representative democracy—reform of the local electoral process to increase public participation and interest—has been neglected until recently. Instead, governments have sought to correct local failings by transferring functions to other (unelected) bodies, imposing national standards of service or periodic structural reviews of all or part of local government. However, if belatedly, the local electoral system is now under reform.

Predictably, the adoption of proportional representation in local elections is advocated by the Liberal Democrats. It is supported by evidence which suggests that there is little relationship between proportion of the vote cast and council seats obtained by political parties.[43] As with national electoral disparities, this is a product of the First Past the Post system operating within electoral wards of different electoral complexions and sizes.[44] The Commission for Local Democracy advocated the adoption of a single transferable vote system of elections based on multi-member wards.[45] This proposal was intended to produce an electoral system whose outcomes better reflect the wishes of the whole electorate, while retaining a clear connection between individual councillors and local wards.[46] In its 1995 policy document on local government the Labour Party argued that all councils should be required to adopt annual elections in a third or quarter of all council seats, to increase local accountability.[47] Significantly, however, this proposal was made within the context of retaining the First Past the Post system; the Commission for Local Democracy, on the other hand, argued that annual elections would weaken responsiveness within a reformed system of voting based on proportional representation, and preferred elections to be held for all council seats at the same time.[48] The

[41] Miller, op. cit., 21.

[42] Ibid. 31, 36, 237–8.

[43] See CLD, *Taking Charge: The Rebirth of Local Democracy* (London, 1995), 11, for examples.

[44] C. Rallings and M. Thrasher, *Electoral Reform for Local Government* (London, 1991).

[45] CLD, *Taking Charge*, 25–6.

[46] The alternative of a party list across the whole council would increase party patronage, while weakening the local connection of councillors. The Commission also proposed a system of directly elected council leaders, based on the Alternative Vote system: ibid. 27.

[47] Labour Party, *Renewing Democracy, Rebuilding Communities* (London,1995), 5 and 14.

[48] See CLD, op. cit., 28.

debate boils down to a choice in the form of local democracy between retention of strong party control (modified by more frequent consultation of the electorate) and a system which would increase the number of councils in which no party was in overall control, but where the composition of the council would be more representative of the community as a whole.

In government, Labour set out its proposals on reform of local elections in its 1998 White Paper.[49] A change to proportional representation was not supported, but the proposals included more frequent elections and ideas for easier ways of voting. It is proposed that all unitary councils, including the London boroughs, will move to the system prevailing in metropolitan district councils, and some shire unitary district councils, of electing by thirds. The 'fallow' year is to be used for other elections; for example, in unitary councils with a directly elected mayor, the mayoral election would occur then, as would the elections for the Mayor and Assembly of the Greater London Authority. In two-tier areas, in order to avoid having annual elections for councils in both tiers, elections will be held in districts and counties by halves in alternate years. This will reduce the frequency of elections in some shire district councils, where elections are currently held in three years out of four, but increase it in the remainder and in the counties.[50]

Additional changes are planned in order to encourage people to register, to remove disincentives to vote, and to make voting and counting easier. A two-pronged approach was planned, with the government encouraging local authorities to maximize registration and participation through guidance, and legislation to enable councils to engage in ministerially sanctioned experiments in the way local elections are conducted.[51] The latter might include: use of electronic voting, extending the vote over a number of days, conducting entire elections by postal vote, the use of mobile polling stations or enabling voting at any polling station in the authority, and electronic or mechanical counting of votes. The electoral register will become a 'rolling' document instead of the old system of an annual registration date.[52]

[49] *Modern Local Government: In Touch with the People*, Cm. 4014 (1998), ch. 4.

[50] The changes are implemented under ss. 85–6 Local Government Act 2000 which give power for the Secretary of State to specify which of 3 schemes for elections is to apply to the various categories of councils. The options are: election of the whole council every 4 years by thirds in 3 years out of 4; or by halves biannually.

[51] Powers were granted to conduct pilot schemes under the Representation of People Act 2000, s. 10; ministers are given power to amend procedures generally in the light of the result of these schemes under s. 11. The first such experiment was in the conduct of elections in May 2000, when voters could vote up to a week before the poll day and votes for the Mayor of London and the Greater London Authority were counted electronically.

[52] Representation of the People Act 2000, s. 2. Further changes in local elections will be brought about as a result of the recommendations of the Committee on Standards in Public

The low voter turnout in local elections may be partly attributable to the public's difficulty in understanding the system.[53] If so, the government's proposals for annual elections may not succeed in increasing turnout: in fact it seems that where elections for the whole council are held every four years, participation rates among voters are higher than in districts opting for the system of elections by thirds. Annual elections may, however, make councils more responsive to the electorate. Nor is it guaranteed that the introduction of directly elected mayors and cabinets[54] will reinvigorate voter interest. In one sense they may harm local democracy by increasing the number of councillors who do stand for re-election (currently about 40 per cent), if back-benchers do not feel they have a worthwhile job to do.

From the place of elections in local democracy we turn now to questions of institutional design. In the remainder of the chapter we shall consider the place given to local government within the constitutional hierarchy and the extent to which this allows for pluralism, experimentation, and responsiveness to local needs. We begin with the review of local government structure carried out in 1992–6 by the Local Government Commission. Later we will examine the position of councils in the new order of devolved chambers and regional bodies. Finally, discussion will move to the question of constitutional recognition for local government.

## THE ARCHITECTURE OF LOCAL DEMOCRACY: REORGANIZING THE STRUCTURE

Local government reorganization occurs with predictable regularity. Equally predictable is the tendency of the supposed panaceas to come full circle. Thus, the review undertaken by the Local Government Commission[55] in 1992–6 was partly driven by a desire to return to unitary authorities abandoned as recently as 1974 (the county boroughs).

The Local Government Commission's review was driven by an undigested mix of policy factors.[56] It was initiated by the government at the same time as a review of local government taxation, which resulted in the replacement of the Community Charge with the Council Tax in the Local Government Finance Act 1992. Considerations of economy and financial

Life, to introduce controls on the funding and campaigning of political parties taking part: Political Parties, Elections and Referendums Bill 2000 (note especially the inclusion of local elections as 'relevant elections' under cl. 20(3)(f)).

[53] Thrasher and Rallings, op. cit., 72. In 1998 turnout averaged 29% with variations from 25 to 34% in metropolitan districts and unitary authority and just 11% to 45% in others.

[54] See pp. 230–46 below.

[55] LGA 1992, pt. II.

[56] S. Leach, 'The Strange Case of the Local Government Review', in J. Stewart and G. Stoker (eds.), *Local Government in the 1990s* (Basingstoke, 1995).

accountability were as present in the structural review policy as in the parallel taxation one. This was a factor which the Local Government Commission was required by legislation and ministerial guidance to consider, and projections of estimated savings featured prominently in its proposals.[57] Further divergent policy influences were the enthusiasm of Michael Heseltine (who as Secretary of State launched the review) for elected mayors—an organizational reform which was consistent with the adoption of a unitary structure—but a preference not shared by his cabinet colleagues or ministerial successors, Michael Howard and John Gummer. Broader changes in the role of local government also featured: policy documents referred to the emphasis on 'enabling'[58] but with little clarification of what the term meant in this context or of its structural implications.[59] Indeed, it could be argued that reform of tiers and boundaries of local government was something of a distraction at the time from more fundamental changes in the role of local authorities brought about by compulsory competitive tendering, consumerist legislation, and changes in relations with central government.

By comparison with most local government legislation, the 1992 Act provisions, governing the process, were curiously brief and simple. A mere sixteen sections sufficed to inaugurate the biggest programme of revision for two decades. The 1974 reforms were preceded by five years of agonized debate and a royal commission (which guaranteed a place in the collective cultural memory for its Chairman, Lord Redcliffe-Maud). The abolition of the GLC and the metropolitan county councils in 1986 provoked vigorous debate, even if the proposals were introduced without real consultation.[60] Perhaps the memory of these political battles influenced the government's strategy on this occasion. It offered no overall blueprint except a preference for unitary authorities of some kind and left the exercise to an independent body.

Superficially the Local Government Commission was a more attractive vehicle of reform, since it had the air of political independence, operated procedures for consultation with those affected, and had the ability to produce results flexibly tailored to local circumstances in a way that uniform patterns imposed from above might not. The Commission replaced the Local Government Boundary Commission, but the types of review it undertakes are fundamentally different in kind from those of its

[57] However, Leach criticizes the prominence which the Commission gave to consultant's estimates of savings and the emphasis on economy, rather than cost effectiveness: ibid. 58–60.

[58] See p. 306 below.

[59] Leach, op. cit., 51–2, argues that the emphasis on enabling related only to questions of service provision and neglected the structural significance of council functions of regulation, strategic planning, and acting as a focus for promotion of their area.

[60] DoE, *Streamlining the Cities: Proposals for Reorganising Local Government in London and the Metropolitan Counties*, Cmnd. 9063 (1983).

predecessor body, since they are concerned not merely with geographical but also with structural boundaries between authorities. This is an important point since it broke with the previous assumption that there ought to be national policies approved by Parliament according to which the structure of the second tier of government was organized, even if they took account of geographical differences. In basing itself, at least legislatively, on an extreme atheoretical and pragmatic approach the Conservative government rejected this tradition. The result can fairly be described as 'structural pragmatism'—a policy of no policy. As a political strategy this approach also had the advantage that local government reorganization became a series of minor local skirmishes over the proposals for each area with an independent body as a buffer, rather than a national contest in which local authorities or their representative associations could find political allies to engage the government directly.

However, simplicity and flexibility were purchased at the expense of democratic legitimacy. The reason for the brevity of the provisions in the 1992 Act dealing with structural reform was that all the crucial details of the principles governing the Commission's work were omitted. The Act dealt only with the relevant procedures by which the Commission was to conduct a structural review of local authority areas at the request of the Secretary of State.[61] This review could result in the Commission recommending either the replacement of two tiers in a non-metropolitan area with a single, unitary authority, the revision of boundaries between existing authorities, or no change. The minister can give effect to these recommendations with or without modifications,[62] and does so by laying a draft statutory instrument for parliamentary approval.[63]

Where the legislation was virtually silent was on the substantive principles to guide the Commission's work. It stated merely that the Commission was to :

> have regard to the need—
> (a) to reflect the identities and interests of local communities; and
> (b) to secure effective and convenient local government.[64]

These aspirations were sufficiently general to be politically uncontroversial. The first reflected the government's view that some of the post-1974 local authorities had failed to find acceptance in their communities, and that return to more traditionally recognized units of local government might be in order. This was widely interpreted at the time (prophetically) as serving notice on some of the newer counties, such as Avon, Cleveland,

[61] LGA 1992, s. 13. In addition the Commission is charged with regular reviews (on a 10–15-year rolling programme of local electoral arrangements (in this capacity the Commission replaced the Local Boundary Commissions).

[62] LGA 1992, s. 17.

[63] Ibid. s. 26.

[64] Ibid. s. 13(5).

and Humberside, and heralding the revival of ancient titles like Rutland.[65] In interpretation of the second criterion much depends on semantics: effectiveness can be measured in terms either of value for money or of simple economy, ignoring questions of quality.[66]

The Department of the Environment's 1991 consultation paper *The Structure of Local Government in England* expressed a preference for unitary authorities, but with no fixed view on whether the district or the county level should be abolished over the country as a whole and the possibility that in some places two tiers might be retained. All this was to be left to the Commission. However, the chairman (Sir John Bainham, a former Director-General of the CBI) was appointed by the Secretary of State for the Environment, who also issued guidance on the Commission's work.[67] Although the legislation gave the minister a large measure of discretion, there was nevertheless an inherent tension in the statutory scheme because of the independent position of the Commission. This led to many subsequent difficulties. There was no precedent for Parliament to hand a blank cheque of this kind to a minister to reorganize an entire tier of government. Perhaps parliamentarians should have been grateful at being spared having to decide who was to maintain the cemeteries, catch stray dogs, and license tattoo parlours. Equally, though, who was to run schools and social services and repair roads were vital questions on which one might expect central government to have a view and Parliament to have an interest in. The attempt to forestall debate on such vital constitutional questions by resort to administrative discretion and ministerial guidance was regrettable. The subsequent history shows, however, that to a large extent it rebounded, and that the government came to rue the failure to spell out more explicitly its preference for unitary authorities in the legislation.

The Commission ran into both political and legal controversy. In 1993, when its recommendations for the reorganization of Derbyshire departed from the government's preferred pattern, it was asked to reconsider. Revised guidance was issued by the government to the Commission in October 1993. This gave greater emphasis to the expectation that the LGC would recommend unitary authorities (with retention of the existing two-tier system seen as exceptional), a presumption against very large unitary authorities (thus making unitary districts more likely than unitary counties), and a preference for 'intermediate' solutions, i.e. medium-sized

[65] The Welsh review similarly resulted in the names of the medieval kingdoms adopted by the counties in the 1974 reorganization being largely jettisoned.

[66] Cf. Leach, op. cit.

[67] S. 13 (6) of the LGA 1992 provides for the Secretary of State to issue directions to the Commission, and these directions may require the Commission to have regard to any guidance issued by the minister.

unitary authorities combining districts. Leach argues that the revised guidance crossed the line from concern with the input criteria which the Commission was to consider into dictation of ministerially preferred outcomes.[68] A significant judicial rebuff to the whole process came when this new guidance was held to be ultra vires by the courts in January 1994.[69] In a challenge brought against the Commission's proposals by Derbyshire and Lancashire, the Secretary of State's guidance was found to have gone too far in constraining the independence of the Commission in a manner inconsistent with the statutory criteria. The guidance had expressed the government's preference for unitary authorities by stating:

> In some areas the Commission may wish to recommend a continuation of the existing two-tier structure. But the government expects that to be the exception, and that the result will be a substantial increase in the number of unitary authorities in both urban and rural areas.

The court took the view that this sentence undermined the statutory criteria and exceeded the minister's powers.

The judgment represented a welcome affirmation of constitutional proceduralism, which in effect put the government to its election between the options of amending the legislation to reflect legally their policy or withdrawing the offending guidance. It chose the latter option. Subsequently, an attempt to have the revised policy guidance declared unlawful failed, when the High Court held that no fair reading of the guidance could lead to the conclusion that the minister was seeking to enforce a unitary system in the case of twenty-one district council areas referred back to the Commission in June 1995.[70] This does not mean, however, that political independence in the review process ultimately prevailed. Instead, the government changed tactics and made extensive use of its power to refer back recommendations of which it disapproved. It was forced to do so because its other powers under the Act were limited. On these, Jowitt J had commented in the Lancashire case:

> although the secretary of state had wide powers to modify the commission's recommendations, he could not transform them so that they became a different animal. He might modify a recommendation of no change by, for example, altering a boundary, but it was difficult to see how he could lawfully modify a recommendation for no change so that it became a recommendation for change from a two tier to a unitary structure for local government.

Referrals back especially affected those reports of the Commission which recommended continuation or minor variation of the existing dual-tier arrangements. The differences of opinion became so heated that they

[68] Leach, op. cit., 63–4.

[69] *R v SSE ex p. Lancashire CC and Derbyshire CC*, [1994] 4 All ER 165.

[70] *R v SS for the Environment ex p. Lancashire CC*, *The Times*, 9 Dec. 1995.

culminated in March 1995 in the removal of the chairman, Sir John Banham, whose 'resignation' was welcomed in a parliamentary statement by the Secretary of State for the Environment.[71] His replacement was David Cocksey, another businessman and a former chairman of the Audit Commission. According to Banham, the Commission's mistake had been to give preference to local public opinion, rather than to politicians with vested interests.[72] The government, however, took the view that the Commission had mismanaged the review process, which had become unduly convoluted. Inter-council strife was also rife: at one stage the Association of District Councils reported a number of county councils to the Audit Commission, alleging that they had misused millions of pounds of public money in opposing reorganization.

Predictably the controversy spilled over into the courts, in a number of (mostly unsuccessful) judicial review actions against the Commission by local authorities. In all but one case (the Lancashire decision, already noted), the courts refused to intervene in attacks made on the Commission's procedures. In one, Laws J argued that the court should be loath to intervene because the Commission was not a decision-making body since it merely made recommendations to the Secretary of State, who was the more appropriate person to whom to address objections to the proposals.[73] The courts also affirmed the wide statutory powers the minister enjoyed over when to refer proposals back to the Commission.[74] When the Commission reported back in September 1995 on the twenty-one cases referred that June, it recommended that eight of these districts should become unitary authorities and a further four councils should merge to form two new unitary authorities.

To the Commission's credit it made strenuous efforts to fulfil its duty of consultation under s. 13(5) of the Act by a wider variety of means than is customary in such exercises. These included not only the inevitable public meetings and invitations for written representations but also extensive public opinion polling and use of postal questionnaires. These can be seen as an attempt to go beyond elected councillors (who, it might be fairly said, were far from disinterested participants) directly to the public.[75]

[71] HC Debs., vol. 562, cols. 1128 ff. (21 Mar. 1995).

[72] *The Times*, 3 Mar. 1995.

[73] *R v LGC ex p. N. Yorks. CC* (unreported decision, QBD, 11 Mar. 1994, affirmed 20 Dec. 1994, CA), citing with approval the dictum of Simon Brown J on the LGC's predecessor in *Ex p. Hart DC* (unreported decision of 9 Dec. 1987).

[74] *R v LGC and Another ex p. Cleveland CC*, *The Times*, Law Report, 4 July 1994, QBD, holding that the minister had power under ss. 17(4), 19 and 26(4) of the Act to refer back recommendations previously accepted with modifications.

[75] However, the Commission's tendency to give decisive influence to questionnaire responses about the affiliation of the respondents to particular areas has been criticized, both in terms of ambiguity of the data and because other aspects of 'community' ties, notably employment, shopping, and leisure patterns, were neglected. See Leach, op. cit, 60.

Attempts to base legal challenges on information leaflets[76] and questionnaires[77] disseminated by the Commission as part of this process failed. Likewise, an attack on the more limited consultation undertaken by the Commission following the referral back of its recommendations by the Secretary of State failed.[78]

The Commission's work has been criticized, however, for demonstrating inconsistencies in the approach to essentially similar problems in the solutions adopted for different counties. Leach ascribes this to different approaches by the Commissioners involved, and to the failure to spell out in the legislation, in the ministerial guidance, or by the Commission as a whole, what the defining role of the restructured local authorities was to be.[79]

In the final analysis four counties disappeared completely, to be replaced by unitary districts (Berkshire, Cleveland, Avon, and Humberside). A further fifteen counties lost part of their territory to enhanced districts. A total of fifty new unitary districts was created. The direct cost of the exercise was in the region of £15 million. The first elections to the new authorities took place in May 1996. By contrast in Scotland and Wales a consistent system of unitary district authorities was imposed by the Secretary of State through primary legislation, following a consultative exercise. In Wales this involved the replacement of eight county and thirty-seven district councils with twenty-two unitary authorities.[80] In Scotland twenty-eight new unitary authorities replaced twelve regional and fifty-two district councils. It is questionable whether at the end of the day the solution adopted in the Celtic fringes of ministerial diktat was any less legitimate than that followed in England, where ministers tampered repeatedly with a supposedly independent process when it failed to produce their preferred recommendations.

## REGIONALISM

In this section the reasons for the establishment of regional agencies and assemblies in England are first examined, together with the provisions of the Regional Development Agencies Act 1998. An assessment is then

[76] *R v LGC ex p. Cleveland CC* (unreported decision of 8 Feb. 1995, CA). Although the Divisional Court had had 'serious reservations' about financial information contained in a leaflet summarizing the Commission's proposals, the CA held that this did not amount to a procedural impropriety, since there were other aspects to the consultation process, including a MORI poll.

[77] *R v LGC ex p. N.Yorks. CC* (unreported decision, 20 Dec. 1994, CA).

[78] *R v LGC ex p. Gloucester City Council* (unreported decision, 4 Nov. 1994, QBD).

[79] Leach, op. cit., 53 and 58.

[80] Implemented by the Local Government (Wales) Act 1994.

made of the implications for local government. A similar, briefer, discussion of devolution follows.

The main pressures for the introduction of regional government stem from dissatisfaction with central rather than local government. The principal argument is that it allows for expression of political identity even where the central government at Westminster fails to reflect the political mood of the regions. Regional government therefore counteracts a feeling of political disenfranchisement and allows for pluralism. A further argument relates to the lack of regional democratic accountability for central government offices dispersed regionally and regional quangos. Oversight of such bodies featured prominently in the proposals for regional government from the independent think-tank the Constitution Unit.[81] However, the subsidiary arguments for regional government relate more strongly to issues about local government functions, and focus on the need for strategic planning in such areas as land use and transportation and the need for coordination at the regional level of economic development and bids for and implementation of EU funding. Here there may be a risk that, as well as 'drawing down' functions from the centre, regions may 'draw up' functions from local authorities.

In June 1996[82] the Constitution Unit published a developed set of proposals which seems to have influenced the Labour government's subsequent White Paper and Regional Development Agencies Act 1998. It proposed initially a move to Regional Chambers, which would be indirectly elected, that is composed of representatives from local authorities in the region. The report recognized that there was insufficient demand for full-blown Regional Assemblies in England enjoying legislative powers. The proposals envisaged that directly elected Regional Assemblies might develop unevenly: the north of England was seen as a likely early contender whereas the south-east (outside London) was relatively unenthusiastic. The policy could be flexible. Regional Chambers could be a transitional phase, to be replaced with Assemblies fairly rapidly, or alternatively, development might never proceed beyond the Regional Chambers stage. The possibilities were left open because fundamental questions remained unanswered about whether central government would be prepared to give up its powers to elected Assemblies, and if so, what the relationship to local government should be (for example, should

[81] Constitution Unit, *Regional Government in England* (London, 1996).

[82] Earlier proposals were made in the 1970s. In a minority dissenting memorandum to the report of the Royal Commission on the Constitution, Crowther-Hunt and Peacock proposed that there should be eight English provincial authorities and that the Upper Chamber of Parliament should be amended to include a strong provincial presence, which would give it an indirectly elected character by being drawn from regional assemblies: Royal Commission on the Constitution 1969/73, vol. ii: *Memorandum of Dissent*, Cmnd. 5460-i (1973).

Regional Chambers continue as a forum for regional local government), and what the source of finance for Assemblies would be.

The Labour government's plan for regional government in England ranks modestly within this range of options. The Regional Development Agencies Act 1998 provided for the establishment of agencies for London and eight regions.[83] The main brief of the new RDAs is regional economic development; accordingly, they are business-led and dominated boards, although it is intended that the membership will also contain local authority members and representatives of other regional interests, such as the education and voluntary sectors. The government intends that one-third of members should be drawn from local councillors in the region which the agency serves, to reflect the size of local authorities, geographical spread, and political balance.[84] The RDAs replace some existing actors (for instance, English Partnerships and the Rural Development Commission) and will be the lead agency in other areas, notably in coordinating bids for funding from the European Structural and Regional Funds and in distributing Single Regeneration Budget Challenge funding. In addition, the legislation envisages the possibility of further transfer of central government functions to the RDAs by ministers where it is expedient to do so.[85] This opens the possibility of uneven, or asymmetrical, development between different English regions: where an individual RDA consents, functions may be delegated to it without being given to RDAs generally.[86] The provisions for delegation are similar to those provided in relation to the transfer of functions to the Welsh Assembly.[87]

In its proposals the Constitution Unit had suggested that the Chambers would essentially act as strategic coordinating bodies, reliant on the cooperation of the constituent local authorities. If no legislative backing were given to the Chambers, their powers would be limited to those currently enjoyed by local authorities. Funding might come from a precept on local authorities, and the powers of the Chamber would be limited to those of

[83] RDA Act 1998, s. 1 and sched 1. The regions are the East Midlands, Eastern, North East, North West South, East South West, West Midlands, and Yorkshire and Humberside. With the exception of the North West Region, the boundaries are intended to mirror the existing areas of the relevant Government regional offices: White Paper, para. 2.2. Separate arrangements for London apply under the GLA Act 1999: see pp. 242–6 below.

[84] White Paper, *Building Partnerships for Prosperity*, Cm. 3814 (1997), para. 10.8.

[85] RDA, s. 8(1).

[86] Ibid. s. 6(3). Delegation of functions may be made simultaneously to all RDAs without their consent. Equally, however, delegation may be withdrawn, provided (where an RDA does not consent) it is withdrawn from all RDAs simultaneously: s. 6(4). Although the scheme therefore involves a high degree of executive largesse and is open to easy amendment by a new administration unsympathetic to a regional structure, it does have a form of constitutional safeguard: primary legislation is required before regions can be penalized selectively for party political disagreement with Westminster. This may become important in any future regional–central conflict.

[87] GWA 1998, ss. 22–5 and sched. 3.

the councils represented in it. The Constitution Unit envisaged that a Chamber of this kind would have the function of strategic coordination of land-use planning, transport, environmental and economic development, and European funding bids, with the intention of establishing a regional strategy. Any oversight of devolved central government powers would, necessarily, be limited to questioning local representatives, and, even for this, statutory powers to obtain information might be necessary. The political representation and balance of a Regional Chamber would reflect the composition of the constituent local authorities on some agreed pattern.

The legislation is both vaguer and weaker than even this outline plan. It provides for ministerial designation of Regional Chambers 'if the Secretary of State is of the opinion . . . 'that there is a body which is representative of those in a regional development agency area and with an interest in its work' and which is 'suitable to be given the role'.[88] These indirectly elected consultative assemblies are likely to be mainly drawn (although this is not a legislative requirement) from members of the local authorities in the region. The DETR published criteria in August 1998, which regional chambers would have to meet before recognition for consultative status.[89] These included:

> the chamber's constitution should provide for representation from local authorities on the basis of broad political support across the region; the local government members should be in the majority within the chamber. Non-local government members would be expected to comprise no less than 30 per cent of the chamber; it will be for the regional partners to decide whether voting arrangements are necessary, but all chamber members should have the opportunity to contribute to debates and for their views to be reflected in published statements.

Where a Regional Chamber is designated[90] the RDA will be under a duty to consult it. However, Chambers are envisaged, at least initially, as voluntary bodies with no statutory powers of their own.[91] Where a Regional Chamber is designated, ministers *may* at a later point require an RDA to take account of its views in formulating strategy.[92] In the absence

[88] RDA Act, s. 8(1).

[89] DETR, *Regional Development Agencies Guidance on the General Principles of Designation of Voluntary Regional Chambers*, 7 Aug. 1998.

[90] By July 2000, Regional Chambers had been recognized by the Secretary of State in the following areas: East Midlands, West Midlands, the North West, North East, Eastern, South East, and South West England, and Yorkshire and Humber.

[91] The exception is London, where a new directly elected Greater London Authority and directly elected mayor will have specific powers relating to the London Development Agency. This role is described in the White Paper as 'setting the agenda' for the Agency, whereas the RDA Act 1998 reserves powers for ministers to direct and approve strategy for other RDAs: ss. 7(2) and 18.

[92] Ibid. s. 8(2).

of a Regional Chamber, RDAs can be required to consult local opinion in other ways.

In comparison with the directly elected chambers introduced in parts of the United Kingdom, the RDAs and Regional Chambers look like poor relations. It is true that the arrangements are highly flexible, enabling the government to respond differently to variations in demand for regional demand in different parts of England. This is achieved, however, at the cost of excessive ministerial powers to recognize the Chambers and to alter the roles and powers of the RDAs. When combined with the power of patronage in making appointments, the result is a long way short of the democratic ideal. The Regional Chambers lack any powers over central government regional offices, in contrast to the accountability of the Scottish Executive to the Scottish Parliament and the powers of the National Assembly in Wales. They go only modestly further than the most advanced example of voluntary regional consultation and cooperation, prior to 1998, namely, the Northern Regional Assembly, a body of local authority representatives in the north of England. In the longer term, however, the government has signalled its preparedness to consider elected regional government in parts of England which can demonstrate demand for it. The initial step would be to hold regional referendums.

In this mild initial form regional government is scarcely a threat to a local government. Regional Chambers will essentially be controlled by local authorities rather than supervising or taking over their powers, and have no powers of their own in any event. Longer-term, there is potentially a significant overlap between the supervision of quangos at a regional level and the broader vision of community leadership for local government now being promoted by legislation.[93] In both cases the emphasis is on an elected public body (whether directly or indirectly) seeking information about the policies and actions of other unelected bodies. If they were established, Regional *Assemblies* would be quite different. They would be independent of local councils, since they would derive their powers direct from central government and might take over the task of allocating funding to local authorities. Such a development would alter totally the nature and position of local government.

We can postulate three options for regional–local relations. First, a pattern of regions could be superimposed upon a uniform layer of local government, with the competence of both tiers fixed from the centre: this would be like the post-1972 dual-tier local government writ large. Secondly, a variable geometry of regional and local government might be imposed from above. Thirdly, the composition of local government could itself be one of the devolved responsibilities of regional government, as it

[93] See pp. 59–65 and 336–7 below.

is in the devolution legislation for Scotland and Northern Ireland. In the second and third scenarios different regions might develop significantly differing patterns of local government. However, there is an important difference: in the second scheme, regional variations in local government would result from national legislation and be under the control of central government, whereas in the third they would be a product of regional initiative and experimentation. In practice, as a result of the asymmetrical scheme of devolution and regionalism which has now taken effect, a pattern based on a mix of the second and third alternatives is emerging. One attraction of all three arrangements, unlike the pattern of central–local relations, is that the regional authorities' powers over local government might also be limited, providing a form of constitutional guarantee for local authorities, with or without a broader constitutional settlement. We shall return to that topic in conclusion after briefly reviewing the relationship of local authorities and the new devolved bodies in Scotland and Wales.

## Devolution

The establishment of devolved government is generally seen as a reaction to the shortcomings of Westminster, in particularly its failure to satisfy cultural and regional distinctiveness and the feeling of political disenfranchisement of parts of the United Kingdom whose political sympathies have diverged over long periods from the remainder of the country.[94] However, it suggests also that local government institutions alone had failed to satisfy these aspirations to *difference*. In part this may be due to a common cause: the centralizing tendencies of postwar administrations have restricted local authority discretionary powers; also, it is possible that in a different climate local government might have acted as something of a safety valve for the pressures which fed demands for devolution.

In both Wales and Scotland, the devolved bodies are, like local authorities, constitutionally speaking, subordinate and limited governmental institutions. They enjoy powers only under the terms of the devolution legislation, and if these are exceeded their actions may be declared ultra vires by the courts.[95] Westminster will be able to amend their powers, to

[94] See the White Papers: *Scotland's Parliament*, Cm. 3658 (1997); *A Voice for Wales*, Cm 3718 (1997).

[95] Under the Scotland Act 1998, s. 28, laws emanating from the Scottish Parliament are described as Acts of the Scottish Parliament and become law when they have been given the Royal Assent. However, such legislation is only law if within 'legislative competence' of the Scottish Parliament (ibid. 29(1)). Although much has been made of the difference between the so-called 'primary' law-making powers of the Scottish Parliament and the 'secondary' powers of the National Assembly under the Government of Wales Act 1998, in constitutional terms each is a species of delegated legislation (i.e. the power is derived from an enabling

legislate ignoring the division of functions between the regions and the centre, or, indeed, to abolish regional government altogether without legal impediment in the same way that it has been unconstrained in adding or subtracting functions to local authorities or reorganizing the whole tier at will. This, at any rate, is the legal theory. In practice, the Scottish Parliament may prove to be a much more equal adversary in the constitutional crisis that would no doubt be engendered by any such move. The result of the referendum held in September 1997, in which 74.3 per cent of those voting (on an electoral turnout of 60.4 per cent) approved the establishment of the Parliament, acts in effect as a political entrenchment of constitutional reform.[96] The National Assembly is in a substantially weaker position—fractionally over 50 per cent voted in favour in the equivalent Welsh referendum and its lawmaking powers are minor in any event. As a body with executive rather than legislative powers, the Assembly appears to resemble a second-tier[97] local authority, rather than a parliamentary body. Indeed, the government's initial proposals were for a committee structure in the Assembly indistinguishable to the average municipality,[98] although the Government of Wales Act 1998 ultimately adopted a cabinet-style arrangement.

The second interesting feature of devolution is the relationship between the new bodies and local government. Responsibility for local government falls within the powers of the Welsh Assembly[99] and is within the legislative competence of the Scottish Parliament.[100] The National Assembly is required to make a statutory scheme for how it proposes in the exercise of its functions to sustain and promote local government in Wales.[101] There is also a Partnership Council, comprising members of the Assembly and members of Welsh local authorities, to advise both the Assembly and local authorities, but specifically able to 'make representations to the Assembly about matters affecting, or of concern to those involved in local government in Wales'.[102] The Partnership Council seems to be modelled in part on non-statutory arrangements introduced by the Labour government for consultation with local authorities. The Scottish Parliament has also been active in reviewing its relations with local government since its formation. Even before the Parliament was operative a commission was established

statute). Significantly, and in distinction from Westminster legislation, Acts of the Scottish Parliament and of the NI Assembly are treated as subordinate and not as primary legislation under the Human Rights Act 1998, s. 21.

[96] The corresponding figures in Wales leave the Assembly in a much weaker position: on a turnout of 50.1%, only 50.3% voted in favour in the referendum.

[97] Post-1996, all councils in Wales are unitary authorities.

[98] *A Voice for Wales*, Cm. 3718, 1997.

[99] GWA, s. 22 and sched. 2.

[100] Scotland Act 1998, s. 29. See further: C. Himsworth, 'Local Government and the Scottish Parliament' (1999) 2 JLGL 9.

[101] GWA 1998, s. 113(1).

[102] Ibid. s. 113(2) and sched. 11.

(the McIntosh Commission) to review local government and its relations with the new institutions.[103] It recommended that the Scottish Parliament and the councils should commit themselves to a joint agreement setting out the basis of their working relationship, and that a standing Joint Conference be established as a place where parliamentarians and local government representatives could engage in dialogue on a basis of equality.[104] In addition, relations between local government and the Scottish ministers should also be governed by a formal working agreement.[105]

Other recommendations from the McIntosh report underline the possibility of local government developing quite differently north of the Border than in England. It was recommended that legislation should be introduced to provide councils with a statutory power of general competence.[106] The Commission recommended the introduction of proportional representation for local government elections. A review was to determine the most appropriate voting system according to the following criteria: proportionality; retaining the councillor ward; fair provision for independents; allowance for geographical diversity; and a close fit between council wards and natural communities.[107] Councils were also to review their management of business and working practices, under the guiding principles of accountability and accessibility.[108] Although it was recommended that councils consider formalizing the political leadership as an executive, it was suggested that they should also be able to consider other options.[109] If implemented[110] these would all be appreciable points of difference to the reformed English local government system, which is to have a revised power of community initiative rather than a power of general competence, where the electoral system is to remain First Past the Post, and where separate political executive are being imposed.[111]

## CONCLUSION: CONSTITUTIONAL RECOGNITION FOR LOCAL GOVERNMENT?

One reason why much of the account in this chapter has been in terms of the values recognized by and supporting local democracy in the UK is the absence of a clearer constitutional purchase. The UK lacks a written constitution, and it is trite that under the doctrine of parliamentary sovereignty local government could legally be abolished at a stroke. However,

[103] *Report of the Commission on Local Government and the Scottish Parliament*, June 1999.
[104] Ibid., para. 34.
[105] Ibid. para. 45.
[106] Ibid. para. 52.
[107] Ibid. para. 89.
[108] Ibid. para. 94.
[109] Ibid. paras. 106 and 110.
[110] See *Report of the Commission on Local Government and the Scottish Parliament: The Scottish Executive's Response*, September 1999.
[111] See respectively, pp. 52–64 below, 14–16 above, and 230–2 below.

a re-evaluation of the constitutional position of local government is now overdue. Concern about the perceived erosion of the powers of local authorities since 1979, the rise of quangos, and a growing debate about the place of regionalism in any new constitutional settlement have provided the impetus. The concern here is not with the perennial issue of the mechanics of constitutional entrenchment, but rather with the possible objectives of and form of any such protection.

Reconsideration is timely also in view of the UK's obligations under the European Charter of Local Self-Government 1985, which it ratified in 1998. This is a treaty defining among the signatory states the constitutional status to be accorded to local government and providing, among other things, a guarantee of adequate finance.[112] Its provisions include in Article 4 a right for local authorities to exercise general competence to initiate matters promoting the general welfare of their inhabitants. Article 4, paragraphs 3–5 of the Charter state:

> 3. Public responsibilities shall generally be exercised, in preference, by those authorities which are closest to the citizen. Allocation of responsibility to another authority should weigh up the extent and nature of the task and the requirements of economy and efficiency.
> 4. Powers given to local authorities should normally be full and exclusive. They may not be undermined or limited by another, central or regional, authority except as provided for by the law.
> 5. Where powers are delegated to them by central or regional authority, local authorities shall, insofar as possible, be allowed discretion in adapting their exercise to local conditions.

In addition Article 9 guarantees the freedom to determine expenditure priorities and to raise adequate resources.

However, these are principles stated at a high level of generality, and mere signature of the Charter has little or no domestic legal impact. Treaties are not self-executing in UK law, and in the absence of some act of legislative incorporation the sole domestic legal effect of the Charter would be as a marginal influence on the interpretation of statutory provisions. Where possible, the courts interpret UK legislation consistently with treaty obligations. In the case of a clear conflict, however, the statute will prevail. At the international level the Charter has little bite either, because, in the absence of any enforcement machinery giving standing to local authorities, its status is simply an agreement between sovereign states. Theoretically, a contravention by one state in relation to its local authorities could be subject to international adjudication brought by another signatory state, but this prospect strains credibility.

[112] See: C. Crawford, 'European Influence on Local Self-Government', (1992) 18 (1) LGS 69.

Constitutional recognition of local government is normal in other countries. For example, in the French Constitution of the Fifth Republic, the historic units of local government, from departments through to the smallest municipalities, receive recognition.[113] Provisions on local government feature regularly in the post-1988 constitutions of the new Eastern European republics.[114] Naturally, the exact form varies, although some statement of the collective nature of local government, limits to interference by the central state, and budgetary or fiscal freedom are common. In the Federal Republic of Germany, for example, under Article 28 of the Basic Law, at the level below the *Länder* (Provinces), elected counties and communities are guaranteed the right to regulate their own affairs. They may apply to the Federal Constitutional Court under Article 93. 4b to enforce this right in so far as they are unable to do so at the provincial level, before a Land constitutional court.

The key virtue of constitutional protection for local government in the UK would be the enshrinement of pluralism within the state. The minimum necessary to achieve this would be a commitment to *elected* local government (a local stratum composed entirely of authorities run by ministerial appointees would not suffice) with some form of safeguard from central domination of the functions assigned to local authorities. However, this second factor is the cause of potentially endless difficulties. Taking a global view, there is considerable divergence in the tasks assigned to local government. Even within twentieth-century British experience, the remit of local authorities has fluctuated markedly: for example, with the removal of municipal electricity and gas companies, and of local hospitals earlier in the century, but the addition, more recently, of community care. Moreover, even if a list of quintessentially local functions could be devised either on some principled or historical basis this would not be the end of the difficulties. Experience suggests that local responsibility and accountability for services can be undermined not only by frontal attack but also by the creation of or government sponsorship of parallel providers: this has happened in the recent past with the shift in the financing of social housing by redirecting grants away from local authorities to be distributed instead by the Housing Commission to Housing Associations, and the creation of a Grant-Maintained school sector funded directly from central grant.[115]

Should local authorities be given exclusive powers within their domain, or concurrent powers with regional or central government? Advocates of

[113] Constitution of the Fifth Republic 1958, art. 72.

[114] See e.g. the Constitution of Bulgaria (12 July 1991), arts. 135–46; the Constitution of the Czech Republic (16 Dec. 1992), arts. 99 ff.; and the constitution of Lithuania (25 Oct. 1992), ch. 10: Council of Europe, *The Rebirth of Democracy: 12 Constitutions of Central and Eastern Europe* (Strasburg, 1995).

[115] See pp. 149–51 below.

entrenchment of local government might prefer the former, but there would inevitably need to be a concurrent list also (transport, on the current division of powers, would be one obvious area). On the other hand, it would be difficult to prescribe the areas in which local government had legal freedom to act without also some comparable delineation of the role of central government and the new Regional Development Agencies. Something along these lines already exists, in the devolution legislation, between Westminster and Edinburgh under the Scotland Act, although it does not purport to limit Westminster and is not immune (in legal theory at least) from later change or repeal by that Parliament. However, a binding constitutional settlement defining the respective spheres of competence of central, regional, and local government is not at present in the realm of practical politics in the UK. What *would* be possible to imagine is concurrent freedom to act within a broad sphere where local authorities, RDAs, and central government enjoyed overlapping powers. This would be in the spirit of the current vogue for 'joined-up' (or collaborative) government. It would not require a formal constitutional settlement of spheres of competence, but some thought would need to be given to possible conflict between local initiatives and central government and regional policies or future initiatives.

Leaving aside the difficulty of lists, it would be necessary also to add something about finance. To establish local government endowed with constitutionally protected functions but denied central funding or the capacity to raise local taxation to undertake them would be a mockery. The fiscal disability would undercut the constitutional competence. The most obvious form of protection would not be a general statement about access to adequate funding, which would be a blank cheque that any government would be loath to grant. Rather, the constitutionally recognized power of local taxation (if necessary, within limits[116]) would be preferable and would enhance the pluralist nature of the enterprise.

However, a danger of constitutional protection should also be borne in mind. Pluralism is only one of the values to be preserved, and a constitutional provision which gave that aspect over-rigid protection might threaten other values such as responsiveness and flexibility. A constitutional provision which prevented, for example, a future reorganization of a form of local government which because of social changes had become unresponsive would be a mixed blessing.

Difficult as it may be, the idea of a constitutional guarantee should not be rejected out of hand for the UK. The deceptively simple statement that the UK lacks a written constitution, which was always misleading because of the large body of identifiable constitutional law, is becoming less true

[116] Cf. Scotland Act 1998, s. 73 (power to vary income tax by 3p).

almost by the month as a result of the reform programme of the Blair government. With devolution, the Human Rights Act, reform of the House of Lords, and freedom of information, much of the previously unwritten constitution has been set down and clarified, although, because of the dominant doctrine of parliamentary sovereignty, none of it is entrenched nor enjoys a higher status than other law as regards Westminster. Nevertheless, we are rapidly reaching the position where it would be relatively easy to bring these constitutional laws together into a single document, irrespective of its precise legal status.

In the early 1990s the Institute for Public Policy Research proposed a draft written constitution for the UK, which included a constitutional guarantee for local government.[117] It was proposed that the exact functions, boundaries, and tax-raising powers would be specified by regional assemblies, which would also be responsible for equalizing grants between council areas, something currently undertaken at central government level. However, councils would have had some guaranteed powers under this scheme: a general power of competence and an independent power to levy rates (i.e. a property tax), irrespective of the other taxation powers granted by the region.

Nothing like this is currently proposed by the government, and the idea may sound implausible. If so, it perhaps reveals more about our lack of commitment to local democracy, compared to other aspirations such as devolution, supremacy of European law, and protection of human rights, than it does about the constitutional feasibility of the proposal.

[117] Institute for Public Policy Research, *A Written Constitution for the United Kingdom* (London, 1991), 95 and 221–2.

# 2

# *The Powers of Local Government*

## INTRODUCTION: THE CORPORATE MODEL

All local authorities are corporations: artificial entities imbued with the characteristics of legal personality—the ability to create liabilities and enforce rights. Corporate status is a life-form that councils share with other fictions and office-holders such as companies, the Crown, and bishops. The implications of this form of legal personhood cannot be overemphasized in understanding local government law and politics. Councils are legally distinct from those who finance, staff, elect, and control them. They can have rights and duties towards these people and each other, those they contract with, those they wrongfully injure, and central government. This has both benefits and detriments. If corporate status is a kind of gigantic fiction, it is perhaps unsurprising that the disadvantages come from taking the analogy with real people a stage too far. Corporate status can become a cloak to cover the real exercise of political power by flesh-and-blood individuals. The idea of personality may take on a life of its own and, like Frankenstein, give rise to unexpected consequences—for example, the controversy over whether councils have corporate 'governing reputation' which can be protected through an action for defamation.[1]

The usefulness of corporate status varies according to the context in which it is found. For instance, where an office may be held by successive individuals (such as the Crown or an ecclesiastical appointment), corporate status provides legal continuity to cover events such as death, resignation, and abdication, since a corporation never dies. In local government, the council endures although the members of the corporation (councillors) can be replaced at the pleasure of the local electorate. A change in the composition of a council or of political control does not, therefore, affect the authority's legal obligations, although they may have

[1] Answered negatively: *Derbyshire CC v Times Newspapers*, [1993] AC 534 (see pp. 41 and 79 below); and see *R v London (North) Industrial Tribunal ex p. Associated Newspapers Ltd*, *The Times*, 13 May 1998, holding that Camden LBC was not a 'person affected' for the purpose of a reporting restriction relating to an allegation of sexual misconduct in a tribunal case brought by one of its employees arising from the alleged actions of another council officer. On the other hand, note the surprising seventeenth-century decision in which the City of London was held guilty of seditious libel: see W. Holdsworth, *History of English Law* (London, 1926), ix. 50–1.

been entered into under different political control and now inhibit the political freedom of action of the present members of the corporation.[2]

A second advantage of corporate status lies in its usefulness as a vehicle for collective action. In this respect local authorities resemble companies.[3] The history of the corporation in local government has two intersecting plots, each based on urban collective action. The older tradition, going back to the medieval period, was of boroughs granted the status of corporations under royal charter, in the same way as mercantile guilds of the same period. The later urban growth caused in the eighteenth and early nineteenth centuries by the Industrial Revolution did not correspond with the older centres of population, which enjoyed borough status, and even where the old boroughs were vastly enlarged a whole host of new social and public health problems was created. Attempts to improve these conditions led to a mix of corporations created by local initiative and to single-purpose boards imposed from above. Ultimately, multi-functional local corporations emerged in the nineteenth century and came to dominate local government by the early twentieth.[4]

As with companies, local corporations were formed initially to enable groups of local worthies to engage in large-scale collective projects, especially those of public health, transportation, and education, which were beyond their individual resources or powers. This was especially the case where these public works required some form of compulsion, for example, raising finance through local taxation, compulsorily acquiring land, or extraordinary powers of inspection, demolition, or entry on to private land. The public corporation was a convenient vehicle through which to pursue such objectives and on which to confer coercive powers of this kind. What began as voluntary initiatives was progressively standardized in the nineteenth and early twentieth centuries through the central creation of first single-function, then multi-purpose, corporations on which not only powers but also duties were conferred by Parliament. The individual service to the community and philanthropy which had provided the earlier impetus became legitimated with the grafting on of a democratic system of choosing the members of the corporation through local

[2] See p. 282 below, dealing with contracts.

[3] For a valuable account which explores a number of parallels between company law and administrative law: M. Stokes, 'Company Law and Legal Theory', in W. Twining (ed.), *Legal Theory and Common Law* (Oxford, 1986); see also R. Grantham and C. Rickett (eds.), *Corporate Personality in the 20th Century* (Oxford, 1998).

[4] See M. Loughlin, *Legality and Locality: The Role of Law in Central Local Government* (London, 1996), ch. 1; e.g. the responsibility of the parishes for highways passed first, in the urban areas, to local boards of health (Public Health Act 1848) and then to the Urban Sanitary Authorities (Public Health Act 1875) and, in rural areas, to highways boards (Highways Acts 1862 and 1864) then to Urban District Councils under the Local Government Act 1894. In education, the Elementary Education Act 1870 established local school boards, whose responsibilities were transferred to education authorities by the Education Act 1902.

elections. The end result of the process was a system whereby all local authorities are now statutory corporations with a complex range of standardized duties and powers.

The ability to use the corporation for collective initiative, which persists in the case of commercial corporations, has, in the case of local government, been mainly lost through tightening of the legislative regime to iron out significant variations. Whereas in company law the legal regime is concerned with procedural matters only, leaving the *raison d'être* of the enterprise to those who control and own it, in local government the law governs both. However, a degree of flexibility in the use of corporate powers, subject to minimum standards, maximum limits to powers, and financial constraints, still remains,[5] justifying (although, some would argue, barely) the retention of a system of electoral choice of the members of the corporation (councillors).

This discussion raises the issue of how suitable the corporation is at the present time to reflect different local interests. We can identify several categories: councillors, officers, local taxpayers, local electors, local service users, individuals or companies in a commercial relationship with the council, and local inhabitants affected by the council's decisions. Councillors and officers are the human decision-takers and executors of the corporation, although in law it is the councillors alone who are its members. In practice, as we shall see in Chapters 6–8, local government law has developed a body of complex internal rules to govern these relationships, notably to safeguard the position of individual councillors, by giving rights to information and imposing corresponding duties on officers. Although there is a parallel between these rights and duties and the position of the board of directors and protection for minority shareholders in commercial corporations, there are important differences also. In local government the 'insiders' represent public interests which are in many instances non-consensual: unlike the case of the private corporation, the relationship of an 'outsider' with a local authority is often *unchosen*. Moreover, the range of public interests represented are infinitely more complex than the protection of investors or creditors. The position of local taxpayers and of people contracting with councils is, however, similar to such financial interests. The specific protection given to the former group (on which see Chapter 4) can be explained to a large degree by the perceived failure of the local government corporate framework to reflect their interests. Individuals and companies dealing commercially with local authorities are in a clearly subordinate position: the public interests in ensuring that councils behave within the limits of their legal powers, do

[5] On provisions expressly permitting local initiative, see pp. 50 ff. below. Note also that a local authority has power to promote or oppose local legislation: LGA 1972, s. 239.

not unlawfully restrict future freedom of action, and do not misuse public money have resulted in a rigid regime where the financial loss arising from unlawfully incurred municipal liabilities has, until recently, fallen on the outsider.[6] This is the direct counterpart of the doctrine of limited liability and separate legal personality which was the nineteenth century's contribution to the development of private corporations.

Local electors are represented in the corporate model only indirectly and peripherally: it is they who choose members of the corporation (councillors) at regular intervals. The formal decision-making processes provide them with few legal entitlements between elections. As with the position of other outsiders, their interests are subordinated.[7] More cynically, the fiction of corporate status can be seen as creating an artificial barrier between the electorate and the real individuals who take and execute decisions for the council—a screen to mask the real exercise of power. In Chapter 6 the implications of this are discussed in relation to the power of the party political group, whose real influence has been largely ignored in law, thanks to the outworking of the fiction of corporate personality. Greater realism has prevailed in the facility (available since 1928 but soon to be abolished) of 'lifting the corporate veil',[8] to attribute the unlawful decisions of the council to individual councillors or officers, who might then be made personally financially liable for loss arising.[9] Service users, equally, have no formal place with the corporate structure of governance. In some instances the terms of the council's duties towards them may be sufficiently precise to be legally enforceable, but more often these will give a large measure of discretion. The recent growth of consumerism in local government to represent such interests[10] is attributable directly to the failure of the conventional corporate model adequately to represent the interests and preferences of service users.

In summary, while corporate status was well adapted to answer questions of liability between members of a corporation and private law issues in relation to outsiders, it was less well adapted to concerns of public law accountability. This is no doubt in part because popular elections and party group discipline are relatively modern features of local government which have been added to a much older institutional framework. It can be argued, then, that corporations are inappropriate vehicles for representing democratic interests. Their historical value was as a legal representation of collective invention and initiative, rather than for delegation from above

[6] See Ch. 9. Reforms through a system of 'certified contracts' which enable recovery of loss by the contractor are contained in the Local Government (Contracts) Act 1997, discussed at pp. 298–9 below.

[7] See p. 73 below for discussion of *Bromley LBC v Greater London Council*, [1983] 1 AC 768.

[8] An expression more commonly used in company law.

[9] See discussion of the surcharge in Ch. 4.

[10] See Ch. 5.

of powers and duties by Parliament, as is currently the case. It is noticeable that where corporations have been used elsewhere by the state in the twentieth century (for example, for regulatory bodies) it is the formal independence, whether from government or industry, which follows from their separate legal personality, which is valued. Corporations are less suitable for representing community interests since they aggregate different interests as though they were shares under the statutory decision-making processes of majority voting.[11] This effect is exacerbated by the First Past the Post system through which individual councillors are elected, with the result that minority electoral opinion is wholly discarded in corporate decision-making.

## ULTRA VIRES AND CORPORATIONS

As an artificial person lacking in the natural and inherent abilities of an individual, the corporation may only act as empowered in law: action beyond its powers is unlawful. The ultra vires concept is one common to the public and the private spheres, with the objective in each of ensuring that the corporation does not take on a role beyond that intended. There is, however, one crucial difference between the two sectors. The all-important practical question is who has the ability to define and change the authorized objectives and powers of the corporation. In company law the question is largely technically redundant, because of the standard use of wide objects clauses in the memorandum and objects of incorporation which reserve the power to conduct all foreseeable kinds of business acccording to commercial opportunity and need. Likewise, although government departments labour under judicial supervision through ultra vires, among other aspects of judicial review, access through ministers to the parliamentary process through which first to obtain wide grants of power (and, only very rarely in their case, duties) and then to change any found to be unduly restrictive, gives the doctrine a totally different flavour. In local government, on the other hand, the doctrine is of daily significance, because the legal parameters are imposed in tightly drawn statutory powers and duties which are incapable of being changed by the corporation itself.[12]

[11] LGA 1972, sched. 12, para. 39, provides that all questions before an authority are to be decided by the votes of a majority of members present at a meeting.

[12] Professor Martin Loughlin has argued that critics who rail against the doctrine are guilty of neglecting the point that, even in the absence of the ultra vires rule, councils would be restrained by their lack of privileges (i.e. exceptional powers or exemptions from the law applicable to natural persons): *Legality and Locality* (Oxford, 1996), 46. It is argued below (pp. 41–6), however, that the courts have turned the point on its head by using ultra vires to impose *additional* restrictions on the normal powers of a legal person (e.g. contract or ownership of land) when these are exercised by a local authority.

The control of local authorities under the ultra vires rule has developed lineally from nineteenth-century legal doctrines concerning the powers of corporations. The same body of rules that controlled the actions of public and private corporations in the nineteenth century branched in very different directions: ultra vires was applied increasingly liberally in relation to companies in the early twentieth century and was finally abolished by legislation, whereas in the case of public bodies it became an increasingly potent method of judicial control. The reasons for these very different trajectories reveal much about the legal status of local authorities as political entities and the difference in judicial attitudes to public and private power.[13]

Prior to the nineteenth century the use of incorporation as a method of organizing collective or communal enterprise, whether for municipal benefit or private profit, was strictly controlled as a royal favour: corporations had been formed under charter for both purposes since at least the sixteenth century. These charter corporations were treated in law as possessing all of the attributes of a natural person; for example, contracts entered into by them were binding unless illegal according to normal principles. Following the South Sea Bubble, it became common for private corporators to petition Parliament for statutory powers. In company law these statutory companies were succeeded as the nineteenth century came to a close by registered companies. In the local government sphere, statutory corporations ousted chartered corporations later.[14]

The change in the legal source of power, from the prerogative to legislation, brought a substantial difference in judicial approach to the powers of corporations. Until comparatively recently prerogative powers have been treated as unreviewable by the courts. Statutory interpretation, however, formalized into a discipline in the nineteenth century. Judicial control of statutory corporations can be justified constitutionally as the corollary of parliamentary sovereignty, but this oversimplifies the creative potential for different judicial approaches to statutory construction or interpretation.[15] The potential for differing judicial approaches is shown by the debate in the second half of the nineteenth century over whether a wide or narrow version of the ultra vires rule was appropriate: the former

[13] The account of nineteenth-century company law below is derived from: H. Rajak, 'Judicial Control: Corporations and The Decline of Ultra Vires' (1995) 26 Cambrian Law Review 9.

[14] All local authorities now enjoy their powers solely under statute: LGA 1972, ss. 2(3), 14 (2), and 21(2). The Act extinguished the claim that boroughs created under Royal Charter possessed the powers of an ordinary person and so were not subject to ultra vires; and see *Hazzell v Hammersmith LBC*, [1992] 2 AC 1, 39–43 per Lord Templeman.

[15] The history of the control of corporations is therefore intimately bound up with larger movements in judicial temperament. Rajak also connects the rise in judicial control of statutory corporations in the nineteenth century with a philosophical preference for individualism: Rajak, op. cit., 15.

would strike down as unlawful any acts of the corporation not expressly authorized by legislation, the latter would only do so where legislation expressly or impliedly prohibited the action in question. After some vacillation, in company law it was the wide view which prevailed; however, it was quickly modified by the introduction of the incidental powers rule, which in turn laid the intellectual foundations for a distinction between a company's powers and objects which was exploited by draftsman and resulted in first the independent objects doctrine and then subjective objects. Together these developments emptied the doctrine of any further inconvenient consequences in the private sphere.

One can only speculate what might have been the outcome if the narrow rather than the wide version of ultra vires had prevailed in public law. The crucial turning-point came with the replacement of charter corporations with statutory corporations. In the celebrated *Ashbury Railway* case Blackburn J had argued at first instance that there was no difference between the common law position of a charter corporation and a statutory one, and that each should be endowed with natural faculties, except to the extent expressly or impliedly restricted.[16] This endorsement of the 'narrow' view rested fundamentally on an assumption that statutes should be regarded as an accretion to the common law, except where they necessarily prevail over it. However, when the case reached the House of Lords it was the 'wide' version of the doctrine which prevailed.[17]

Several possible explanations may be offered for the more restrictive approach subsequently taken to public corporations by the courts. Regardless of the method of incorporation, public corporations display much more homogeneity than private ones, a factor tending to discourage judicial endorsement of wide discretion. One reason why the doctrine was cut back in company law was the commercially inconvenient effects: many of the cases arose from challenges brought to otherwise unimpeachable contracts. This was a lesser factor in public law, although it is noticeable that business competitors were keen to challenge emergent local authority services through the Attorney-General's relator action.[18] The non-voluntary nature of financial contributions to local authorities may also have encouraged a different approach: in company law judges emphasized, for example, that the shareholders had *chosen* to subscribe to a company whose constitution gave wide discretion to the directors, and so needed less protection from the courts.[19] Local taxpayers, however, have no comparable choice: those who are electors may only choose *between*

[16] *Ashbury Railway Carriage Co. v Riche*, (1874) LR 9 Ex. 249.
[17] (1875) LR 7 HL 653.
[18] e.g. *AG v Fulham Corp.*, [1921] 1 Ch. 440; *AG v Manchester Corp.*, [1906] 1 Ch. 643; *AG v London County Council*, [1901] Ch. 781; *AG v Leeds Corp.*, [1929] 2 Ch. 291.
[19] Dankwerts LJ in *Bell Houses Ltd v City Wall Property Ltd*, [1966] 2 QB 656, 683–4.

rival councillors. Councils are unable to control the powers conferred upon them since these are laid down in central legislation. Finally, public corporations have greater potential for interference with private rights than do companies, and this colours the courts' attitude towards them.

This debate about the nature of corporate powers and judicial control is not merely a footnote in the legal history of public law. Fundamentally, the same choice between the wide and narrow versions of ultra vires remains today. We shall see later how it is relevant to proposals to reform the powers of local authorities. Certainly some of these suggestions amount to a retracing of the legal steps back to the *Ashbury Carriage* case, to take the road untravelled. First, however, we shall examine how the same issue has recurred in relation to whether a council is free to use its property or other rights for the political ends of the councillors in charge.

## THE LIMITS OF LEGAL PERSONALITY: LOCAL AUTHORITIES AS PUBLIC BODIES

If corporate status is intended to confer legal personality on the council, how far does this extend? Does a council have the same rights as a natural person?[20] The courts have sought to limit the effects on third parties of the fiction of corporate status by pointing to the status of local authorities as *public bodies* as a reason for denying to them the normal incidents of legal personality. Thus, in the *Derbyshire* case the House of Lords held that a local authority was not entitled to sue in defamation; Lord Keith of Kinkel stated, among other reasons, that the council as such did not have a reputation which could suffer in the same way as the reputation of a natural person.[21] Furthermore the need for public bodies to remain open to public criticism meant that there were strong policy reasons why defamation should not extend to them.

Likewise, in 1995 the Court of Appeal affirmed the view of the High Court[22] that a local authority had acted ultra vires in forbidding

[20] In the late nineteenth and early twentieth centuries a substantial theoretical literature on the nature of corporate personality arose, chiefly as a response to developments in company law. A key disputed point was whether corporations were real (since they arose from a collective enterprise of living people) or fictitious entities (whose decisions, actions, and their consequences were distinct from those constituting the corporation), see: G. Williams, *Salmond on Jurisprudence* (11th edn., London, 1957), 362–3.

[21] For other aspects of the judgment see p. 79 below.

[22] *R v Somerset CC ex p. Fewings*, [1995] 1 All ER 513; for discussion see: G. Nardell, 'The Quantock Hounds and the Trojan Horse', [1995] *PL* 27; M. Loughlin, *Legality and Locality: The Role of Law in Central-Local Relations* (Oxford, 1996), 174–5 and 412–14; R. Thomas, 'Stag Hunting, Irrelevant Considerations and Judicial Review', [1996] 3 *Web JCLI*; D. Cooper, *Governing Out Of Order: Space, Law and the Politics of Belonging* (London, 1998), ch. 7; I. Cram, 'Public Authorities, Political Protest and Judicial Review', (1995) 24 Scots Law Times 213.

deer-hunting on common land held by it. The Court drew a distinction between the powers of a private landowner and those of a public body. In the High Court Laws J based the principle on the doctrine of the rule of law:

Public bodies and private persons are both subject to the rule of law. . . .But the principles which govern their relationships with the law are wholly different. For private persons, the rule is you may do anything you choose which the law does not prohibit. . . . But for public bodies the rule is opposite, and so of another character altogether. It is that any action to be taken must be justified by positive law. A public body has no heritage of legal rights which it enjoys for its own sake; at every turn all of its dealings constitute the fulfilment of duties which it owes to others; indeed, it exists for no other purpose. . . . . It is in this sense that it has no rights of its own, no axe to grind beyond its public responsibility: a responsibility which defines its purpose and justifies its existence. Under our law this is true of every public body. The rule is necessary in order to protect the people from arbitrary interference by those set in power over them.[23]

This led to the outcome that ' a public body. . . . has no possession of legal rights, akin to a private person, which are truly its own'.[24] Whereas a private landowner would have been permitted to prevent deer-hunting because of a moral objection to it, this was not a course open to the council, notwithstanding a widely worded power which allowed it to appropriate land 'for the benefit, improvement or development of their area'.[25] A majority in the Court of Appeal endorsed Laws J's reasoning and affirmed the decision, although on slightly narrower grounds.[26]

If this is, as is claimed, a constitutional principle, it has not been consistently applied to other public bodies.[27] Moreover, the approach gives scant recognition to the political context in which such powers are conferred on local authorities. The limits of councils' powers and the danger of abuse should be understood in the context that they are elected bodies,

[23] [1995] 1 All ER 513, 524. [24] Ibid. 525. [25] LGA 1972, s. 120 (1)(b).

[26] Laws J held that the council had unlawfully given way to its moral repugnance at deer-hunting, which was irrelevant under s. 120 LGA 1972. In the Court of Appeal the majority construed that provision more widely so that councillors' view of the cruelty of deer-hunting was not necessarily irrelevant. Instead the council had acted unlawfully because of the failure of the councillors to consider the provision at all in their discussion of the deer-hunting ban: [1995] 3 All ER 20, 28 (per Sir Thomas Bingham, MR) and 35 (Swinton Thomas LJ). The council's assertion of its discretion as a landowner was a symptom of this failure to consider the powers correctly. In a dissenting judgment Simon Brown LJ held that the councillors' view of the morality of hunting was either directly relevant or, at least, not irrelevant to their powers over the land, and that the council were not *obliged* to allow hunting on the land in the absence of a positive legal right to hunt: ibid. 33.

[27] *Malone v Metropolitan Police Commissioner* (No. 2), [1979] Ch. 344 (state phone tapping not unlawful because no express law prohibiting it); on the basis of *Malone* Harris argues for the opposite conclusion to Laws J, that the government is able to take any action not otherwise prohibited: B. Harris, 'The "Third Source" of Authority for Government Action' (1992) 108 LQR 626. Cf. the discussion of the 'narrow' form of ultra vires: p. 40 above.

intended at law to have some degree of freedom to pursue political objectives unless they are plainly unlawful, and to be accountable to the electorate for the choice of policies among those lawfully open to them. This principle does not yield a determinative answer on the exact scope of a particular statute, any more than Laws J's approach does, but it is a reason to give the benefit of the doubt to the local authority when construing statutory powers. Laws J considered this argument in *Fewings* and rejected it in part because it would require differential treatment of bodies under the ultra vires doctrine according to whether they were elected.[28] While it might mar the intellectual symmetry of administrative law, such a distinction would, nevertheless, have much to commend it on constitutional grounds.

Underlying this point are interesting questions about the democratic nature of local government. In a nineteenth-century case upholding a local authority by-law the judges of the Queen's Bench Division suggested that the courts should be loath to interfere with such decisions by councils, because they were made by people who had been elected as local representatives and who must be presumed to have knowledge of local conditions.[29] It is significant that the by-law in question was made by a county council and that this decision came within a decade of the introduction under the Local Government Act 1888 of elected county councils. However, as familiarity with elected local government has grown it would seem that judges have become less deferential to local democracy.

In the High Court in *Fewings* Laws J regarded with suspicion the suggestion that, having regard to their role as elected representatives, councillors could form their own view of the desirability of deer-hunting which they might apply to the question of whether the community would benefit by prohibiting it on council land. Counsel for the local authority had argued that the council should represent the feelings, including the ethical perceptions, of the electorate, and that the capacity of local councillors to reflect views which were strongly held in the locality was an important dimension of local democracy. However, the judge saw this as raising the danger that the councillors would give priority to their own personal moral preferences, something which he thought was impermissible.[30] The decision was upheld on narrower grounds in the Court of Appeal. Simon Brown LJ, dissenting, found it 'impossible to say that the councillors must shut their minds to the cruelty argument, still less that they must do so as a matter of strict construction' of the relevant provision.[31]

[28] [1995] 1 All ER, 529. Cf. the dissenting judgment of Mathew J in *Kruse v Johnson*, (1898) 2 QB 91, 111.

[29] Ibid. 98–9 (Lord Russell) and 104 (Sir F. H. Jeune), Mathew J dissenting.

[30] [1995] 1 All ER 513, 527ff.

[31] [1995] 3 All ER 20, 31.

There are large questions about law and morality at stake in this difference of opinion which, in part, go beyond the differing conceptions of local democracy. It is plain that Laws J felt that in some sense that for councillors to act in accordance with their moral convictions was tantamount to imposing them on the community, or at least on a minority (those who wished to hunt deer), and that this would require a quite explicit statutory basis for it to be lawful.[32] This was linked to a view which saw the morality of hunting as a contentious issue *nationally*, which in turn made it unlikely that Parliament had intended to confer discretion on local authorities to form differing perceptions about hunting; if deer-hunting was to be banned, it should be by legislation.[33] This was a view echoed by Swinton Thomas LJ in the Court of Appeal.[34] As is customary, the judges in *Fewings* stated that it was not their role to judge the morality of hunting, merely the legality of the council's action.[35] This is fully in line with the Liberal conception of what judicial review involves: judging the legality of action, not its merits on political or other grounds. This disclaimer is normally made to safeguard the constitutional neutrality of the judiciary, in view of the fact that, although unelected, they may displace the judgments of elected politicians. However, it is questionable whether in this case the approach did involve taking a morally neutral stance, since it presumed that the morality of hunting was a matter of *private* personal opinion.

Also questionable is the equation of a prohibition of an activity on council land with a 'ban'. At one level this involves an elementary semantic confusion. The council did not have the power (nor had it attempted) to criminalize deer-hunting locally, or even to prohibit it throughout its area. The issue was much narrower: whether the absence of such a power should prevent it from regulating the land which it did control. It is curious to equate the decision with *imposing* the council's morality: even assuming deer-hunting to be in some way a morally protected activity, people in Somerset would have remained free to undertake it on non-council land. Arguably the judges' approach itself imposed morality, by *requiring* the council to *allow* deer-hunting on land it controlled, although it disagreed with it. In other words, the decision imposed the moral view that hunting is within the sphere of private morality and so cannot be prohibited by a public landowner.[36] According to this line of criticism, if Laws

[32] [1995] 1 All ER 513, 530. [33] Ibid. 531. [34] [1995] 3 All ER 20, 36.

[35] [1995] 1 All ER 513, 515–16 (Laws J); [1995] 3 All ER 20, 24 (Sir Thomas Bingham MR), 33 (Swinton Thomas LJ).

[36] Nardell has pointed to the similarity between this outcome and the 'public fora' doctrine in US constitutional law, which extends constitutional protection for rights such as freedom of speech and assembly to public property: Nardell, op. cit., 31–3. The connection seems appropriate in view of Laws J's own view, expressed extra-judicially, about the capacity of the common law to protect constitutional rights: Sir J. Laws, 'Is the High Court the Guardian of Fundamental Constitutional Rights?', [1993] PL 59. However, even assuming the

J and the majority in the Court of Appeal had wished to behave in a morally neutral way they should have left the matter to the council. The judgments are unconvincing because they disregard the subtle difference in the degree of recognition that different laws may give to a moral position by collapsing several alternatives into the misleading description of 'banning' an activity.[37]

The morality argument is intimately connected with the issue of legal personality and corporate nature—it is because councils are seen by the courts as less morally autonomous than private persons that they are denied the capacity to make legally enforceable judgments by reason of moral conviction. A different frame of judicial reference which was aware of its own moral preconceptions might have seen the wisdom of leaving locally elected politicans to make such decisions. Leaving aside considerations labelled as 'moral', the issue boils down to whether a local authority should be free to express strongly held local feelings on issues which may vary between areas. It is an argument about whether local democracy is representative in character.

The same judicial tendency to limit the powers of a public authority can be seen in another much-celebrated case. The House of Lords struck down a council's decision to revoke the licence (in a property law sense) of a rugby club to use a training-ground when the club failed to condemn unreservedly the actions of several of its players in taking part in a rebel tour of South Africa.[38] The judges stressed that in their view since the rugby club was doing no wrong, the council could not use its discretion to manage land under the Open Spaces Act 1906 to terminate the licence to use the training ground.[39] However, irrespective of this aspect, the procedure which the council had adopted, by insisting on public denunciation by the rugby club of their players and on an affirmative response to specific questions concerning apartheid, was treated as ample evidence of an unfair and unreasonable approach. If these factors had not been present the underlying rationale would have been much less persuasive, since it

desirability of displacing the views of elected councillors to protect judge-made rights of this kind, the approach must be questionable on the facts of *Fewings*. A constitutional right to pursue recreational activity (or to hunt deer, to state it more narrowly) is arguably less worthy of protection than e.g. a right to protest.

[37] Sir Thomas Bingham argued for a more complex position. In his view the council's error was in failing to distinguish adequately between their view of the immorality of hunting and the further step of whether this required the prohibition of hunting. He read the power in s. 120 of the LGA 1972 as requiring a form of stronger conviction of the second kind: [1995] 3 All ER 20, 28. There are strong echoes here of the law/morality debates between Hart and Devlin of the 1960s. Although more subtle, the argument is no more neutral than those already discussed, since it operates within the same frame of reference which compartmentalizes morality into subdivisions of private belief and public benefit and imposes the judge's version of this in determining the legality of the council's action.

[38] *Wheeler v Leicester City Council*, [1985] 2 All ER 1106.

[39] See esp. Lord Templeman at 1112–13.

suggests (like *Fewings*) that a council's discretion in management of property should be limited according to the legal character of the other party's action.[40] At a certain point such an argument must inevitably fail: there could be any number of competing lawful activities which might take place on a council recreation ground which would be mutually exclusive; the more significant question is what factors the *council* may consider in choosing between them to manage the land.[41]

This discussion has shown that courts limit the powers of local authorities in ways which would not apply to private individuals, because of their character as public corporations. However, this tendency shows a distinct ambivalence—essentially their powers are restricted when the interests of private individuals might be adversely affected by their actions. In a different sense, however, the public character of councils as elected bodies, properly representing their communities, is ignored by the courts.

## LOOSENING THE ULTRA VIRES DOCTRINE

In this section attempts to allow a measure of flexibility in local authority decision-making are discussed. The first, section 111 of the Local Government Act 1972, enables a local authority to do anything 'which is calculated to facilitate, or is conducive or incidental to, the discharge of any of their functions'. This provision is intended to soften the rigour of the ultra vires rule by making lawful actions which are ancillary to an express statutory power. The power is subsidiary in nature[42] and cannot be used to override specific limitations in the 'parent' provision. Despite its apparently technical formulation, the rule has over the decades been the site of numerous skirmishes over the proper line between public-sector provision and the private sector.

[40] In another instance, the House of Lords held that a rating authority which had received an overpayment of rates because of a mistake of law wrongly exercised its statutory discretion in resolving not to return the money, although a private litigant would not have been obliged to do so in comparable circumstances: *Tower Hamlets LBC v Chetnik Developments*, [1988] 1 All ER 961. Lord Bridge argued that Parliament intended such councils to behave in a 'high-minded' way whereas a private individual might behave 'shabbily' if they so chose: ibid. 969–70. See also: *R v Crawley BC ex p. Arthur Prince (Turf Accountants) Ltd* (QBD, unreported decision of 18 Aug. 1989), obiter of Nolan J that a local authority's refusal as landlord of a commercial property to consent to change of user might be susceptible to judicial review, since a public landlord was in a different position to a private landlord in holding public property.

[41] In fact this understates the issue in *Wheeler*; since good race relations was not merely a permissible factor to be considered, it was expressed in terms of a *duty* imposed on the council under s. 71 of the Race Relations Act 1976.

[42] See the comments of Woolf J in *Hazell v Hammersmith and Fulham LBC* [1990] 2 QB 697, 722–3 (approved by the Court of Appeal at [1990] 2 QB 697, 785 and by the House of Lords at [1992] 2 AC 1, 29).

This power was introduced in 1972 and followed earlier decisions in which the ultra vires rule had been applied legalistically to strike down local authority operations beyond the strict letter of the enabling Act. Thus, in one case a council laundry service was found to be outside the terms of the Baths and Wash Houses Act 1846, since the council was enabled to provide facilities for washing clothes but not to charge.[43] In another, a power to carry parcels on a municipal tram service did not entitle the council to run a parcel delivery service by tram.[44] Both these decisions were reached on interpretation of the common law rule permitting a corporation to carry out actions 'reasonably incidental' to those authorized in its constitution.[45] In the tramways case the judge pointedly differentiated between business which could be conveniently combined with that authorized (which a parcels service could) and what was incidental.

The effect of these decisions—prompted by the complaints of local tradespeople—was to prevent local authorities from expanding their activities into services which could be provided by the private sector. On the other hand, the ancillary functions rule did not require a local authority to use private services in preference to its own. Thus, a council's internal printing and bookbinding service which required printing in a challenge instigated by local printers was held to be incidental to the council's duties.[46] Legislation would be required to compel local authorities to 'contract out':[47] it would not be brought about by judicial interpretation. An analogy with the probable behaviour of a private-sector landlord was expressly rejected in a decision upholding a local authority's policy of arranging group insurance for its council house tenants, which was held to be incidental or consequential to its duty to manage its housing stock.[48] The decision has the paternalistic feel of a different political era, since the court was particularly impressed by the argument that the council had a legitimate interest because of the probability that a tenant suffering uninsured loss would replace lost furniture by going into rent arrears.[49]

In considering whether actions undertaken by a local authority are conducive to or calculated to facilitate some other statutory function, the

43 *AG v Fulham Corp.*, [1921] 1 Ch. 440.

44 *AG v Manchester Corp.*, [1906] 1 Ch. 643; see also *AG v London County Council*, [1901] Ch. 781. However, see *AG v Leeds Corp.*, [1929] 2 Ch. 291, where a power to run a bus service outside the city boundary along authorized tramway routes was held to authorize incidentally a minor (40 yards) deviation from the tram route.

45 From *AG v Great Eastern Railway*, (1880) 5 App. Cas. 473.

46 *AG v Smethwick Corp.*, [1932] 1 Ch. 562.

47 See Ch. 10.

48 *AG v Crayford UDC*, [1962] Ch. 575.

49 Cf. a decision in which Dyson J held that a housing authority had no power under section 111 to pay interest on housing benefit withheld pending the settlement of a dispute between the tenant (claimant) and his landlord, notwithstanding that a court might order payment of interest against the tenant: the payment of interest on the benefit would not facilitate its payment, although it might assist a broader purpose of ensuring that the tenant did not get into debt. *R v Kensington and Chelsea Royal BC ex p. Brandt*, *The Times*, 21 Dec. 1995.

courts are able to assess the true purpose of transactions entered into and to strike down those which appear to be a sham.[50] Hence, in the interest rates swap case, the House of Lords held that while financial transactions of this kind could be within section 111 if entered into in order to limit the council's exposure in the money markets, the transactions in question had gone beyond this and, hence, were not ancillary to other functions.[51]

In another case it was held that a local authority could not guarantee a bank loan to a company which it had itself formed, when the company was engaged in a development (the building of timeshare apartments) which would have been ultra vires the authority.[52] In so holding, the Court of Appeal took a restrictive view of the council's powers. Whereas the High Court had held that the council was entitled to perform its functions through the medium of a company and that the illegality subsisted in guaranteeing the company's debts,[53] the Court of Appeal held that the building of the timeshare was ultra vires, whether carried out by the council itself or through the medium of a company.[54] Moreover, the scheme could not be rescued by invoking section 111 since there was no primary statutory function which the council could lawfully undertake in relation to the timeshare, to which it would be subsidiary. In the Court's view the whole scheme had been entered into for the purpose of avoiding the controls on capital expenditure to which the council was subject at the time of

[50] See e.g. *R v Wirral MBC ex p. Milstead*, 87 LGR 611.

[51] *Hazzell v Hammersmith LBC*, [1991] 1 All ER 545; see the detailed study by Loughlin, op. cit., ch. 6.

[52] *Credit Suisse v Allerdale BC*, [1996] 4 All ER 129, CA.

[53] At first instance (*Credit Suisse v Borough of Allerdale*, [1995] 1 Lloyd's Rep. 315) Colman J was careful to note that this did not mean that all guarantees by local authorities of loans to companies established by them were ultra vires; rather it was necessary to consider whether the obligation the performance of which was guaranteed would be ultra vires the council. This was applied in a later case to uphold a council guarantee and indemnity for repayments of a loan made to a company established to acquire properties which were then leased to the council to provide homelessness accommodation: the guarantee was held to be ancillary to the council's statutory duty to house the homeless under section 65 of the Housing Act 1985: *Credit Suisse and Another v Waltham Forest LBC*, [1996] 4 All ER 176.

[54] The judges reached this conclusion after analysis of s. 19 of the Local Government (Miscellaneous Provisions) Act 1976, which provided: 'A local authority may provide . . . such recreational facilities as it thinks fit and . . . the powers conferred by this subsection to provide facilities include the powers to provide buildings, equipment, supplies and assistance of any kind . . .'.

The scheme constructed was for a combined timeshare and leisure pool complex: whereas the section expressly allowed for provision of swimming pools. The judges held that the timeshare part of the complex did not fall within the scope of facilities provided 'in connection with any other recreational facilities', as permitted under section 19(1)(f), and was not a recreational facility in its own right. The only connection between the two parts of the development in the court's view was their financial interdependence: it was intended that the sale of the timeshare units would finance the building of the leisure facilities. A further argument grounded on the section was also rejected: the guarantee of the loan could not fall within the terms of 'assistance of any kind' since the assistance had to be given to those using the recreational facilities, rather than a third party which was 'providing' them itself.

the scheme. Even had the judges found that there was a primary statutory power which enabled the council to undertake the development through participation in a company, whose loan it guaranteed, the same reasoning would have rendered the scheme unlawful. The objective of avoiding statutory controls would have been regarded as an improper purpose, and this would have been a separate ground for holding the scheme ultra vires.

The restrictive view of local authority powers in the Court of Appeal's judgments suggest that the notion of the 'enabling authority'[55] is far from being judicially accepted. The antipathy towards such an approach is present both in the judicial interpretation of 'assistance' (section 19 of the 1976 Act) by restricting it to a direct relationship between the council as service provider and the user of leisure facilities with no legal space for the participation of an intermediary, in the restrictive attitude towards section 111, and in the ruling that any attempt to broaden the council's powers through use of a company amounted to an improper purpose. This last point is especially important: it substantially inhibits the potential role which a local authority might play as coordinator and supporter of local initiatives, whether coming from the public or private sector in its locality. The decision illustrates the difficulties of a wide version of 'enabling'.[56] Later cases applying these principles have failed to develop a coherent framework in which section 111 could be used to advance the notion of the 'enabling authority', by financially guaranteeing the liabilities of arm's length organizations, since each example turns on its own particular statutory context.[57]

The question of ancillary powers has arisen also in relation to service users. In *McCarthy and Stone (Developments) v Richmond upon Thames LBC*[58] the House of Lords held that the council could not lawfully charge for the provision of pre-application planning advice. In the view of Lord Lowry the council was permitted under section 111 to provide the advice, since this facilitated its statutory function of determining planning applications, but not to charge, since this only facilitated the giving of the advice and, hence, was beyond the permitted range of activities under section

[55] See pp. 54 and 306 below.

[56] See Ch. 10 for discussion of contracting out and for further discussion of the importance of *Alledale* in a contractual context.

[57] Cf. *Credit Suisse v Waltham Forest LBC*, [1996] 4 All ER 176 with *Morgan Grenfell v Sutton LBC*, (1996) 95 LGR 574, where it was held that a similar guarantee to an unregistered housing association was ultra vires because section 111 could not be used to override a specific limitation on loans and indemnities in s. 60 of the Housing Act 1985. *Allerdale* was distinguished in a case in which an indemnity of a contractor's loan was upheld, since the company was not one controlled by the council: *City Centre Leisure (Holdings) Ltd. v Lord Mayor and Cititizens of the City of Westminster*, unreported decision QBD, 5 Apr. 1995.

[58] [1991] 4 All ER 897. Cf. *R v Hereford and Worcester Local Education Authority ex p. Jones*, [1981] 1 WLR 768, where an education authority's decision to charge fees for individual and group music tuition was held to be unlawful.

111.[59] He relied upon well-known authority requiring clear legislative authorization for taxation[60] for the proposition that clear statutory authority was necessary for the charge to be imposed. He also rejected the council's contention that since it was not under a duty to provide the service it was free to set the terms under which it did so.[61] The decision has been criticized for failing to recognize an 'implied functions' doctrine.[62] It was left to Parliament to give express power to authorize councils to charge for services of this kind.[63]

The limited scope of section 111 was further demonstrated when the Court of Appeal held that it could not be utilized by a council to validate voluntary severance payments made to staff in excess of the statutory maximum to which they would have been entitled under redundancy and superannuation legislation.[64] Despite the apparently open-ended discretion to appoint staff on conditions which it thought fit, the Court of Appeal held that the conditions for dismissal could not be grounded in section 112 of the 1972 Act, and had instead to be founded on section 111, which had primacy over the other provision. Section 111 was itself subject to limitations appearing in 'other provisions' (whereas section 112 was not) and, consequently, was subordinate to other employment legislation. This was a remarkable feat of statutory interpretation: the outcome was that section 111, which was intended to soften the ultra vires rule, restricted a *wider* specific power in the same Act. This was highly inventive, and all the more so for ignoring the view expressed clearly in the House of Lords only months earlier that section 111 was to be regarded as subsidiary to other statutory provisions.[65] A better explanation perhaps lies in the role of the court in protecting the interests of local taxpayers.

A second potential source of flexibility is the power of discretionary expenditure under section 137 of the 1972 Act. This gives a power of discretionary expenditure within set financial limits (calculated on a per

[59] [1991] 4 All ER 902 and 906 (where his Lordship described it as 'incidental to incidental').

[60] *Attorney-General v Wilts. Dairies*, (1921) 37 TLR 884.

[61] [1991] 4 All ER, 903. The council's argument had earlier prevailed in the Court of Appeal, where Slade LJ had equated the position of the council to a contractor who could offer to supply the service on a 'take it or leave it' basis: *R v Richmond upon Thames LBC ex parte McCarthy and Stone (Developments) Ltd*, [1990] 2 All ER 852, 859–60.

[62] *Cross on Local Government Law*, para. 1–25.

[63] Local Government and Housing Act 1989, s. 150 (power for the Secretary of State to authorize authorities to charge in respect of designated functions).

[64] *Allsop v North Tyneside MBC*, (1992) 90 LGR 462; Parker LJ justified the use of s. 111 rather than s. 112 by arguing that the power to employ staff did not contain an implied power to dismiss them, which could only be derived from the former provision. See also *Hinckley and Bosworth BC v Shaw and Coker*, [2000] LGR 9.

[65] *Hazzell v Hammersmith LBC*, [1991] 1 All ER 545.

capita basis[66]) and has been widely used as an instrument of local initiative.[67] The section also allows local authorities to make donations to charities.[68] Case law is sparse, but in one case a council grant to the British Olympic Association towards the costs of sending a team to the Moscow Olympics was upheld.[69] The provision was also controversially used to establish a trust to provide free or assisted places at independent schools in a dispute in Manchester between the Conservative-controlled metropolitan County Council and the Labour City Council.[70] The City Council brought an action for declarations that the County Council had acted beyond its powers in passing the resolutions of April 1978 to establish a trust (to which it later paid £1.12 million). As the case made its way through the courts several different arguments about the scope of the power of discretionary power were considered and rejected. First, the County Council's powers were not limited by the fact that it was not an education authority, while those of the district councils in its area were.[71] Secondly, it was held that the County Council had power to establish the trust as being incidental to or consequential on the power under the section; the trust was regarded as the means of achieving the council's legitimate end, rather than a distinct objective in its own right. A third objection, to the money being applied over seven years to pay the educational costs of the children starting school in 1978, also failed: a single payment from the council within the current year was permissible, even if the trust were to use the money over a longer period. The Court of Appeal held that there was no general principle that a local authority could not enter into a commitment which would continue beyond the life of the currently elected body.

Since these decisions, however, the scope of section 137 has been progressively limited. The section has been revised so that there must be a 'direct benefit' to some or all of the inhabitants of the area and the benefit must be 'commensurate' to the expenditure involved, introducing, in

[66] LGA 1972, s. 137 (as amended by LGA 1986, s. 3 and LGHA 1989, ss. 36 and 37). The power was first introduced by s. 6 of Local Government (Financial Provisions) Act 1963. The Local Authorities (Discretionary Expenditure Limits) Order 1993, SI 41 (1993), sets the limit per authority. See also Local Authorities (Discretionary Expenditure Limits) Order 1995, SI 651 (1995).

[67] For a study of the operation of the power in its previous guise, see C. Crawford and V. Moore, *The Free Two Pence* (London, 1983).

[68] LGA 1872, s. 137 (3)(a).

[69] *Lobenstein v Hackney LBC* (unreported Divisional Court judgment of 16 July 1980). In view of the subsequent tightening of s. 137, it is doubtful if the case would be decided in the same way today.

[70] *Manchester City Council v Greater Manchester MCC*, (1980) 78 LGR 71, CA; (1980) 78 LGR 560, HL.

[71] At first instance Smith J held that the actions of the county council were ultra vires because education was not one of their functions, but this was rejected on appeal since limitation under s. 137 only apply to actions forbidden to the authority in question: s. 137(1).

effect, a statutory requirement of value for money or proportionality. These restrictions, together with a specific regime for local authority participation in economic development projects (Local Government and Housing Act 1989, Part III) have diminished the appeal and perhaps the need for a discretionary power of expenditure. Research published by the DETR[72] found that (in contrast to the proposed new duty and power of community concern, discussed below) section 137 was seen by councils in a negative light, hedged around by restrictions, irrelevant to their situation, and unlikely to encourage innovation. However, the same study found that few local authorities use anything approaching the permitted levels of expenditure under the section.[73] Following the introduction of the new power of community initiative (below), section 137 will be largely superseded.[74]

Other existing legal powers enabling some local flexibility are either difficult to use or inadequate. Local legislation is expensive and time-consuming to promote and unlikely to receive parliamentary approval if contentious. By-laws are subject to confirmation under the Local Government Act 1972, section 236.[75] Where the by-law is made for the purpose of good rule and government or the suppression of nuisance, the Home Office is the confirming authority. In practice, confirmation acts as a more stringent control on the substance of such by-laws than does judicial review; the Home Office is reluctant to confirm by-laws which depart from the terms of its 'model by-laws' even on topics as mundane as dog-fouling or control of ice-cream van chimes. Moreover, by-laws operate within a limited sphere by criminalizing minor forms of undesirable activity; they contain no power to promote positive initiatives. The existing powers all operate within the existing understanding of the ultra vires doctrine, and none affects the constitutional arrangements in which local government plays a subservient role.

## REFORM OF THE ULTRA VIRES RULE

A number of problems with and limitations in the ultra vires doctrine have emerged from the discussion so far: it engenders an excessive concern with legality, gives too little recognition to local diversity and no deference

[72] N. Mason, R. Turner, and Michael Dodd Consulting Ltd, *Local Authority Activity under Section 137, Local Government Act 1972* (London, Mar. 1999).

[73] Discussed below at pp. 65–6.

[74] LGA 2000, ss. 2(b) and 8.

[75] Councils are, however, permitted to promote or oppose local legislation under LGA 1972, s. 239.

to representative democracy, lacks innate powers, and draws too sharp a boundary between the corporation and other actors.

Dissatisfaction with the rigidity of ultra vires is long-standing. Calls for its relaxation go back to Private Members' Bills introduced in the 1920s and 1930s.[76] Both the Maud Committee and the Redcliffe-Maud Commission recommended that a general competence power be granted in which local authorities would be able to undertake activities which they considered to be in the interests of their area.[77] It was intended that this power should be free of financial limits or ministerial approval and that it would operate as an adjunct to specific statutory functions and duties. Local authorities would then be able to take the initiative in responding to local pressures and circumstances. However, the Widdicombe Committee argued that such a new general power would be irreconcilable with the continued existence of a framework of specific functional powers, and preferred instead the extension of a financially limited general discretion by way of reform of section 137.[78] Despite Widdicombe's objections to the principle of a power of general competence, various recent proposals have been made for reform of the doctrine. These include: a widening of 137;[79] granting a power of general competence to undertake any activities considered to be in the interests of the area unless specifically prohibited by law;[80] licensed experiments granting additional powers to selected

[76] M. Loughlin, 'Ultra Vires: Hail and Farewell' in Local Government Information Unit, *A Framework for the Future* (London, 1997).

[77] *Report of the Committee on the Management of Local Government*, 1967, para. 283; *Report of the Royal Commission on Local Government in England*, Cmnd. 4040 (1969), ch. 8, para. 323 (a general power to incur expenditure for the benefit of its inhabitants and the area without limit, subject only to national economic and fiscal objectives); see also the Wheatley Commission proposals for Scotland: *Report of a Royal Commission on Local Government in Scotland*, Cmnd. 4190 (1969), para. 640.

[78] Paras. 8.26ff. The committee preferred future difficulties over the source of funding or legality of borderline activities to be resolved by non-statutory guidance giving practical advice on the use of s. 137 in relation to functional powers in areas of particular concern.

[79] The Association of Metropolitan Authorities considered a proposed Local Government (Enabling) Bill prepared by Professor Martin Loughlin, and modelled on the Republic of Ireland Local Government Act 1991, to revise s. 137. However, unlike that provision, the draft did not impose a financial ceiling. It specifically authorized a range of activities (including undertaking works, providing buildings, equipment, and services), rather than merely authorizing expenditure, and would have relaxed the requirements of 'direct benefit' to the council's area and proportionality related to expenditure which were introduced in 1989. The proposed power was intended to work in conjunction with s. 111. It had the underlying purpose of returning to what was described earlier as the 'narrow' version of ultra vires, where councils are free to undertake activity unless specifically prohibited by legislation. It included also a representative role, which would have allowed local authorities to represent the interest of the local community 'in such manner that they think appropriate', and, specifically, to undertake research, surveys of studies connected with the local community to ascertain and disseminate the views of the local community of matters affecting them, and to 'facilitate and promote interest and involvement in local government affairs'.

[80] Commission for Local Democracy, *Taking Charge: The Rebirth of Local Democracy* (London, 1995); House of Lords Select Committee, 'Rebuilding Trust', HL 97 (1995–6).

councils, as in the Scandanivian 'free commune' schemes;[81] and a stronger presumption of legality.[82] Two factors have given the present debate cogency and urgency. As we have seen, a series of court decisions earlier in the 1990s gave a restrictive interpretation of the ancillary powers under section 111 of the Local Government Act 1972 on which many local government practitioners had pinned their faith.[83] Secondly, the past decade has seen a growing consensus that the role of councils has changed and that new powers are needed as a consequence; this issue is explored below.

In recent years the role of local authorities has changed dramatically, away from being the sole or main providers of local services towards the concept of the 'enabling council'. Used as a rallying call by the New Right in the early 1980s, it signified an emphasis on new modes of service delivery, where the council became a purchaser and regulator of services delivered by the private sector through contracting out. However, a more recent, communitarian version, which has become the current orthodoxy, is much broader. It sees the council as a 'community leader'[84]—the advocate, representative, and coordinator of a range of services delivered by the local public, private, and voluntary sectors to the local community.[85]

In 1996 a House of Lords Select Committee made a number of proposals grounded on the recognition of an emerging new order—that of 'local governance', in which local services were provided by a variety of bodies: elected councils, appointed local quangos, and the voluntary sector. Councils would continue to play a part within this new order as significant service providers, but the new and challenging role for them was that of community leadership—brokering, facilitating, and influencing all those involved in 'local governance', thus spreading democratic accountability. Councils are seen as the natural community leaders within this differenti-

[81] See Kitchin below; L. Rose, 'Nordic Free-Commune Experiments: Increased Local Autonomy or Continued Central Control?' in D. King and J. Pierre (eds.), *Challenges to Local Government* (London, 1990).

[82] Cf. 'certificated contracts' under Local Government (Contracts) Act 1997; p. 298 below.

[83] *Hazzell v Hammersmith and Fulham LBC*, [1991] 1 All ER 545; *McCarthy and Stone v Richmond upon Thames LBC*, [1991] 4 All ER 897; *Credit Suisse v Allerdale BC*, [1996] 4 All ER 129; *Credit Suisse v Waltham Forest LBC*, [1996] 4 All ER 176; *Morgan Grenfell v Sutton LBC*, (1996) 95 LGR 574.

[84] See esp. J. Stewart and G. Stoker (eds.), *Local Government in the 1990s* (Basingstoke, 1995), ch. 14. For official endorsement see: *Modernising Local Government: Local Democracy and Community Leadership* (Feb. 1998), esp. paras. 1.9 and 6.5; *Modern Local Government: in Touch With the People* (1998), paras. 8.1 ff.

[85] A parallel in the existing law is with the power under s. 222 of the LGA, which allows a council to bring or defend legal proceedings or make representations at a public inquiry where the authority considers it expedient for the promotion or protection of the interests of the inhabitants of their area. This is in a literal sense a representative/advocacy role for the local community; see B. Hough, 'Local Authorities as Guardians of the Public Interest', [1992] PL 130.

ated world of 'local governance' because, being elected, they are open to a degree of democratic accountability, and, unlike most local agencies, they are multi-functional, with a broader interest in the local area.[86] This analysis was partially accepted by the Conservative government.[87] For the Select Committee, the new power of general competence, coupled with greater acceptance of local diversity and freedom to experiment with new administrative and electoral arrangements,[88] would all play a part. As we shall see, the incoming Labour government adopted most of this reform agenda.

In the ensuing debate over a power of general competence, several issues emerged as critical: the relationship between the power and more detailed powers enjoyed by councils, financial implications of money spent under the power, the effect on other tiers of government, potential conflict with central government policy, and electoral and financial accountability for use of the power. These suggest that whether the leadership role was conceived as one of direction, policing, or umpiring, it would have natural limitations within the existing statutory and constitutional arrangements. It would be possible, however, to imagine concurrent freedom to act within a broad sphere where local authorities and central government each enjoyed power. This would not require a formal constitutional settlement of spheres of competence, but some thought would need to be given to possible conflict between local initiatives and central government policies or future initiatives. Any general power of competence carrying with it freedom to make discretionary expenditure would also have implications for central government control of local taxation.

An alternative proposal was a power to waive or lift specific restrictions under which councils work. Inevitably, this would require the cooperation of central government in order to be effective. Hilary Kitchin suggested that it should take the form of a discretion for the Department of Environment to relax statutory provisions on an experimental basis for individual councils.[89] These experiments might involve exemption from national legislation or regulations, or the conferral of additional powers. Applications from councils would be subject to a local consultation process, including the involvement of the voluntary and business sectors, public-sector trade unions, and other affected government departments. It was envisaged that the Secretary of State for Environment would make the

[86] 'Rebuilding Trust', paras. 4.37 ff. The CLD suggested that councils should have a statutory entitlement to monitor and comment on the actions of local quangos and governmental agencies: ibid., para. 6.16.

[87] *Government Response to the Report of the House of Lords Select Committee on Relations Between Central and Local Government 'Rebuilding Trust', HL 97 (1995–96)*, Cm. 3464 (1996), para. 4.45.

[88] See ch. 7 below.

[89] H. Kitchin, 'A Power of General Competence for Local Government', in L. Pratchett and D. Wilson (eds.), *Local Democracy and Local Government* (Basingstoke, 1996), 223 ff.

final decision on any experiment, and that he or she would be accountable to Parliament for these decisions and for the operation of the experimental programme.[90]

Questions of potential conflict with the government's economic priorities and with government policy would be less problematic here than in the case of a general power of competence. In the context of limited experiments in individual councils, the government's interest in control on general economic grounds should in principle be weaker than when considering functions and expenditure across the sector as a whole. Obviously, experiments could not carry an automatic entitlement to additional central government grant, but, equally, if there were no freedom to raise additional finance the scope for experimentation would be severely limited. Plainly, government may be concerned that freedom to experiment should not be used to escape the limitations on expenditure and local tax generally. One way of reconciling these conflicting demands would be to allow for specifically 'earmarked' or 'hypothecated' local taxation for approved local experimental schemes. This would have the advantage of directly involving the local community through the normal electoral accountability mechanisms; experiments would be financially transparent and capable of being audited for their effectiveness and value for money, but would not constitute a general escape route from the rigours of financial control. Any such power could be combined with approval of spending on experimental schemes through a local referendum. The question of conflict with local government policy in relation to delivery of local services is perhaps more theoretical than real. Schemes which involved simply a repatriation of local government powers of regulation and service delivery would be unlikely to be approved. The most likely types of experiment are those involving increased cooperation with the local private and voluntary sectors and quangos in ways not currently envisaged.

## IMPLEMENTING REFORM[91]

With the election of the new government in 1997 the context for the debate altered considerably: the 1998 White Paper[92] wholeheartedly embraced

[90] An alternative was suggested by Professor Malcolm Grant, namely approval of experimental programmes by a Select Committee: see M. Grant, *The Rehabilitation of Local Government, Vires or Virus* (London, 1990). However, this had several difficulties, not least that these bodies are normally involved (somewhat imperfectly) in scrutiny and accountability of government departments, rather than in the permissive role envisaged. Moreover, as Kitchin argues, it risked substituting direct accountability to Parliament for accountability to the local electorate.

[91] For earlier evaluation of the government's proposals: C. Crawford, 'Powers for the New Vision', (1998) 1 JLGL 31; T. Child and B. Schwehr, 'Power to the People' (1998) 1 JLGL 71.

[92] *Modern Local Government: In Touch with the People* (July 1998).

the notion of councils as community leaders within a broader vision of the renewal of local democracy, as had been urged by a number of recent reports.[93] Some of the more commercially inconvenient results of the courts' interpretation of local government powers were removed through the introduction of a system of 'certificated' contracts under the Local Government (Contracts) Act 1997.[94] The United Kingdom signed the European Charter on Local Self-Government.[95] Prior to the 1997 election the Labour Party had proposed that there should be an overall duty to promote the social, economic, and environmental well-being of the community coupled with a general power of community initiative.[96] After the election the government published its proposals for reform of the executive structures of local government and for a new ethical framework, together with draft legislation.[97]

The community leadership role had four significant features under the 1998 White Paper, both structural and functional: new legal duties and powers; as a part of these, the development of a community strategy; greater opportunities for local organizations and the agencies to explain their policies and actions to the community (for example, through non-statutory local public forums); and greater freedom to enter into partnership arrangements.

Relaxation of the ultra vires rule was proposed in three distinct ways. First, by expanded discretionary powers to enter into partnership arrangements with other local bodies, organizations, or agencies. These were intended to remove the present uncertainty over the legality of some of

[93] CLD, op. cit; House of Lords Select Committee, op. cit.; Local Government Information Unit, *A Framework for the Future* (1997); *Modernising Local Government: Local Democracy and Community Leadership* (London, Feb. 1998).

[94] See p. 298 below.

[95] Note esp. Article 4(1): 'The basic powers and responsibilities of local authorities shall be prescribed by the constitution or by statute. However, this provision shall not prevent the attribution to local authorities of powers and responsibilities for specific purposes in accordance with the law.

(2) Local authorities shall, within the limits of the law, have full discretion to exercise their initiative with regard to any matter which is not excluded from their competence nor assigned to any other authority.'

Art. 5. 'Where powers are delegated to them by central or regional authority, local authorities shall, insofar as possible, be allowed discretion in adapting their exercise to local conditions.' However, the House of Lords Select Committee accepted the DoE's argument that the ultra vires rule was consistent with these provisions and that a power of general competence was not a requirement of the Charter (*Rebuilding Trust*, para. 3.28). This seems hard to reconcile with the plain text of Art. 4(2).

[96] *Renewing Democracy, Rebuilding Communities* (London, 1995). While the proposals were at a formative stage it was suggested that these might take the form of local referendums, followed by ministerial approval of individual schemes and a system of annual review: see H. Kitchin, 'A power of community initiative?', 1996 Local Authority Law 3, 7.

[97] *Local Leadership, Local Choice* (London, March 1999); Local Government (Organisation and Standards) Bill.

these cooperative ventures.[98] Secondly, the introduction of a general duty and linked power of community initiative to apply to all councils. The new duty on councils to promote the economic, social, and environmental well-being of their areas was intended to enshrine in law the role of the council as 'the elected leader of their local community'.[99] It was to be 'underpinned' by a power enabling councils to act for the well-being of their area and for those who live, work, and visit there. The Green Paper[100] described the new duty as an intended spur to the community leadership role, which would remove uncertainty without significantly extending local authority powers. This power was to be limited so that it could not be used to 'prejudice' other council functions or those of other statutory bodies,[101] and the Government would retain a reserve power.[102]

The third proposal took the form of a ministerial relaxation of controls for authorities which could demonstrate that they deserved greater freedom because of their strong existing performance ( 'Beacon Councils'[103]). 'Beacon Councils' are the Labour government's version of the Scandinavian 'Free Local Government' initiatives. The scheme is envisaged in two distinct phases:[104] a first stage in which councils are identified as performing strongly in particular services (or exceptionally, overall) and are commended and encouraged to share best practice with other authorities, through open days, seminars, staff exchanges, and so on. The Local Government Improvement and Development Agency will foster these efforts. The second stage involves the possibility of conferring on beacon councils greater freedom from statutory controls. This would be done under a statutory scheme for ministerially licensed experiments for a period of perhaps three to five years (subject to continued satisfactory performance), with the vetting of proposals and recommendations by an independent panel. It is envisaged that the freedoms conferred might include relaxation of ministerial consent requirements and the conferral of new powers. This is a less cumbersome means to the acquisition of special powers than the promotion of local legislation. There is also the added

[98] The 1998 Green Paper proposed a modest reform of s. 111. The purpose was twofold: to broaden so that ancillary power could be more than one step removed from the primary power (i.e. ancillary to ancillary) and to resolve doubts over use of s. 111 for cooperation and partnership activities, including participation in companies: Green paper, para. 6.13. The second of these is followed through in ss. 2 (4) and 4 LGA 2000; the first appears to have been abandoned.

[99] White Paper, para. 8.9.

[100] *Modernising Local Government: Local Democracy and Community Leadership*, para. 6.10.

[101] The proposed limitation for other public bodies was omitted from LGA 2000, ss. 2 and 3.

[102] For discussion see pp. 59–66 below and I. Leigh, 'The Proposed Duty of Well-Being: Comparable Powers and Duties' in Local Government Information Unit, *Turning Community Leadership into Reality* (London, 1999).

[103] DETR, *The Beacon Council Scheme: Prospectus* (London, Feb. 1999).

[104] Ibid.

incentive of financial rewards. The award of beacon status might at this stage be relevant to decisions taken about resource allocation and auditing: the Local Government Act 1999 allows for flexibility to take account of beacon status under the 'best value' regime and under the new council tax reserve powers. Powers have aready been taken to allow ministers to set aside legal constraints on forms of service delivery by local councils where these cut across 'best value'.[105] The White Paper also proposed that Beacon Councils should have greater freedom to set local business rates.[106]

The 'Beacon' proposals differ from the new power of community initiative: the former will be a route by which councils can achieve relaxation of other statutory controls, whereas the new power will be subject to other legislation. There will, therefore, be a natural hierarchy in the new proposals: innovation may first be attempted under the power to promote community well-being and, if this gives insufficient flexibility, an application made for ministerial relaxation of constraints. Under the community initiative power the weighing of the social, economic, or environmental benefits will be for the council itself (subject to judicial review and audit), whereas consideration of these matters is likely to form the core of the external approval process for 'Beacon' applications. Obviously, guidance on any potential overlap between the powers would be highly desirable in order to avoid confusion.

## THE NEW POWER TO PROMOTE COMMUNITY WELL-BEING

All local authorities are to have power under section 2(1) of the Local Government Act 2000 to do anything which they consider is likely to promote or improve the economic, social, or environmental well-being of their area.[107] When exercising the power (or considering whether to do so) an authority must consider the effect on the achievement of sustainable development in the United Kingdom.[108]

Under Section 2(2) the power may be exercised in relation to, or for the benefit of, the whole or any part of the area or all or any persons resident or present in it. The latter allows councils to exercise the power for the

[105] LGA 1999, s. 16(1); ministers may also confer additional powers on authorities by order where it is considered to be necessary or expedient in order to permit or facilitate compliance with best value: ibid., s. 16(2). Further powers are contained in the LGA 2000, s. 5 (general power to allow Secretary of State by order to remove enactments which obstruct authorities from promoting the well-being of their communities) and s. 6 (allowing the Secretary of State to suspend requirements to prepare statutory plans or strategies).

[106] Paras. 10.20–6.

[107] The power does not confer an independent power of borrowing: s. 3(2).

[108] Ss. 2(3) and 4(1).

benefit of visitors and those working within the area, as well as residents and council taxpayers. Moreover, under subsection (5) it is clear that an authority can do anything in relation to, or for the benefit of, any person or area situated outside their area if it considers that it is likely to promote the well-being of its area. There is a risk of incompatibility here with the focus of the fiduciary duty upon local taxpayers' interests.[109] It might be doubted whether the power to act in the interests of people visiting and working in an area, as well as those living there, voting, and paying council tax, does enough to displace judicial preference for taxpayers' interests under the common law fiduciary duty. On balance, however, the clear intention is that these provisions should be taken as a signal that Parliament means councils to have the discretion to benefit their areas through measures targeted at such groups.

Linked to the power is a specific duty to 'prepare a strategy for promoting or improving the economic, social and environmental well-being' of the authority's area (s. 4(1)). In so doing the council may consult widely and must have regard to ministerial guidance. The strategic plan is intended to provide focus for the leadership and coordinating aspects of the community leadership role. Apart from a specific power to incur expenditure, detailed powers to enter partnerships also feature prominently.[110] These, however, are illustrative only in an attempt to prevent the general power being read down by the judges.[111]

The success of the new power will depend largely on the constraints within which it operates. In its response to the Hunt Committee, the previous government argued that any general power of competence would need to be constrained so that it did not detract from national economic objectives (for example, control of public expenditure) or national aims for local services (for example, recent reforms in education over the national curriculum and schools testing).[112] The limitations proposed on the new power in the Labour White Paper were less onerous (and, of course, are in addition to the 'Beacon Council' scheme). It proposed that the power be limited so that it could not be used to prejudice other council functions or those of other statutory bodies, and the Government would retain a reserve power. The relationship between the power and more detailed powers enjoyed by councils, and the probable attitude of the courts, need to be considered also.

[109] See pp. 131–8 below.

[110] The power includes specific ability to give financial assistance, enter into arrangements or agreements, cooperate with, or facilitate or co-ordinate the activities of any person, exercise on behalf of any person any functions of that person, and to provide staff, goods, services, or accommodation to any person: s. 2(4).

[111] S. 2(6).

[112] *Government Response to the Report of the House of Lords Select Committee on Relations between Central and Local Government 'Rebuilding Trust'*, Cm. 3464 (1996), para. 39.

Various limitations on the new power to promote well-being have been incorporated under section 3 of the Local Government Act 2000. Specifically excluded is anything subject to a 'prohibition, restriction or limitation on their powers which is contained in any enactment'.[113] This will prevent councils from using the general power to override national limitations in other specific powers, on the grounds that the council thought that they were inappropriate in local conditions; for that, ministerial relaxation under the Beacon scheme will be necessary. There is a danger that the new power of community concern will fall short of the radical initiative which is apparently intended and will amount to little more than a symbolic change on top of the plethora of specific legislation which already binds local authorities. The drafting is less restrictive, however, than the equivalent restriction under section 111, which made the power 'subject . . . . to the provisions of any other enactment'.[114] Whereas the latter restriction was in keeping with the subsidiary nature of the power (s. 111 is retained), the former suggests that the council will have free-standing power to act for the community's well-being, unless there is a specific provision to the contrary. It also compares favourably with section 137, which was only available to be used where the expenditure in question was not authorized under another provision.[115] On the whole, it is less restrictive than the White Paper suggested.

On the other hand, ministers have a wide power to exclude activities by delegated legislation.[116] This could easily be used by a future government less benevolently disposed towards the vision of community leadership to empty the new power of content. Earlier proposals to set a financial limit to protect national interests seem to have been dropped, however. The shadow of central government is also cast by a requirement that before exercising the power, a local authority must have regard to ministerial guidance about its exercise.[117] Conversely, however, under section 5 ministers are given a wide power to remove or amend enactments which they think prevent or obstruct local authorities from exercising their community well-being power. It is envisaged that this could be used selectively in relation to individual local authorities, as well as local government as a

[113] S. 3(1). This applies to existing and future legislation ('whenever passed or made') and to subordinate legislation also (subs. 6).

[114] In *Allsop v North Tyneside MBC*, (1992) 90 LGR 462, it was held that 'enactment' included delegated legislation so that the council could not use s. 111 to give redundancy payments which were more generous than those permitted under a statutory instrument. In *Morgan Grenfell v Sutton LBC*, (1996) 95 LGR 574, Peter Gibson LJ accepted (at 584) that where other legislation prescribed the means by which a statutory function was exercisable s. 111 could not be used to undertake the same function by alternative means.

[115] S.137 is largely superseded by the new power except in the case of parish and community councils, which will not have the new power.

[116] S. 3(3).

[117] S. 3(5).

whole; it therefore provides statutory underpinning for the 'Beacon Council' scheme.

A key issue will be the attitude of the judiciary towards the new power. On one view the administrative law Bar might face mass redundancy if the result of reform was that the ultra vires principle were rendered otiose at a stroke for a whole tier of public authorities. This seems improbable. Presumably, in most instances councils would continue to act under specific, detailed, and limited statutory powers, where judicial review has a well-established role. There would then be an issue of how these specific powers and the new general power fitted together. Experience with comparable statutory provisions where local authorities have power to act in the interest of the community or the area is not encouraging. We have seen already the restrictive interpretation given to the seemingly broad power to do anything 'which is calculated to facilitate, or is conducive or incidental to, the discharge of any of their functions' under section 111 of the Local Government Act 1972. Similarly restrictive treatment has been given the apparently widely worded power to acquire and use land for community purposes under section 120(1)(b) of the 1972 Act, which allows a council to appropriate land 'for the benefit, improvement or development of their area'. As we have seen, in the *Fewings* case[118] the Court of Appeal held that a local authority acted ultra vires in banning deer-hunting from common land held by it. The council's assertion that it had merely used the width of its discretion as a landowner was taken as symptomatic of its failure to consider the powers correctly. The restricted treatment of such seemingly wide powers by the judges suggests that any attempt to overlay a general power of community initiative on top of the existing closely confined statutory powers may not create a new atmosphere of judicial deference to local discretion.

There may be a better prospect of the judiciary deferring to local judgment if councils help themselves by considering overtly and recording the legal basis for the initiatives that they take, i.e. the supposed specific benefit to the community and the factors considered in reaching the decision (so overcoming in part the objection in *Fewings*). Arguably, the new power will require a conscious decision by the council to exercise it in any event, otherwise the preconditions of considering the promotion of well-being will not be met. Moreover, failure to consider ministerial guidance or the effect on sustainable development would render it liable to challenge.

[118] *R v Somerset CC ex p. Fewings*, [1995] 3 All ER 20. See pp. 41–5 above.

### 'AN OVERARCHING DUTY'?

In some respects the new power looks less radical than the White Paper proposals. First, the idea of it underpinning a duty has been abandoned. This is probably a mainly cosmetic change, since it is unlikely that a legal 'duty' expressed in such general terms would have been enforceable. However, it was also suggested that the new power would be 'overarching': that it would bring together the various specific functions of councils in disparate fields. There is a clear need for such a mission statement because, unlike company law, local government law lacks a distinction between objects and powers. A clear distinction between a 'function' and 'powers' and 'duties' (the terms used in the legislation) is hard to discern from the statute book.[119]

In the light of such confusion there is a compelling case for a systematic review of the legislation.[120] If one could start from a clean sheet, a tidy, hierarchical arrangement would be a threefold distinction between purposes, functions, and powers and duties. The notion of community leadership would be expressed at the purposes level, as it is in the GLA Act (below). Functions would refer to the particular specific areas of work delegated to councils (such as education and planning), and these would be fleshed out in more detail by specific powers and duties. Purposes and functions could then form the higher-order norms against which powers and duties were construed by the courts. In the present regime, however, the first level is entirely missing: it is the lack of any public and authoritative statement of the constitutional purpose of local government which has led to the present debate over community leadership, in an attempt to find a rationale which is more than the sum of the various council functions. At the second level, functions can be found in the present statute book, but they are often expressed in the form of unenforceable general duties. Specific powers and duties abound, with huge variations in the detail with which they are expressed and relatively little legislative explanation of their comparative importance. Perhaps it is little wonder that the courts have failed to find the key and have treated what were intended to be broad powers in a restrictive way.

The government may have been chastened by the cautionary lesson of an earlier overarching *duty*: section 71 of the Race Relations Act 1976. This

[119] Indeed, in interpreting s. 111 of the LGA 1972 'function' has been equated by the courts with 'the multiplicity of specific activities the council is expressly or impliedly under a duty to perform or has a power to perform'. Woolf J in *Hazell v Hammersmith and Fulham LBC*, [1990] 2 QB 697, 722–3 (approved by the Court of Appeal at [1990] 2 QB 697, 785 and by the House of Lords at [1992] 2 AC 1, 29).

[120] C. Grace, 'Local Government Law: Components of a New Framework' in Local Government Information Unit, *A Framework for the Future* (London, 1997).

requires local authorities, in relation to the exercise of their 'functions', to promote good race relations. As we have seen, in *Wheeler v Leicester CC*[121] the House of Lords considered this provision when striking down the council's decision to revoke the licence of a rugby club to use a training-ground.[122] Several judges rejected the argument that the duty under section 71 was 'inward-looking' (for example, concerned only with the council's employment policies). However, they gave it little weight when compared to the lawful activities of the rugby club. This approach effectively devalued section 71: the promotion of good race relations was not merely a permissible factor to be considered, it was expressed in the legislation as a *duty* imposed on the council. This decision underlines the need for any new 'overarching' duty and power to be of an unmistakably different character to the remainder of the legislation applicable to local councils. It also suggests that the drafting would need to be quite explicit in order to persuade the courts that Parliament intended that councils should be able to displace the otherwise lawful activities of private individuals for the benefit of the community. This example makes the courts' approach to any fresh 'overarching' provisions difficult to predict, and perhaps explains why the idea was not pursued.

A quite different approach is taken in the Greater London Authority Act 1999, section 30. This states that the principal *purposes* of the Authority are the promotion of economic and social development, wealth creation, and the improvement of the environment in Greater London. The Authority has power to do anything which it considers will advance these purposes. The drafting makes clear that these purposes are the end result which any person exercising the powers of the Authority must keep in view, and also relevant considerations in determining whether to exercise any of its powers in the first place (s. 30(3)). The authority also must consider the desirability of maintaining a 'reasonable balance' between the purposes over time. Whereas it would be difficult legally to challenge the overall impact of any single action of the Authority for failure to promote the social or economic development or the environmental improvement of the area, it might be easier to demonstrate that these factors have not been considered, or not considered in a balanced way.[123]

[121] [1985] AC 1054.

[122] pp. 45–6 above.

[123] S. 30(7) gives the Secretary of State powers to issue guidance, which the Authority must consider under s. 30(8) in relation to the use of these powers. On the connection between these purposes and the political structure of the GLA, see pp. 242–3 below.

The power is constrained under s. 31 in a way which makes it clear that it is intended primarily to operate where other public authorities do not have jurisdiction. Expenditure on housing, education services, social services, and health services which could be undertaken by a London Borough is forbidden, as is expenditure on anything which may be undertaken by another functional body (Transport for London, fire, and police). In addition, the Mayor is to '*seek to secure*' that the Authority does not spend money on anything which could be

More radical still would be to give a fresh start by legislation which is earmarked as constitutional in nature or equivalent to an Interpretation Act for local government.[124] Under the doctrine of parliamentary sovereignty, any general power will always be vulnerable to express repeal by later legislation. However, constitutional experience in the case of the European Communities Act 1972 (and, it is hoped, with the Human Rights Act 1998) suggests that workable solutions can be found to guard against the risk of *implied* repeal by inconsistent later legislation—a real risk in view of the frequency, volume, and complexity of local government legislation. One possibility would be an explicit direction to the courts (as in the Acts mentioned) to construe legislation in the light of the council's wide powers of community initiative; a direction of this type could always be expressly overridden in a later legislation if Parliament so desired. Nothing like this currently exists, and the idea may sound implausible. If so, it reveals more about the lack of commitment to local democracy, compared to other aspirations such as supremacy of European law and protection of human rights, than it does about the constitutional feasibility of the proposal.

## CONCLUSION

Research published by the DETR[125] found that (in contrast to the power of discretionary expenditure under section 137) the proposed new duty was seen by councils as a positive power which expressed the confidence of central government in them and signified a change of mood in central–local relations. It was seen by a number of authorities as a 'useful external stimulus to the re-prioritisation of their activities and budgets', as a boost to the confidence of officers and members, and as enhancing the credibility of the council with other agencies.

In the longer term, however, the test of these new powers will be whether they succeed in reviving local self-confidence and initiative so

undertaken by the London Development Agency. None of this, however, prevents the Authority from spending money in 'co-operating with, or facilitating or co-ordinating' such activities (s. 31(6)). This saving provision underlines the role of the Authority in strategic leadership among other public bodies in London. S. 34 mirrors the incidental powers rule under s. 111 of the LGA 1972, but without the qualifications 'subject to the provisions of this Act and any other enactment passed before or after this Act'.

[124] As proposed by Colin Crawford, 'Powers for the New Vision' (1998) JLGL 31, 33. Note that the courts have been directed concerning interpretation in the case of the Scottish Parliament to read provisions 'as narrowly as is required for it to be within competence, if such a reading is possible': Scotland Act 1998, s. 101 (2); and see Northern Ireland Act 1998, s. 82(3). These provisions apply in the case of bodies with limited legislative competence, but the approach might nevertheless be adaptable to local government.

[125] N. Mason, R. Turner, and Michael Dodd Consulting Ltd, *Local Authority Activity under Section 137, Local Government Act 1972* (London, Mar. 1999).

that the flagging interest of the local electorate is restored and local authorities attract members and officers of high calibre. Three factors will contribute to this process. First, the question of financial freedom is crucial—any new power to innovate worthy of the name must carry the freedom to back new ideas with the necessary investment. Significantly, the DETR study on section 137 found that most authorities which responded raised concerns about resources in relation to the new duty. Second, the spirit in which central government approaches the exercise will determine whether councils see it as merely cosmetic or as a real opportunity to bring forward new ideas. The drafting of ministerial guidance on use of the new power and use of ministerial restrictions will be all-important. The ability to exclude certain functions from the scope of the power could too easily allow for future resumption of central control, without recourse to Parliament. Thirdly, the legislation needs to send the correct messages to the judiciary about the legitimacy of local democracy: where councils have tried to use apparently widely worded powers in the recent past the courts have been too ready to find the action unlawful. There could still be a mismatch in the interaction of very specific statutory schemes construed according to the conventional principles of public law and broadly worded general powers.

Overall, the White Paper's proposal of an 'overarching duty' suggested a provision of quasi-constitutional significance, defining the mission of local government. This has not been delivered, but in its place is a useful power which will stand in the place of section 137 and give scope for partnership with other agencies to give credibility to community leadership.

Part II

# Accountability to the Public

# 3

# *Information, Public Participation, and Accountability*

## CONTEXT

The representative model of local democracy depends crucially on public access to information about local government and on participation in local affairs. In the discussion that follows the voluntary release of information is first examined; this section explores both the uses of political manifestos in local government and controls on political advertising by councils. Discussion then moves to instances in which the flow of information is legally compelled; public rights of access to information and duties to consult the public are examined in turn. Use of information does not map tidily on to a theoretical distinction between accountability within representative democracy and consumer accountability. Some duties to provide information or to consult plainly have a consumerist version of accountability in mind. This is particularly the case where the purpose of duties to supply information is to enable an informed opinion about the council's efficiency in service provision, or where they are linked with a choice open to service users. These procedures are discussed in Chapter 5, although the general principles described here also apply to them.

Before discussing the legal regulation of particular practices concerning information, the context in which they operate is briefly considered. The geographical accessibility of local institutions is an important practical factor affecting the public's opportunities for observing and participating in local decision-making. In some respects this is an argument for unitary authorities—one criticism of the post-1972 county councils was that, because of their demographic base, they were inevitably more remote centres of decision-making than the districts. The organization of the local franchise into local wards is a strength of the system, giving ready access to local elected representatives. However, at one councillor to approximately 1,200 people, council wards in Britain are still large by continental standards. Some authorities have attempted to increase local responsiveness and accessibility by organizing services on a neighbourhood basis, and in some instances, devolving the administration and decision-making to area committees and offices.[1]

[1] See Ch. 7.

Much public consultation occurs spontaneously and organically in local government: its ethos is pervasively and fundamentally different from that of Whitehall. At central government level consultation is mainly of sectional interests such as pressure groups; while these certainly do operate at local level, there is also more opportunity for direct contact with individual members of the public. The law establishes a (mostly statutory) minimum both by requiring councils to publish certain kinds of information and by allowing access to meetings and documents which are involved in decision-making. Many of the obligations of the former kind have been introduced either to require often unwilling local authorities to publicize central government reforms or as part of the consumerist underpinning of the Citizen's Charter.[2] Examples include the detailed requirements to publish information about the setting of the level of Council Tax, about school examination results, and about performance indicators. The most conspicuous of these concerns information to be sent out with the annual council tax demand,[3] but other requirements exist for information about annual reports and financial statements, manpower information, and the handling of planning applications.[4]

The role of the local press is another important contextual factor.[5] In practice, relatively few members of the public attend council meetings or councillors' surgeries, and so their main source of information about the local council is through a local newspaper.[6] As we shall see, local journalists have important legal rights of access to papers and meetings which can be used in their investigation and reporting of local politics. Stories about the local council are one of the largest categories of local news.[7] In addition to conventional regional daily and weekly newspapers, there has been a growth in recent decades of free local papers. Funded by advertising, the capacity of these organs to act as independent sources of information and criticism of local politics is minimal. Research has shown that they rely heavily for 'news' on press releases from local government public relations officers, which are often reproduced more or less verbatim.[8] In addition, many councils distribute free municipal newspapers; because

[2] See further Ch. 5.

[3] Under regulations made under the Local Government Finance Acts 1988 and 1992; see the Council Tax and Non-Domestic Rating (Demand Notices) (England) Regulations 1993, SI No. 191, para. 3(4) and sched. 3 (as amended by the Local Government Changes for England (Council Tax and Non-Domestic Rating, Demand Notices) Regulations 1995, SI No. 23, to take account of local government reorganization).

[4] See S. Bailey, *Cross on Principles of Local Government Law* (London, 1992), para. 4-102.

[5] See B. Franklin and D. Murphy, *What's News? The Market, Politics and the Local Press* (London, 1991).

[6] Franklin and Murphy (ibid. 7) argue that it is newspapers, rather than local radio or television, which is the source of most local news.

[7] Ibid. 64.

[8] Ibid. 100–4.

of the controversy these have aroused, they are discussed below in connection with controls on political advertising.

The extent to which local authorities are free to attempt directly to influence public opinion by the supply of information, or indeed argument, about their own or central government's policies goes to the heart of the debate about their political status. Two contrasting positions can be sketched. On the one hand, it may be argued that the desire to persuade the public follows inevitably from the party political nature of local government, and that restrictions on such activity are not only impracticable but also undesirable, in a pluralist democracy. The alternative perspective characterizes activity of this kind as 'propaganda on the rates', and argues that councillors should be strictly neutral in their use of public money and public facilities. This view is associated closely with the position that councils exist to provide services to the public and not to pursue some wider party-political agenda. Even this narrow view, of course, recognizes the reality of party-political campaigning about local government. However, it presupposes a strict division between the local party-political machine (which may engage in this) and a local authority's formal powers and resources, which should not be deployed for this purpose. This discussion deals first with information distributed for an avowedly party-political purpose directly related to the electoral process—party group manifestos. It then moves to deal with information distributed in the name of the council as a whole. There then follows a brief treatment of the similar issue of attempts in the name of the council as a whole to suppress criticism through the law of defamation.

## LOCAL MANIFESTOS

One study suggests that local manifestos should be understood as part of the process of 'reappraisal' of the political role of local government by the major parties following the 1972 reorganization.[9] According to this view, the introduction of local manifestos marked a shift from 'local administrative politics' to 'ideological politics' by providing a programme of specific commitments which the political party would implement when in control of the council. One of the earliest such examples was the manifesto of the Labour Party at the election of Nottinghamshire County Council in 1973, which ran to a policy statement of more than 30,000 words and was formally adopted after the election as council policy. The preparation of manifestos has become increasingly formalized, with some Labour local

[9] J. Gyford, S. Leach, and C. Game, *The Changing Politics of Local Government* (London, 1989), 17.

parties engaging in an extensive programme of working parties and consultation to draft proposals on different policy areas.

The preparation of manifestos raises particular difficulties for officers of the council. Whereas there are considerable advantages in officers advising on the feasibility of specific manifesto proposals before they are formally adopted, there is also the risk of appearing to compromise officers' political neutrality. This is most likely to occur when officers advise only the present ruling group on the council prior to an election. It can be overcome, however, by providing equal access to officer advice for all parties.[10]

The process of drawing up and implementing a local manifesto may raise tension between the party group of councillors elected to the authority and the wider local political party. This is particularly so in the case of some Liberal Democrat and Labour authorities, where the role of the local party is seen as being that of monitoring implementation of the manifesto by the party's councillors.[11] The constitutions of the main political parties make it plain that it is the responsibility of local parties (rather than party groups of councillors) to campaign for the successful election of the party candidates. Likewise, it is the local parties which will be responsible for selection of prospective candidates (whether or not they are sitting councillors). The Widdicombe Committee found that responsibility for drawing up a manifesto varied according to each party, with Labour local parties playing a more active role in manifesto formulation than local Conservative associations as regards their respective councillors; with the Alliance (as it was then) a wide process of consultation was normal.[12] Although the Committee found that local manifestos were becoming more common, their influence on group policy after election was often slight. It was exceptional rather than normal for groups systematically to review manifesto implementation. Significantly, though, individual councillors did often see themselves as somehow 'bound' to implement the manifesto.[13]

The courts have vacillated in their attitude. In the *Tameside* case[14] both Scarman LJ in the Court of Appeal and a majority of the Law Lords referred to the fact that the policy of the council (to retain grammar schools) could not be said by the Secretary of State to be 'unreasonable' within section 68 of the Education Act 1944 *because* it had been endorsed in a very recent local election. Lord Wilberforce[15] referred to the council

[10] J. Gyford, S. Leach, and C. Game, *The Changing Politics of Local Government* (London, 1989), 132–43.

[11] Ibid. 169–72.

[12] See Widdicombe Report, research vol. i. 92–5.

[13] Ibid. 92.

[14] *Secretary of State for Education and Science v Tameside MBC*, [1977] AC 1014.

[15] Ibid. 1051 and 1052.

being 'in a sense bound' by the promise to the electorate. For Scarman LJ the fact that the education authority was democratically elected was a reason why its opinion should be respected by the Secretary of State.[16] Likewise, Lord Diplock considered that the minister was bound to consider the mandate the council had received.[17] For Lord Russell of Killowen the endorsement of the council's policy by the electorate was a reason why it could not be said to be unreasonable.[18] Lord Salmon and Viscount Dilhorne confined themselves to referring to the fact that the policy had a mandate.[19] The judgments demonstrate a sense of profound respect for the legitimacy of the democratic process in local government. One interpretation is that the House of Lords implied limitations into a statutory ministerial discretion so as to preserve the declared preference of the electorate for the policy of a controlling group on the council. The contrast with *Bromley v GLC*[20] is striking.[21] There the House of Lords implied a limitation (the fiduciary trust of the council to its ratepayers) so as to protect ratepayers from the effect of a policy similarly endorsed by the electorate, the reduction of transport fares in London by 25 per cent. Far from the mandate clothing the decision with legality, both the Court of Appeal and three of the Law Lords found the council's adherence to it ultra vires. All three members of the Court of Appeal found that the council had given undue weight to the manifesto in regarding itself as bound to implement it.[22] In the House of Lords, Lord Wilberforce argued that electoral approval could not confer legality on an otherwise illegal policy, and distinguished *Tameside* on the basis that it was concerned with reasonableness.[23] Both Lord Diplock[24] and Lord Brandon of Oakbrook[25] acknowledged that the council could properly take account of the electorate's choice (Lord Diplock went so far as to describe it as a 'weighty factor'), but were not bound by it.

The outcome is confusion, certainly when viewed from the perspective of representative democracy, if not of administrative law doctrine. No doubt the electorate is sophisticated enough to know that politicians at whatever level sometimes promise more than they are able to deliver, although the constraints are generally economic and practical rather than

[16] Ibid. 1033. [17] Ibid. 1066. [18] Ibid. 1074.
[19] Ibid. 1067, 1073 (Lord Salmon), 1055 and 1061 (Viscount Dilhorne).
[20] [1983] 1 AC 768.
[21] Cf. McAuslan, 'Administrative Law, Collective Consumption and Judicial Policy', (1983) 46 MLR 1, 14–20 and H. Brayne, 'The Local Government Mandate and the Courts', (1986) Law Society's Gazette 514.
[22] [1983] 1 AC 768, 776–7, per Lord Denning MR; Oliver LJ, 795 (but acknowledging that the Court should be slow to interfere with the decisions of elected bodies); Watkins LJ, 796.
[23] Ibid. 814. Unless the intention is that the mandate should operate differently in relation to different grounds of review (for which no explanation is offered), the reasoning is circular.
[24] Ibid. 829. [25] Ibid. 853.

legal. Equally, once it is accepted that local government is a legally subordinate and limited sphere, it follows that locally elected politicians ought not to be able to enlarge their powers simply by electoral endorsement of a potentially unlawful manifesto. The balance of other interests in local democracy, especially those of local taxpayers and service users, and the relatively low level of interest in local elections all support this position. The principle underlying the *GLC* case is, therefore, uncontentious, although the application of it by the judges to the particular statutory scheme and facts were far from clear-cut. In reality, many cases will fall into this legal penumbra where there is scope for legitimate debate about the extent of an authority's powers, and the *Tameside* approach of giving local politicians a wide discretion has much to commend it. Nevertheless, there may still be unsatisfactory instances in which local politicians make wide promises to pursue a policy which would be clearly unlawful if elected, and then shrug off responsibility once in office, blaming the courts, the auditor, or central government. The only safeguard against exploitation of the electorate's gullibility is vigilant political opposition. Too often, however, local election campaigns fall far short of an informed debate about local politics.[26]

## COUNCIL PUBLICITY AND POLITICAL ADVERTISING

The position of free newspapers distributed by councils to households within their area has proved especially controversial. Some of these have larger circulation figures (albeit much more infrequently) than some national dailies. A study by Franklin and Murphy found that Labour authorities were three times more likely than Conservative councils to distribute a newspaper.[27] There were other clear differences also: newspapers from Labour councils devoted space to issues not featured in those from Conservative councils: unemployment, benefits, sexuality, and racial issues, whereas those from Conservative councils were more taken up with advertising, leisure facilities, and a consumerist slant on local services.[28] In short, the style of the newspaper tended to reflect the concerns and policies of the council and hence, indirectly, of the majority party. This was so although in most cases the paper was edited by an officer (normally the public relations officer), who might, however, be subject to pressure from leading councillors or officers to include certain items; inevitably, items critical of council policy did not feature.[29] Franklin and Murphy concluded that, understood within a pluralist framework in which they stood

[26] See Ch. 1.
[27] Franklin and Murphy, op. cit., 136.
[28] Ibid. 143.
[29] Ibid. 148–50.

alongside commercial local newspapers and central government's own information and persuasion efforts, to describe such newspapers as 'propaganda on the rates' was generally unhelpful.[30]

Controversy has arisen over the extent to which it is permissible for a local authority to use its position to further the party political ambitions of the controlling group by publicity or deployment of other council resources.[31] Legislation governing political propaganda by local authorities and the use of contractual power for political purposes has sought to curb this. The issue came to a head in the mid-1980s, due to government annoyance at the political campaigning of groups of Labour-controlled authorities against rate-capping and the abolition of the Metropolitan county councils.

Previously the legal position had been ambivalent. The GLC's use of some £7.6 million in a campaign against its abolition was found by the District Auditor to be unlawful.[32] In Scotland, however, in *Meek v Lothian Regional Council*[33] the Outer House held that an authority's publicity was not ultra vires section 88 of the Local Government (Scotland) Act 1973 since, in the words of Lord Ross:

> Parliament must have appreciated that party politics do prevail in local government and that a majority group in local authority might well select for publication, information on matters relating to local government which would show or tend to show the majority group in a favourable light.[34]

The party political content of the publicity in question in that case was held, however, to support a particular candidate for the purpose of election expenses under section 63(1) of the Representation of the People Act 1949. In *Re Cook's Application*[35] the Court of Appeal of Northern Ireland held that expenditure by Belfast City Council on a banner reading 'Belfast says No' (to the Anglo-Irish agreement) was not so unrelated to local government business as to be ultra vires. However, in *R v ILEA ex p. Westminster City Council*[36] Glidewell J held that expenditure purportedly

[30] Ibid. 153.

[31] The Widdicombe Report recommended the introduction of a general prohibition on the use of discretionary power to secure an electoral advantage: para. 8.89.

[32] See H. Thompson and C. Game, 'Section 137: Propaganda on the Rates?', (1985) Local Government Studies 11, 12–13. The Auditor found that the campaign was beyond s. 142 LGA 1972 since its purpose was to persuade and not to inform (cf. the *Westminster* case below). However, he argued that the expenditure might have been lawful under s. 137 LGA 1972, except that the GLC had already used its permitted expenditure under that provision.

[33] [1983] SLT 494. But see n. 36 below.

[34] Ibid. 495.

[35] [1986] 1 NIJB 43 (affirming the decision of Hutton J, 3 NIJB 43).

[36] [1986] 1 All ER 19. See also *R v GLC ex p. Westminster City Council*, *The Times*, 22 Jan. 1985, in which an interim injunction was granted to restrain the council from engaging advertising agencies for the purpose of a campaign against its abolition on the basis that such expenditure would not be 'incidental' to the authority's powers under s. 111 of the Local Government

incurred under section 142 of the Local Government Act 1972 was ultra vires because the purpose was not merely to inform the public but also to influence it in opposition to cuts in central government grant. The judgment is consistent with a view of local government which is limited to the delivery of services (and information about those services). The argument that the campaign was an indirect method of increasing the revenue available for service delivery was not canvassed. The overall effect of these decisions was that the legality of expenditure depended, first, upon which statutory provision the authority sought to rely[37] and, secondly, on the view of the proper role of local government taken by the court in question. Certainly the outcomes seem inconsistent: it is difficult to conclude, for example, that opposition to the Anglo-Irish agreement was substantially more related to local government affairs than a campaign (as in the *ILEA* case) against the effects of rate-capping.

The Widdicombe Committee was established immediately following the 1984 Conservative Party Conference at which strong disapproval of local authority campaigning had been expressed by a number of delegates.[38] The Committee were required to deliver an Interim Report on local authority publicity in advance of their main report on local politics generally. The Interim Report[39] took a middle course between the two poles identified. It endorsed the principle that local authorities had a broader interest than merely the administration of a series of statutory services. It also argued that local government had a duty to inform the public in its area not only about the exercise of its own functions but also with

Act 1972. *In Stated Case by the Commission for Local Authority Accounts in Scotland relating to City of Edinburgh District Council* (*The Times*, Scots Law Report, 18 Apr. 1988) it was held by the Second Division of the Inner House of the Court of Session that expenditure by the council in adopting and using the slogan 'Edinburgh District Council—Improving Services—Creating Jobs' was ultra vires s. 88 of the Local Government (Scotland) Act 1973 (the equivalent to s. 142 of the LGA 1972). Lord Ross held that although s. 69 of the Act (the equivalent to s. 111 of the LGA 1972) conferred a slightly wider power than s. 88, the lawful purpose of expenditure under that section was publication of information. On the facts he was satisfied that the purpose of the slogan was to rally support for the council in opposition to the Secretary of State, rather than to inform.

Cf. cases in which the courts have held that some restrictions may be imposed on the political purposes which a council allows its staff to engage in. Hence, a decision by ILEA to release one officer to a joint organization representing trade unions could be justified by an implied power to promote good industrial relations, but in the same case a decision of the GLC to give 7 staff paid leave to work for the same body to campaign against abolition of the council was unlawful: *R v GLC ex p. Westminster CC, The Times*, 27 Dec. 1984; see also *R v District Auditor ex p. W. Yorks MCC*, (1985) 26 RVR 24. Likewise, *R v GLC, ex p. Bromley LBC, The Times*, 27 Mar. 1984, in which Forbes J held that donations by a council to an association of London authorities designed to put forward Labour policies were ultra vires.

37 It was on this basis that Hutton J in *Re Cook's Application* (see n. 35 above) distinguished the *ILEA* case.

38 See Gyford et al., op. cit., 279ff.

39 *Interim Report of the Committee of Inquiry into the Conduct of Local Authority Business, Local Authority Publicity*, 1995.

regard to local government matters generally, including support or opposition to proposed changes in the law. It stated, however, that local authorities should act within the existing law and that publicity should not be used to promote the interests of a political party. This approach recognized the importance of information in enhancing public awareness and openness about local government, and attempted to achieve an approximate equality of arms with the power of the central government to publicize the merits of its own policies (including those relating to local authorities). The Committee recommended a statutory prohibition on publicity promoting the interest of individual politicians or political parties. However, it wanted councils to continue to be free to provide information to the public on matters relating to local government.

The Conservative government took a much more stringent view. Legislation was introduced to prohibit publicity designed to affect public support for a political party or a body, or a cause or campaign identified, or likely to be regarded, or identified, as a political party. The test of whether the material has this effect is not merely whether it refers to the party but also whether it refers to persons 'identified with a political party' or 'promotes or opposes a point of view on a question of political controversy which is identifiable as the view of one political party and not of another.'[40] Widdicombe's emphasis upon the legitimacy of a broader role for council information was disregarded, and permissible information was confined to the councils' functions or services within their area.

Most contentious of all was the introduction of a ministerial Code of Practice on the content, style, distribution, and cost of local authority publicity. The Committee had taken the view that such matters could be dealt with by self-regulation or through agreement at the level of the local authority associations. However, the government preferred compulsion. The House of Lords amended the 1986 Local Government Bill so as to make the Code of Practice advisory rather than mandatory, but ministers eventually prevailed when further amendments to this scheme were introduced in the 1988 legislation, imposing a mandatory Code.[41] The current provision requires local authorities to 'have regard to the provisions' of the Code.[42] As might be expected, the Code stresses the need for information to be 'objective, balanced, informative and accurate'.[43] It suggests that campaigns should not be used solely for the purpose of persuading the public to adopt a particular view on matters of policy. Stress is placed on

[40] LGA 1986, s. 2(2), as amended by LGA 1988, s. 27(1).

[41] For discussion of the earlier legislation see: H. Rawlings and C. Willmore, (1987) 50 MLR 52.

[42] LGA 1986, s. 4, as amended by the LGA 1988, s. 27(2). Discussion of the Code is taken from P. Birkinshaw, *Government Information: Law Relating to Access, Disclosure and Regulation* (London, 1990), 100–1.

[43] DoE Circular 20/88, para. 13.

the need for cost-effectiveness in the use both of publicity and advertising. The emphasis should be on the council as a whole rather than individual councillors.

The political advertising provisions have been attacked for their breadth and vagueness. The criticism receives some indirect support from a High Court decision in which a series of comparable conditions imposed on political activity and representation at a community festival in a local authority park were held to be meaningless.[44] Local authorities are not alone in facing restrictions on political advertising. However, these provisions go much further than comparable legal restrictions on trade unions[45] and charities[46]

There is a stark contrast between these restrictions and the representative role of local authorities envisaged under the new power of community well-being.[47] This reform gives substance to a much wider vision for local authorities than that underlying the current political advertising restrictions.[48] It is at present unclear how the tension is to be resolved, but presumely this is one of the matters that ministerial guidance about use of the new power will address.

## FREE SPEECH AND LOCAL DEBATE

One area in which the interests of the local authority, of the party group, and of individual politicians are apt to become confused is in dealing with unwelcome criticism. For individuals the law of defamation exists to provide a remedy for written or spoken comment damaging to reputation, usually through monetary recompense (an award of damages) and, quite exceptionally, through prior restraint (the issue of an injunction). However, the danger of inhibiting the political process through limitations on freedom of speech is well recognized; established defences of absolute and qualified privilege extend to cover speech on certain occasions where a public interest is served by the unrestricted flow of infor-

[44] *R v Barnet LBC ex p. Johnson*, (1991) 89 LGR 581, 590–1, per Purchas LJ (holding that conditions in a Council grant to a community festival prohibiting use by any organization promoting or opposing any political cause were ultra vires).

[45] Trade Union Act 1913, s. 3(3), as amended by the Trade Union Act 1984, s. 3. In *Paul and Fraser v NALGO*, [1987] IRLR 413, a campaign 'Make People Matter' by NALGO in the run-up to the 1987 local and general elections was held to be unlawful; the High Court found that the campaign went beyond expressing legitimate concern over public services, or exerting pressure on the public or the government, and into the forbidden territory of persuading people to vote against the Conservative Party.

[46] Restrictions flow from the general proposition that a trust for a political purpose (including furthering the objects of a political party) is not charitable: Halsbury's Laws of England (4th edn., reissue), v (2), para. 60.

[47] See Ch. 2.

[48] See pp. 59–62 above.

mation and criticism. It is the defence of qualified privilege, requiring an absence of malicious intention, which particularly applies to criticism by and of local politicians.[49] Qualified privilege extends to remarks made during council meetings. Adverse comment in ombudsman reports attracts additional protection in that it is absolutely privileged.[50]

Perhaps because an action for defamation is costly, fraught with risk (especially against a wealthy defendant, such as a newspaper), and is ineligible for legal aid, politicians may be tempted to argue that actionable remarks refer to them in a public capacity and that litigation should be publicly funded. However, to permit councillors to use public position and money may be to grant immunity from public criticism. The House of Lords recognized this when it held that Derbyshire County Council was not entitled to bring proceedings in the name of the authority (and at public expense) against the *Sunday Times* for an article criticizing its handling of a pension fund.[51] A similar action had been brought by the Leader of the Council, the Labour politician David Bookbinder, arising from the same article.[52] Overruling earlier authority,[53] the Lords held that ambiguities in the law of defamation should be resolved in favour of free speech and found that a local authority could not bring such proceedings.[54] The public interest did not favour the extension to governmental bodies of a right to sue. On the contrary, Lord Keith stressed the importance of not inhibiting public criticism of bodies which were democratically elected and organized on party political lines.[55] Public corporations should not be treated in every respect as possessing the same rights as private persons where it

[49] *Horrocks v Lowe*, [1975] AC 135; *De Buse v McCarthy*, [1942] 1 KB 156. On qualified privilege, see generally *Reynolds v Times Newspapers*, [1997] 3 WLR 1010, where the House of Lords declined to create a general defence covering publication of political information and reiterated that qualified privilege requires a duty to publish the information and a legally recognized interest in receiving it, taking account of all the circumstances.

[50] LGA 1974, s. 32; these reports now name individual councillors found to be responsible for maladministration: p. 173 below.

[51] *Derbyshire CC v Times Newspapers*, [1993] 1 All ER 1011; Morland J decided at first instance that the Council was entitled to sue to protect its governmental reputation ([1991] 4 All ER 795), but this was reversed by the Court of Appeal ([1992] 3 All ER 65). For discussion see: E. Barendt, 'Libel and Free Speech in English Law', [1993] PL 449; I. Loveland, '"Defamation of Government": Taking Lessons from America', (1994) 14 Legal Studies 206; J. Cumberbatch, 'The Quiet Revolution in Freedom of Speech: A Comment on Derbyshire CC v Times Newspapers', (1994) 45 NILQ 219; E. Grant and J. Small, 'Derbyshire CC v Times newspapers in the House of Lords: Molecular Rather than Molar Motion', (1994) 14 Ox. JLS 287.

[52] See also: *Goldsmith and Another v Bhoyrul and Others*, *The Times*, 20 June 1997 (political party cannot sue in libel).

[53] *Bognor Regis UDC v Campion*, [1972] 2 All ER 61.

[54] The question of defence of a council's 'trading reputation' was left undecided, but is potentially important where DSOs and DLOs continue to operate following abolition of CCT. Cf. also *Manchester Corp. v Williams*, [1891] 1 QB 94, 63 LT 805 (holding that a municipal corporation may sue for a libel affecting its property).

[55] [1993] 1 All ER 1017.

was contrary to the public interest.[56] His Lordship referred expressly to the danger of confusing governing interests with those of the politicians temporarily in power:

> In the case of a local authority temporarily under the control of one political party or another it is difficult to say that the local authority as such has any reputation of its own. Reputation in the eyes of the public is more likely to attach itself to the controlling political party, and with a change in that party the reputation itself will change. A publication attacking the activities of the authority will necessarily be an attack on the body of councillors which represents the controlling party, or on the executives who carry on the day to day management of its affairs. If the individual reputation of any of these is wrongly impaired by the publication any of these can himself bring proceedings for defamation. Further it is open to the controlling body to defend itself by public utterances and in debate and in the council chamber.[57]

A corporate action for defamation was therefore unnecessary and undesirable. Although an alternative approach would have been to extend to the newspaper the defence within the law of defamation of fair comment[58] (which expressly exists to protect public discussion of matters of public interest), the House of Lords' solution is neater. The judgment rests firmly within a pluralistic liberal democratic understanding of the position of local government, but the outcome is somewhat at variance with other pronouncements, for example, those in the political advertising cases discussed in the previous section, subordinating its governmental role.

From consideration of controls on voluntarily distributed information and on criticism, we move now to discussion of positive legal entitlements to information held by local authorities.

## PUBLIC RIGHTS OF ACCESS TO INFORMATION

Freedom of information legislation has been recently promulgated by the Blair government for all levels of the public service.[59] Local government was the one area of the British state where fully fledged freedom of information legislation already existed, and the Freedom of Information Act will add to these rights. For this reason we shall consider first the earlier legislation before discussing the implications of the new Act.

Rights for the public and press to attend council meetings have existed for most of the modern life of local government. The right for accredited

[56] [1993] 1 All ER 1019.

[57] 1020, per Lord Keith.

[58] This was the approach advocated in an earlier Canadian case raising the same question: *City of Prince George v British Columbia Television System Ltd*, (1979) 95 *DLR* (3d) 577, 585 per Atkins, JA.

[59] *Your Right to Know*, Cm. 3818 (1997), Freedom of Information Bill 2000 (see note, p. x).

members of the press to attend council meetings was introduced in 1908;[60] however, the legislation did not impose a duty to admit the public at large. In 1960 the right was introduced for members of the public to attend council meetings by a piece of Private Member's legislation promoted (ironically, in view of her subsequent attitude to open government) by the back-bencher Margaret Thatcher.[61] The right was extended to council committees in 1972[62] and to sub-committees in 1985.[63] The current legislation requires a minimum of three clear days' public notice for council meetings to be given,[64] with the agenda and papers to be referred to available for public consultation. The structure of the Act suggests that these procedures are strongly protected, and the consequence of disregarding them will be to render void any decision reached at meetings which do not comply.[65] In view of the predominance of meetings in the committee structure of local government, this provision gives deeper access to the corridors of power than might be at first apparent, or than would be the case in central government.

Prior to the Freedom of Information Act, the rights of the public to documents flowed largely from this model, and hence were mainly rights to documents considered or to be considered by *meetings* of councillors. This may seem odd compared with foreign models of freedom of information legislation which either give rights to documents or records per se or to information in government possession. However, it should be remembered that it is impossible for a council to take even the smallest action involving expenditure or affecting an individual without a proper delegation of power and

[60] Local Authorities (Admission of the Press to Meetings) Act 1908. It was held in *Tenby Corporation v Mason*, [1908] 1 Ch. 457, that the public had no right to attend.

[61] Public Bodies (Admission to Meetings) Act 1960.

[62] LGA 1972, s. 100 (now amended by the Local Government (Access to Information) Act 1985).

[63] LGA 1972, ss. 100A and 100E (the right also extends to meetings of Joint Authorities and joint committees), introduced by the Local Government (Access to Information) Act 1985. The 1985 Act was introduced as a Private Member's Bill and followed the model of an earlier experiment in Bradford: A. Clipson, 'Bradford's "Open Government" Experience', in R. Chapman and M. Hunt, *Open Government* (Beckenham, 1987). For studies of openness before and after the legislation, see respectively P. Birkinshaw, *Open Government, Freedom of Information and Local Government* (London, 1985), P. Birkinshaw, 'Open Government—Local Government Style', (1988) Public Policy and Administration 46, and P. Birkinshaw, *Freedom of Information: The Law, the Practice and the Ideal* (2nd edn., London, 1996), 138–42, 190–9, and 239–47.

[64] In *R v Swansea CC ex p. Elitestone Ltd*, (1993) 66 P & CR 422, it was held that the requirement was for 3 working days' notice (excluding weekends).

[65] S. 100B, esp. subs. (4), which debars meetings from considering items for which proper notice has not been given, subject to stringent exceptions for urgent business. It is likely that this provision would be held to constitute a mandatory procedural requirement: it was so treated at the leave stage of an application for judicial review in *R v LB of Lambeth ex p. Boston* (unreported decision of the QBD, 25 Apr. 1986). If so, any decisions taken at such a meeting would be ultra vires.

decision-making through the chain of meetings.[66] This follows from the legal conferrment of powers on the council as a whole, and it differs markedly from the central government position, where a welter of statutory powers are exercisable by the Secretary of State. (The position is now, of course, changing owing to implementation of the executive structure reforms.[67]) In addition, there are a number of disparate entitlements where an individual is permitted to have access to information held on council files about him or her personally;[68] these are best understood as a recognition not of public accountability (the rights are personal to the 'subject' of the data) but rather of privacy, and so are not discussed in depth here.

There were, however, some important omissions from and exceptions to these public rights. The rights were only triggered by meetings: the essential criterion seemed to be a gathering of councillors, and hence working parties and working groups were in an anomalous position. These operate as mixed bodies where the officers debate issues with members rather than merely advising them, and where the members are more actively involved in policy development and execution, rather than approval, as in a traditional committee. Although such groups may exercise considerable de facto power, they did not attract access rights.[69]

In one instance, a 'working party' of an education committee was held to be outside the legislation despite the fact that nine of its ten members were councillors who sat on the education committee; Simon Brown J held that the subjective intention of the local authority, rather than an objective assessment of the group's composition and function, determined whether the statutory rights applied.[70] Here, in view of the nature of the group, it could have been established either as a committee or as a working party, but in the absence of any unlawful intention the council's intention to create a working party prevailed. This unfortunate decision created a considerable loophole in the legislation; the result seemed to suggest that it was a matter of discretion whether a council chose to use a consultative body open to full public scrutiny or to work in private. A much stronger statement of the importance of public access rights in how a council arranges its business would have been preferable and in keeping with the spirit of the legislation. It would, for example, be open to a court to hold on normal administrative law principles that the formation of a working party is unlawful if it is done to avoid public scrutiny (there was no evidence of

[66] See Ch. 7.

[67] See pp. 230–46 below.

[68] Data Protection Act 1998; Education Act 1996, s. 563; and see *Gaskin v UK*, (1990) 12 EHRR 36.

[69] Cf. *R v Eden District Council ex p. Moffat*, *The Times*, 24 Nov. 1988, CA (refusing access to a councillor because of the lack of a need to know under the common law); P. Birkinshaw, *Government and Information: The Law Relating to Access, Disclosure and Regulation* (London, 1990), 144–5; T. Harrison, *Access to Information in Local Government* (London, 1988), 5ff.

[70] *R v Warwickshire DC ex p. Bailey*, [1991] COD 284.

this in the *Warwickshire* case) or if the council fails to consider the effect on public access in making a decision to proceed in this way. These factors weighed heavily in another decision in which a council's homelessness decision was held to be unlawful when made in accordance with the policy of a 'Homelessness Board' which was neither a committee or sub-committee, but comprised four members from the majority group of councillors and two officers, and whose papers were not available for public inspection.[71] Sedley J held that the taking of decisions on policy or practice by a group of this kind was a grave abuse of power precisely *because* it was beyond the rights of public access.

Extensive use of wide delegation to officers[72] could also be used to inhibit public access, but such arrangements are unlikely to appeal in practice to politicians wishing to keep hold of the chains of office. Delegation of decisions to officers 'in consultation' with individual members (typically to chief officers in consultation committee chairmen) may be a more effective way of preserving secrecy while retaining a measure of control.[73] Decisions taken at meetings of political groups were (and still will be) beyond the reach of access to information legislation, and there is a clear danger, especially where one party is in a secure and permanent majority, that the real debates take place behind closed doors within the group meeting, but that public discussion in council or committee meetings is carefully orchestrated. Much depends on the size and vigour of the minority parties.

The legislation also contained a lengthy list of factors justifying refusal of public access.[74] These fall into two categories: mandatory exemptions and those which are merely discretionary. The former cover mostly matters supplied by central government under some legal condition of secrecy, whether in the criminal law or an obligation of confidentiality:[75] these are uncommon in practice. The discretionary exemptions cover, as one might expect, situations in which the council is discussing personal or financial information about the recipient of some council service.

Equally predictable is the discretion to keep confidential matters of commercial sensitivity; this applies both to the affairs of those negotiating with the authority and to those of the authority itself. For instance, premature disclosure of the council's negotiating position could clearly prejudice its own financial interests, and disclosure of the financial details of third

[71] *R v LB of Tower Hamlets ex p. Khalique*, (1994) 26 HLR 517.

[72] See Ch. 7.

[73] See pp. 209–10 below; Harrison, op. cit., 9–11.

[74] LGA 1972, sched. 12A. A shorter list of possible exclusions applies to councillors: see below. It has been held that the mere fact that material is 'exempt information' under the Act does not preclude a court from ordering disclosure of it in other contexts, such as subsequent litigation: *West Midlands Police Authority and Another v Walsall MBC, The Independent*, 26 Feb. 1992.

[75] Described in the legislation as 'confidential information': LGA 1972, s. 100A(2) and (3).

parties to their competitors could deter them from seeking local government work. Nevertheless, these exemptions were introduced before the substantial shift towards delivery of local services through CCT,[76] and there is a danger that the cumulative effect may be to inhibit public accountability for the legal arrangements governing the execution of local services; these are issues in which the public and local service users have a legitimate interest.

Other exemptions concern advice about pending legal action to which the authority is a party[77] (otherwise the legislation would undermine the authority's legal privilege from disclosure under the rules of evidence) and reports about the imminent service of statutory notices, since in some cases prior knowledge could lead to the intended recipient taking avoiding action. As with the commercial exemptions, the purpose is that a third party should not gain additional rights to information for *private* advantage, because he or she happens to be dealing with a public authority.

Mention should be made of one exception which might have been expected but did not exist. Whereas freedom of information legislation often contains exemptions to protect the confidentiality of the policy-making process, no such protections existed under the local government legislation. This was perhaps indicative of a failure to recognize the political legitimacy of the decision-making process (or at least to value it less than public accountability). As we shall see, this is one aspect which will change under the new regime.

Public access is required not merely to agendas and minutes of meetings and reports referred to, but also to 'background papers',[78] other material on file used to compile the report. The requirement does not give unrestricted public access to all council filing cabinets and computer disks: 'background papers' will not be disclosable if the relevant report is not disclosable, and the Act acknowledges that 'background papers' may be exempt because of the details they contain even where the report is not. Moreover, the duty to provide such documents applies as soon as is reasonably practicable, allowing lawful delay to identify the 'background papers' and to weed them for exempt material. Some local authorities implemented the Act by making structural changes in the way they recorded information, to make it suitable for public access and disclosure, with parallel closed files containing exempt information, as necessary.

[76] See Chs. 7 and 10.

[77] This exemption was held to be properly invoked although no proceedings had been begun, to enable legal advice from the council's officers to be given on a planning application: *Stoop v Council of the RB of Kensington and Chelsea*, [1992] PLR 1.

[78] S. 100G LGA 1972; background papers must be available for a 4-year period. Councillors enjoy wider rights under s. 100F to *any document* in the possession of the council or under its control containing material relating to business to be transacted at a meeting of the council: see p. 223 below.

The council is required to designate a 'proper officer'—an official with the task of certifying that an exemption applies, where the exclusion relates to access to documents.[79] Decisions to close part of a meeting to the public must be taken in public—i.e. by a resolution which formally records which of the grounds for exclusion is invoked.[80] This duty is much more satisfactory than the one it replaced, which gave wide discretion to exclude the public by reason of the confidential nature of the business to be transacted or for 'other reasons'.[81]

There is little hard data on use of the legislation, and few reported cases have reached the courts. However, one commentator has highlighted a number of practices by which authorities have either grudgingly implemented the legislation or attempted to sidestep it. These include: minimizing publicity concerning rights under the legislation, charging exorbitant fees for copies of documents, circulating papers 'for information only' to members and not as a matter of report, and increased use of working parties.[82]

These rights are to be extended by the new Freedom of Information Act,[83] which will apply to all public authorities, including local

[79] The same applies to refusals of requests by councillors for access to documents.

[80] A narrow exception may be where because of public disruption of a meeting it is impossible to take a resolution of this kind. In *R v Brent Health Authority ex p. Francis*, [1985] 1 All ER 74 a meeting held behind closed doors (following disruption of previous meetings) where the first item on the agenda was to approve the exclusion of the public was found not to be unlawful. Although the decision was made under the former legislation, the Local Government (Access to Information) Act 1985 expressly retains common law rights to exclude the public.

[81] Public Bodies (Admission to Meetings) Act 1960, s. 1(2). The section was found by the Court of Appeal to be satisfied when a local authority wholly excluded the public because there was insufficient space in the chosen meeting room to accommodate all who wished to attend: *R v Liverpool CC ex p. Liverpool Taxi Fleet Operators Assn.*, [1975] 1 All ER 379. Although the Court of Appeal found no evidence of bad faith, the precedent was clearly adaptable to creative misuse and seemed to affirm the paradox that the greater the degree of public interest, the easier it would be to exclude the public. The Court also held that the section imposed no duty to specify the nature of the special reason in the resolution.

[82] P. Birkinshaw, 'Open Government—Local Government Style', (1988) Public Policy and Administration 46.

[83] See generally Campaign for Freedom of Information, Freedom of Information Bill, Briefing for Second Reading, 7 Dec. 1999. References are to the latest version of the Bill, available in July 2000.

The legislation had a lengthy and chequered period of gestation. A draft Freedom of Information Bill was published in an annexe to the consultation paper Freedom of Information, Cm 4355, May 1999. This draft Bill was considered by the Select Committee on Public Administration, 3rd Report, 1998–99, Freedom of Information Draft Bill, HC 570-I, and in the House of Lords by the Report from the Select Committee appointed to consider the draft Freedom of Information Bill, 1998–9, HL 97. For discussion see P. Birkinshaw and N. Parry, 'The End of the Beginning? The Freedom of Information Bill 1999', (1999) 26 J. of L. and S. 538; P. Birkinshaw and N. Parry, 'Every Trick in the Book: The Freedom of Information Bill 1999', [1999] EHRLR 372. The Bill departed in several respects (described in the text below) from the earlier White Paper: *Your Right to Know*, Cm. 3818 (1997). For discussion of the White Paper see: P. Birkinshaw, [1998] PL 176; S. Palmer, 'Freedom of Information—Principles and Problems: A Comparative Analysis of the Australian Proposed UK Systems', in University of

authorities.[84] The legislation gives a general right (subject to exemptions and to the payment of a fee) for an applicant to be told whether the authority holds the information requested and, if so, to have it communicated to him or her.[85] Public authorities receiving requests under the legislation are required to determine promptly whether an exemption applies, and in any event within twenty working days,[86] but where the duty to consider discretionary disclosure applies there is no further specific time limit; instead, the decision must be reached within a reasonable time.[87] Applicants disappointed by an authority's refusal to disclose information can appeal to an independent official, the Information Commissioner. The Commissioner has powers to obtain information and to serve decision and enforcement notices on a public authority.[88] Appeal lies either by the authority or a complainant to a tribunal and, on a point of law, to the High Court.[89] Public authorities are also required under legislation to adopt, follow, review, and publicize a 'publication scheme' of the types of information they intend to publish routinely;[90] the scheme must be approved by the Information Commissioner or be one of the models already approved by the Commissioner. If the schemes are widely drafted they are likely in practice to be more significant than information requests from individuals in encouraging greater openness.

In the case of local government, the legislation will not replace the existing access rights, so that access to meetings and information relating to reports discussed at meetings will continue to be governed by the 1985 Act.[91] Nevertheless, an authority will have a duty to consider discretionary disclosure under the Freedom of Information Act as well in these

Cambridge Centre for Public Law, *Constitutional Reform in the United Kingdom: Practice and Principles* (Oxford, 1998).

[84] Freedom of Information Bill 2000, cl. 2 and sched. 1, pt. II, paras. 8 and 9. The legislation does not apply to Scotland, where it has been proposed that public authorities be governed by legislation stronger than that in England and Wales: Scottish Executive, 'An Open Scotland.:Freedom of Information: A Consultation Paper', SE/1999/51 (Edinburgh, Nov. 1999).

[85] Ibid., cl. 1. Exemptions to the right of access are provided for by cl. 1(4) and pt. II; exemptions to the right to 'confirm or deny' apply by virtue of cl. 1(5). Information is treated as 'held' by public authority if it is held on its behalf by another person: cl. 2(2)(b). This means that the authority may be liable under the Act for information held by a contractor or other partner (whether in the public, private, or voluntary sectors) where it relates to the authority's functions under contracting out or some partnership arrangement. Contractors can also be designated as subject to the legislation in their own right under cl. 4(1)(b) where they are providing a service which is one of the local authority's statutory functions under a contract with the authority.

[86] Ibid., cl. 9.

[87] Cl. 1 3(6).

[88] Cll. 51 and 52.

[89] Cll. 56–9. There is no direct civil action against an authority apart from these provisions: cl. 55.

[90] Cl. 17.

[91] This follows from cl. 19, which exempts information reasonably accessible to the public by other means; under cl. 19(2)(b) information required to be open for inspection is to be treated as reasonably accessible.

cases.[92] It must have regard to all of the circumstances of the case and to the desirability of communicating information wherever the public interest in disclosure outweighs that in maintaining the exemption. Where, however, the earlier legislation does not apply, the new Act may. This is likely to be particularly important in the case of information held under the new executive structures, which are to be exempted from the reach of the 1985 Act,[93] although, as we shall see shortly, a significant further exemption applies in their case.

A number of exemptions under the Act are broadly similar to those under the 1985 legislation. This includes: information held for the purposes of criminal investigations or proceedings, information the disclosure of which would be likely to prejudice law enforcement or regulatory functions, personal information falling under the Data Protection Act, information provided in confidence, information covered by legal professional privilege, and information the disclosure of which would prejudice the commercial interests of the public authority or another person.[94]

Protection of administrative and political advice has proved one of the most controversial areas of the proposed exemptions. Local government cannot take advantage of the exemption for policy discussion drafted for the protection of government departments. However, something similar applies in a provision which allows authorities to withhold information if, in the 'reasonable opinion' of a 'qualified person', disclosure would inhibit the free and frank provision of advice or the exchange of views for the purposes of deliberation, or would prejudice 'the effective conduct of public affairs'.[95] It is unclear who will be designated as the 'qualified person' for these purposes by ministerial order. The provisions allow it to be either a minister or an officer of the authority (perhaps the 'proper officer' designated under the 1985 Act).[96] In either event, however, it will be difficult for an applicant successfully to challenge such an opinion before the Information Commissioner. A further exemption allows information to be embargoed for disclosure where it is intended for later publication and it is reasonable in all the circumstances that it should not be published until the later date.[97] A clear weakness in this formulation is that there is no requirement that a firm date for publication be identified. This raises the

[92] Cl. 13 (1). The drafting of this provision is particularly unfortunate and contains an apparent contradiction. It applies *inter alia* to information covered under cl. 19 (i.e. to be treated as accessible to the public because it is open for inspection), provided disclosure of the information is 'not otherwise required by law'. It is submitted that the fact that disclosure of the information is required under the 1985 Act should be considered only under the first limb of this test and not under each part, or the apparent objective would be defeated.

[93] See p. 233 below.

[94] Respectively cll. 28, 29(1)(g), 38–41.

[95] Cl. 34(2)(a)–(c).

[96] Cl. 34(4)(m); in relation to the Greater London Authority it is the Mayor of London: cl. 34(4)(k).

[97] Cl. 20.

risk that the provision could be used as a cover for delaying embarrassing disclosures.[98]

As with the ombudsman, normally applicants will be required to exhaust an authority's own internal complaints procedures (which must be established under the Code of Practice accompanying the Act) before complaining to the Commissioner.[99]

The Commissioner's power to review an authority's use of an exemption varies according to which is invoked. In the case of the claims that disclosure would prejudice the exercise of regulatory functions or commercial interests, the Commissioner can overrule the authority's decision as to whether harm would be caused. Powers in relation to use of the other exemptions are more limited: here the Commissioner may only order disclosure if he or she finds that the information withheld does not fall into the class of information concerned. The legislation is at pains to stress, however, that a public authority's refusal to disclose on a discretionary basis in the public interest information falling within an exemption cannot be reviewed by the Commissioner.[100] This flaw undermines the strength of the Commissioner's other powers, which include the ability to obtain information from the authority[101] (and so to see that the information which it claims should be withheld) and to issue decision and enforcement notices requiring an authority to follow the Act and which are backed by judicial sanctions.[102] The Commissioner's decisions are subject to appeal to the Information Tribunal,[103] which has the power to substitute its own decisions for those of the Commissioner; and the Tribunal's decisions in turn can be challenged, on a point of law, in the High Court.[104]

Compared with some other countries, and, indeed, with the government's own initial proposals in its White Paper,[105] the Freedom of Information Act amounts to a half-hearted attempt to legislate for open-

[98] There is, however, a requirement that the embargo be imposed before the access request is received: cl. 20(1)(b). Although the section does not cross-refer to the authority's publication scheme (cl. 17), presumably the Information Commissioner will do so in assessing reasonableness under cl. 20.

[99] The Commissioner is not required to determine a complaint where the applicant has not done so: cl. 50(2).

[100] See cll. 50(7) and 52(2).

[101] The Commissioner's powers are exercisable by service of an 'information notice' under cl. 51 (to which the only exceptions are those for confidential legal advice between the authority and its advisers). Appeal against an information notice lies, under cl. 56, to the Information Tribunal.

[102] Under cl. 53(3), where the Commissioner certifies that an authority has failed to comply with a notice it is to be treated by the court as contempt.

[103] Cl. 56.

[104] Cl. 58(1).

[105] Commentators have attributed this backtracking on earlier policy undertakings to the transfer of responsibility for freedom of information in 1998 from the Cabinet Office to the Home Office, following the removal from office of the minister responsible for the White Paper, Dr David Clark.

ness. Two features of the White Paper proposals had suggested that the scheme would be much more robust: the claim that there would be no 'class' exemptions so that public authorities would nearly always have to satisfy the requirement that the particular disclosure would be damaging, and the proposed power of the Information Commissioner to order disclosure of information, subject only to judicial review of the Commissioner's decisions. Both aspects have been abandoned. In their place is a proliferation of class exemptions,[106] combined with a discretionary disclosure test which leaves the public authority itself as the arbiter of the public interest, with little scope for review by the Information Commissioner. The most that the Commissioner will be able to do is to *recommend* disclosure in the public interest where an exemption applies, but the public authority will be free to ignore such advice. This undermines the whole principle of the legislation: local authorities should not be free to determine for themselves whether the public interest would be served by disclosure of exempt information which they may find embarrassing. Political self-interest hardly encourages clear calculation of the public benefit and detriment in such cases. The case for an independent official having the power to compel disclosure is overwhelming.

The government seems to have been guilty of backsliding on this principle because of misgivings about an unelected official having powers to overrule the normal processes by which public authorities are accountable. This, however, is not a convincing justification, in general and certainly not in the case of local government. The White Paper proposals already contained a generous (and controversial) exemption protecting the interests of central government in keeping policy advice confidential. In the translation from legislative proposals to the form in the Bill the Information Commissioner's powers have been similarly weakened across most of the exemptions and in relation to all public authorities. The result is a tautology: effective accountability of public authorities depends on public access to information, but for most purposes the Freedom of Information Act leaves public authorities themselves as the gatekeepers over access to the necessary information. The argument that the public authority is more accountable for its decisions than the Information Commissioner is, therefore, circular and self-serving.

Moreover, the way in which the legislation has been applied to local government by overlaying the existing rights of access to meetings and related documents is not merely untidy but also likely to confuse applicants who wish to challenge council decisions to withhold information. If the information to which access is sought relates to a council or committee

[106] Moreover, for exemptions where a harm test has been retained the criteria have been weakened from the proposed test of 'substantial harm' to a requirement of 'prejudice'.

meeting, an applicant may be better off applying under the 1985 Act, since the range of exemptions is narrower than under the Freedom of Information Act, because the exemption for information the disclosure of which would prejudice the effective conduct of public affairs does not apply. Similarly, if the applicant is a councillor or can enlist a councillor to make the application, a narrower range of exemptions will apply under the 1985 Act.[107] However, the Freedom of Information Act will apply in situations where the 1985 Act does not (for example, to information about decisions taken by a member of the council executive or an officer under delegated powers, or where the document or information is not a 'background paper').

Challenges under the 1985 Act will continue to lie in the courts, although it would seem that the Information Commissioner also can question whether, notwithstanding the availability of an exemption under that Act, the public authority should nevertheless make discretionary disclosure in the public interest. There will, however, be a fundamental difference in outcomes according to which route is used: if the High Court finds that the authority's claim to exemption is misguided, the council will have acted ultra vires and decisions taken at any meetings concerned will be unlawful. The court has no formal power to order disclosure of the information concerned, but it could grant the prerogative orders of certiorari (to quash the unlawful decision) and mandamus (to require it to be retaken according to the law). On the other hand, if the Commissioner disagrees with the authority's decision, the power will vary according to the reason why the authority has gone wrong. If no exemption under either piece of legislation applies, then the Commissioner will be able to order disclosure. If the Commissioner disagrees with the authority's assessment of the public interest concerning disclosure, then the limitations already described will apply. In total, this is a long way from being a route for challenging council bureaucracy which is simple and easy to understand and use.

## CONSULTING THE PUBLIC

From duties to provide information we move now to consider another aspect of local democratic practice: consultation of the public. This is an area only partially covered by legal requirements and which in recent years has seen increasing experimentation by local authorities, in an effort to supplement the input from councillors and to obtain the views of sections of the public which are normally less vocal or visible in the democratic process.

[107] See pp. 221–4 below.

Consultation of the public is a routine feature of local government decision-making. Consultative exercises may to an extent take the place of representation of community interests by councillors, or they may, conversely, be a means by which councillors inform themselves of public feeling on certain issues. It is important to remember that consultation can take many different forms: testing the views of service recipients generally (for example, by the equivalent of customer care questionnaires in the private sector), or more narrowly (for instance, the views of tenants in a particular housing block or estate on proposed refurbishment, or of parents at a particular school), or of members of the public in a particular ward affected by a given proposal (such as planning or highways schemes); or more general attempts to consult, for example, on a structure or local plan;[108] or with a specific section of the public (for instance, taxi licence-holders before a change in policy affecting them). The objective may be to involve the public or sections of it in the policy-making process, or simply to test the opinions of particular groups, or to obtain feedback on defined issues or areas of council performance. Quite apart from variations in geographical reach or sectional interests, consultative exercises also vary in their time-frame, for example, from single-exercise focus groups and citizens' juries to consultative panels which may be questioned repeatedly over a period of months.

There is a growing number of areas in which consultation is a statutory requirement before a decision is taken which affects a given area or individual. For example, the duty to give public notice of planning applications has been considerably expanded, from narrow categories such as unneighbourly development and alterations affecting the appearance of a listed building to a duty governing all planning applications, with more onerous requirements applicable to some categories. These notice provisions are strengthened by a formal prohibition on the council considering the application within fixed times from the notice and a requirement to consider representations made as a result.[109] Specific duties to inform and consult their secure tenants are also imposed on local authorities under housing legislation.[110] These include a duty to make standing arrangements to consult tenants on questions concerning housing management[111] and a requirement to publish a summary of the council's rules on

[108] Planning and Compensation Act 1991, sched. 4, para. 17; although this provision is narrower than the duty it replaced (Town and Country Planning Act 1971, s. 7; and see DoE Circulars 52/72 and 23/81).

[109] S. 16(2) Planning and Compensation Act 1991; see: S. De Smith, H. Woolf, and J. Jowell, *Judicial Review of Administrative Action* (5th edn., London, 1995), 435–6. However, where a local planning authority had voluntarily adopted a practice of consulting neighbours beyond that then required, this did not create a legitimate expectation that it would be followed: *R v SSE ex p. Kent*, [1990] JPL 124, CA.

[110] See Birkinshaw, *Freedom of Information*, 196–8.

[111] Housing Act 1995, s. 105.

allocation of its housing stock and on transfers (to and from other areas) and tenants' exchanges of housing.[112] However, the value of these consultation provisions is doubtful in view of a general reluctance to respond except where a matter directly affects an individual tenant, despite the creation of tenants' associations and co-option of tenants' representatives on to housing committees.[113] There is also some ambivalence in the policy underlying these duties, bearing in mind that legislation also permits councils to dispose of their housing stock to new landlords with minimal consultation of sitting tenants.[114] These provisions follow earlier and barely used powers to ballot tenants on the proposed establishment of a Housing Action Trust.[115]

Wider consultation is often a requirement under the growing number of statutory plans. Here consultation is an attempt to encourage the coordinated response of different agencies to social problems that cut across the institutional boundaries of government. A plan may also serve to make transparent the objectives of public bodies, to structure discretion, and to provide a measure for audit and performance review. Such a plan often requires consultation of the public and of other stakeholders about the provision of public services and coordination of efforts among public authorities and other service providers in tackling intractable cross-cutting social problems, especially in the areas of crime, social exclusion, and health. The archetype of planned cooperation is a provision requiring local authorities in formulating a community care plan to consult voluntary organizations representing likely users of community care and their carers.[116] The position of voluntary bodies under these various existing plans, strategies, and reviews is generally fairly weak: there may be a procedural right to be consulted, but even the choice of bodies consulted may be within the discretion of the public authority.[117]

The spirit in which a consultative exercise is undertaken is largely beyond the reach of the law. The strongest protection is in cases where a statutory duty is imposed to consider representations and to give reasons

[112] Housing Act 1995, s. 106. Excessive secrecy surrounding such policies underlay the earlier *Tower Hamlets* case (n. 71 above).

[113] Birkinshaw, *Freedom of Information*, 197.

[114] *Short v Tower Hamlets LBC*, (1985) 18 HLR 171, interpreting Housing Act 1985, s. 105; see also ibid., s. 106A and sched. 3A.

[115] Housing Act 1988, s. 61.

[116] National Health Service and Community Care Act 1990, s. 46(3).

[117] For recent examples see Crime and Disorder Act 1998, s. 5(3), requiring chief police officers and local authorities in devising a strategy for reduction of crime and disorder in their locality to invite participation from specified categories of bodies; Schools Standards and Framework Act 1998, s. 6. A rare example of a stronger right is the position of diocesan authorities (voluntary sector providers of church schools) where there is in effect a right of review before an Adjudicator: Education (School Organisation Plans) England Regulations 1999.

for the resulting decision. However, this does not prevent a council from overriding the weight of opinion of consultees, and in many situations the statutory underpinning for the exercise is markedly weaker. The law will, however, attempt to ensure that sufficient time is allowed for consultation in order for the person consulted to give helpful advice rather than a cursory response.[118] Likewise, there are judicial statements to the effect that consultation must be genuine in the sense that it takes place before a council's mind is effectively made up.[119] The position has been succinctly summarized in terms of four requirements:

> First, that consultation must be at a time when proposals are still at a formative stage. Second, that the proposer must give sufficient reasons for any proposal to permit intelligent consideration and response. Third, that adequate time must be given for consideration and response and finally, fourth, that the product of the consultation must be conscientiously taken into account in finalising any statutory proposals.[120]

However, these requirements should not be taken too rigidly: they are adaptable to the type of consultation and may depend on the status of the body that a council uses for consultation.[121] It has been said that the central question is 'whether the consultation process as a whole resulted in unfairness'.[122]

In the education field, the courts have imposed some consultation requirements in addition to those appearing in legislation, even in relation to the development of formative proposals by a Local Education Authority in reviewing its schools stock.[123] This emphasizes the need for consultation to occur while the council's policy is still at the formative stage, in order to have real influence on the decision-making process.[124] It has been held that a pattern of previous consultation may give rise to a legitimate expectation in the parents that they would be consulted, which the court would enforce. Subsequently, a statutory duty to consult 'such

[118] *R v SS for Social Services ex p. AMA*, [1986] 1 WLR 1, per Webster J at 14.

[119] *R v Gwent CC and SS for Wales, ex p. Bryant*, [1988] COD 19; *R v Camden LBC ex p. Cran*, (1995) 94 LGR 8; *R v Devon CC ex p. Baker*, [1995] 1 All ER 73.

[120] *R v Brent LBC ex p. Gunning*, (1986) 84 LGR 168, 189, per Hodgson J.

[121] Where a working party is used to gather opinion and does not possess deliberative powers, the requirements may be amended accordingly: *R v Warwickshire DC ex p. Bailey*, [1991] COD 284.

[122] *R v Governors of Haberdashers' Aske's Hatcham Schools ex p. Inner London Education Authority*, [1989] COD 435, per Kerr LJ.

[123] *R v Brent LBC, ex p. Gunning*, (1986) 84 LGR 168; see also: *R v Sutton LBC, ex p. Hamlet* (unreported decision of 26 Mar. 1986); *R v Northants. CC ex p. Tebbutt* (unreported decision of 26 June 1986).

[124] But see *Nichol v Gateshead MBC*, (1989) 87 LGR 435, where the Court of Appeal held (reversing McCowan J) that the local authority was not required to consult on each possible option for school organization which it identified, merely its preferred option.

persons as appear to [the council] appropriate' before publishing proposals has been introduced.[125]

Similar criteria for consultation have been applied where a council was considering plans for the closure of an old people's home; it was held that the council should give early notice to the residents in advance of the final decision, that there should be a reasonable time to make objections, and that these should be considered by the council.[126] Applying these principles to the facts, the court held that a meeting of residents of a home with officers or councillors was sufficient opportunity to voice objections and there was no obligation to grant each resident an individual interview. Nevertheless, it found in the case of one of the closures challenged that a mere five days' notice (including a weekend) by letter before the committee took the decision was insufficient consultation.

It has been stated that 'consultation is not and should not be a referendum'.[127] A council may take account of its officers' professional advice in preference to objections from those consulted. However, when a council's treatment of consultees over the introduction of an on-street parking scheme suggested that it had a closed mind and was applying an inflexible borough-wide policy irrespective of local circumstances, and officers failed to reflect fairly objections received in a report to councillors, the consultation was found to be inadequate.[128]

## OTHER PARTICIPATORY MECHANISMS

Traditionally the public's voice was heard in the town hall through their elected representatives—councillors, who retained a monopoly on participating in the formal decision-making processes of the authority. However, two recurring recent trends, pioneered mainly by Liberal Democrat-controlled councils, have been the introduction of standing orders allowing for a public question time at council meetings[129] and the creation of neighbourhood committees or forums allowing more direct involvement of the community alongside councillors in tailoring council-wide policies to smaller localities. There is currently also considerable interest in other devices designed to allow for direct, participatory demo-

[125] Now contained in the Education Act 1996, s. 35(5).

[126] *R v Devon CC ex p. Baker*, [1995] 1 All ER 73; see esp. Dillon LJ at 83 and Simon Brown LJ at 91–2.

[127] *Nichol v Gateshead MBC*, (1989) 87 LGR 435, 454 per O'Connor LJ.

[128] *R v Camden LBC ex p. Cran*, (1995) 94 LGR 8, 71–5 per McCullough LJ.

[129] See also the requirement for a 'People's Question Time' under the Greater London Authority Act 1999, s. 47.

cracy, especially local referendums and 'citizens juries or panels'.[130] The government has proposed increased use of consultative devices such as citizens' juries, service user panels, neighbourhood and issues-based community forums, and advisory panels (drawn from local employers, trade unions, and training bodies) as a method of increasing the responsiveness of councils outside the electoral process.[131]

Proposals for regular use of local referendums featured in the Commission for Local Democracy's package of measures for greater citizen involvement in local affairs.[132] It is doubtful whether specific legal power is necessary. Some local authorities have resorted in the past to local referendums on single controversial issues, and it can be argued that this benefits the local community (under section 137 of the Local Government Act 1972) or is conducive to the exercise of some other specific function (section 111 of the same Act), even in the absence of a specific power or duty of consultation. Where legal regulation may be useful, however, is to regulate the use of public funds in campaigning for one position or another, especially in view of the detailed legal regime already covering political advertising,[133] and to govern procedural questions, such as who may initiate a referendum and the time-scale involved. A number of detailed proposals have been made to regulate the use of referendums at a national level and ensure fairness and consistency. These concern questions such as the phrasing of the question, campaigning, distribution of information at public expense, campaign expenditure, and access to the media.[134] Comparable issues need to be addressed in local government if local referendums are to be used as a regular means of direct participatory democracy. Specific legislation governing local referendums already exists in two fields. Parents of children at schools maintained by a Local Education Authority can trigger a ballot of all such parents on the question of whether selection by academic aptitude should be retained at grammar schools within the authority.[135] This is not a full referendum, since only a limited class of service users is entitled to vote, but it extends further than

[130] See M. Geddes, *Extending Democratic Practice in Local Government* (Commission for Local Democracy research report no. 17) (London, 1996), 17–18; L. Pratchett, 'New Fashions in Public Participation: Towards Greater Democracy?', (1999) 52 (4) Parl. Affs. 616; S. Leach and M. Wingfield, 'Public Participation and the Democratic Renewal Agenda: Prioritisation or Marginilisation?', (1999) 25 LGS 46.

[131] Labour Party, *Renewing Democracy, Rebuilding Communities* (London, 1995), 15; DETR, *Guidance on Enhancing Public Participation in Local Government* (London, 1998).

[132] Commission for Local Democracy, *Taking Charge: The Rebirth of Local Democracy* (London, 1995), 30–1. The limited use of 'Citizen Ballots'—a common practice in the US where questions on specific issues are also put to the electorate along with a choice of candidates—is also advocated.

[133] See pp. 74–8 above.

[134] *Report of the Commission on the Conduct of Referendums* (London, 1996).

[135] Schools Standards and Framework Act 1998, ss. 105 and 106.

the usual focus of consulting parents at an individual school about its future. The first authentic general referendum requirement will be introduced as part of the reform of local executive structures. This will require a local authority to hold a referendum on changing the form of executive structure if it decides to adopt an elected mayor, if 5 per cent of local electors petition, or when the Secretary of State so demands.[136] Outside these specific instances, the government in the 1998 White Paper argued that local referendums should play a larger part in local democracy and promised to introduce legislation to confirm the power of councils to hold them.[137]

'Citizens' juries' have been widely used in the United States and in Germany and are generating substantial interest in the UK. These involve an in-depth discussion of a local issue by a hand-picked, representative group of citizens; exercises which have been run by councils include deliberations on waste management in West Hertfordshire and on drugs policy in Lewisham.[138] Panels of this kind are seen as a way of involving the local community to supplement the knowledge and experience of local councillors. Members of these 'juries' are paid for participating, hear and are able to 'cross-examine' expert evidence (although they lack the formal legal powers of a court), and operate with the assistance of professional moderators who guide the discussion and produce a report. However, concerns have been raised about how representative these exercises are, in view of the small numbers of individuals involved (typically there will be a panel of twelve to sixteen) and because people in full-time employment may be deterred from participating in hearings which may take several whole weekdays. Citizens' juries are best seen as an opportunity for an injection of 'lay wisdom'—an alternative viewpoint, though not necessarily a representative one—into the policy-making process.[139]

Other councils (notably, Kirklees and Bradford) have established larger standing consultative panels of citizens (numbering respectively 1,000 and 2,500) on whom proposals can be market-tested. Panels of this kind work by periodic postal surveys. They can be constructed to be representative of different social and economic groups within the area, although there may be a difficulty in recruiting some groups, notably younger people. It is said, however, that such panels have a limited shelf-life, since there is a

[136] LGA 2000, ss. 26–33. See further p. 231 below.

[137] *Modern Local Government: In Touch With the People*, para. 4.8. Although specific legislation to govern referendums has been introduced (see the Political Parties, Elections and Referendums Bill 2000), the lowest level of referendum to which this applies is one throughout the whole area of a Regional Development Agency: ibid., cl. 97(1)(c). In the absence of specific authority a council might rely on s. 2 LGA 2000, but note that no specific constraints on the referendum would then apply. Perhaps this is less significant, since these referendums would be voluntary and non-binding.

[138] *The Times*, 11 Nov. 1996.

[139] Pratchett, op. cit., 624–5.

tendency for the members, through their involvement, to become increasingly familiar with the council and its policies, so that they quickly become unrepresentative of the local community from which they were drawn.[140]

The use of 'focus groups' is an importation from marketing practice. In contrast to citizens' panels, these are small, unrepresentative groups (normally drawn from a specific locality or socio-economic group) which meet informally, normally on a single occasion. The purpose is to allow politicians and those involved in policy-making to see how particular groups are likely to react to policy initiatives. Where a number of these groups with differing compositions are convened, it may allow for the systematic mapping or 'segmenting' of public opinion.

Use of one or more such mechanisms is now widespread among local authorities: Pratchett's 1999 study found that in the preceding year 18 per cent of councils responding had used citizens' panels, 5 per cent had used citizens' juries, 47 per cent had community focus groups, and 45 per cent had engaged in some form of community planning (with 26 per cent using 'visioning'—consultation over long-term priorities and objectives).[141] Innovative as such developments are, commentators have pointed out that they go no further than considering the issues which the council has predetermined. Councils are also free to choose the mode of consultation. Any enthusiasm for what may appear to be direct democracy should be tempered by a more sophisticated analysis of the suitability of particular techniques for different objectives and exercises. Whereas citizens' panels, for example, may rate highly in terms of representativeness, they give fewer opportunities for responsive participation than unrepresentative citizens' juries. Claims that councils have more democratic legitimacy because low electoral turnout is offset by use of such methods have to be treated sceptically, therefore.

The Commission for Local Democracy has suggested that a range of consultative processes (including electronic consultation, local 'phone-ins', and citizen monitors) should form part of an annual 'Democracy Plan' to be introduced by the Leader of the council and presented to the electorate as a form of democratic audit.[142] The influence of this idea is to be found in the government proposal for a 'Community Plan', to bring together local stakeholders to identify needs and aspirations of local communities and to improve service provision in response to those needs and aspirations.[143] It is to be developed with local people, local business, and with the public and voluntary sectors. The White Paper suggested that there would be some freedom about the content of the Community Plan and the process of its preparation. Although the plan would have no direct

[140] Ibid. 623.

[141] Ibid. 628.

[142] Commission for Local Democracy, op. cit., 32–3.

[143] *Modern Local Government: In Touch with the People* (July 1998), ch. 8.

effect, it would be considered when applications were made for special funding and would be a background consideration to other statutory plans which the council was required to prepare for particular services or functions.[144] These proposals are translated into law by a new statutory duty to prepare community strategies[145] which runs in parallel with the new power for councils to promote or improve the economic, social, or environmental well-being of their communities; in preparing such a strategy councils may consult or seek the participation of such persons as they consider appropriate and must have regard to any guidance issued by ministers.[146] Although it is a tangible legal manifestation of the more amorphous vogue for collaborative (or 'joined-up') government, the duty places no corresponding obligation on other bodies to cooperate.[147] It is doubtful if the duty adds much: a council must surely have had the ability to devise such plans under its general and implied powers in any event. There is, however, a new requirement duty to follow ministerial guidance in preparing the strategy. It is clear, then, that councils have retained a large degree of discretion over consultation, even within the legislation for democratic renewal.

## CONCLUSION

If it is true to say that information is power, it follows that control over the flow of information is the key to democratic accountability. This insight can be applied to the three distinct areas that this chapter has considered: attempts by a council to influence public perception through its own release of information or through controlling its release by others, access by outsiders to information in the hands of a council, and the openness and responsiveness of a council's own processes to members of the public and to those who use its services. In the first of these areas, because of tight controls on political advertising and the protection of freedom of expression, local authorities have relatively little control. In the second, the lengthening reach of freedom of information legislation has diminished

[144] A different approach is taken in the case of the new strategic authority for London, where the Greater London Authority Act 1999 does not require the preparation of an overall plan. Instead there are to be a series of strategies dealing with spatial development, transport, waste management, air quality, and ambient noise.

[145] LGA 2000, s. 4.

[146] Ibid., s. 4(2).

[147] The White Paper also commended the establishment by councils of non-statutory local public forums, to allow for public debate and education on issues of concern; in some instances these have included giving public or private bodies the opportunity to respond to local concerns about their actions or proposals. However, these are not to be a statutory requirement nor underpinned with powers, e.g. to compel the attendance of, and information or evidence from, other local actors, such as quangos and privatized industries (e.g. water companies): Green Paper, paras. 6.25–7.

the ability of local authorities to control the flow of information from their files and computers, although the exemptions, particularly those under the new legislation, preserve a considerable area in which local politicians can operate free from the public gaze. In the third area, apart from a few specific requirements to consult particular groups or bodies, councils still have a high degree of discretion over whether and how to consult the public.

Issues concerning the accessibility, transparency, and responsiveness of councils are of fundamental importance to local democracy, whether it is conceived in terms mainly of the accountability of elected representatives or of financial or consumer accountability. In an environment where councils increasingly attempt to establish credibility and democratic legitimacy by being open and responsive to the public, the significance of legal controls in this area can only grow.

# 4

# *Financial Accountability*

## INTRODUCTION

Questions about the source of local government finance are inevitably closely connected with debates about the proper form of local government, the extent of its political autonomy, and its responsibility to the electorate and to local taxpayers. This chapter first considers the accountability issues raised by local taxation and central government grant funding of local government. Discussion then moves from local revenue to local expenditure, dealing with the place of audit as an accountability mechanism, the role of the Audit Commission, and with the judicially created fiduciary duty owed by a council to its taxpayers.

Any discussion of financial accountability should begin by acknowledging the extent to which local government is dependent upon central government grant for its financial needs. Currently, over 50 per cent of local government money comes from central government through such grants, and a further 25 per cent is under central government control through the National Non-Domestic Rate.[1] All claims that local taxation is a mechanism of local democratic accountability must be measured against the truism that three times as much money is allocated centrally (and comes indirectly through national taxation) as is raised directly by local authorities. The proportion of centrally funded local expenditure also gives central government a considerable stake in the financial probity of local government in order to protect the interests of national taxpayers.

The second contextual feature is the cumulative effect of the actions of local authorities, whether in the capital or revenue fields, on national finances; this applies to the macro-economic effects of expenditure on the money supply (in the case both of capital and revenue expenditure), the inflationary effect of local taxation, and the implications of capital loans for the Public Sector Borrowing Requirement. This is not to take any particular political stance on the legitimacy of different governments' economic policies in relation to the public sector as a whole, but simply to recognize that local finance cannot be treated merely as a local phenome-

[1] In 1998/9, of £50 billion spent by local authorities on local services £12 billion came from council tax (including £2 billion in council tax benefit reimbursed by central government); the remainder came from business rate and government grants (half of this £38 billion came from revenue support grant): DETR, *Modernising Local Government: Improving Financial Accountability*, Consultation Paper (London, 1998), para. 2.6.

non. A recent consultation paper from the Labour government argues that, since local government expenditure makes up about one sixth of public spending, 'it is of considerable importance within the Government's plans for the delivery of its goals for the economy. The Government therefore must remain concerned to ensure that spending by local government should be stable, predictable and consistent with its own economic policies and targets.'[2] On the other hand, critics suggest that attempts to reinvigorate local democracy will fail unless councils regain a measure of control over their finances. Nearly a quarter of a century ago the Layfield Report set out a clear choice between systems of local and central responsibility.[3] The Labour administration, which received that report in 1976, fudged the issue, as have all successive governments. In 1999 a Select Committee report again called for a return to local control to enhance local accountability and to halt what it perceived as a long-term slide from local democracy towards local administration. The Committee specifically linked financial and electoral accountability, arguing that the financial reforms should dovetail with greater consultation on the setting of local budgets and Council Tax levels and with more frequent local elections.[4]

Bearing in mind this web of overlapping interests, it is not surprising that arguments about the control of local taxation and expenditure by central government, and the relative limits of local autonomy, have proved some of the fiercest of constitutional battlegrounds of the last two decades. The account here begins with a sketch of the different local taxes introduced in that period.

## FROM RATES TO COUNCIL TAX, VIA THE POLL TAX

This section does not attempt to chart in detail the shifts in legislation concerning local government finance. To do so would be unnecessarily complex and, in view of several changes of policy, of merely historical interest. Nor is it intended to provide a comprehensive account of the numerous central–local conflicts played out in the courts in the last two decades concerning the increasingly opaque legal powers over local expenditure, whether the allocation of central government grants or controls over local taxation. While an expedition into this virtually impenetrable terrain would yield many lessons of interest from the viewpoints of legal history, public law, public administration generally, and central–local relations

[2] Ibid., para. 2.7.

[3] *Report of the Committee of Inquiry into Local Government Finance*, Cmnd. 6453 (1976).

[4] Environment, Transport and Regions Select Committee, *Local Government Finance*, HC 78-I (1998–9), para. 95. See further pp. 113–14 below.

more specifically, it would be a significant detour.[5] Instead, the focus is the extent to which the various pieces of legislation have strengthened or weakened financial accountability as a vehicle of local democracy.

The Thatcher government took office in 1979 with the system of local rates in place, just as it had been for more than a century. As a property tax computed according to an index related notionally to the market rental value of the property (although somewhat unsatisfactorily, since the register was out of date), rates had a number of inequities, both for local authorities and taxpayers. Because of the linkage with property values, a local authority with a high total rateable value of property needed to charge a correspondingly lower-rate poundage[6] in order to raise an equivalent amount to a council with a lower total rateable value. The total rateable value was wholly unrelated to local needs and dependent largely upon geographical accident; one of the functions of grants from central government was, therefore, to compensate for these arbitrary differences.[7] Since rates were based upon the size and type of property, they were essentially unrelated either to the number of people in occupation or to the demands made by the household upon the local community. The apparent unfairness had, however, over the years been softened by a complex system of rebates, designed to take account of factors such as income and the number of dependants of the householder. Moreover, the system had some advantages which were often overlooked by critics: there was often an approximate correlation between a person's income or wealth and the value of the property they occupied, and the tax was simple to collect, inexpensive to administer, and virtually impossible to evade.

Although the rates system was plainly unsatisfactory, successive governments had fought shy of reforming it for lack of a clear, viable alternative. The gap between local taxation and financial accountability was further increased by the proportion of rates paid by local businesses on commercial and industrial properties. Grant argues that: 'this large divide between funding and electoral accountability undermined the constitutional foundation of local government by weakening its political legiti-

[5] For a detailed account which sketches the place of law in regulating central–local relations over finance, see: M. Loughlin, *Legality and Locality: The Role of Law in Central–Local Relations* (Oxford, 1996), ch. 5.

[6] The amount by which the rateable value was multiplied in order to produce the tax owed.

[7] These factors remain important within a reformed local taxation system. The Consultation Paper (n. 1 above) argued: 'High levels of grant are needed because the total of council spending would be too great for a property based tax like the council tax to bear and because the uneven distribution of needs and resources between local authorities would lead to large variations in tax levels across the country. Without central support many areas of the country would not be able to provide services to the standards required by statute' (para. 2.6).

macy'.[8] The Layfield Committee had recommended in 1976 that if the intention was to strengthen local responsibility, then a form of local income tax should supplement rates.[9] However, an additional tax would have inevitably involved increased administrative costs for a marginal gain in fairness, and the recommendation remained unimplemented. The Thatcher government seemed unable to produce any better proposals when it published its 1981 Green Paper *Alternatives to Domestic Rates*,[10] despite canvassing options involving combinations of property tax, income tax, and what it described as a flat-rate poll tax, i.e. a tax levied on electors as such. The government was forced into precipitate reform, however, following an outcry in Scotland caused by the updating of the index of rateable values. This exercise had produced a dramatic realignment in rates liability, since the rateable values of older properties had tended to lag significantly behind inflation, whereas new properties had been added to the index at current rateable values. The government moved to reform,[11] introducing in the Community Charge an option which it had initially rejected several years before in England and Wales. Subsequently, this ill-fated tax was also introduced south of the Border by the Local Government Finance Act 1988.

The intention behind the tax was in many respects laudable on constitutional grounds, since it was to strengthen the link between financial and democratic accountability of local government by broadening the tax base.[12] One can applaud this objective without also accepting the Conservative government's background assumption: that local electors would choose lower local expenditure once they were more clearly collectively responsible for local taxation. Nor does acceptance of the principle mean approval of the form in which it was implemented, namely through a regressive, flat-rate payment to which there were very few exceptions. In detaching tax liability from ability to pay, the government was flying in the face of the redistributive ethic which motivated many local politicians, whatever their political affiliation. It was, however, consistent with the government's own view that social redistribution should be a matter of central government policy and not for local taxation. A further rationale was that the tax should be a form of charge upon those who used local

[8] M. Grant, 'Central–Local Relations: The Balance of Power', in J. Jowell and D. Oliver (eds.), *The Changing Constitution* (2nd edn.) (Oxford, 1989).

[9] *Report of the Committee of Inquiry into Local Government Finance*, Cmnd. 6453 (1976), ch. 15, para. 44ff.

[10] Cmnd. 8449 (1981).

[11] Abolition of Domestic Rates Etc. (Scotland) Act 1987; discussed in C. Himsworth and N. Walker, 'After Rates? The Community Charge in Scotland', [1987] PL 586.

[12] *Paying for Local Government*, Cmnd. 9714 (1985). See also D. Mason, *Revising the Rates System* (London, 1985), a response to the 1981 Green Paper (n. 10 above), published by the Adam Smith Institute.

services. In this it was necessarily flawed and, instead, liability reflected more directly the entitlement of the charge-payer to vote, hence its pejorative label, the 'poll tax'.[13]

Whatever the purity of this idea, it became politically compromised by attempts to soften the transitional impact of the new tax upon those who would face the largest increases. Apparently the government did not sufficiently trust the mechanisms of accountability which it had established to allow them free rein. Ministers retained in the new legislation powers to limit the maximum level of local taxation (capping powers) which they had first taken under the unreformed rating system.[14] The retention of these powers in effect to override the decisions of local politicians, accountable (if imperfectly) to the local electorate, flew in the face of the arguments for the legislation. Ministers tried to justify the contradiction by claiming that the power would be needed in the transitional period while the Community Charge was phased in to 'protect' charge-payers from budgetary recklessness by councils.[15] In addition, however, when faced with the electoral unpopularity caused by the changes in local tax liability, the government cushioned the effect by, first, giving substantial additional grant aid to local authorities, and then by transferring the financing of education expenditure from local to central control (this necessitated adding 2.5 per cent to the rate of VAT). The consequence was that only 14 per cent of local expenditure was financed by the Community Charge by the late 1980s. An incidental effect of this strategy should have been that because of the very high 'gearing' of the tax (a Community Charge increase of 7 per cent was needed to produce a net increase in council income of 1 per cent), the incentive for the electorate to return lower-spending local authorities was enhanced. In practice, though, there was little evidence of the electorate penalizing councils for setting high Community Charge levels, and in any event the government restrained such actions through the use of its capping powers. The unpopularity of the tax rebounded on the government, and after a prolonged campaign of mass protest and civil disobedience, the Community Charge was replaced in 1992 by the Council Tax.

Ironically, in the Council Tax (which was introduced in the Local Government Finance Act 1992) the government reverted to a fairly inflexible property tax. Under the scheme properties are divided into seven value bands, unrelated directly to ability to pay. The tax attempts to avoid the worst inequalities of the rating system, however, by taking more

[13] See D. Butler, A. Adonis, and T. Travers, *Failure in British Government: The Politics of the Poll Tax* (Oxford, 1994).

[14] Local Government Finance Act 1988, Pt. VII; capping was first introduced in the Rates Act 1984; see p. 106 below.

[15] See C. Himsworth, 'Poll Tax Capping and Judicial Review', [1991] PL 76, 78.

account of the occupancy of individual properties. It is assumed that a property is occupied by two taxpayers, and a reduced rate is payable for single occupancy; if more than two persons are in occupancy, the tax does not increase. This system has remained largely unchanged since its introduction. The Labour government's White Paper argued that the Council Tax was 'working well as a local tax' and posed 'no fundamental problems', although not everyone agrees.[16] Nevertheless, following the period of turbulent change which saw the revision and repeal of the Community Charge, the Council Tax appears to be a more enduring alternative to rates as a local tax.

## CENTRAL CONTROL AND LOCAL EXPENDITURE

Several conflicting factors underlie central government's concern with local finance. Historically, central government grants have served the function of attempting to equalize local disparities in the tax base so that local authorities are equally able to implement national desirable legislation. However, a significant shift has occurred. Early in the twentieth century the focus of such grants was to provide a national minimum level of service which local authorities were free to exceed and finance through local taxation. In the 1980s, on the other hand, grants became used increasingly to prescribe a *maximum* level of local expenditure by councils. This transition is explained by the growing influence of macro-economic concerns about local expenditure and taxation. Central government's concern does not end with the portion of local expenditure which it finances directly; equally, conflicting concerns arise in relation to local taxation. Again at a macro-economic level, central government is concerned with the total amount of public-sector expenditure and borrowing, however, raised. Central government grants can also be used to strengthen or weaken the process of local accountability through local tax. The greater the proportion of local expenditure financed through central government grant, the more unstable local taxation will be, since, in order to produce a small overall increase in the money available to a council, a proportionately larger increase in its local tax will be required; this is the phenomenon known as 'gearing'. In addition, central control may attempt to 'protect' local taxpayers from the inflationary effects of high local tax rises.

All of these factors, of course, are interrelated, and there is a danger that an attempt to use central controls to pursue one objective will have undesirable side-effects. The failure to resolve the issue is now generally agreed

[16] *Modern Local Government: In Touch with the People*, paras. 5.21 and 5.22. The Select Committee suggested, however, that revisions of the tax bands might enable a higher proportion of local income to be raised through council tax: n. 4 above, para. 101.

to underlie the unsuccessful attempts by the first two Thatcher governments to limit local expenditure. In Loughlin's words, 'the Government became caught in a vortex leading to an irresistibly increasing centralisation of control'.[17]

The first moves towards centralization came with the introduction of the block grant mechanism in the notoriously complex Local Government Planning and Land Act 1980, Part VI. Although introduced by the new Conservative government, the system followed an approach (a central grant derived from an assessment of each council's spending needs) which had been proposed by the Department of Environment to the Layfield Committee under the previous Labour administration.[18] The Conservative legislation implemented this scheme with a high degree of ministerial discretion.[19] In addition, the legislation contained incentives designed to influence the level at which councils set rates, through a system of 'clawback' of grant, related to increases in the total expenditure of the council. Whereas, ostensibly, block grant was allocated on the basis of assessment of need, the clawback provisions were triggered by comparison with historical expenditure of the council in question. The effect of the clawback was that any council wishing to exceed the expenditure target effectively prescribed for it by central government had to increase the total yield from its income derived from rates not merely by the difference between the two but also by the amount of grant lost. It was assumed that councils would baulk at the large rates increases necessary in order to maintain expenditure plans radically different from government targets. In the case of a number of councils, however, in the early 1980s this proved incorrect, and rate increases of up to 60 per cent were implemented. The government now took the next, and fundamentally different, step of obtaining statutory power to limit (or 'cap') local tax levels.[20]

The Rates Act 1984 contained two schemes for rate-capping or limitation: one was a scheme of selective rate-capping (this was the scheme in fact used by the government) and the other was a scheme for universal rate-capping (which was never implemented). The selective scheme was

[17] Loughlin, op. cit., 272.

[18] *Report of the Committee of Inquiry into Local Government Finance*, Cmnd. 6453 (1976), ch. 12. The Committee, however, proposed the consideration of new forms of local taxation in order to combat the inexorable drift towards central control through the then Rate Support Grant. The Labour government failed to respond decisively in either direction, preferring instead to retain the flexibility of a mixed system: *Local Government Finance*, Cmnd. 6813 (1977), para. 2.8.

[19] See the powers to determine 'relevant expenditure' and 'total expenditure' in relation to individual councils, to set principles for determining the grant, and thereafter applying a 'multiplier': respectively, Local Government, Planning and Land Act 1980, ss. 56(8), 54(5), 57–9.

[20] See generally Loughlin, op. cit., 300 ff.; M. Grant, *Rate Capping and the Law* (2nd edn., London, 1986).

complex but essentially worked in two stages. Under the first stage the Secretary of State could designate authorities whose expenditure seemed likely to exceed the Grant Related Expenditure Assessment (GRE) and to be excessive, designating a level of maximum expenditure for these councils.[21] A council could challenge this expenditure level by an application for redetermination. However, if it did so the Secretary of State had the power to set a lower level than that originally determined, and was given enhanced powers to interfere in the management of the council's expenditure. This was a considerable disincentive for councils to apply for redetermination. Once the maximum expenditure level was established, and the Rate Support Grant deducted from it, the maximum permitted rate for the council could be calculated. This rate was enforced by provisions absolving ratepayers from paying more than the maximum permitted under the designation.

As with the earlier legislation, the Rates Act constituted no more than a shell to be filled by ministerial discretion: the Secretary of State was to act in accordance with the 'principles determined' by him in considering the critical questions of designation and determining the maximum expenditure level.[22] Where a council did not consent, the final stage in the process, rates limitation, was effected by an order approved by the House of Commons. The whole legislative scheme, with its emphasis upon economic and political judgment by the minister concerning excessive expenditure, and the approval of designation by Parliament, suggested that councils would have difficulty in successfully challenging capping in the courts. This proved to be the case. The Divisional Court held that, although parliamentary approval of the limitation order did not prevent the court from reviewing its reasonableness, Parliament was the best place to address criticisms of the minister's judgment; review of the maximum precepts for the GLC and the ILEA was refused.[23] In this case, and also in a later one brought by Greenwich,[24] the judges refused to order the minister to disclose the underlying factors behind the formula used in designation and limitation. Since the councils designated were almost exclusively Labour-controlled, there were inevitably allegations that the powers were being used for partisan political purposes.

Capping was retained, with variations, under the 1988 legislation which introduced the Community Charge. Under this scheme it was the

[21] Rates Act 1984, s. 2(2).

[22] 1984 Act, ss. 2(4) and 3(2).

[23] *R v Secretary of State for the Environment ex parte GLC and ILEA* (unreported decision of the QBD, 3 Apr. 1985). Note also *R v Secretary of State for the Environment ex parte London Borough of Islington*, unreported decision of the QBD, 26 Mar. 1986, where a challenge to the minister's maximum expenditure determination failed; the court held that the appropriate remedy was for Islington to apply formally for redetermination.

[24] *London Borough of Greenwich v Secretary of State for the Environment*, *The Times*, 19 Dec. 1985.

maximum amount of council expenditure which could be capped, rather than the maximum charge level. The minister could exercise these powers where he was of the opinion that the council's budgeted expenditure was 'excessive' or that there was an 'excessive increase' on the budget for the previous year.[25] Although the retention of these powers seemed to contradict the underlying logic of the Community Charge, the government argued that it was necessary, especially in the transitional period following the introduction of the tax. Predictably, the designation of nineteen councils for the financial year 1990/1 was challenged in the courts. The House of Lords held, as in the previous local government finance cases, that the minister could not be said to be acting irrationally, illegally, or with procedural impropriety, and that fundamentally the issue boiled down to a matter of political judgment.[26] Capping was again retained when the Community Charge was replaced by the Council Tax under the Local Government Finance Act 1992. However, from 1991/2 until very recently the government has announced in advance of council budgets being set its proposals for maximum expenditure levels, with the result that almost all councils have set budgets within these limits so as to avoid later capping. This system has been described as one of 'universal capping'.[27] The Labour government, with the support of the Local Government Association, changed this practice by not announcing in advance capping levels for the financial year 1999/2000. It argued that this would encourage local authorities to exercise budgetary discretion themselves. In the event no council was capped, and the government pronounced itself satisfied that the 'vast majority of councils exercised this new discretion sensibly'.[28]

We shall return to consider the options for reform of capping after discussing another key piece of the apparatus of central control: Standard Spending Assessments.

## SSAs

Central to understanding the distribution of grant to local authorities and capping of their own taxation is the system of Standing Spending Assessments (SSAs). In essence these are the Treasury's determination of what each council 'needs to spend' in order to maintain a standard level of service. They are the latest of a series of acronyms for formulae (the imme-

[25] Local Government Finance Act 1988, s. 100(1).

[26] *Hammersmith and Fulham v Secretary of State for the Environment*, [1990] 3 All ER 589; for discussion see C. Himsworth, 'Poll Tax Capping and Judicial Review', [1991] Public Law 76.

[27] Loughlin, op. cit., 313.

[28] *Government Response to the Environment, Transport and Regional Affairs Committee Report 'Local Government Finance'*, (1999), para. 6.6.

diate predecessor was GRE) whose fundamental purpose is to reconcile geographical, demographic, and social disparities between councils so that central government grants can 'equalize' differences in the local tax base, when compared to local needs. The SSA is subject to parliamentary approval, and the courts have cited this as an 'almost insuperable' obstacle to legal challenge.[29] SSAs are divided into seven sub-blocks: education, personal social services, police, fire and civil defence, highway maintenance, 'other services', and capital financing. These sub-divisions have in turn proved controversial, since, although they play no part in determining the legality of an authority's expenditure on any particular item, there has nevertheless been a tendency in some government departments to view them as benchmarks for that particular service, so diminishing the ability of councils to prioritize their own expenditure.

Most criticism of SSAs has arisen from the perceived change in their use, involving a shift from assessment of need as a norm to their becoming treated as a maximum, with the implication that authorities which spend more are, by definition, 'over-spending'. Such reasoning fundamentally undermines the legitimacy of local democratic decision-making. Studies by several external sources, notably the Environment Select Committee, the House of Lords Select Committee, and the Audit Commission, concluded that SSAs were being abused in this fashion.[30] The intention is that SSAs should equalize needs so that local authorities in differing circumstances spending at the standard rate would set the same council tax for a band D house. However, this standardization does not successfully translate into a similar comparability for authorities spending above or below the standard levels; here, the high 'gearing' of the tax produces wide discrepancies between authorities. In addition, there has been a tendency, arising from the use of SSAs to establish maximum budgets subject to capping, for SSAs and capping to converge, with the result that a number of authorities are capped at the level of their SSAs. For these councils, local discretion over expenditure means only the ability to set a budget below the capping level or to distribute expenditure in a different manner from that envisaged by the SSA blocks between services.

[29] *R v Secretary of State for the Environment ex parte Avon CC*, unreported decision of the Divisional Court of 31 July 1990.

[30] *First Report from the House of Commons Environment Committee, Session 1993–1994, Standard Spending Assessments* (HC 90); *Report of the Select Committee on Relations between Central and Local Government, 'Rebuilding Trust'*, (1995–6) HL Paper 97; Audit Commission, *Passing the Bucks: The Impact of Standard Spending Assessments on Economy Efficiency and Effectiveness* (London, 1993). See also Loughlin, op. cit., 313–18. A challenge to the government's use of SSAs in capping on grounds of unreasonableness failed in *Hammersmith and Fulham LBC v SSE*, [1990] 3 All ER 589 (HL), 637 per Lord Bridge (and see ibid. 618–19 (CA) Lord Donaldson MR) on the grounds that this was a policy decision entrusted by Parliament to the minister under the statutory scheme.

The central interest of SSAs for this study is their effect on local accountability, a subject explored critically by the Audit Commission and by the House of Lords Select Committee. The Audit Commission identified five distinct stresses arising from the use of the SSA system: the increased proportion of local expenditure funded from central grant leading to a high rate of 'gearing' and loss of local accountability; the effect of capping; the increasing tendency towards earmarking (or 'hypothecation') of particular blocks of expenditure with a corresponding loss of local discretion; the growing use of SSAs by central government as a measure of performance in local authorities; and the consequences of the local government reorganization of 1992–6 (especially the break-up of large shire counties).[31] The Commission's conclusions concerning the effect of combining SSAs with capping on accountability were particular damning. Stressing that their interest was in the effect on economy, effectiveness, and efficiency, the conclusions are nevertheless a devastating, penetrating critique which is worth quoting extensively:

> Central government often seems content to let councils accept a cosmetic accountability to the services, for it obviates government responsibility, even if in practice ministerial decisions on resources are pre-eminent in shaping the character of the service which the public experiences. Councils appear to accept this partly because the law positions them to do so, but also because they are reluctant to admit their loss of discretion over policy and resources. The consequence is a system in which councils assume a degree of accountability out of proportion to their ability to control services. Central government chastises local government when local activity deviates from the models' predictions; local government plays the same game and negotiates with central government over the models' characteristics. Central government avoids responsibility for its own effects on local services by pleading the models; local government likewise blames SSAs for the local changes in services. The public is presented with the conclusion that neither tier is accountable but that the models are the all-powerful cause of changes in services. SSAs should not be a substitute for political accountability but rather should be an aid to it.[32]

Despite these criticisms, the Audit Commission felt unable to offer a clear solution. Instead, it suggested three lines of reform, each of which would clarify accountability in differing ways. The first was to increase central control. This might be achieved partly through removing whole services such as education from the calculation of local government finance.[33] Other centralizing stratagems (each, admittedly, controversial) would be to reserve part of the central grant for overtly discretionary distribution by ministers outside the formula basis used in SSAs or the use of contracts

[31] Audit Commission, op. cit., 11–15. [32] Ibid., para. 61.

[33] Education is often seen as a candidate for such treatment because of the degree of national control over the delivery of education and over specific reform proposals (closure or amalgamation of schools) at central level.

between government departments and local authorities for individual services. The second alternative was to restore local control over accountability for expenditure. Here proposals centred on modification of the system of grant distribution[34] or removing or modifying capping (discussed below).

A third alternative was some form of independent mechanism for allocating grants and setting expenditure levels. The Audit Commission discussed the possibility of an independent grants commission which would allocate grants within an overall total determined by central government. The advantages of such a body would be that it would clearly operate in a non-partisan manner, and that the criteria for allocating grants could become more transparent than at present. However, the Commission noted that an independent body would probably tend towards more formula-based methods of allocation, with a resulting increase in complexity, and would be unlikely to entirely depoliticize the exercise or defuse arguments about fairness, which are inherent in the process of resource allocation. In similar fashion, the House of Lords Select Committee envisaged Parliament, through an oversight committee on central–local relations, playing an independent part in determining whether a local authority budget was 'clearly unreasonable'.[35]

## Reform Proposals

Proposals for reform have centred on the restoration of local autonomy through increasing councils' discretion over local finance. This section will discuss in turn proposals for the abolition of capping and then for shifting the balance of local revenue from the centre back to individual councils.

The Commission for Local Democracy argued:

> The capping of budgets, revenue and expenditure is wholly incompatible with democratic accountability. It is as offensive to local government as capping by Brussels would be to national government. While government argues for capping on macro-economic grounds, it uses it to produce a maximum of local conformity and uniformity in standards. This is equally offensive to local diversity as it is to local autonomy.[36]

The House of Lords Select Committee on Central–Local Relations recommended that the use of capping as a standard procedure be discontinued,

[34] The Commission considered a two-tier method of distribution in which central government decided upon distribution to regional 'clusters' of councils who then negotiated further distribution at a second stage might restore accountability; but this involves an over-optimistic view of how such councils would cooperate in the process.

[35] *Rebuilding Trust*, paras. 2.70, 5.34. The Conservative government, however, was unprepared to establish a wide-ranging committee of this kind: *Government Response*, paras. 25–9.

[36] *Taking Charge: The Rebirth of Local Democracy* (London, 1985), 42.

but that a reserve power should be retained to cap where a council set a 'clearly unreasonable budget'; it suggested that this decision should be for a new parliamentary committee, rather than for the Secretary of State alone, with criteria for reasonableness clearly stated in a formal concordat between central and local government.[37] These proposals were summarily rejected by the Conservative government, which claimed that capping was still necessary.[38]

In opposition the Labour Party produced a policy document in 1995 containing passages endorsing the macro-economic arguments which led to capping in the first place, although it did suggest that use of these powers should be exceptional rather than routine.[39] Labour proposed that the power to cap would be subject to investigation by the Audit Commission and to scrutiny by the House of Commons Select Committee on the Environment. There was also a commitment to more openness about the determination of the criteria.[40] Other Labour proposals included a promise to return the business rate to local control, but with provisions for greater consultation with local businesses.[41]

In government, Labour committed itself to the end of 'crude and universal capping', while nevertheless asserting that the proportion of local government finance derived from central grants gives it a justifiable interest in the efficiency, effectiveness, and economy of local authorities, which justifies the retention of reserve powers. A consultative paper on financial accountability expressed the hope that the powers would be used 'rarely if at all', where 'budgeting decisions are excessive or where authorities fall short of the standards of efficiency and economy that people rightly expect from their public services'.[42] Paradoxically, however, it then argued that the existing legal powers were too inflexible for this type of sporadic intervention since they involved stipulating in advance what level of expenditure the government regarded as excessive for all local authorities and applying the capping principles used for a single council to all authorities within that class, whereas what was envisaged was ex post facto intervention in a possibly wider range of situations.

Among the proposals for 'flexibility' were that the minister should be able to consider performance and budget proposals over a number of financial years, a power to limit 'excessive' increases even where these were below the SSA, a power to order reduction of budget below the previous year's (the legislation was concerned only with the level of increase), to exempt certain categories of council (including those with strong performance in delivery of 'best value'), and to simplify the consultation and

[37] *Rebuilding Trust*, para. 5.34.
[38] *Government Response*, Cm. 3464 (1996), paras. 59, 60.
[39] *Renewing Democracy, Rebuilding Communities* (1995).
[40] *Rebuilding Democracy*, 18–21. [41] Ibid. 19. [42] Op. cit. (n. 1 above), para. 6.6.

designation processes and trigger a local referendum.[43] In part these reflected the emphasis elsewhere in the consultative paper that central government powers should be used to protect the interests of local service users and not merely taxpayers.[44] However, they also suggested a dangerous erosion of the procedural safeguards put into place because of the exceptional nature of capping. These 'flexible' powers raise the risk of political abuse in central–local conflict. No mention was made of the role of the Audit Commission or the Environment Select Committee. Sir Humphrey Appleby would surely marvel at the ease with which Labour's opposition to capping turned into a plea for substantially increased powers of intervention, backed by the promise that they would be used with more discrimination. Powers in substantially the form described have now become law.[45] The government defended the legislation in the face of criticism of the retention of capping powers by the Environment Select Committee, stating that it did not believe that 'it would yet be defensible to rely exclusively on voters' ability to exert influence on council taxes via the ballot box because it is not yet clear that voters fully understand where responsibility lies for increases in council taxes and because of low turnout in local elections'.[46]

A recurrent plea from bodies recommending reform is to decrease local government dependence on central grant. The report of the House of Lords Select Committee recommended increasing the proportion of local authority expenditure funded from the Council Tax, and restoring local government control over the National Non-Domestic Rate. It estimated that together these moves could achieve their desired objective of giving councils control over some 50–55 per cent of their revenue, thus restoring local discretion. In its response to the Select Committee report the Conservative government roundly rejected these arguments, because of the Treasury's need to retain control over total council expenditure on macro-economic grounds (reasons which the Select Committee had already considered and found unconvincing).[47]

A recent report by the Environment Select Committee advocated the return of the National Non-Domestic Rate to the control of local authorities

[43] Ibid. 6.11.

[44] This suggests a blurring of central control with the role of value for money audit (pp. 115 ff. below) carried out by the auditor.

[45] LGA 1999, ss. 30 and 31 and sched. 1. These contain no provisions, however, for triggering a local referendum on council tax. Increased accountability is, however, provided for Wales since the National Assembly, rather than the Secretary of State, exercises the powers: ibid. s. 31(13).

[46] *Government Response* (n. 28 above), para. 6.7.

[47] See *Government Response to the Report of House of Lords Select Committee on Relations Between Central and Local Government 'Rebuilding Trust'*, Cm. 3464 (Nov. 1996), paras. 62–5; House of Lords Report, paras. 5.13ff.

as the 'least worst' short-term option for shifting the balance.[48] In the longer term the Select Committee proposed a package of reforms including adjustment of the Council Tax bands, greater use of charging by local authorities for their services (subject to means testing) so that councils could choose to exceed national minimum service standards, a greater emphasis on fairness (rather than the government's preferred emphasis on transparency) in the continuing review of the SSA, and the abolition of central capping powers.

Some commentators have claimed that local control of taxation and local democracy are not necessarily connected. In evidence to the Select Committee Professor Gerry Stoker argued that there was no correlation between voter turnout at local elections and the source of funding for local government and that, rather, innovation and accountability were strengthened by control over *marginal* shifts in spending. The Select Committee specifically rejected this.[49] In its response the government reiterated that there was no clear evidence that previous large shifts in the balance of funding affected accountability, but conceded that it was likely that a major shift to funding through local taxation would make people more aware of the activities of councils. It rejected, however, adding to the burdens on council taxpayers or full localization of the business rate.[50]

A consultation paper issued in 1998 by the new Labour administration contained other proposals.[51] Although macro-economic arguments for central control featured prominently and the need to retain a reserve power of capping was rehearsed, the consultation paper acknowledged the need for change in order to clarify accountability.[52] It proposed a series of steps to achieve this: duties to consult specific service-users about levels of service provision; amendment of the electoral cycle so that all councils face the electorate annually at budget time; the possible use of local referendums to consult the electorate specifically on budget and local tax options;[53] transfer of responsibility for Council Tax benefit from central to

[48] Government grant would have continued in order to equalize differences in non-domestic rateable values between areas. The government would also have ensured that the burden of increases in local tax was fairly divided between the non-domestic rate and the council tax: n. 4 above, para. 96.

[49] Ibid., paras 12–20.

[50] DETR, *The Government's Response to the Environment, Transport and Regional Affairs Committee's Report Local Government Finance* (London, 1999), paras. 12 and 13.

[51] N. 1 above.

[52] e.g. para. 4.2, admitting that gearing 'can mean that to local people it looks as if changes in their council tax bills are driven more by the decisions of central government than by the decisions of their own councils'; para. 5.1: 'Local accountability is not strong enough and central government exercises its powers in a way that is disproportionate to achieving its objectives.'

[53] Paras. 5.9 ff. These might be consultative only, and so not legally binding, or a statutory requirement, triggered by a proposal to exceed a budgetary ceiling or on demand by a prescribed number of voters, so acting as a legal prerequisite for certain budgetary decisions

local government above a guideline figure for council tax.[54] On SSAs, a three-year programme of research by central and local government was proposed to find a 'simpler, more stable, more robust and fairer' alternative for distribution of revenue support grant.[55]

From the examination of accountability in the context of local revenue, we turn now to the mechanisms for ensuring accountability for local expenditure.

## THE PURPOSE OF AUDIT[56]

Although the purpose of local government audit was at one time merely to check that money was spent lawfully, in accordance with the ultra vires rule and without fraud (sometimes described as 'regulatory audit'), it now goes far beyond this. The notion of legality of expenditure is not confined to straightforward unlawfulness, but also includes unreasonable discretionary expenditure. It is in this area that conflict is most likely to occur between the exercise of a council's political judgment and the auditor's duties with regard to financial accountability. Audit now also monitors value for money and effectiveness in the delivery of services.[57] The current provisions in the Audit Commission Act 1998 reflect this emphasis: the auditor is required to satisfy himself that proper arrangements have been

(although the consultative paper adds the important qualification 'subject to reserve powers', i.e. capping: ibid., para. 5.16).

[54] It is suggested that this would sharpen accountability by removing an artificial cushion which currently applies where local authorities decide to increase council tax: ibid., paras. 5.26ff.

[55] N. 1 above, para. 4.5. The Environment Select Committee, while welcoming the review of SSAs, argued that any reform should emphasize fairness rather than simplicity: n. 4 above, para. 103.

Principles laid down in a Council of Europe Recommendation on the Equalization of Resources Between Local Authorities (R (91)4 adopted by the Committee of Ministers on 22 Mar. 1991) are relevant to this exercise. These included a recommendation that any system of equalization 'does not undermine local autonomy by inducing local authorities in practice to provide the same level of service or apply the same rate of tax' (para. 2). The need for stability and transparency was also endorsed.

[56] On historical development see: District Auditors' Society, *Watchdogs' Tales: The District Audit Service—The First 138 years* (London, 1986); R. Jones, *The History of the Financial Control Function of Local Government in the United Kingdom* (New York, 1992); on the history of audit as an instrument of central control, see W. Holdsworth, *History of English Law*, xiv (Aberdeen, 1964), 253ff. The standard work on the auditor's powers is: R. Jones, *Local Government Audit Law* (2nd edn., London, 1985). For a scholarly account of recent changes and episodes see: M. Loughlin, *Administrative Accountability in Local Government* (York, 1992), 112–14, 183ff.

[57] The emphasis on value for money derives from the Layfield Committee: see *Committee of Inquiry into Local Government Finance*, Cmnd. 6453 (1976), ch. 6. It argued that the auditor's role in scrutinizing value for money should be enhanced and protected by greater independence.

made for securing economy, efficiency, and effectiveness in the use of the authority's resources.[58] Value for money audit resonated strongly with the reforms of the public sector in the 1980s, which treated local government as a constitutionally subservient part of the state and as a testing-ground for initiatives later to be imported into the Civil Service. Unlike much of the 'New Public Management', however, the audit reforms do not directly reflect market rationality. Audit for effectiveness and value for money have no direct analogue in the auditing of commercial organizations. In the private sector auditing is concerned with the legality of a business's arrangements, to protect the interests of shareholders, creditors, and the exchequer. Although it is tempting for this purpose to equate those commercial interests with those of electors and local taxpayers in the dealings of a local authority, it is misleading to do so. Whereas the financial interests of shareholders and creditors are straightforward (maximizing profits[59] and conserving assets, respectively), the democratic interests which local government audit reinforces are more complex. 'Effectiveness' and 'value for money' are attempts to summarize these interests in a way which allows for measurement of performance without supplanting democratic choice about what service is to be delivered, and how, where, and to whom. In a 1994 newspaper interview the chief executive of the District Audit service stressed that such audit was seen as a means of strengthening the citizen's interest.[60]

A further reason for audit is to ensure that funds voted by Parliament through the central grant mechanism have been properly used. As increases occurred in the statutory functions conferred on local authorities, especially in the realm of education and housing, dependent on central government subsidy, this went hand in hand with increasing powers of independent audit over such expenditure. Audit therefore protects the interests not merely of local electors and taxpayers but also of those who contribute to central government finance.[61]

In this sense the system of audit serves more than one accountability function. A recent study argues that public-sector audit involves overlapping issues about democratic accountability (of government to citizens),

[58] S. 5(1)(e).

[59] Ignoring the problems which 'ethical' investment and business methods cause for auditors.

[60] 'All Change on the District Line', *Independent*, 19 Oct. 1994.

[61] The Court of Appeal has considered to whom an auditor owes duties in carrying out his/her functions. It found that while Parliament did not intend auditors to be liable in negligence to local authority officers (because the auditor should be free to criticize in a report anyone responsible for conduct resulting in loss), nevertheless there was an arguable case that both a council itself and its officers could bring an action for breach of statutory duty. The court found this potential liability in the web of duties contained in what is now Pt. II of the 1998 Act. See *West Wiltshire District Council v Garland and others*, [1995] 2 WLR 439, reversing in part the decision of the High Court at [1993] 3 WLR 626.

managerial accountability (to hierarchical superiors), and legal accountability (the monitoring and enforcement of rules).[62]

The history of the audit power has shown that in the most controversial cases where auditors have used sanctions against elected councillors, they have done so where the council was in conflict with central government policy. The auditor has often been a key player in conflict between individual local authorities and central government. Two of the clearest cases concern opposition by local authorities to legislation passed in the housing field. In *Taylor v Munrow*[63] the local authority was opposed to the policy under the Requisitioned Houses and Housing (Amendment) Act 1955 of increasing the amount paid by tenants occupying requisition housing. Accordingly, it resolved not to review these rents, with the effect that the difference between the amount payable under the Rent Act and that actually charged by the landlord fell upon the council itself. The council was influenced in this policy by its opposition to any form of means testing of the tenants of the requisitioned property. The auditor's surcharge of the councillors involved was upheld by the High Court, which found that they had acted unlawfully in failing to preserve a balance between the duty owed to ratepayers in general and to particular tenants.

A similar instance occurred in the case of the Clay Cross councillors in 1972: the council resolved not to comply with the Housing Finance Act 1972, which required them to increase council house rents. The auditor found that loss had arisen from the negligence and misconduct of the defaulting councillors, whom he surcharged accordingly. The High Court upheld this order, finding that a failure to bring in revenue could amount to loss under the Act.[64] A further illustration of the auditor standing in the middle in central–local conflict arose over the tactics adopted by the

[62] K. Hollingsworth, F. White, and I. Harden, 'Audit, Accountability and Independence: The Role of the Audit Commission', (1998) 18 LS 78, 96ff. The authors find that some local government audit practices, for example non-publication of local value for money reports and of management letters, suggest an undervaluing of democratic accountability and confusion over the intended audience for the 'outputs' of audit.

[63] [1960] 1 All ER 455.

[64] *Asher v Lacey*, [1973] WLR 1412. The legislation empowered the Secretary of State to declare the council to be in default and, if it persisted in its refusal, to appoint a Housing Commissioner who would implement the Act. However, the minister chose instead initially to direct the district auditor to carry out an extraordinary audit of the council's Housing Revenue Account. In a subsequent case the minister's decision to direct the extraordinary audit was itself attacked by the councillors, who had by this time been disqualified (a Housing Commissioner had also been appointed): the Court of Appeal found that the minister was entitled to act in this way. The councillors' argument that in not appointing the Housing Commissioner from the start the minister must have intended to act punitively towards them and that this was unlawful was dismissed; both Lord Denning MR and Lawton LJ found that the minister could properly direct the extraordinary audit with a view to having the councillors disqualified due to their disobedience of the law: *Asher v Secretary of State for the Environment*, [1974] 2 WLR 466, 474, & 479. Subsequently, the incoming Labour government passed legislation indemnifying the councillors concerned.

councillors in Lambeth and Liverpool in refusing to set a rate for the financial year 1985/6. The courts upheld the district auditor's finding that the councillors were responsible for the loss due to wilful misconduct arising from their improper and extraneous motive, in delaying making the rate so as to put pressure on the Secretary of State in their dispute over central funding.[65] The decision set clear limits on the extent and type of political tactic to which local authorities can resort, because of their duty owed to ratepayers. Such decisions do not mean that audit is simply a mechanism of central government control of local authorities.[66] Rather, it should be recognized that in central–local relations the interests are unevenly balanced: central government can usually enforce its will through proscriptive legislation, and the effect will be to cast non-compliant authorities as law-breakers.

Nevertheless, auditors should not generally be seen as acting under governmental dictation. The legal and administrative arrangements go to considerable lengths to emphasize the independence of the auditor, not only from ministerial instruction but also from the authority which is being audited. Auditors act under statutory powers conferred directly upon them and not as the delegates of ministers. However, they are required to perform their duties in accordance with a Code of Practice prepared by the Audit Commission under the 1998 legislation. The Audit Commission itself was established as a mechanism to ensure independence; early proposals for the control of audit had suggested that central supervision should be used under the overall control of the Comptroller and Auditor-General. The government rejected this proposal as undermining the constitutional independence of local authorities.[67] Ministers enjoy substantial powers, however, in relation to the Commission, notably an unfettered power to appoint members[68] and to require the Commission to direct an extraordinary audit and to follow (published) ministerial directions; the latter two powers have never been exercised and the relevant government departments have, together with the Commission, produced a joint statement of responsibility and accountability, stressing the

[65] See *Smith v Skinner, Gladden v McMahon*, (1986) 26 RVR 45, DC; *Lloyd v McMahon*, [1987] AC 625, HL.

[66] Loughlin, op. cit., however, argues that inconsistencies in the actions of the Audit Commission towards councils which delayed passing a rate resolution as a tactic in their dispute with central government over finance in 1984/5 may have been motivated by a desire 'to make an example of the most confrontational councils of the councils by ensuring the surcharge and disqualification of councillors'.

[67] Rejected by the Government, paras. 93ff.; see *Government Observations on the Eleventh Report from the Expenditure Committee, Session 1976–1977, HC535* Cmnd. 7117 (1978).

[68] Hollingsworth et al., op. cit., 82–5 and 98–100.

Commission's independence and accountability to Parliament (it does not, however, fall within the remit of the Public Accounts Committee).[69]

### POWERS OF THE AUDITOR

Traditionally, the auditor has acted retrospectively and on an annual basis: audit is the process of finally reconciling the annual accounts of the authority to judge their accuracy and legality. Hence, the statutory powers of the auditor refer specifically to the legality of the inclusion of items of account. The auditor has power to apply to the High Court where it appears that an item of account is 'contrary to law'.[70] If the High Court finds that an item is contrary to law it may order those responsible to repay any loss arising (this power is exercisable both against officers and against members of the authority).[71] The controversial power of surcharge arises in the more limited cases where loss is in the auditor's opinion due to the 'wilful misconduct' of officers or councillors.[72] This finding is subject to appeal in the High Court. Where, in the case of members, the amount charged is more than £2,000, councillors will be automatically disqualified from holding public office for five years. Disqualification was introduced in 1927 when it was felt that the power of surcharge by itself was insufficient deterrent to unlawful action by councillors by modest means.[73]

In addition to the formal procedures which can be initiated by the auditor, members of the public have long enjoyed statutory rights in relation to local government accounts. All 'persons interested' can inspect the accounts and related documents and make copies.[74] In addition, a local government elector for the area concerned has the right to question the auditor about the accounts and to object to the inclusion of individual items.[75] This procedure is used surprisingly often in practice,[76] and the

[69] Ibid.

[70] Audit Commission Act 1998, s. 17(1). Previously the auditor had direct power to disallow items of this kind and to surcharge those responsible (with the onus on them to appeal to the courts); under the post-1972 law this power is only available where loss arises from 'wilful misconduct', considered below .

[71] An order may not be made if the court is satisfied that the person responsible for organizing the expenditure acted 'reasonably or in the belief that the expenditure was authorised by law'. In any event the court is to consider all the circumstances including the means and ability of the person concerned to repay: s. 17(3) Audit Commission Act 1998.

[72] S. 18(1) (b) Audit Commission Act 1998.

[73] Audit (Local Authorities) Act 1927, following the *Poplar* case (pp. 132–3 below); see also Jones, para 1.32.

[74] Audit Commission Act 1998, s. 15.

[75] Ibid., s. 16.

[76] For a research study on use of the procedures see B. Walker, S. Delay, and A. Marsh, *Challenges to Local Authority Accounts* (London, 1997). Questions were raised on the accounts of 34% of local authorities (excluding parish councils), and 34 councils attracted 88 objections to their accounts in 1994/5. In each case members of the public with no direct involvement

courts have held that it is preferable to resolve disputed factual issues before the auditor than by way of judicial review.[77] The fact, though, that it is uncommon for objections to succeed led the Audit Commission to suggest that the procedure should be reviewed[78]—a proposal taken up by the Nolan Committee.[79] The Committee found that the process for objection to the accounts, although valuable, was being misused by people who disagreed generally with a decision of the council, or to pursue personal grievance or obtain confidential commercial information. It is therefore proposed that the auditor should be able to decline to investigate for good reasons and that the procedure itself should be simplified.[80] The government appeared to accept the need for reform and promised to legislate, but no proposals emerged in the Local Government Act 2000 (which otherwise implements Nolan's recommendations), and the government appears to have concluded that auditors have sufficient discretion within the existing regime.[81]

Other additions to the auditor's powers came about following the Widdicombe report. These include the ability to bring proceedings for judicial review against a council and to restrain prospective unlawful action and expenditure by the service of a 'prohibition notice'.[82] The latter is soon to be reformed, at the suggestion of the Nolan Committee, which felt it to be an anomalous power, confusing accountability by carrying the auditor into realms more properly the responsibility of the council. The prohibition notice was also used inconsistently by different auditors. It is to be replaced by an 'advisory notice' which the auditor will be able to issue if it appears that the council is proposing to act unlawfully. Under this process it is not mandatory to follow the notice: the council can override the auditor's opinion, but before it does it must consider the advisory notice.[83] This restores responsibility where it should lie—with the authority itself.

The auditor also enjoys less formal reporting powers: an annual management letter is issued at the conclusion of the audit and this may include

in the issue were the largest source of objections, followed by people directly affected and then local or national politicians; this appears to undermine the claim (see below) of abuse of the process.

[77] See *R v Westminster City Council ex parte Hilditch* [1990] CD 434, where the court accordingly refused to exercise its discretion to allow judicial review proceeding out of time (preceding the District Auditor's report into the designated sales of the Westminster CC—see below).

[78] See M. Loughlin, *Administrative Accountability in Local Government* (London, 1992), 58–9.

[79] *Third Report from the Committee on Standards in Public Life, Standards of Conduct in Local Government in England, Scotland and Wales*, Cm. 3702 (1997).

[80] Ibid., paras. 4.6–8.

[81] DETR, Consultative Paper: *Modernising Local Government: The Ethical Framework* (1998), ch. 4; *Modern Local Government: In Touch with the People*, Cm. 4014, (1998) paras. 6.36 and 6.37.

[82] Audit Commission Act 1998, s. 20.

[83] Green Paper, paras. 4.4 and 4.5. Local Government Act 2000, s. 91.

recommendations which must be published;[84] local value-for-money studies may be undertaken. A statutory power also exists to issue a public-interest report, which must be debated by the council in public.[85]

The account here deals first with the history and use of the surcharge, before discussing wider reforms following the creation of the Audit Commission.

## THE SURCHARGE[86]

The history of the surcharge confirms its roots as an instrument of central government control. It is a relic of a system of accounting devised in the feudal period which has been adapted and grafted into the very different statutory context of modern local government, chiefly through reforms in the nineteenth century. Even today it is unique among methods of governmental accountability. The politicians and officials who administer central government are not subject to an equivalent personal sanction and it is noticeable that the exponential growth in appointed bodies (quangos) in the last twenty years has taken place without any similar mechanism of accountability being put into place. This lacuna seems anomalous, because in many cases quangos perform functions formerly undertaken by elected councils and, in effect, they are subject to fewer controls, because the electorate has no opportunity to pronounce upon their financial stewardship. Far from being extended, however, at the time of writing the days of the surcharge are numbered,[87] following its controversial use in the Westminster case (discussed below).

The feudal system of charge/discharge accounting was the precursor of the surcharge: under this system a local official (steward) would be 'charged' with monies paid from the central exchequer. This liability only ceased when he could demonstrate in the annual reckoning that the sum granted had been properly spent, and therefore that the charge was 'discharged'. If a payment could not be justified, under this system, the effect was to disallow it and consequently to impose a personal liability on the official.[88] This

[84] S. 11(3), 1998 Act.

[85] Ibid., ss. 8, 11, and 12.

[86] Although the usage of referring to 'surcharge' is followed in this account, that term is no longer used in the statutes, which give instead the power to apply to the court for declaration in the case of legality and 'certification of sums due' from persons responsible for loss of rising from their misconduct. (Prior to 1972 there had also been a concept of liability to surcharge for negligence—this finds no equivalent in the post-1972 law.)

[87] Local Government Act 2000, s. 90 confirms its abolition. The Maud Committee recommended as long ago as 1967 that the power of surcharge should be abolished because it inhibited members and officers, without contributing positively to the management of council.

[88] See R. Jones, *The History of the Financial Control Function of the Local Government Accounting in the United Kingdom* (New York, 1992), chs. 2 and 3, esp. 43, 66, and 72.

quasi-judicial power of disallowing items of expenditure, and hence surcharging, without recourse to the courts was inherited by an official, who was recognizably the predecessor of the district auditor in the Poor Law Amendment Act 1844. It is this power, now limited to cases where the auditor is of the opinion that 'wilful misconduct' has led to loss, which now survives.[89]

In the mid-nineteenth century the monies distributed under the Poor Law were by far the largest sums administered locally. The same system of district audit came to be applied to local boards of health, under the Public Health Act 1848, to school boards under the Elementary Education Act 1870, and to sanitary authorities under the Public Health Act 1872. The new county councils created under the Local Government Act 1888 were subject to the jurisdiction of the district auditor. Curiously, however, the county boroughs retained the option (only abolished in 1972) of 'elective audit'—a system under which the audit was carried out by two elected representatives (not actually councillors but 'representing the ratepayers'), together with a councillor nominated by the mayor.[90] It was open to local authorities to adopt an alternative system of audit under legislation where they were subject to elective audit, and by the 1930s many had done so, promoting powers of 'professional audit', i.e. audit by a qualified accountant of their choice.[91] A key distinction between the systems of elective audit, professional audit, and the district audit system was that the powers of disallowance and surcharge were only exercisable by the district auditor. Thus, for county boroughs, this was effectively a voluntary jurisdiction. This bewildering and inconsistent set of choices was rationalized in 1972 with the abolition of elective audit. Choice of auditor between a private-sector accountant and the district auditor was extended to all local authorities.[92] The Layfield Committee had argued in 1976 that it was wrong in principle for a public body to be in the position of choosing its own auditors.[93] The choice was effectively removed by the Local Government Finance Act 1982, which introduced the present arrangements and standardized the powers of auditors, however appointed, so

[89] Under section 18 of the Audit Commission Act 1998 (see below).

[90] The auditors so-called did not have to be professionally qualified, leading one judge to describe the system in 1906 as an illusory mechanism of control: *Attorney-General v DeWinton*, [1906] 2 Ch. 106, 119 per Farwell J.

[91] Legislation in 1933 gave these boroughs the option of adopting either audit by the district auditor or professional audit, without the need for local legislation.

[92] The new Conservative government of 1979 had a strong preference as part of its privatization policy for the use of private-sector accountants, and attempted to overcome the reluctance of local authorities to choose such people as auditors by itself appointing a number of them as additional district auditors: the decision to do so was unsuccessfully challenged in the courts in *Derby City Council v Secretary of State*, (1982) 81 LGR 134.

[93] Layfield suggested standardization under a national system governing both local and central government, but this was rejected by the government.

removing a long-standing anomaly.[94] Under the current legislation (section 3 of the 1998 Act) auditors are appointed for each local authority by the Audit Commission after consulting the council (usually for a term of five years) and may be either members of District Audit[95] or private accountants.

The technical language in which the auditor's and High Court's powers are clothed masks some important issues about the nature of local democracy. One example is the expression 'item of account contrary to law', used in relation to the auditor's power to apply to the High Court for a declaration under the 1998 Act. Controversy revolves around whether legality is to be considered solely from the viewpoint of the propriety of an entry in the accounts, or whether broader questions concerning the council's decision to undertake the activity resulting in the expenditure, which may render it ultra vires, are relevant.[96] Where auditors find expenditure to be unlawful on the basis of an unreasonably exercised discretion or because expenditure on a lawful item was excessive, a judgmental exercise is involved. This goes beyond the simple issue of whether a line should appear in the accounts, and there can be a danger that auditors and courts supplant the judgment of elected politicians with their own, under the guise of illegality. The issue also raises the question of whose interests are to be protected through the audit process. Jones argues that the narrow (Beecham) approach to unlawful items of account is consistent with protection of the interests of the ratepayers, since it excludes expenditure where it is to their detriment, but not otherwise.[97] On the other hand, the broader approach imports into the audit process the rights of other individuals, such as members of the public or users of council services.[98] The position is further complicated by cases in which the courts have explicitly stated that the council must balance a variety of interests in the exercise of a discretionary power in order to act lawfully. A clear example is the creation within audit cases of the fiduciary duty to ratepayers.[99] However, there is some justification for such an approach where the statutory

[94] R. Jones, *Local Government Audit Law* (2nd edn., London, 1985), 3–19.

[95] Members of District Audit are formally Audit Commission employees but District Audit has agency status in relation to the Commission: Hollingsworth et al., op. cit., 85–6.

[96] The former view was preferred by Boreham J in *Beecham v Metropolitan District Auditor*, (1976) 75 LGR 79, 83 where he found that the council's expenditure on demolishing houses owned by them was lawfully entered as an item of account, although the failure to obtain planning permission may have been unlawful (see Jones, *Local Government Audit Law*, 137–9, drawing a distinction between acts which are ultra vires and items of account which are unlawful).

[97] The difference in emphasis between protecting the ratepayers from loss and simple ultra vires can be further illustrated where contracts are found to be beyond the powers of the council. The 'interest swap' cases involved transactions carrying millions of pounds of liability which were found to be ultra vires. The loss fell upon the banks who had transacted with the councils concerned and not upon the authorities (see pp. 283–4 below).

[98] See Jones, *Local Government Audit Law*, 139.

[99] See pp. 131–9 below.

language itself refers to the concept of reasonableness, as was the case in legislation governing the level of council house rents. In these instances the courts have held the council was obliged to balance the financial interest of their tenants and of ratepayers in a reasonable way.[100]

**Westminster**[101]

A report by the District Auditor into Westminster City Council found three councillors (including the former leader, Dame Shirley Porter) and three officers (including the former chief executive) to have committed wilful misconduct. The auditor surcharged all six for approximately £31 million for unlawful expenditure and losses arising from the council's 'designated homes' policy during the 1980s. The policy had involved discounted sales of council houses and flats as they became vacant on designated housing estates. Although the policy had been in place since 1972, it was greatly extended by the council's Housing Committee in 1987, with the objective of raising sales from some 10–20 each year to a target of 500. The policy had been adopted across the borough, but the District Auditor concluded, in a 2,000-page report after an investigation which lasted six years, that its adoption following the 1986 local election was a direct attempt by the ruling Conservative group on the council to influence the social composition of marginal wards to their own electoral advantage. Documents found by the auditor demonstrated that the objective was to replace council tenants with home-owners who, it was felt, would be more inclined to vote Conservative. In the process, the council's duty to house homeless people in its area was given a low priority and strenuous efforts were made to 'export' such people to other areas. The losses of £31 million resulted partly from lost capital receipts on the discounted house sales, but also from lost revenue in rents, and officers' salaries in implementing the policy. The District Auditor concluded that the principal participants were aware that it was unlawful to pursue council policies for electoral advantage, but nevertheless continued, at the very least, recklessly.

The auditor concluded that although the council did have power to sell the designated houses, the Housing Committee's decision of July 1987 to do so was unlawful for a number of reasons. The council had misdirected itself by proceeding as though it was entitled to *balance* the need to pro-

[100] See *Evans v Collins*, [1965] 1 QB 580, where a court refused to interfere with the District Auditor's decision that the London County Council had failed to balance in this way by charging unduly low council rents. See likewise *Giddens v Harlow District Auditor*, (1972) 70 LGR 485.

[101] *Independent*, 10 May 1996. A further councillor, named in the provisional report, Barry Legg MP, was not surcharged because although the auditor found in the final report that he had been aware of the policy and knew that it was improper, the auditor accepted that he had not realized that he had a duty to report it.

mote home-ownership and the needs of homeless families, whereas it owed a duty[102] to the latter group to ensure that suitable permanent accommodation became available for their occupation. A number of aspects of its functions under homelessness legislation which the council should have considered were neglected. In the same way, the committee's decision was inconsistent with the statutory duty in choosing its tenants to give reasonable preference to those occupying various types of unsatisfactory housing.[103]

In two respects the auditor found the council's policy to be irrational, arising from the additional cost of housing homeless families in bed-and-breakfast accommodation rather than in council dwellings. The spiralling expense (an additional £1.5 million each year above the preceding year) of the policy was such that the council in adopting it was in breach of its fiduciary duty owed to local taxpayers. Moreover, it was inevitable that the expense involved would force the council to stop short of its stated objective of selling all the flats in designated blocks as they became vacant, notwithstanding assurances given to earlier purchasers. Furthermore, the operation of the policy in increasing the number of properties designated for sale, and in selecting blocks in key politically marginal wards, was 'influenced by an irrelevant consideration, namely the electoral advantage of the majority party',[104] which the auditor found to be the 'driving force' behind the policy. In his words: 'My view is that the Council was engaged in gerrymandering, which I have found is a disgraceful and improper purpose, and not a purpose for which a local authority may act.' The council had made unlawful capital payments to induce secure council tenants to move out and purchase non-council property, and, once again, an improper purpose had intruded. Unlawful expenditure had also been involved in the preparation by officers of papers for discussing means of promoting the electoral advantage of the Conservative majority.

In many ways the Westminster case illustrates the dangers of close political control by a small party caucus of councillors in collusion with senior officials. The documents appear to indicate that a predetermined strategy of gerrymandering (a description used not only in the auditor's report but also in some of the council's own notes of meetings), decided upon by core members of the Conservative group of councillors, was the hidden agenda behind the policies steered to approval through the formal decision-making machinery of the council and its committees. The District Auditor was only able to uncover this shadowy policy because of oblique

[102] Housing Act 1985, Pt. III. [103] Ibid. s. 22.

[104] The Widdicombe Committee had earlier argued that that there should be a declaratory statutory provision embodying the common law prohibition on use of discretion for the main purpose of securing electoral advantage for a particular candidate or political party: *The Conduct of Local Authority Business*, Cmnd. 9797 (1986), paras. 8.91–100.

references in notes of meetings, which led him to request information about party group meetings. In doing so he faced not only considerable attempts at legal obstruction, but also more straightforward techniques of evasion, such as incomplete answers in interviews and in response to requests for documents, and attempts to smear him personally and to have him removed from the investigation. He was forced in return to adopt police-style tactics of unannounced visits to seize documents before they were shredded, and to use private investigators to locate witnesses reluctant to give evidence.[105]

When the auditor's decisions were challenged in the High Court the appeals of Dame Shirley Porter and the Deputy Leader of the council, Mr Weeks, were dismissed, but those of one member who had become chairman of the Housing Committee and of two officers, director of housing and the managing director of the council, were allowed.[106] The court found that Porter and Weeks had lied, both to the auditor and in evidence on appeal that the gerrymandering policy had been abandoned following legal advice. Rather, they were content that the policy be 'dressed up' to disguise it: 'Their purpose throughout was to achieve electoral advantage. Knowledge of the unlawfulness and such deliberate dressing-up both inevitably point to . . . wilful misconduct on behalf of each of them.'[107] In the case of those whose appeals were allowed, however, the auditor was found to have given too little weight to the impact upon them of legal advice that the designated sales policy would be lawful if implemented over the borough as a whole; the successful applicants may have been guilty of misconduct but it was not wilful within section 20.[108]

The appellants attempted unsuccessfully to attack the fairness of the auditor's procedure, either for bias or a breach of Article 6 of the European Convention on Human Rights. The court described the auditor's roles 'of investigator, prosecutor and judge which might be thought an almost impossible burden'.[109] Both the duration of the investigation[110] and the auditor's conduct of a press conference at which he presented his provisional findings were criticized. Although the latter was ill-judged, the court found that the auditor had nevertheless approached the subsequent decisions with an open mind.[111] The court found that for the purposes of

[105] See further Ch. 8.

[106] *Porter and Others v Magill*, (1998) 96 *LGR* 157, QBD, Rose LJ giving the joint judgment.

[107] Ibid. 185.

[108] Ibid. 174, 194, 199, 202. Nevertheless, the court found that attempts in their evidence to distance themselves from improper motive, of which they were aware, were 'less than frank'.

[109] Ibid. 168, noting the recommendation of the *Third Report of the Committee on Standards in Public Life*, Cm. 3702–1 (1997) that the surcharge be abolished.

[110] Ibid. 161 and 169 (but the delay did not cause prejudice (ibid. 169) and was not itself a violation of Article 6 (ibid. 173).

[111] Ibid. 173–4.

Article 6 the audit was not criminal in nature; the purpose was compensation for the council's loss, not punishment of a wrongdoer.[112] Moreover, fairness under Article 6 was to be equated with the common law standard. Any tension in the various roles of the auditor arose from the statutory scheme and could only be resolved if the auditor only ever used the powers under section 19 of the LGFA (as investigator and prosecutor) but not under section 20 (as judge). This would be contrary to the statutory scheme.[113] In any event, appeal to the High Court could correct any defects in procedure and for the purpose of Article 6.[114]

The appeals by Porter and Weeks were, however, allowed in the Court of Appeal by a majority.[115] Kennedy LJ regarded as 'unreal' the suggestion that a councillor who gives any thought to the electoral advantage before deciding on a course of action is guilty of misconduct. Some means of securing re-election were, of course, unlawful, but it was primarily for Parliament to lay down the parameters of acceptable conduct. Schiemann LJ took a similar view. Robert Walker LJ, dissenting, held that there was no basis for the Court of Appeal to depart from the lower court's assessment, based on hearing the evidence, that leading members of the majority party had formulated their housing policy with the overriding (rather than incidental) objective of securing electoral advantage, which they had tried to cover by 'widespread and persistent pretence' and, subsequently, by lying to the Divisional Court.

Whereas the Divisional Court found that Porter and Weeks knew that the policy was unlawful and had attempted throughout to conceal their true purpose of gaining an electoral advantage under a veneer of legitimate housing reasons, Kennedy LJ and Schiemann LJ took a different view. They concluded that since the Divisional Court had regarded the legal advice obtained by the council as providing a proper foundation for the views of some of the officers that the proposed action was lawful, it was inconsistent to take a different view of the liability of Porter and Weeks. Robert Walker LJ argued, dissenting, that there was little evidence that the legal advice had a significant effect on the thinking of Porter and Weeks. The treatment of the officers by the lower court was perhaps motivated by an element of mercy (which he described as 'absolution by association') in view of the possibility of intimidation by the councillors.

**Reform**

The scale of the penalties and the length of the investigations in Westminster inevitably prompted calls for reform. The Nolan Committee

[112] Ibid. 171. [113] Ibid. 172. [114] Ibid. 169 and 171–2.

[115] *Porter v Magill*, [2000] 2 WLR 1420; for discussion of other aspects, see pp. 266–7 below.

recommended abolition of the surcharge and its replacement by a new criminal offence of misuse of public office.[116] The proposal should be understood in the light of other proposals to strengthen the ethical framework of local government by giving councils themselves greater disciplinary powers over councillors through local Standards Boards.[117] The case against the surcharge was that as a restitutionary order it is unrelated to any personal gain derived by the individual councillor or officer by the misconduct, to the gravity of the misconduct, or to the ability to pay. The consultative paper laid emphasis on punishing wrongdoing involving personal gain, and on the uniqueness of the system to local government, which made it appear anomalous. Arguably, this reasoning is confused. It may be unfashionable to defend the surcharge, but one of its strengths is that, ultimately, individuals are personally responsible (whether or not they gain financially) for decisions in which they participate. If anomalous, it is perhaps symptomatic of weaknesses in the mechanisms for holding politicians and officials to account elsewhere in the public sector rather than indicating that those in local government are excessive; ministerial responsibility, for example, has been steadily emptied of rigour in the postwar period. It is at least arguable that some ill-judged central government decisions about public expenditure might have benefited from the discipline of a well-founded risk of personal liability.[118] The government's intention is that orders of compensation might still be made against individuals where they have gained personally. These could be made either through auditor-initiated procedures or by a court order of compensation on conviction of the new offence of misuse of public office.

Imposing criminal liability certainly fulfils the objective of strengthening personal responsibility, but it is likely to bring further difficulties. The area of unlawful expenditure currently covered by the surcharge ranges from straightforward fraud, through political abuse of power and funds, to ill-advised decisions, and those technically ultra vires. The element of wilfulness in the misconduct under section 18 of the Audit Commission Act 1998 relates to knowledge or recklessness that the expenditure was

[116] *Porter v Magill*, *The Times*, Law Report, 6 May 1999, paras. 4.9–16; *Third Report of the Committee on Standards in Public Life: Standards of Conduct in Local Government in England, Scotland, and Wales*, July 1997, Cm. 3702; the Law Commission has also produced proposals for the reform of corruption: *Corruption*, Consultation Paper No. 145 (1997) (on which see G. R. Sullivan, 'Reformulating the Corruption Laws: The Law Commission Proposals', (1997) Crim. LR 731) and *Legislating the Criminal Code: Corruption*, Report No. 248 (1998); see further Home Office, *Raising Standards and Upholding Integrity: The Prevention of Corruption* (London, 2000).

[117] See p. 173 below.

[118] e.g. the use of billions of pounds of currency reserves in the abortive defence of the pound's membership of the European Exchange Rate Mechanism on 'Black Wednesday' in Sept. 1992.

unlawful.[119] If this were adopted as the basis of the new offence there might be great difficulties in securing convictions. A new form of white-collar crime would have been created, with all the attendant difficulties of investigation and problems in persuading juries to regard the perpetrators as real criminals. Furthermore, if the legality of the expenditure were one element of the actus reus of the offence local government would still be treated anomalously, because legal regulation of local authority powers is closer than elsewhere in the public sector. The Westminster case illustrates this: if central government were to set out to target their policies on a particular social group in the hope of attracting their votes at the next general election, it might colloquially be described as a form of bribery, but it would be unthinkable that the ministers responsible would be indicted for misuse of public office. The boundaries between acceptable political behaviour and corruption are very difficult to draw, and depend to a large extent on a value judgment about the legitimacy of political activity in local government. Imposing criminal liability will, on balance, probably result in more questionable behaviour being condoned because of reluctance to invoke the sanction or to instigate a prosecution because of the probability of an acquittal. In practice, however, most cases of alleged abuse in local government will probably fall to be handled under the new ethical framework put in place by the Local Government Act 2000 and not through the criminal process. Certainly this was what the government envisaged in its White Paper.[120]

## THE AUDIT COMMISSION

The creation of the Audit Commission[121] in the Local Government Finance Act 1982 marked a decisive watershed in the nature and function of public sector auditing. It had been preceded by several years of debate, prompted by the Layfield Committee report of 1976, over the best way to achieve greater independence in local government audit. In the event the model followed what was in some respects similar to that already prevailing in Scotland—the creation of a new and independent body, with responsibility for appointing auditors to local authorities. This removed the historic choice which many local authorities had over this decision, but

[119] Cf. the Court of Appeal in Westminster (above).

[120] White Paper, paras. 6.19–30. The proposals were described as the government 'response' to Nolan; the proposals for reform of the corruption laws or the new misuse of public office offence were described as still under consideration: ibid., para. 6.30. See further, p. 173 below.

[121] On the Commission's role see: M. Radford, 'Auditing for Change: Local Government and the Audit Commission', (1991) 54 MLR 912; M. Loughlin, n. 56 above; Hollingsworth et al., op. cit.

on the other hand fell short of direct central government interference in the process. Nevertheless, the Commission, whose membership is appointed by the Secretary of State from the ranks of industry, management, and local government,[122] has enthusiastically promoted the values of the new public-sector management, along the lines of the reforms introduced by the Conservative Governments since 1979. The most significant feature of the Commission's work has been its proactive role in disseminating management practice, ostensibly under the authority of its statutory functions of promoting value for money. The Commission has spread this message through two means: first, its role in overseeing and coordinating auditors under a Code of Practice, and secondly, through statutory studies into specific local services and into the effect of central government policies on local government. Members of the Commission are not themselves involved in carrying out audits. A review of the Commission's work published at the end of 1998 confirmed the need for an independent body fulfilling these functions and reflected a high degree of satisfaction with the Commission's performance.[123] The confidence which government has in the Commission can be gauged from the considerable expansion of its role under the 'best value' regime.[124]

Auditors are legally obliged to follow the Commission's Code of Audit Practice.[125] Although the code states that the auditor's function is not to question policy, it nevertheless encourages auditors to measure the effects of policies and to examine the arrangements by which decisions are reached. This suggests a fine line between monitoring whether an authority has successfully and efficiently achieved its policy objectives and questioning those objectives.

The Commission is given the statutory brief of undertaking 'comparative and other studies' to enable it to make recommendations for improving economy, efficiency, and effectiveness in the provision of local authority services.[126] A number of comparative studies has been undertaken, focusing on specific statutory functions and comparing a variety of types of authority. The results of these studies are published, with the intention of disseminating to other authorities good practice, so promoting value for money. These studies also provide a focus for the training of auditors and the findings inform subsequent audits of local authorities: in this way the Commission's role in undertaking special studies links with its central place in the practice of audit. In the years since 1983 virtually every field of local authority activity has been subject to a special study.

[122] Hollingsworth et al., ibid. 82–3, note the unfettered nature of ministerial patronage in contrast to the appointment of the Comptroller and Auditor-General.

[123] DETR, *Quinquennial Financial Management and Policy Review of the Audit Commission: Prior Options Assessment* (London, 1998).

[124] See pp. 339–43 below.

[125] Audit Commission Act 1998, ss. 4 and 5(2).

[126] Ibid., s. 33.

This comparative role of the Commission was substantially strengthened in 1992 by the legislation providing for the collection and publication of performance indicators.[127] The Commission also undertakes another form of special study, namely of the effect of central government policy on economy, efficiency, and effectiveness of local government.[128] In the past these studies have been sharply critical of the use of central government financial policy tools such as the Standard Spending Assessment.[129]

The Audit Commission claims to have facilitated savings of many hundreds of millions of pounds in local government through its value for money studies. What is more doubtful is whether the managerial style advocated by the Commission can be said to be technocratic and value-free. Indeed, the Commission has embraced new management concepts such as the enabling authority and the contractor/client split. Emphasis on customer satisfaction has also been a key Commission *nostrum*. However, the democratic role of the elected councillor emerges less clearly from the Commission's reports.

Recent legislation broadens the Commission's power to make comparative reviews to embrace the 'functions' of councils, rather than merely the provision of local authority services.[130] This technical and semantic point underlines the expansive and changing nature of audit under the 'best value' regime. We shall return to this point when considering 'best value' in the concluding chapter.[131]

## THE FIDUCIARY PRINCIPLE

Perhaps the most spectacular judicial creation in local government law is the principle that a local authority is in a sense a trustee of money it receives from local taxpayers. The principle requires a council to balance taxpayers' interests against those of others, such as service recipients, in decisions involving expenditure.[132] Since this principle's innate tendency is against redistributive policies, it has been dubbed 'the Rule against Socialism'.[133]

Ever since the publication of John Locke's *Second Treatise on Government* the notion of trusteeship has been a powerful metaphor in political

[127] See now ss. 44–6 of the 1998 Act, discussed in Ch. 5.

[128] Under s. 34, Audit Commission Act 1998.

[129] See p. 110 above.

[130] S. 19, LGA 1999.

[131] See pp. 139–43 below.

[132] Three other implications of the duty are cited in M. Supperstone and J. Goudie, *Judicial Review* (London, 1992), 267: a principle of statutory interpretation; a duty not to act thriftlessly and (positively) to use resources to the best advantage; a mandatory relevant consideration for *Wednesbury* purposes when an authority reaches decisions on financial questions.

[133] P. Fennell, 'Roberts v Hopwood: the Rule against Socialism', (1986) 13 J. of Law and Society 401. For a detailed account of the history and development of the doctrine see M. Loughlin, *Legality and Locality* (Oxford, 1996), ch. 4.

discourse. In the Lockean version the trust is a mechanism for ensuring the continued consent of the beneficiaries (political subjects) to government; in the last analysis the sovereign may be removed for breach of trust, if necessary by revolution. While the notion of the public trust, derived perhaps from such auspicious constitutional revolutionary credentials, has been influential in the United States, Australia, and Canada, Finn has noted its absence in UK law.[134] Local government is an exception, but there the judicial version is altogether more prosaic and less democratic. Its modern purpose is to protect the property rights of the electorally powerless from majoritarianism. It is a reworking of the revolutionary adage 'No taxation without representation'.

In the nineteenth century local government reforms (such as the Municipal Corporations Act 1835) had ensured that the franchise and liability to rates were coterminous. It is no accident that the notorious use of the fiduciary principle by the House of Lords in 1925 in the case of the Poplar councillors[135] came hard on the heels of electoral reforms introducing near-universal suffrage and removing property disqualifications from local electors. These created the serious prospect for the first time that these electors might choose a council which would act against the financial interests of local businesses, which paid rates but had no vote.[136] The Lords' decision was to uphold surcharges imposed by the District Auditor on the grounds that the councillors had acted unlawfully in refusing to deflate the wages of their manual workers in line with the recessionary market rates of pay. The payments were found to be arbitrary and not related to work done (hence the characterization of them as 'gifts' in the judgments), but also objectionable as excessive expenditure on a lawful purpose. It was this second limb which constituted the breach of the fiduciary duty.[137] The doctrine was fashioned by the courts from earlier authority holding that corporations which attempted to resist local gov-

[134] P. Finn, 'Integrity in Government', (1991) 3 Public Law Review 243.

[135] *Roberts v Hopwood*, [1925] AC 578. For an account of 'Poplarism' see J. Griffith, *Judicial Politics since 1920* (Oxford, 1993), 1–11 and the sources cited there.

[136] Cf. Professor Martin Loughlin's placing of the emergence of the doctrine: 'A transition was taking place from a nineteenth-century local government system based on the idea that the right to vote was conditional on making a direct contribution to the funds which a local authority administered, to a twentieth-century system in which ratepayer democracy was being replaced by representative democracy' (*Legality and Locality*, 226).

[137] The Divisional Court had endorsed the principle: *The King v Roberts ex parte Scurr and others*, [1924] 1 KB 514, 522 per Sankey J. The Court of Appeal had found for the councillors, *R v Roberts ex parte Scurr*, [1924] 2 KB 695 (Bankes LJ dissenting). Atkin LJ pointed out the shortcomings of the trust analogy: 'That trust and confidence are bestowed on them [the councillors] is true; that they may not use the powers so entrusted to them for their own advantage is also true. But for the proposition that there are any equitable rights in the ratepayers as such, which can be enforced by the interference of a court of equity with the honest administration of affairs, I know of no such authority. The duty of the council is to the local community as a whole' (ibid. 725–6).

ernment reform (the Municipal Corporations Act 1835) by alienating their assets were bound to return them since they acted as trustees *for the new corporations*.[138] In *Roberts v Hopwood* the ratepayers rather than the corporation become the beneficiaries of this trust.

Having earlier described the approach of the council in setting wages as 'guided . . . by some eccentric principles of socialist philanthropy, or by a feminist ambition to secure equality of the sexes in the matter of wages in the world of labour',[139] Lord Atkinson continued:

> the indulgence of philanthropic enthusiasm at the expense of persons other than the philanthropists is an entirely different thing from the indulgence of it at the expense of the philanthropists themselves. The former wears quite a different aspect from the latter and may bear a different legal as well as moral character. A body charged with the administration for definite purposes of funds contributed in whole or in part by persons other than the members of that body, owes, in my view, a duty to those latter persons to conduct that administration in a fairly businesslike manner with reasonable care, skill and caution, and with a due and alert regard to the interest of those contributors who are not members of the body. Towards these latter persons the body stands somewhat in the position of trustees or managers of the property of others.[140]

Stated in this form, the principle emphasizes that councillors are responsible to ratepayers as a whole for the use of the taxes paid. It presupposes that ratepayers' interests will always lie in the most economical use of their money according to the supposedly neutral principles of the market (used, in this instance, to determine the wage rate for manual workers). It ignores collateral accountability through the ballot box and the fact that many ratepayers were also electors who had chosen to vote for the council's policies. In Fennell's words, the decision amounted to an elevation of duties to ratepayers as 'shareholders' in local government over any duties owed to the electorate—a triumph of legal over political accountability.[141]

However, in later formulations the rule has been restated as the duty of councillors to balance the interests of different groups.[142] In *Prescott v Birmingham Corporation* it was so used to declare unlawful (in the absence of explicit statutory authority) the policy of a local authority in providing free travel on council buses to pensioners.[143] Invoking the analogy of the trust, Jenkins LJ characterized the scheme as 'the making of a gift or

[138] Fennell, op. cit., 408–9, Loughlin, *Legality and Locality*, 222–3. *AG v Aspinall*, (1837) My. & Cr. 613; *AG v Wilson* (1840) Cr. & Ph. 1 (40 ER 389). Significantly, in the later case of *AG v Brecon*, (1878) 10 Ch. 204, Jessel MR had stated that this did not create a remedy for ratepayers (at 228).

[139] [1925] AC 594. [140] Ibid. 595–6. [141] Fennell, op. cit., 405.

[142] Loughlin, *Legality and Locality*, 213ff., helpfully distinguishes between two objectives underlying the fiduciary duty: efficient financial management and non-discrimination.

[143] [1955] Ch. 210. Following the judgment such schemes were expressly authorized by the Public Service Vehicles (Travel Concessions) Act 1955.

present in money's worth to a particular section of the community at the expense of the general ratepayers'.[144] A very similar situation arose in relation to a different piece of local legislation authorizing public transport in the famous 'Fares Fair' case.[145] The House of Lords struck down a scheme for subsidized transport in London on a variety of grounds, including a failure to balance between the financial interests of transport users and ratepayers. Lord Scarman described the fiduciary principle as 'no more than common justice—especially where, as is the case under the existing law, those who provide the greater part of the rates have no vote in local government elections'.[146]

The alleged unfairness which the rule seeks to correct is that while many local taxpayers are also local electors, some, within a system of local tax rebates, enjoy representation without taxation and so do not bear the financial consequences of electorally approved policies, and a minority of taxpayers (businesses) have no vote. The shareholders' analogy is apposite: the protection of the courts is equivalent to that developed in company law to protect minority shareholders from the decisions of an oppressive majority. The need for protection is clearly contingent on the particular electoral and taxation arrangements at a given time. When the franchise and local tax liability coincide, the doctrine is to some extent unnecessary. In this sense the ill-fated community charge would have been a safeguard in its own right against the 'abuse' of an electorate voting in a financially irresponsible way for policies funded by others, since the voters themselves would also bear the financial consequences. However, even in such a regime the danger remains of a majority voting for policies which financially penalize a minority whose party was unsuccessful at the ballot box. Another response is to limit local authority discretion to tax local businesses—the introduction of the National Non-Domestic Rate does this. However, even where businesses contribute at a standard rate to local taxation, this still leaves some scope for application of the fiduciary concept as regards discretionary use of the money raised by local taxes, notwithstanding that the intended use would not result in a tax increase. Whether the courts would explicitly take account of these arguments to restrict the future application of the doctrine is doubtful,[147] but the result is that con-

144 [1955] Ch. 236.

145 *Bromley LBC v Greater London Council*, [1983] AC 768. The case involved detailed analysis of the powers of the GLC and the London Transport Executive under the Transport (London) Act 1969. Only the parts of the judgments touching on the fiduciary duty are discussed here. On the treatment of the question of the electoral mandate, see Ch. 3.

146 [1983] AC 838. Lord Brandon of Oakbrook took the view that for the council to persist with its scheme after it was aware that it would lead to substantial loss of government block grant (thereby nearly doubling the cost to ratepayers) meant that it had failed to balance these interests: ibid. 853. See also Lord Wilberforce, ibid. 820.

147 Cf. Loughlin, *Legality and Locality*, 259, who argues that the repeal of the Community Charge and its replacement by Council Tax renders unnecessary any further judicial

flict between the interests of taxpayers and electors as distinct groups is less likely to occur, and if it does, is more likely to be met with a judicial affirmation of the discretionary nature of the council's powers.

There is another sense in which the *Fares Fair* case represents a significant widening of the concept. In *Roberts v Hopwood* the fiduciary trust was introduced in the context of the auditors' powers to surcharge councillors for unlawful expenditure. It therefore appeared within the framework of a statutory regime whose objects could be said to ensure financial accountability for the protection of interests of local taxpayers (and electors). The lack of an explicit legislative basis for the fiduciary duty was therefore excusable, as it could be said to be implied from the logic of the auditor's powers. However, later judgments have dislodged it from this context and treated it as a freestanding concept: *Prescott* was an action brought by an aggrieved ratepayer, *Bromley* was brought by one of the borough councils which would be subject to the proposed supplementary rate precept. If the fiduciary principle is seen as supplementing audit law by giving added protection for taxpayers, the first extension at any rate seems unobjectionable. However, if the principle is seen as merely consistent with audit principles it amounts to an extension, in view of the weaker procedural position of local taxpayers. For, while any interested person (including a local taxpayer) is entitled to all documents to be audited, only electors for the area are entitled to object to items of account before the auditor.[148] The omission of specific rights for ratepayers could be interpreted either as a legislative indication that their rights were to be subordinate to those of electors or as a gap in the scheme, appropriately filled by the courts with the fiduciary duty. If the first approach is taken, the effect of the fiduciary concept is directly to undermine a legislative preference for electors.

The fiduciary duty has been criticized as having the potential to supplant decisions about economic priorities arrived at by elected councillors with those made by unelected auditors or judges.[149] Some judges have been alert to this danger from the beginning. In the Court of Appeal in *Roberts v Hopwood*, both Atkin LJ and Scrutton LJ emphasized the council's character as a representative body entrusted by Parliament with discretionary powers as a reason for non-interference.[150] Likewise, when a local

invocation of the fiduciary duty as a residual device to achieve fairness between taxpayers and electors.

148 See pp. 119–20 above.

149 For a classic and powerful argument in this vein see H. J. Laski, 'Judicial Review of Social Policy in England', (1926) 39 Harv. LR 832. In one of the finest of many rhetorical passages Laski cited the instance from 1912 of an auditor who 'ruled that such items as cod-liver oil, malt extract, and fruit did not come within the definition of food [under the Education (Provision of Meals) Act]; and it was only after a struggle that he was persuaded to abandon his objection to fruit in return for the surrender by the County Council of its enthuasiasm for malt extract and cod-liver oil' (ibid. 840).

150 [1924] 2 KB, 725, 718–19.

authority's wage settlement was attacked in 1983 as unduly generous, the Divisional Court held that the settlement was within the discretion of the council. Lord Justice Ormerod stated that the fiduciary duty did not 'open[s] up a route by which the courts can investigate and, if thought appropriate, interfere with any exercise of their discretionary powers by local authorities'.[151] Loughlin argues that this decision and others after the *Bromley* case show the courts cutting down the apparent width of the doctrine to reconcile it with more modest claims for judicial review, along conventional *Wednesbury* lines.[152]

To invoke the private law concept of the trust as a mechanism of accountability in public law seems particularly inapposite for several reasons. First, it involves a deliberate judicial lifting of the corporate veil of local authorities. One might have expected that the position of local taxpayers would be dealt with solely on the basis of the relevant legislation authorizing the collection of local taxes, and quite separate from the powers of the local authority to incur expenditure, which would depend on interpretation solely of the legislation purportedly authorizing the expenditure. Although in each case naturally the general principles of administrative law would inform the analysis, taxation and expenditure would be treated as discrete activities undertaken by an artificial entity, the corporation, with questions about how the money was obtained irrelevant to the question of the council's authority to spend. Instead, the fiduciary duty suggests that the corporation is under continuing duties once taxation is in its hands (and legally its property) to those from whom taxation was raised, or that prospective spending decisions can be attacked because of their taxation implications.

Secondly, the trust is too narrow a conceptual device to take proper account of the complex and diverse range of legal and political interests which impinge on the decisions made by local councillors. In private law the only purpose of the trustees' legal powers is to manage the trust property for the beneficiaries. Local authorities are subject to a web of other interests, many of them contained in legislation, beyond those of local taxpayers.[153] Moreover, having gained as it were a toehold through the device of the ratepayers' trust, some of the judicial dicta about the careful

[151] *Pickwell v London Borough of Camden*, [1983] QB 962, 1003.

[152] Loughlin, *Legality and Locality*, 250–7, discussing *Pickwell v Camden LBC*, [1981] 1 QB 962 (see esp. Forbes J at 988 and Ormerod LJ at 1004); *British Leyland Cars v Birmingham DC and Coventry CC*, [1982] RVR 92; *R v GLC ex p. RB of Kensington and Chelsea*, *The Times*, 7 Apr. 1982; *R v Greenwich LBC ex p. Cedar Transportation Group Ltd*, [1983] RA 173. He concludes (at 256) that the *Bromley* decision was an 'aberration'.

[153] Cf. the comment of Forbes J that the concept had to be viewed in the light of other duties imposed by Parliament on the council 'to provide a wide range of services for its inhabitants, be they ratepayers, electors or neither': *Pickwell v London Borough of Camden*, [1983] QB 962, 987.

use of resources are none too discriminating about the source of the finance concerned (bearing in mind that three-quarters of local expenditure comes out of central grant). Invocation of the fiduciary duty can too easily be a form of political table-thumping or queue-jumping on behalf of one sectional local interest. This danger is exacerbated by the tendency of the courts in each of the *Poplar, Birmingham,* and *GLC* cases to use the fiduciary duty as an overriding canon of construction by which to cut down apparently wide discretionary statutory powers enjoyed by the councils.[154]

Thirdly, the fiduciary concept gives priority to a too narrow set of questions about the use of statutory powers, whose focus is solely on what is economical. Broader social objectives, such as those disparaged by Lord Atkinson in *Roberts v Hopwood*, are taken to be either impermissible or subordinate. Even the characterization of local taxpayers' interests is a narrow one; they are presumed to be solely concerned with minimizing their tax liability, rather than, for example, achieving value for money or quality of service. However, there is no clear and overarching legislative or constitutional ground for a judicial ranking of values (for such it is) of this kind.

The most fundamental objection to the fiduciary principle, however, is its manifest distrust of representative democracy.[155] To assert that liability to tax alone is sufficient claim to establish an overriding protection from the implications of democratic decisions suggests deep judicial distrust of socially redistributive government. The true measure can be best appreciated by a hypothetical comparison: would the courts entertain a challenge to a discretionary spending decision by central government acting under statutory powers because it was to be funded by an increase in income tax or corporation tax? Matters of this kind are regarded as self-evidently within the proper realm of political judgment at central government level, and there is no suggestion of a fiduciary duty owed to taxpayers. There is no constitutional reason for a difference of approach to discretionary decisions taken by local authorities similarly taken within powers granted by Parliament. Yet it is apparent that the judiciary is very much more loath to interfere with central government financial decisions than with their local equivalents.[156]

[154] e.g. the comments of Lord Scarman, [1983] AC 838–9, suggesting that express statutory wording would be necessary before the principle would be displaced.

[155] Cf. Laski, op. cit., esp. 845), who argues that it flies in the face of 'the Anglo-American idea' of 'experimental local government', i.e. a version of Millian local democracy (pp. 7–10 above).

[156] See e.g. *Nottinghamshire CC v SSE*, [1986] AC 240, 250 per Lord Scarman and *Hammersmith and Fulham LBC v SSE*, [1990] 3 All ER 589, 637 per Lord Bridge; but for a bold counter-example see *R v SS for Foreign and Commonwealth Affairs ex parte World Development Movement*, [1995] 1 All ER 611.

It has been argued, however, that properly understood the doctrine imposes no more than a procedural requirement.[157] Certainly post-*Bromley* decisions show more judicial self-restraint, but the earlier dicta, several from the highest courts, still stand as good law. Nor is there any sign of the fiduciary duty falling into disuse. Although an occasional visitor to the courts, it still exercises real power. In a recent instance the High Court struck down the purported exercise by Rochester City Council of a power under the Highways Act 1980 (section 274) to contribute towards expenses incurred by a highway authority if 'in the opinion of the council such expenditure would be of benefit to its area'. Among the reasons given were that the council could not have reasonably concluded that it would benefit its council taxpayers (note, not 'the inhabitants of its area') to contribute to a scheme already approved and budgeted for by the highway authority.[158] Moreover, auditors, political opponents, and even officers can, and do, appeal to the doctrine in circumstances where many councillors uncertain of the precise boundaries of their discretion feel unwilling to press the issue (especially when under the current law the result could be surcharge and disqualification from office). In this sense the doctrine may act as a form of self-censorship on innovative local political leadership, and the uncertainty about when it may be invoked only adds to the deterrent effect.

The fiduciary duty also looks anomalous in view of the new 'best value' duty and mechanisms, but it would be premature to assume that the courts will take a lead from these to pronounce the death sentence: the doctrine has survived previous amendments to the audit and local taxation regimes. The government's consultation paper on finance claimed that 'best value' reinforced rather than replaced the fiduciary duty, although it also describes it as giving statutory effect to the common law duty.[159]

The doctrine may also represent a real obstacle to the full implementation of the proposals for a new duty of community initiative;[160] a power like that proposed in the White Paper to act in the interests of people visiting and working in an area, as well as those living there, voting and paying council tax, may therefore need explicitly to relax the common law fiduciary duty if it is not to be hamstrung by the deeply ingrained fiscal prudence in the judiciary. This is not to argue for a power for councils to spend uneconomically, but there is a risk of incompatibility between the focus of the fiduciary duty upon *taxpayers'* interests and the broader range of groups in whose interests the power of community initiative is to be exercised.

[157] Loughlin, *Legality and Locality*, 253, and see n. 152 above.
[158] *Rochester City Council v Kent County Council*, *The Times*, 5 Mar. 1998.
[159] Green Paper, paras. 2.2 and 3.5.
[160] See pp. 59–65 above.

Our discussion of the fiduciary duty underlines a persistent theme of this chapter: the tension between considerations of financial accountability and representative democracy. We have seen how, in relation to local taxation, a clear sense of local accountability, let alone responsiveness, has been repeatedly undermined by central intervention and control, especially the effect of the distribution of central grants and of capping. In a different way the same is true of expenditure: the use of the auditor's powers and the operation of the fiduciary duty cut directly across the responsibility of councillors to the electorate. This is a recognition that local democracy involves much more than simply the interests of the electorate, and the effect of decisions on other people, especially taxpayers, must be considered also.

# 5

# *Consumer Accountability*

## INTRODUCTION

This chapter is concerned with one facet of 'direct' democracy,[1] namely, the legal mechanisms open to users of local public services to express their preferences, and to influence and complain about those services. The consumerist movement has many organic connections with the participatory innovations discussed in Chapter 3, especially a dissatisfaction with the responsiveness of representative democracy to the wishes of those for whom public services are provided. Its practical origins were ideologically modest: they lie in experimental attempts by local authorities to be more responsive to the wishes of local people; initiatives of this kind gained momentum in the late 1970s as a development of public participation.[2]

Whatever its roots, public-sector consumerism in Britain is now irrevocably associated with the Citizen's Charter introduced by the Major administration,[3] which was itself a continuation of New Right-inspired public-sector management reforms drawing from the wells of public choice theory.[4] The introduction of consumerist initiatives within the public sector was, of course, ideologically motivated by the strong preference of the Thatcher and Major governments for the private sector. Where simple privatization was seen as unworkable market-type solutions were imported into the public sector instead, sometimes involving ingenious attempts to reproduce competitiveness and market discipline (the creation of an 'internal market' within the National Health Service was a prime example). In part this must be seen also as a reaction to the perceived inadequacies of the traditional methods of accountability—the electorate and the courts.

[1] Rather than 'representative democracy: see pp. 94–8 above. On the distinction in this context see: V. Lowndes, 'Citizenship and Urban Politics', in D. Judge, G. Stoker, and H. Wolman, *Theories of Urban Politics* (London, 1995).

[2] A theoretical basis for responding at a local level to the group interests of local government consumers could be found in the early ideas of 'functional representation' developed in the 1920s and 1930s by the socialist G. D. H. Cole. Cole argued that representative democracy was inadequate to capture the full basis of fraternity, which required other forms of group representation and influence (e.g. workers' guilds) in addition to the franchise: D. Hill, *Democratic Theory and Local Government* (London, 1974), 31–2.

[3] *The Citizen's Charter*, Cm. 1599 (1991).

[4] Discussion of public choice literature is beyond the scope of this chapter; see further: P. MacAuslan, 'Public Law and Public Choice', (1988) 51 MLR 681; N. Lewis, *Choice and the Legal Order: Rising Above Politics* (London, 1996).

For the purpose of the discussion here it makes sense to proceed like an archaeologist: to start near the surface before digging deeper. Before more detailed consideration of mechanisms for expressing consumer choice and voicing complaints, therefore, we will begin with the Citizen's Charter.

## THE CITIZEN'S CHARTER

This programme, announced as government policy in 1991 by the Major administration, brought together into an umbrella policy many of the trends in the reform of the public sector of the preceding years.[5] It has been continued by New Labour with some difference of emphasis (especially as regards consulting service users and, incidentally, strengthening central control) under the title 'Service First' as part of the 'Better Government' initiative.[6] Much of the Charter programme concerns the central state (in both Whitehall departments and the burgeoning agencies), privatized and public-sector utilities, and quangos, although the programme is intended equally to apply to local government. A number of the criticisms that have been made of it[7] (for example, the lack of legal basis and legally enforceable entitlements) are much less applicable to local government than to the other spheres.

The policy focuses on six key principles.[8] First is the setting and publication of standards which users of public service can reasonably expect and the monitoring and publication of performance against these standards. Secondly, clear information is to be provided about public services, how much they cost and who provides them. The third principle focuses on consulting users of public services about their preferences, and embodying these views in choices that are made about standards. The fourth embodies standards of courtesy and helpfulness from those who deal directly with the public and the expectation that such services will be arranged for the convenience of the public, not those who run them. The fifth is concerned with putting things right when service is inadequate, with a guarantee also of a full explanation and a speedy apology. The sixth

[5] *The Citizen's Charter: Raising the Standard*, Cm. 1599 (1991).

[6] Cabinet Office, *Service First: The New Charter Programme* (1998), para. 2.7. For analysis, see: C. Scott, 'Regulation Inside Government: Re-badging the Citizen's Charter', [1999] PL 595.

[7] For reviews, see A. Barron and C. Scott, 'The Citizen's Charter Programme', (1992) 55 MLR 526; G. Drewry, 'Mr. Major's Charter: Empowering the Consumer', [1993] *PL* 248. N. Lewis, 'A New Way of Governing?', (1992) 64 *Pol. Q.* 316; N. Lewis, 'Reviewing Change in Government', [1994] *Public Law* 105; C. Willett (ed.), *Public Sector Reform and the Citizen's Charter* (London, 1996); C. Harlow and R. Rawlings, *Law and Administration* (2nd edn., London, 1997), ch. 5.

[8] Restated in *Service First*.

promises value for money and independent validation that this is being provided. The extent to which these very different themes may conflict was not explored, no doubt because of the need to present the policy as a coherent whole. The six principles restated and repackaged what were for local government long-established models of public consultation, financial accountability, and complaints redress, with a new emphasis on consumer choice and information.

In the sense that no political party is likely to campaign for low-quality, distant, arrogant, secretive, and profligate government services, these principles are surely uncontentious; the only surprise is that no previous government had thought to state them explicitly and insist on making them a priority. They should be almost apolitical. The controversy perhaps lay in their emphasis. Two general points may be made.

The first is what has been referred to as the 'apostrophe question' (the Citizen's Charter, not a charter for citizens): the vision of citizenship, and corresponding responsibility of government, implicit in the programme is focused on accountability to individual service users, to the citizen as customer and consumer. The ideal 'citizen' of the Charter dislikes queues, official delays, and nameless bureaucracy. She writes as 'disgusted of Tunbridge Wells': it seems unlikely that she camped at the gates of Greenham Common, protested at Twyford Down, or withheld her poll tax. Critics have argued that the vision of citizenship is an impoverished, individualistic one that neglects community interests and falsely atomizes service users.

At the purely practical level, this vision of consumer accountability may be inappropriate to a number of governmental activities which are not provided (or provided only incidentally) to identifiable individuals. Who, for example, are the recipients of administration of the economy, the conduct of foreign affairs, or the maintenance of defence? Although at the local level most functions do have identifiable service recipients—for example, parents of school-age children, council tenants, applicants for planning permission—some clearly do not. The more strategic functions (planning, highways, local economic development, waste disposal—rather than waste collection) are undertaken in the interests of the locality as a whole. Protection of the environment also obviously transcends such individual interests. Nor does emphasis on consumer rights tackle the question of what level of service should be provided in terms of the resources devoted to it. In the real market the consumer is able to choose between a cut-price, basic version of a product and a more expensive but higher-quality model. The strict central control on local authority finance since the 1980s has denied to consumers of local government service the option of going up-market. Crude measures such as the criteria for allocating central grant to local authorities (through the Standing Spending

Assessment[9]) or the use of Performance Indicators[10] seem to carry the implicit message that political choices about the level of service provision (irrespective of efficiency, consumer responsiveness, and value for money) are not officially encouraged, especially if they involve additional spending.[11]

The Citizen's Charter initiative should be understood as a refocusing of earlier concerns in the New Public Management—namely, the introduction of market mechanisms in the delivery of public services and a system of rewards and incentives for managers of those services. As initially drafted, only a few of the strands of the programme were directly focused on individual citizens and even these placed the citizen in the position of reacting to poor service delivery, rather than participating directly in decisions about the standard or quality of service. The requirements to publish performance targets, information on standards, and details of complaints procedures all fall into this reactive category.

However, the movement towards charters in local government preceded the government's own initiative. It was also considerably more diverse: while some local charters (especially those of Conservative-controlled County councils) focused on the position of a citizen as consumer of local services, others took a broader view of citizenship of the council's own area. Foremost in this latter approach is the council which claims to have invented the phrase 'Citizen's Charter'—York City Council.[12] According to Prior, the York Charter focuses on a broader statement of civic rights which follow from citizenship of the city.[13] This emphasis sits alongside statements relating to customer entitlement, so that Prior has suggested that the York scheme involves 'dual status', where some people have rights as 'citizens' (for example, in relation to broader matters of council policy), others have rights as 'customers' in relation to specific services which they use (for example, a leisure centre); other rights overlap both categories, because some services are provided universally (for example, street cleaning or refuse collection). In contrast, the Hertfordshire County Council Citizen's Charter relates solely to services and the

[9] See p. 108 above. [10] See pp. 144–7 below.

[11] This is something of a generalization, since value for money and performance indicators as concepts would be capable of sophisticated interpretation, which took account of conscious choices about allocation of resources according to political priorities. It remains to be seen whether the 'best value' regime (pp. 146–7 below) succeeds in fostering public or political debate at this level.

[12] See D. Prior, 'Citizens' Charters', 90ff., in J. Stewart and G. Stoker (eds.), *Local Government in the 1990s* (Basingstoke, 1995), ch. 6.

[13] Such as rights to be heard, to know about and to influence decisions, to be treated honestly, fairly, and courteously, to participate, and to be represented. In addition to the legal entitlements, mechanisms are established whereby such rights can be implemented, for example, area committees allowing consultation in decisions affecting a particular neighbourhood.

rights of the citizen as consumer of them: to high-quality services with targets specified, clear information about services, information about complaints, and consultation as a customer. The consultation aspect was stronger, however, than in the central government Citizen's Charter, and it is on this basis that Prior argues that Hertfordshire's charter was concerned with citizenship within a service context.[14] Prior argues that for such charters to justify the tag of citizenship, rather than merely remaining a managerial tool, they need to demonstrate true responsiveness to citizens' concerns about quality of service and quality of government.[15]

Consumer choices depend, if they are to be realistic and informed options, on adequate knowledge about the product and alternatives. Interest in the assessment of performance of local services is therefore an underlying theme on consumerism and, as we have seen, the first charter principle. We turn now to consider the issue of statutory performance indicators.

## PERFORMANCE INDICATORS

The publication of performance indicators has an overtly consumerist objective—in the words of the Audit Commission, it is to enable citizens to 'decide whether your council is giving you a good service'.[16] From 1994 onwards councils were required to publish data about prescribed issues (such as response times) in education, social services, waste disposal, public libraries, fire, police, housing, refuse collection, development control and local plans, council tax, housing benefit, and council tax collection. In 1995 trading standards, highways, street lighting, parks and leisure, street cleaning, environmental health, and public toilets were added to the list.

The Audit Commission has readily acknowledged the limitations of this approach. Nearly half of a pamphlet it issued to the public ('How Is Your Council Performing?') was devoted to explaining why simple comparisons cannot be made between councils because of local circumstances. Variables include: population density (leading to increased time and cost in delivering services in rural areas), social deprivation, seasonal changes in population (for example, due to tourism), variations in the age of population, language and cultural differences (large Welsh-speaking or ethnic communities may require multilingual staffing), geographical differences,

[14] The Hertfordshire document was paralleled by the council's Community Government project which considers the effect of services on a particular neighbourhood in aggregate rather than in relation to atomized functions with the emphasis more on control, and influence for service users rather than on simple notions of quality, efficiency, and effectiveness.

[15] Prior, 'Citizens' Charters'.

[16] Audit Commission pamphlet, 'How Is Your Council Performing?'; and see the more detailed handbook, Audit Commission, *Watching Their Figures* (London, 1994).

differences in the age and type of housing stock, and regional pay and costs differences. Despite these shortcomings, however, the raw figures alone were published and the public were merely advised to 'think about' these factors when attempting to compare the different standards of service of local authorities. No data about the difference were published in parallel to provide the context for such comparisons, despite the fact that the government does have data of this kind available (and uses it in compiling the Standard Spending Assessment of each council).[17] Moreover, as with any system of measurement, considerations of quality are harder to convey than mechanical, external criteria. To take a simple example, comparisons of the time taken on average to answer a phone call or letter give no indication of the politeness or thoroughness with which enquiries are dealt with in different authorities.

In some cases the indicators allow the council to specify a target for performance, and then the published figures measure how successfully this target has been reached. This approach allows more scope for political choice by a council about which areas to prioritize in the light of local factors than does a simple flat-rate measure. It could, for example, open a fruitful debate about why one council has decided that all letters should be acknowledged within five days whereas in another it is fourteen. The degree of success in meeting the target may also give some indicator of the effectiveness of the council's management. Plainly, however, success may also be a measure of how ambitious the target was in the first place; there is plenty of scope for setting targets below current performance rates to produce an impressive-looking statistical outcome.

On the other hand, as already explained, flat-rate targets are too blunt a measure in many cases to take account of local differences. There would be a further fundamental objection, even in a sophisticated system of performance indicators, which weighted results for such factors. The assumption that there exists a nationally optimum level of service provision seriously constrains local political choice. Politics, whether nationally or locally, is the process of allocating benefit and opportunities between the competing claims of different groups: a move to nationally accepted performance criteria would seriously undercut the point of elected local government. Unless local politicians enjoy some freedom and bear some responsibility to the electorate to put forward different priorities from those of the parties they vanquished at the polls, elections are reduced to a contest about which personalities can best be trusted to carry out predetermined objectives. Whether *elected* local government is necessary at all for what is essentially managerial accountability of this kind is questionable.

[17] See Ch. 4.

However, the information available in the performance indicators can be put to another use—as a tool for calling officials and councillors to justify their priorities, compared with those of other councils. In this sense even seriously incomplete information is a tool for accountability, since it establishes an initial case which councillors may be able to answer by providing more complete information about local factors and priorities. In reality it may also lay bare local disparities in service provision, which are not the product of conscious choice at all. The requirement to monitor performance may aid political control by giving politicians clear evidence of how officers are performing. The factors will also be useful in comparing an authority's performance from one year to the next: they could, in time, become an indispensable part of the electoral armoury in defending or attacking political stewardship of the council.

Although performance indicators are flawed, then, they are not beyond redemption. Such thinking underlay the endorsement of modified use of performance indicators by the Labour Party when in opposition. It envisaged retaining the Audit Commission's role in publishing performance indicators for the purpose of comparison, but consulting the local community and service users in the setting of targets as part of a Local Performance Programme.[18] The tension in these proposals between universality and locality was to be resolved by the setting of national *minimum* standards for some services and the publication of national tables of comparators of councils in similar circumstances. The Audit Commission's role would be redirected from concern primarily with value for money towards acting as a standards inspectorate to report to local councils and people on how the council was performing against its published targets.[19]

The Labour government's policy of 'best value' (introduced under the Local Government Act 1999) maintains continuity with a number of the themes of the previous Conservative administration, especially the emphasis on consumer consultation and performance indicators. It also integrates them, however, in a new way through a statutory planning and performance review process, new developments in quality audit and assurance, and powers or intervention in cases of failing performance.[20] In many ways it represents a blending of user accountability and financial accountability. Unlike previous initiatives involving performance indicators, however, it is claimed that the policy is sensitive to local political choices about distribution of resources and service levels, and to differing modes of service provision.

[18] Labour Party, *Renewing Democracy, Rebuilding Communities* (London, 1995), 9–10.

[19] It is envisaged that such reports might form one of the sources on which the Audit Commission might draw in intervening in the case of uneconomic or failing services: ibid. 11.

[20] These aspects are dealt with at pp. 339–43 below.

Measures of performance work in a complex way under the legislation: some ('performance indicators'[21]) are merely intended to allow comparison between councils, while others ('performance standards'[22]) are ministerially prescribed targets which the council must meet in exercising the relevant function. If it fails to do so it will be in default of the 'best value' duty.[23] Formal responsibility for prescribing performance indicators is transferred from the Commission to the minister. However, the Commission will continue to analyse performance data and to make recommendations for amendment or adjusting the indicators and standards. In setting indicators and standards, the Secretary of State must have regard to the general nature of the duty of best value and also to any relevant recommendations of the Audit Commission.

It is time now to move from the general policy underpinnings of consumerism and the provision of information to some of the more specific entitlements which individual service users possess. One, now classical, typology expresses consumer attitudes and choices in terms of exit, voice, and loyalty.[24] The first two, especially, are discussed here: individual and collective exit rights conferred by legislation on users of local authority services and opportunities to be heard and to complain about poor performance. The latter theme gives rise to an extended discussion in the second half of the chapter of the local ombudsman and the remedy for maladministration.

## EXIT AND CHOICE

One feature which clearly distinguishes consumerism from simple participatory democracy is the emphasis on conferring individual or collective legal rights on those affected. While some of these rights are procedural (especially rights to various categories of information), others are more tangible (for example, the limited right to a choice of schools). In particular, the legislative schemes introduced by the Thatcher governments of the 1980s were designed to replicate market choice within the public sector (especially in the fields of housing and education).[25] These took various forms.

[21] LGA 1999, s. 4(1).

[22] Ibid., s. 4(2).

[23] Ibid., s. 4(5). The basic duty is, under s. 3(1), to make 'arrangements to secure continuous improvement in the way in which its functions are exercised, having regard to a combination of economy, efficiency and effectiveness'.

[24] A. Hirschman, *Exit, Voice and Loyalty: Responses to Decline in Firms, Organizations and States* (Cambridge, Mass., 1970).

[25] For a general overview, see: K. Walsh, *Public Services and Market Mechanisms: Competition, Contracting and the New Public Management* (Basingstoke, 1995).

The earliest might be described as the provision of 'exit' choices—the right (or perhaps inducement would be more accurate) to withdraw from a publicly provided service and to receive it instead from a private-sector (or independent) supplier. Such choice was nothing new as such—people had always had the right to choose to buy private education or healthcare, for instance, notwithstanding state provision. However, anyone exercising such a choice would remain liable to pay through taxation for the state service they had chosen not to use. What was new was the concept of state assistance for those who preferred private to state provision. This could take the form of tax assistance in reliefs against income tax (as for private health insurance) or a transferable state set-off against the full private-market cost of the service. A much-discussed, but never fully implemented idea of the early 1980s was the provision of education vouchers, to be 'cashed in' by parents at the school of their choice, in part-payment of private school fees or full payment in the state sector. Two educational schemes, comparable to vouchers, do however deserve brief mention.

The Assisted Places scheme,[26] whereby the government subsidized the cost of a place at an independent school on a scale dependent on parental income, was the nearest equivalent, but involved small numbers of places (about 30,000 per annum). The arrangements between the Department for Education and individual schools offering places are contained in a participation agreement. The relationship between a parent taking advantage of the scheme and a participating school is contractual.[27] The scheme is currently being phased out. One of the first statutes promoted by the Blair government discontinued the scheme for new children from September 1997.[28] One area in which vouchers proper were introduced was in a short-lived scheme for nursery education. The Major government introduced a scheme giving vouchers for 4-year-olds which parents could use with a local authority or towards purchasing private provision.[29] Since at the time councils were not obliged to offer nursery places to all 4-year-olds, the scheme did not operate as a straightforward 'exit' ticket from state provision; nevertheless, where councils did provide a large number of (free) places, the effect was that parents were given a state-subsidized private alternative. The scheme was abolished by the incoming Labour

[26] The scheme was initially introduced under the Education Act 1980, s. 17 (latterly the Education Act 1996, ss. 479–81 and sched. 35) and SI 1995/2016.

[27] It has been argued, however, that the statutory underpinning ought to have the consequence of making an independent school which participates subject to judicial review: E. Batey, 'The Assisted Places Scheme: Crossing the Public/Private Divide', (1996) 8 Education and Law 191.

[28] See Education (Schools) Act 1997 and *Excellence in Schools*, Cm. 3681 (1997).

[29] Nursery Education and Grant Maintained Schools Act 1996, s. 1, and see Dept. of Education, *The Nursery Education Scheme: The Next Steps* (London, 1996).

administration, to be replaced by an extended duty on local education authorities to provide nursery places.[30]

One politically highly popular 'exit ticket' was the introduction in the Housing Act 1980 of a statutory 'right to buy' for council tenants. Although some Conservative local authorities had been voluntarily selling council houses for many years, the Act required all local authorities to do so to tenants of more than three years' standing and at substantial discounts on the market value of the property, according to how long the applicant had been a council tenant. The result was the transformation of many municipal housing estates within a few years, shifting the boundaries of state and private provision and increasing home-ownership at a speed unrivalled by previous initiatives in housing policy.

In addition to these individual 'exit rights', there were also examples of 'collective exit' rights (and, again, inducements) to use intermediate state suppliers. The most obvious examples are once again in the fields of housing and education. In housing, the creation of Housing Action Trusts (or HATs) under the Housing Act 1988[31] allowed council tenants to vote to remove their estates from local authority control—collectively to become their own landlords. This option was little used in practice, but further legislation allowed for Housing Associations to take control of council housing. The right for schools by parental vote to 'opt out' of local authority control and become grant-maintained,[32] introduced under the Education Reform Act 1988, proved more popular, perhaps because of the financial incentives: grant-maintained schools received their funds direct from central government (or via the independent education authorities).[33] The private-sector model most analogous here is perhaps not the customer, but the shareholder: parents and tenants were given choices not merely to take their custom elsewhere but also to replace the management—the equivalent of dismissing the board of directors within a company.

The Conservative government argued for the introduction of grant-maintained status as increasing parental choice of types of state-funded schools, freeing schools from LEA control so that governors would have the opportunity to create institutions with their own ethos, and making schools more directly responsive to parental concerns.[34] The governors assumed responsibility for matters formerly provided by the LEA

[30] School Standards and Framework Act 1998, s. 118.

[31] M. Davey, 'The Housing Act 1988', (1989) 52 MLR 661.

[32] Education Act 1996, Pt. III; and see generally: P. Meredith, 'Judicial Review and Education', in B. Hadfield (ed.), *Judicial Review: A Thematic Approach* (Dublin, 1995); P. Meredith, *Government, Schools and the Law* (London, 1992), ch. 6, esp. 153ff.; N. Harris, *Law and Education: Regulation, Consumerism and the Education System* (London, 1993), 47ff.

[33] Education Act 1993, Pt. 1. The Funding Agency for Schools was dissolved by the Schools Framework and Standards Act 1998, s. 132.

[34] *Grant-Maintained Schools: Consultation Paper* (London, 1987).

including school meals, financial and personnel matters for employees, cleaning and educational advisory services: in effect they received the funding which would have gone to the LEA to cover these matters, with increased discretion over how it is used. It is a matter of political controversy whether through these calculations (and special capital grants) the government in effect offered financial inducements to opt out.[35]

Governing bodies of county and voluntary schools were under a statutory duty to consider annually whether a ballot of parents should be held on the school acquiring grant-maintained status, and to publish their conclusions in the annual report.[36] However, irrespective of the governors' conclusions a ballot could also be initiated by a request signed by 20 per cent of parents of registered pupils.[37] Other provisions concerned what information had to be made available to parents; these included a power for the Secretary of State to declare a ballot void and require a fresh ballot where, among other reasons, it appears to the minister that 'voting. . . . is likely to have been influenced to a significant extent by the dissemination of information appearing to the Secretary of State to be to a material extent false or misleading'.[38] The governors were given specific power to campaign in favour of grant-maintained status.[39] The Conservative government's preference for grant-maintained schools and distrust of local education authorities was apparent in the procedure; it was noticeable, for example, that GM schools were under no comparable duty to consider returning to the LEA fold. The underlying purpose of these provisions was tested in a challenge to the timing of a ballot of parents in which Rose J upheld the governors' decision, although the effect was that parents of children joining the school in the following year would be unable to vote.[40] The council's argument that the timing of the ballot should be judged against what it claimed to be the legislative policy of maximizing the involvement of parents was rejected: the Act did not make this policy dominant.

[35] Meredith, *Government, Schools and the Law*, 151–2.

[36] Education Act 1996, s. 185.

[37] Ibid., s. 187. The exercise of this right and campaigning in relation to a ballot was facilitated by s. 188, which entitled parents to inspect a list of the names and addresses of parents of registered pupils.

[38] Education Act 1996, s. 192(1)(g).

[39] Ibid., s. 189(6), confirming *R v Governors of Small Heath School ex p. Kahn, Independent*, Law Report, 3 Aug. 1989, where Woolf LJ held that governors were able to campaign actively in favour of GM status to counteract inaccuracies and confusion in the debate. The information distributed by two teacher governors was also challenged for an alleged infringement of the legislative duty to take a politically balanced approach to the curriculum (now contained in the Education Act 1996, s. 407). Woolf LJ held that even if applicable, the provision had not been breached.

[40] *R v Governing Body of Irlam and Cadishead Community High School ex p. Salford CC*, [1994] ELR 81.

As with parental choice of school (below), these provisions considerably undermined the LEA role in managing educational resources as a matter of political responsibility. Inevitably, when LEAs were considering mergers or closures of schools to meet falling numbers of pupils, they often had to contend also with the complication of a proposal from the affected school(s) to opt out. The link between the two procedures appeared clearly in provisions that required LEAs to consult with governors of schools which might be eligible for grant-maintained status before formulating proposals for change.[41] The Secretary of State was required to consider any proposals that came for grant-maintained status together with proposals from the LEA. However, the legislation was less even-handed over consultation, since LEA proposals are subject to a public inquiry but GM status was a matter solely for parental ballot and, thereafter, the Secretary of State.[42] A number of ballots took on the character of a battle between groups of parents and governors and the LEA. [43] In some cases the hostility continued after 'opting out', for example, by denial to opted-out schools of council resources that they had formerly enjoyed and which other LEA schools continued to use.

**Schools Admissions**

Turning from these collective rights to individual consumer entitlements, in education[44] these have predominantly taken the form of creating consumer choice between schools within the state sector. Thus, in the Education Act 1980 parents were given the 'right' to express a preference for a child to attend the school of their choice[45] rather than simply to follow the allocation by the LEA. This can be seen as mirroring within the state sector the choice of a parent buying education in the private sector

41 Education Act 1996, s. 167(3).

42 Meredith, *Government, Schools and the Law*, 157.

43 See e.g. litigation concerning the Beechen Cliff school in Bath: *R v Secretary of State for Education ex p. Avon CC*, (1990) 88 LGR 716; CA, (1990) 88 LGR 737.

44 See generally Harris, op. cit.; M. Feintuck, *Accountability and Choice in Schooling* (Buckingham, 1994).

45 See now School Standards and Framework Act 1998, s. 86; Meredith, *Government, Schools and the Law*, ch. 2; Harris, op. cit., ch. 5; J. Tweedie, 'Rights in Social Programmes: The Case of Parental Choice of School', [1986] PL 407.

Recognition of parental choice based upon religious considerations is complicated by the fact that denominational schools (voluntary controlled and voluntary aided schools) are technically independent of LEAs, although the majority of funding comes from councils and numerous LEA powers apply to such schools. Denominational schools of this kind have been permitted to adopt an admissions policy designed to keep the specific religious character of the school: Schools Framework and Standards Act 1998, s. 86(3)(b); and see *Choudhury v Governors of Bishop Challoner Roman Catholic Comprehensive School*, [1992] 3 All ER 277, HL; *R v Lancashire CC, ex p. F*, [1995] ELR 3.

Further constraints on parental preference arise from the ability of some schools to make limited selection of pupils (Schools Framework and Standards Act 1998, s. 86(3)(c).

between schools. To some degree, indeed, it can be seen as attempting to remove private market anomalies in the allocation of education, since a system of council allocation of pupils to schools according to area of residence merely gives a market advantage to those able and willing to buy houses in proximity to what are perceived to be 'good' state schools. In practice, though, state schools that are over-subscribed continue to give high priority to geographical proximity in allocating places (as they are permitted to do under the legislation) so that a 'school premium' is still a recognizable feature of the housing market. The consumer choice between state schools has been enhanced by statutory duties to publish information about the school including the much-criticized examination performance and truancy 'league tables',[46] thus supposedly enabling an informed choice—in much the same way that a shopper in a supermarket might use the product details, weight, and ingredients contained on the labels of tins to choose between rival brands.

The arguments in favour of consumer choice are that parents are in a better position than the LEA to know what is best for their child, that parents take a more active role in their children's education than when a LEA decides on their behalf, and that schools become more responsive to their 'customers'.[47] Whether the outcome is an overall improvement in education, in response to parental concerns, depends crucially on whether parents are making informed choices and, therefore, on the information available to them about the respective schools. These arguments are a mixture of the descriptive and the prescriptive, but at the very least they assume that actively involved parents and responsive schools are in some sense better than choices made by the LEA on the basis of its overall policy and on the advice of its professional officers.

Indeed, the argument against enthroning parental choice is that to do so may hamper effective planning and implementation of policy by the council. For example, it runs directly counter to any attempt to set admissions quotas for schools well below capacity in order to spread pupils evenly between popular and unpopular schools. Where a policy of that type is operated, parents denied the school of their choice are in effect the casualties of a policy designed to provide a viable or better school for pupils who would be left using the less popular school in any event. Conversely, though, in a public education system which is incapable of meeting adequately all parental preferences, the negative effects of parental choice for those whose children's educations may suffer as their schools lose pupils and resources needs to be counted also against the benefits in assessing the policy.

[46] Under regulations made under what is now the Education Act 1996, s. 537.
[47] Tweedie, op. cit., 430.

In a true market where demand outstripped supply one of two things would happen: either a queue or waiting-list of buyers would form or prices would rise until demand matched supply. As regards the first: in the private education sector queues (such as 'putting a child's name down' at birth for privileged schools) do operate. In maintained schools, however, the annual admissions procedure is designed to prevent a disorderly 'first come, first served'. Although in the private sector fee differentials may dampen excessive demand, this is obviously not an option open to state schools. Other factors which operate to allocate scarce places in higher education, such as ability or academic attainment, are only allowed influence in state schools where procedural requirements for adopting such an admissions policy have been met and only then within prescribed limits.[48] In a sense, then, the statutory admissions procedure places parents in competition with each other for scarce places at popular schools, but without the normal market mechanisms for resolving their competing preferences.

There is something of a mismatch between the statutory procedure, which focuses on the rights of the parent of the individual child who has applied for a place at an over-subscribed school, and the position which routinely confronts appeal committees, where they have to decide between multiple appeals relating to the same school. However, the High Court has, in the absence of a statutory basis for a comparison between cases, refused formally to recognize the competitive nature of appeals. Parents are not allowed access to the cases of other parents' children presented to an Appeal Committee.[49] Nevertheless, Woolf LJ has suggested that an appeal committee is permitted to adopt a procedure of hearing all appeals relating to the same school one after the other, and of deferring decision until they have all been heard.[50] To hear and decide sequentially would prejudice parents whose appeals were heard later.

It has been argued that parental choice of school really amounts to no more than a procedural right to express a preference, which may be overridden by school or local authority policies. These are unlikely to be set aside, provided they do not involve arbitrary discrimination. An appeal against refusal by the LEA of the parents' preferred choice lies to an appeal committee,[51] whose decisions are binding. An apparently technical

[48] School Standards and Framework Act 1998, ss. 86(3)(c) and 99–103.

[49] *R v Education Appeal Committee of Leicester County Council ex p. Tarmohamed*, [1997] ELR 48, QBD.

[50] *Choudhury* (n. 45 above); Harris, op. cit., 158.

[51] School Standards and Framework Act 1998, s. 94 and sched. 24, govern the composition and procedure of these appeal committees. In addition, the Council on Tribunals has issued a non-statutory code of practice: *Education Appeals: Code of Practice on Procedure* (London, 1992). The operation of these committees is examined in: D. Bull, 'Monitoring Education Appeals: Local Ombudsmen Lead the Way', (1985) JSWL 189; T. Buck, 'School Admissions Appeals', (1985) JSWL 227; and Tweedie, op. cit. For a study focusing on Scotland, see: M. Adler, A. Petch, and J. Tweedie, *Parental Choice in Education Policy* (Edinburgh, 1989).

change in the grounds of appeal in relation to the 'prejudice' ground[52] signifies an important change, weakening the parents' position in the case of infants schools appeals. Generally, the appeal has to be allowed unless the committee is satisfied that compliance with the parents' preference would prejudice the provision of efficient education or the efficient use of resources. Where so satisfied, the committee is bound to weigh these factors against the prejudice to the child of refusal, including consideration of geographical factors, place of residence, exceptional medical or social factors, and siblings already at the school.[53] It has been held that an Education Appeal Tribunal should approach the issue in two stages: first, whether evidence exists that the admission of the child would cause prejudice, and, if so, whether on balance that prejudice is sufficient to outweigh the reasons given by the parents for their choice of school.[54] Under the 1998 Act the appeal panel is only to overturn the refusal of a place at an infant school if satisfied that the decision appealed against was not one that a reasonable authority could reach in the circumstances or that the child would have been offered a place if the admission arrangements had been properly implemented.[55] This change follows from the capping of infant class sizes at thirty pupils.

A complication arises because of parental freedom under the legislation to choose schools outside the LEA in which they reside.[56] Here consumer choice and council responsibility for managing education are likely to come into sharp conflict. A local authority whose schools are undersubscribed because parents choose to send their children out of the area has no means of restricting their choice. Pure market theorists would argue that this provides an incentive for it to improve its 'product' to win back consumers. However, a particular school may be less well regarded due to factors beyond the council's control—especially the educational effects of the social composition of its catchment area. Although schools are free to use geographical proximity as an admissions criterion (and commonly do so), the Court of Appeal has held that it is unlawful to adopt a policy of favouring pupils residing in the authority's area.[57]

The potential clash between LEA policy and parental preference has also been acute over the questions of racial integration or segregation.

[52] For this purpose the standard admissions number of pupils at the school determined under the School Standards and Framework Act 1998, s. 93, must be considered.

[53] See further: *R v Commissioner for Local Administration ex p. Croydon LBC*, [1989] 1 All ER 1033.

[54] *R v S. Glamorgan Appeal Committee ex p. Evans* (unreported decision of 10 May 1984), per Forbes J; see also *ex p. M*, *The Times*, 24 May 1994; *R v Appeal Committee of Brighouse School ex p. G and B*, [1998] ELR 39.

[55] School Standards and Framework Act 1998, sched. 24, para. 12.

[56] School Standards and Framework Act 1998, s. 86(6).

[57] *R v Shadow Education Committee of Greenwich LBC ex p. Governors of John Ball Primary School*, (1990) 88 LGR 589.

Respect for parental choice means that the views of parents who do not wish their children to be educated in a multiracial school with a non-English-speaking majority of pupils must prevail if the school of their choice is under-subscribed.[58] The legislation may, therefore, handicap attempts to use schools admissions policies designed to produce racial integration.[59] It has also been held, on the other hand, that a council is not obliged to counteract the effect on schools admissions of de facto racial segregation in housing in the catchment areas by giving priority at over-subscribed schools to disfavoured minorities.[60] Indeed, it is arguable that to do so would itself be unlawful.

Overall, the legislative scheme creates a mixed system in which parental choices are accorded some priority, but councils have a large measure of discretion in the admissions policies adopted once schools reach the level of being over-subscribed, since at this point any policy adopted will disappoint some parents. The outcome is a compromise between LEA control and a parent-led market mechanism.[61] As parents exercise choices for more popular schools their choices may produce a redeployment of teachers, with popular schools receiving additional resources to follow pupils, and less popular schools losing posts. However, the principle operates in a less than perfectly responsive market. There is no obligation to make buildings or site alterations to popular schools to accommodate the pattern of parental preferences. Moreover, paradoxically, the short-term result of a parental move from a less popular to a more popular school may be a decrease in the class sizes at the former and an increase at the latter. Hence, the conclusion of one commentator, Meredith, that parental

[58] In *R v Cleveland CC ex p. Commission for Racial Equality*, (1993) 91 LGR 139, the Court of Appeal held that a local authority did not discriminate on racial grounds when it reluctantly agreed to a parental request for transfer of a child to a school where most children were white and English was the predominant language (unlike her present school); see N. Harris, 'Educational Choice in a Multi-Cultural Society', [1992] PL 522. Meredith argues that the outcome, in this instance the elevation of parental choice, and the lack of legal recognition of a local authority's policy to produce multicultural classes or schools by giving priority over parental wishes, may result in de facto racial segregation: Meredith, 'Judicial Review and Education', 88.

[59] This situation arose in Dewsbury in 1987–8 where a number of white parents challenged the council's admissions policy, which was designed to preserve racial balance in its schools by setting admissions limits which redistributed parental preference before schools in which the majority of pupils were white were full to capacity. Following an unsuccessful appeal to the Secretary of State the council acceded to the parents' requests after admitting procedural errors in its admissions process.

[60] Legal challenges by Asian parents to Bradford's system of operating catchment areas reflecting traditional links with individual secondary schools failed in *R v Bradford MBC ex p. Ali*, *The Times*, 21 Oct. 1993; *R v Bradford MBC ex p. K*, unreported, 11 Nov. 1993, QBD. The parents argued unsuccessfully that the policy was an unreasonable limitation on parental choice of school and amounted to indirect discrimination contrary to the Race Relations Act 1976.

[61] Audit Commission, *Trading Places: The Supply and Allocation of Schools Places* (London, 1996).

choice operates against effective planning and implementation of education policy by LEAs.[62]

Consumers have also been an increasing 'voice' in education through additional powers and responsibilities conferred on parent governors.[63] This development has gone hand in hand with a weakening of the political influence of LEAs in the management of schools and increasing devolution of budgetary (under Local Management schemes), curriculum, and staffing decisions. The Taylor report of 1977 had first suggested an increased role for governors and greater representation of parent governors alongside LEAs, teachers, and the local community.[64] The Education Act 1980 created a separate governing body for each school (previously grouping of schools under a single body had been permitted) and gave enhanced powers to governors, over appointments and curriculum. In 1986 further legislation provided for elected parent governor representation in all LEA schools;[65] LEA representatives became a minority, and the scope for local political influence was diluted accordingly. This was also the effect of judicial decisions limiting the right of LEAs to replace governors representing them who departed from the council's policy.[66]

At the same time governors' powers were increased, especially under the Local Management schemes,[67] which involved the governing body directly in decisions about expenditure and staff recruitment (the latter proved especially controversial in 1996 when it looked as though there might be a national revolt by school governors over the staffing reductions necessary in order to implement budget reduction imposed on LEAs). Doubts have been expressed about whether parent governors are responsive to consumers' concerns or act as a channel of communication between management and parents in the way envisaged; the formal accountability mechanisms comprise little more than the annual governors' meeting, which has been likened to a company's annual general meeting with its shareholders.

Commentators began to fear that the direction of Conservative educational reform amounted to a programme of 'de-democratization'.[68] According to this view the elevation of consumer choice (for example, parental preferences), together with devolution of education management

[62] Meredith, *Government, Schools and the Law*, 48–9.

[63] Harris, op. cit., 67ff.

[64] Report of a Committee of Enquiry, *A New Partnership for Our Schools* (London, 1977).

[65] Education (No. 2) Act 1986.

[66] *Brunyate v ILEA*, [1989] 2 All ER 417 (in which the House of Lords held that the authority had acted unlawfully in removing two Conservative councillors who were its representatives from the governing body of a school for refusing to undertake not to vote in favour of grant-maintained status); see further Ch. 7.

[67] See Harris, op. cit., 78–83. Education Reform Act 1988, ss. 33–47.

[68] S. Ranson, 'From Reforming to Restructuring of Education', ch. 7 in J. Stewart and G. Stoker (eds.), *Local Government in the 1990s* (Basingstoke, 1995), 119–20, citing J. Chubb, and T. Moe, *Politics, Markets and America's Schools* (Washington, DC, 1990).

(through Local Management schemes and grant-maintained status) and increased central regulation (for example, the National Curriculum), amounted to a sustained attack on the principle of local democratic responsibility for education. The reforms seemed to be moving away from the position where councils were the major education providers to one where their role became that of coordinating a diverse range of local providers and acting as a safety net in providing support services, such as special needs, to schools which were otherwise self-governing.[69] Ranson argued, however, that the involvement of the council remained necessary because education is a system (rather than a series of autonomous and self-governing institutions), and because it should be accountable to the local community.[70] This last point is meant as more than an objection to increasing national regulation: it concerns the question of whom education serves. Arguably, the beneficiaries are not merely the children and parents making use of the resource at any given time, and mechanisms designed to reflect the interests of the local community should go beyond those of the immediate consumers.

Critics who fear for the long-term future of the local democratically controlled system of education may not be wholly reassured by the reforms introduced since 1997 by the Labour government.[71] It is true that the policy of opting out has been reversed with the abolition of grant-maintained schools. However, parental rights to choose schools and to adequate information about performance and standards have been retained. In some respects parental rights have been strengthened: for example, through the introduction of ballots on grammar school status[72] and a requirement that parental representatives sit on local education authority committees.[73] The government no longer uses the strident language of consumer choice of its predecessor: it now talks of 'partnership' between councils, schools, and various bodies and people, including parents. A practical manifestation of this is the introduction of home–school agreements.[74] It would seem that, by whatever name, consumerism in education has achieved a bipartisan status.

So far we have discussed the opportunities given to the users of local services to exercise choice and, related to that, to have information about their council's performance in delivering services. We move now to the issue of redress for dissatisfaction. The next section examines mechanisms for complaining, both outside the council to the local ombudsman and the increasingly important topic of internal complaints procedures.

[69] Ibid. 117. [70] Ibid. 122–3.

[71] The developments described in this paragraph were all introduced in the Schools Framework and Standards Act 1998, following the White Paper *Excellence in Schools*, Cm. 3681 (1997). For an assessment of Labour policy, see: (1998) (1) Liverpool Law Review.

[72] 1998 Act, ss. 104 ff. [73] Ibid., s. 9. [74] Ibid., ss. 110–11.

## COMMISSIONERS FOR LOCAL ADMINISTRATION[75]

The Local Commissioner (or ombudsman) is the independent official who investigates complaints of council 'maladministration'. The account in this section opens with a general description of the ombudsman's role and powers, considering especially the connection with consumer accountability and with the position of councillors and officers in resolving complaints internally within the authority. Proposals for reform (especially those emanating from a financial management and policy review for the Department of Environment[76]) are then considered for the light which they shed on the future development of this office and its contribution to local democracy.[77]

The ombudsman's office is now a well-established mechanism for consumer accountability of authorities to their service users. Its creation, however, in 1974 (following the introduction of an equivalent Parliamentary Commissioner in 1967) considerably pre-dated the recent 'consumerist' trend. The ombudsman has no power to award legal remedies but works instead by delivering a public report following investigation. To this extent it operates within the liberal/representative notion of local government by rendering local politicians and officers accountable. The ombudsman has no power, however, to substitute his judgment for that of the authority or to issue formal sanctions. It is assumed that the electorate will hear of maladministration through the local press (there are duties to publish and discuss a report where the authority is proposing not to follow the ombudsman's recommendations) and hold the administration accountable through the ballot box. Lawyers sometimes tend to dismiss this regime as toothless. Nevertheless, the powerful influence on political actors of the desire to avoid bad publicity in the local press following an adverse report should not be underestimated. Moreover, the ombudsman's swingeing investigatory powers and the simple inconvenience and

[75] See: M. Loughlin, *Administrative Accountability in Local Government* (York, 1992), ch. 5; P. Birkinshaw, *Grievances, Remedies and the State* (2nd edn., London, 1995), 218–27; N. Lewis and P. Birkinshaw, *When Citizens Complain* (Buckingham, 1993), ch. 7 and 154–65. P. Watchman and J. Logie, *The Local Ombudsman* (Edinburgh, 1990) is a study of the comparable Scottish office.

[76] Pt. 1 of the review was a 'prior options' review conducted by Sir Geoffrey Chipperfield: *Report of the Financial Management and Policy Review of the Commission for Local Administration in England, Stage One: Prior Options Review* (London, Nov. 1995); see also *Report of the Financial Management and Policy Review of the Commission for Local Administration in England, Stage Two* (London, 1996); the government responded to both phases in: *Government Response to the Financial Management and Policy Review of the Commission for Local Administration in England*, (London, 1996).

[77] The description here is concerned with the 3 investigatory Commissioners who between them cover the English councils; separate commissions exist in Wales and Scotland.

administrative disruption involved in being subject to investigation may have a deterrent effect in their own right.

While it is true that a (very small) minority of authorities reject ombudsman findings and brazen out critical reports, it is more normal that councils try to avoid a complaint being made initially. For this reason many councils have created internal complaints systems and some have appointed internal ombudsmen. Commonly authorities try to anticipate a critical report by putting matters right as soon as possible. These points can be illustrated by figures from complaints handled by the ombudsman in 1998/9: 23.2 per cent of all complaints received were settled voluntarily by local authorities during investigations, without the issue of a formal report, as compared with 4.7 per cent in which a report was made.[78] In the latter group, 331 (3.4 per cent of complaints) reports finding misadministration causing injustice were issued, but no further reports were issued. This is consistent with figures from recent years, which suggest that only a handful of cases lead to an unsatisfactory outcome.

The shift from a democratic representative model towards a consumerist one can be seen as an important change in the legislative scheme. It initially required a complaint to be brought through a councillor (the 'councillor filter'); only where a councillor had declined to forward the complaint could the Local Commissioner receive it direct from a member of the public. The purpose was to encourage the resolution of complaints through the normal democratic channels, with the ombudsman available as a safety net where they had failed. However, one consequence was to place an additional hurdle in the way of potential complainants, and one which deterred many. Since 1988 the commissioners have been empowered to receive complaints direct from the public in addition to the councillor route.[79] The number of complaints rose dramatically in the first two years of the new system (by 44 per cent in 1988–9 and 24 per cent in 1989–90[80]). This suggests that either from lack of persistence, ignorance of local representatives on the part of the public, or the reluctance of councillors to refer cases, there had been considerable unmet need previously.

## Jurisdiction

Although as a matter of legislative history the notion of maladministration was introduced to provide for 'redress of grievances', it, too, should

[78] Commission for Local Administration in England, *Annual Report for 1998/99* (London, 1999), apps. 3(b) and 3(f). The remaining percentage comprised complaints outside the ombudsman's jurisdiction, or where discretion was exercised not to pursue the complaint.

[79] LGA 1988, sched. 3, para. 5(2) (amending LGA 1974, s. 26).

[80] See Commission for Local Administration in England, *Annual Report for 1988/89* (London, 1989), 9, and *Annual Report for 1989/90* (London, 1990), 10.

be understood as fundamentally a consumerist concept. The famous non-statutory catalogue; 'Bias, neglect, inattention, delay, incompetence, ineptitude, perversity, turpitude, arbitrariness and so on',[81] is an increasing litany of the causes of customer dissatisfaction. It is concerned with the way in which a local authority performs, not with the substance of its policies, so far as the law allows it discretion: a finding of maladministration is not intended to supplant political judgment. Hence, questions about the merits of decisions taken without maladministration are excluded from the ombudsman's jurisdiction.[82] Likewise, decisions affecting 'all or most of the inhabitants of the area of the authority concerned'[83] are excluded: these lack the necessary focused detriment to the individual, and by implication are more suitable for political and electoral redress because of their scale and diffuseness. Also excluded from investigation are a number of situations in which the individual's relationship with the authority is not as a service recipient: personnel questions, contractual and commercial decisions, and legal proceedings;[84] internal school matters are excluded because separate complaints mechanisms exist in their case.

In recent years it is complaints arising from budgetary cuts imposed by councils on local services which have raised the most difficult questions about the boundaries of political discretion and maladministration. The questions of whether the council has adequate resources to fulfil its functions or its own priorities in allocating expenditure under its control are political considerations outside the local ombudsman's jurisdiction. The LCA's approach to complaints arising from 'rationing' decisions was developed over several years in consultation with local-authority associations (consultation with pressure groups representing particular categories of service users is not mentioned).[85] The approach in relation to discretionary expenditure (for example, on grants or services) requires the ombudsman to be satisfied:

[81] No definition of maladministration appears in the statute, and the list comes from the speech of the minister (Richard Crossman) when introducing the Parliamentary Commissioner Bill: HC Debs., vol. 734, col. 51 (18 Oct. 1966).

[82] LGA 1974, s. 34(3). Over 50% of complaints received result in termination by the LCA (under s. 26(10)) because there is no maladministration or no or insufficient injustice, e.g. *Annual Report for 1998/99*, app. 3(c); however, the report does not make clear what proportion of this total follows from an appreciation of a council's legal discretion and what proportion is based upon the facts of the case.

[83] LGA 1974, s. 26(7). This ground accounted for termination of about 0.5% of complaints (73 in all) in 1998/9: *Annual Report for 1998/99*, app. 3(c).

[84] LGA 1974, sched. 5 (as amended by SI 1988 No. 242). *The Report of the Financial Management and Policy Review of the Commission for Local Administration in England, Stage II* (London, 1996), 46–53, recommended a number of changes to these exclusions, mostly dependent on consideration of proposals in the Woolf report on the relationship between the ombudsman and the courts (nn. 111 and 112 below).

[85] This account is drawn from Commission for Local Administration in England, *Annual Report for 1994/95*, 5.

that the council has considered the matter and has taken into account the relevant consideration and has excluded any that are not relevant;
the council's decision or policy does not discriminate unfairly against any person;
the council has properly announced and explained its decision or policy;
the council has not fettered its discretion by applying the decision or policy without regard to any exceptional circumstances in a particular case;
the council has implemented the decision or policy fairly and consistently.

There is substantial overlap in this approach with the standards with which a court applying judicial review principles would approach the same issue. It preserves freedom for councils to take policy decisions about targeting scarce resources on particular social groups or in defined circumstances of need, provided individuals are not unfairly treated. The ombudsman's approach to rationing in relation to mandatory expenditure is also flexible:

While a failure to comply with a statutory obligation is prima facie maladministration, in reaching conclusions on each complaint we shall need to consider the particular facts of the case, the totality of the council's available resources, the scale of expenditure involved in relation to those resources and whether section 114 and 115 of the Local Government Finance Act 1988 were relevant to the matter.[86]

These problems have been particularly acute in relation to complaints arising from the management and repair of housing in inner-city areas (housing is, in any event, the service which attracts most ombudsman complaints). A long-term gap between funding and repairs needs, together with the ring-fencing of the Housing Revenue Account and capping of council tax levels, have led to a substantial backlog of repairs which are mandatory under the terms of the tenancy agreements or of housing or public health legislation.[87] This, in turn, can lead to officers viewing these forms of redress with hostility as a type of 'queue-jumping' over the heads of many more equally deserving but more patient or less voluble tenants. However, the CLA has, equally, been critical of delays directly attributable to under-funding by central government of mandatory housing improvement grants.[88] The Commission has issued a Guidance Note on Housing Repairs, although this was given a lukewarm reception in the Chipperfield report.[89]

[86] The duty of the chief financial officer to report on unlawful expenditure (on which see pp. 269–70).

[87] The Commissioner for the North of England commented in the early 1990s that the situation in Liverpool seemed to have reached the position that little attention was paid to tenants' requests for repairs unless they resulted in a complaint to the ombudsman, to a councillor, or in the initiation of legal proceedings: *Annual Report for 1990/91*, 29.

[88] *Annual Report for 1992/93*, 28.

[89] Where the appropriateness of the CLA giving advice on matters of local authority management (of which handling complaints is just one aspect) is questioned: Chipperfield, op. cit., 24.

An important question in view of the proliferation of non-elected local bodies and the changing structure of local authorities due to contracting out is the effect of the structural changes upon the handling of complaints. The Local Commissioners' jurisdiction was extended to include Housing Action Trusts, Urban Development Corporations (in so far as they decide planning questions), the National Rivers Authority (in respect of flood defence and land drainage), and schools (in relation to decisions about the expulsion of pupils). Proposals have been made for further extensions of jurisdiction to all publicly funded schools and tribunals (for example, Housing Benefit Review Boards) examining local government functions.[90]

The effect of contracting out is more problematic for two reasons. First, the exemption from jurisdiction for contractual and commercial matters may inhibit some investigations, although procedures for disappointed tenders under the Local Government Act 1988 will provide remedies in some cases.[91] Where a private company or a DLO or DSO provides services under contractual arrangements the complaints procedure may appear less clear to the public, although the council remains legally responsible for contracted-out services. The danger in contractual arrangements of this kind is that the service user's needs become marginalized: the contractor (whether external or a DLO or DSO) will be primarily concerned with commercial considerations, and the council may see its role primarily in terms of monitoring this contractual performance. With regard to contractors operating on the council's behalf and within areas covered by the ombudsman jurisdiction, the 1974 Act allows the Commissioner to investigate action taken 'by or on behalf of the council'.[92] Formally, the ombudsman's powers of investigation extend to contractors as they do to council officers. The Commission has also suggested that councils should advise contractors of the possibility of complaint and investigation, and should consider reserving in their contractual arrangements the ability to recover payments which they may make to a complainant who has suffered injustice through maladministration.

Rather similar concerns arise from the increasing use of partnerships between councils and other public or voluntary bodies.[93] The CLA has argued that jurisdictional boundaries between the different public sector ombudsmen may make it difficult for the public to know where and how to complain; for example, a person who is mentally ill who is discharged from hospital may deal with the council social services department

[90] *Government Response to the Financial Management and Policy Review of the Commission for Local Administration in England* (London, 1996), 7–8.

[91] See Ch. 10.

[92] See further *Annual Report 1993/94*, 8–9.

[93] See pp. 324–31 below.

(within the CLA's jurisdiction) and the hospital concerned (subject to the Health Services Ombudsman), a housing benefit claimant may find it hard to allocate responsibility between the Department of Social Security (subject to the jurisdiction of the Parliamentary Commissioner) and the council, and so on. To simplify matters and avoid the need for multiple complaints, it has been suggested that there should be a more integrated approach, with a single or unified point of entry for complaints.[94]

**Procedure and Enforcement**

The CLA's procedure is designed to settle complaints without investigation if possible: before the Commissioner conducts an investigation the authority concerned must be given the chance to investigate and reply. This is especially important where complaints come directly from members of the public rather than via a councillor. If the Commissioner decides to embark on an investigation, both the authority and persons concerned must be given the opportunity to comment. Investigations take place in private—an important consideration in making the process 'user-friendly'. In practice, investigations are conducted by field officers who will interview the complainant, read the relevant files, and interview officers and members of the authority as appropriate.[95] A draft report will then be prepared and the authority invited to comment upon its factual accuracy. The report will be approved by the Commissioner in person before being sent to the authority. Where a report finds that maladministration has occurred and that the complainant has suffered injustice as a result, it may contain recommendations, and the authority comes under a specific duty to consider the report and to respond within three months.[96] Typically, a recommendation may suggest an ex gratia payment to a complainant; an authority has specific power to comply with recommendations involving expenditure.

Where the council is proposing not to follow the CLA' s recommendations, the report must be considered by the full council. Recalcitrant authorities who reject such recommendations can be asked to reconsider by way of a further report. If the authority has not satisfactorily responded within three months, the CLA can insist upon publication of the recommendations in a local newspaper (if necessary the CLA can undertake this

[94] *Annual Report for 1998/99*, 4–5; Cabinet Office, *Review of the Public Sector Ombudsmen in England: A Consultation Paper* (London, June 2000).

[95] The Commission has powers to subpoena evidence if necessary. See *Re A Subpoena (Adoption: Commissioner for Local Administration)*, [1996] 2 FLR 629, QBD, where Carnwath J held that public interest immunity was inapplicable to the commission's requests for files on adoption necessary to resolve a complaint, in view of Parliament's intention that there should be free access for the purpose of investigation.

[96] LGA 1974, s. 31 (as amended).

and charge the authority); the council is entitled to incorporate within this notice its reasons for not acting on the report. This procedure respects the ultimate right of an elected body to reject the findings of an unelected commissioner. However, it seeks to build on and mobilize local accountability to force the council at least to justify its position publicly so that the electorate can judge.[97]

The duty to consider a report in the full council and the right of the ombudsman to publish a statement were reforms introduced in 1989 in an attempt to reduce the small but hard core of cases in which the local ombudsman's findings and recommendations are ignored. The CLA has kept its new powers of adverse publicity under review, and has concluded that in practice they have produced little change in the hard core of authorities prepared to ignore a further report. It has therefore raised once again the question of whether powers of enforcement should be introduced.[98] The CLA has also undertaken research into why councils do not comply, finding that the commonest causes are a refusal to accept that maladministration or injustice have occurred; it has subsequently introduced further steps intended to explain its findings and to educate councils in good practice.[99] Possibly as a result of these measures, for the first time in 1998/8, the Commission issued no further reports.

In practice, over 90 per cent of the CLA's workload now comes from direct complaints, rather than those referred by councillors. To some extent, the CLA has become a victim of its own success in cultivating contacts in CABs and other advice centres. The number of complaints has grown out of recognition since the removal of the councillor filter and this has placed considerable strain on the CLA's resources: complaints rose from 8,733 received (with 7,159 determined and 317 formal reports) in 1989/90 to 15,869 received in 1998/9 (of which 15,653 were determined and 459 involved formal reports). Although since 1989 funding for the service has come out of the Rate Support Grant, and so directly from the Department of the Environment, it has not tracked the increase in workload, and in recent years the CLA has had to bear its share of cuts in government funding; with a budget of £7.7 million and a staff of under 200 in 1998/9 the local government complaints service looks to be good value, however, compared with alternatives such as courts or tribunals. This picture suggests that strategic and financial considerations may partially

[97] Before the 1989 amendments, where the LCA was of the opinion that an injustice had been caused by maladministration, the council was under a duty to consider the report and to notify the Commissioner of any action which had been or would be taken; the only further sanction against a recalcitrant authority was for the Commissioner to issue a further report: LGA 1974, s. 31(1) (now amended by LGHA 1989, s. 26).

[98] See *Annual Report for 1993/94*, 71 ff.

[99] *Annual Report for 1995/96*, 4.

underpin the noticeable shift in the CLA's priorities towards encouraging councils to devise their own complaints systems.[100]

Ombudsman complaints were intended to complement rather than to duplicate legal redress. Hence, the commissioners are not empowered to investigate where the complainant has a right of appeal to a tribunal or to a minister, or a remedy in law, unless satisfied that, in the circumstances, it would not be reasonable to require the complainant to use these avenues.[101] In view of the similarities between the grounds for judicial review and 'maladministration' there is considerable potential overlap between the two procedures. For instance, 'bias' and 'turpitude' may in some forms amount to a procedural impropriety, while 'perversity' and 'arbitrariness' may constitute irrationality. However, whereas use of the ombudsman is free, High Court litigation will be expensive, unless the applicant is fully legally aided. The ombudsman also has available inquisitorial powers, to inspect documents and to interview officers and members under oath, which are only exceptionally used in judicial review proceedings. In addition, the time limits are more favourable to the complainant: up to a year is allowed for ombudsman complaints, as against three months for judicial review proceedings. It is true that in the last analysis the ombudsman lacks coercive powers, but, as has been argued, in the majority of cases recommendations are followed. Moreover, a recommendation may be of considerably more use in meeting the practical needs of an applicant than one of the prerogative orders (especially if, as is frequently the case, the order is certiorari, which leaves the authority free to re-take the decision without illegality, to the applicant's disadvantage). In view of these factors, it is fortunate that the commissioners interpret the proviso to the 'legal redress' exclusion generously so as to allow complaints to progress even though many could technically be framed as applications for judicial review.

The relationship between complaining and taking legal action by way of judicial review suggests an indeterminate line between the two methods of redress.[102] The courts have been generally deferential to discretionary decisions by ombudsmen in other fields over whether to commence an investigation.[103] However, there are judicial comments in relation to the Local Commissioner suggesting a stricter approach to the question of an available legal remedy: it has been suggested that the ombudsman should focus not on the probability of success in the courts but simply on the availability of the remedy for the type of issue concerned. Woolf LJ has

[100] See pp. 174–9 below.

[101] LGA 1974, s. 26(6).

[102] A. Bradley, 'The Role of the Ombudsman in relation to the Protection of Citizens' Rights', [1980] CLJ 304, 332; C. Crawford, 'Where Judges Fear to Tread', [1982] JPL 619, 627.

[103] See *R v PCA ex parte Dyer*, [1994] 1 All ER 375, *Re Fletcher's Application*, [1970] 2 All ER 527, both decided in relation to the Parliamentary Commissioner.

stated that the ombudsman should be reluctant to investigate in the case of a specialist body or panel, whose decisions may be better policed by the courts, and should be mindful of the additional safeguards for a public body which operate in the case of judicial review.[104] The court did not in this case hold that it had been incorrect to commence the investigation, although the CLA's finding of maladministration was quashed. Nevertheless, it suggests a more legalistic approach than the Commission had previously taken to alternative remedies. In practice many investigations have been undertaken where the complainant might also have had an (expensive and time-consuming) remedy in public law. Moreover, the suggestion that the ombudsman should not investigate if a legal remedy might have been sought had action been commenced within the appropriate time limit is plainly misconceived. [105] It has the effect of importing into ombudsman investigations the very strict time limit of three months within which judicial review should be sought: the implication is that the non-availability of a legal remedy because of delay in applying for judicial review should itself be a reason for not investigating. Neither the legislation nor principle supports this approach. The 1974 Act sets a time limit of twelve months within which complaints should be brought.[106] This longer time limit is justifiable in view of the different outcomes of a successful application for judicial review and of an ombudsman's complaint. The same risk of disruption to administration by a finding of an unlawful action does not arise in the latter case. Woolf LJ's approach in the *Croydon* case neglects these differences.

Questions of overlap may also arise where a complainant has some tangential interest which can be raised in legal proceedings not centrally concerned with his or her complaint. Two examples may be given: until a change in case law in the 1980s allowed for the possibility of judicial review, the neighbour of a developer granted planning permission by a local authority had no means of challenging the process except by complaint to an ombudsman.[107] Similarly, a parent who wished to complain about the process adopted by a local authority in taking her child into care might raise the issue peripherally in the care proceedings, but the focus of

[104] *R v CLA ex parte Croydon LBC*, [1989] 1 All ER 1033, 1044–5.

[105] However, where an applicant complained to the Commissioner *after* bringing an application for judicial review, the Court of Appeal refused leave to challenge the Commissioner's view that the existence of the alternative remedy prevented investigation: *R v Commissioner for Local Administration ex p. PH* (unreported, 8 Mar. 1999, affirming a decision of Turner J, *The Times*, Law Report, 21 Dec. 1998). The Court rejected the applicant's argument that he should be allowed to proceed because of the possibility that compensation might be obtained if the ombudsman so recommended following a finding of maladministration.

[106] S. 26(4).

[107] M. MacPherson, 'Local Ombudsman or the Courts?', (1987) J. of Pl. and Env. Law 92.

these is on the best interests of the child, and so the courts have held that this possibility should not bar a complaint to the ombudsman.[108]

Local authorities have also exploited the potential overlap between legal proceedings and ombudsman complaints by bringing judicial review proceedings against the Commissioner. In a landmark decision in 1988 underlining the 'juridification' of local government, the Court of Appeal held that actions of the local commissioner were reviewable, notwithstanding the Commissioner's inability to make coercive orders and the absence of a statutory right of appeal against an ombudsman's report.[109] The reasoning was that since Parliament intended that councils should accept and act on the ombudsman's reports, rather than 'appealing' to the media in challenging the findings (which would undermine the process), it was a necessary safeguard that the CLA's actions were subject to judicial review.[110]

However, as will be seen, a minority of authorities not disposed to accept reports do not behave in the way presupposed by the Court of Appeal, and consequently the decision to some degree upsets the balance within the scheme. Moreover, the legislation now formalizes the council's 'right of reply' by the ability to include its reasons for not implementing the ombudsman's report in any published statement, so part of the underlying reasoning for the decision has been removed. It is arguable that the result has been to load the process in the authority's favour, since it may use public money to fight an ombudsman's report with which it disagrees, and nevertheless retains the option of ignoring it should it lose the legal battle. Although, theoretically, complainants are equally able to challenge the CLA if disappointed by the outcome, in practice they are much less likely to do so.

The whole issue of overlap between the ombudsmen and the courts was also explored in Lord Woolf's reports reviewing the civil justice system. The interim report suggested that powers of cross-referral between the courts and ombudsmen would be useful. Ombudsmen would find the power to apply for a ruling on a point of law valuable in the conduct of an investigation, while courts would value the ombudsman's investigative assistance in order to determine disputed factual issues.[111] In his final report Lord Woolf noted the extent to which the Local Commission and the Housing Association Tenants' Ombudsmen already use their discretion to investigate complaints of maladministration involving housing disrepair where a legal remedy would also lie. He recommended that this

[108] *R v LCA for North and East Area of England, ex p. Bradford MCC*, [1979] QB 287.

[109] *R v Local Commissioner ex p. Eastleigh BC*, [1988] QB 855.

[110] See esp. Lord Donaldson, ibid. 867.

[111] Lord Chancellor's Dept., *Access to Justice: Interim Report* (London, June 1995), paras. 16–19.

discretion be placed on a more formal basis and that a power to refer issues of statutory interpretation to the courts should be created, along with judicial enforcement of recommendations of compensation.[112] The Major government, however, while not rejecting these proposals, indicated that other aspects of the reform of civil justice had a higher priority.[113]

The Widdicombe Committee had earlier proposed that there should be a new 'power of assistance' conferred on the ombudsman, to assist individuals in bringing court cases where there were wide implications for a council's services or procedural matters affecting its conduct of business generally, where legal clarification of important issues of principle was desirable, or in cases of persistent breaches of the law.[114] The proposed power was modelled on the powers to assist individual complainants long enjoyed by the anti-discrimination commissions, and would have been in some respects similar to the public-interest power already enjoyed by the district auditor,[115] although not limited to matters of financial propriety. It would, however, have involved a reorientation of the CLA's work towards enforcement rather than investigation, and also away from redress of individual grievances towards the legality more generally of council action. For this reason the CLA was unenthusiastic, and the government did not endorse the proposal.

Similarly, repeated calls for a power of independent investigation have so far failed to bear fruit. The Commission has consistently argued for a power to initiate investigations without a complaint having been made, because of its expertise in conducting investigations, and on the grounds that this would often be cheaper than ad hoc inquiries into matters of public concern set up by local authorities. A number of local authorities have made requests to the CLA for investigations of this kind themselves, but the CLA has no legal power to undertake them at present. The Widdicombe Committee supported this proposal, noting that the present complaints system favours articulate, educated, and determined middle-class complainants and a power of investigation on the CLA's initiative might be in the interest of manual and other economic groups.[116] This recommendation was not implemented, but in its response to the Financial Management and Policy Review the previous government seemed to have

[112] *Access to Justice: Final Report to the Lord Chancellor on the Civil Justice System* (London, July 1996), 218–22.

[113] *Government Response to the Financial Management and Policy Review of the Commission for Local Administration in England* (London, 1996), 6.

[114] *The Conduct of Local Authority Business*, Cmnd. 9797 (1986), paras. 9.87–101.

[115] See Ch. 4.

[116] Widdicombe Report, para. 9.76; see *Annual Report 1992/93*, 6–7, 63.

accepted the case for an independent power, provided it did not deflect the CLA from improving the handling of complaints by individuals.[117]

It has been common among administrative law writers to contrast the role of the ombudsman in developing good administrative practice favourably[118] with the sporadic and peripheral intervention of the courts in the administrative process through judicial review. Underlying this approach is the belief that independent offices like the ombudsman can propagate value-free principles of good administration by reflection and illustration of what constitutes maladministration, to the benefit of the many citizens who never complain. To some extent this reasoning precedes the interest since the late 1980s in consumerism. An academic study of the operation of the local commissioners by researchers at Sheffield[119] advocated the enhanced use of 'administrative audit' involving a revised Code of Administrative Practice, a new and wider formulation of maladministration (it suggested banishing the term entirely), and a power of independent investigation. On the other hand, Loughlin has argued that the local ombudsmen have been relatively unsuccessful in developing good administrative practice. He suggests that, in any event, such a role would conflict with their task of mediation, and that more formal development of administrative principles would probably result in increased conflict with local authorities and challenges to the CLA through judicial review.[120] Nevertheless, the 1989 Act gave authority to promulgate statutory guidance on good administrative practice,[121] which has been used to produce a series of publications, to mixed reviews.[122]

The Commission also has a clear policy of increasing use of recommendations (these are made in about 60 per cent of reports finding maladministration) to improve the future quality of administration. There are other indications of moves towards a more strategic approach. The CLA keeps the pattern of local settlement of complaints under observation, since these may present symptoms of an underlying failure which is not being addressed. A complaint would need to be made which was not settled, however, before the CLA could investigate and suggest improvements.

[117] *Government Response* (n. 113 above), 9. Legislation was promised at 'a convenient opportunity'.

[118] See e.g. C. Harlow and R. Rawlings, *Administration and Law* (London, 1984), 207ff.

[119] N. Lewis, M. Severantne, and S. Cracknell, *Complaints Procedures in Local Government* (Sheffield, 1987): see the detailed discussion and criticism in C. Crawford, 'Complaints, Codes and Ombudsmen in Local Government', [1988] PL 246, 257–61.

[120] Loughlin, op. cit., 107–8.

[121] Local Government and Housing Act 1989, s. 23.

[122] These are a series entitled 'Guidance on Good Practice', and occasional bulletin, *LGO*, giving details of good practice. Chipperfield (op. cit., 24–5) doubted the value of the Guidance Notes. However, the Stage II review was more supportive (n. 76, paras. 427ff.). In any event, the Commission has stated that it intends to target its future guidance towards publication of digests of leading cases and the lessons to be learned: ibid., para. 423.

In addition, recent reports suggests some grouping of complaints which have been investigated in parallel because they relate to the same local authority department or procedure: examples include a major investigation into procedures for handling applications for rehousing in the London Borough of Brent, the administration of Housing Benefit in Ealing[123] and Lambeth,[124] rationing of house renovation grants in Birmingham,[125] and housing transfers in Hertsmere.[126] This approach may be partly a product of the strategic referral by councillors or voluntary agencies of a large number of cases raising a common problem, but it also appears to come from the CLA's own initiative. This development casts the CLA more in the role of an inspectorate rather than a body solely concerned with individual redress of grievance. However, the power to make recommendations still depends on a finding of injustice to an individual complainant caused by maladministration: the CLA is powerless to propose action unless an individual has suffered injustice as a result. In the final analysis, the balance of the CLA's emphasis is, therefore, on individual service users who complain.

In the face of a hard core of about 5 per cent of cases in which councils took no action following an adverse report from the ombudsman, the requirements publicly to consider and respond to the Commissioner's report were strengthened in 1989 in the way described earlier. These provisions were introduced in preference to the Widdicombe Committee's suggestion that the Northern Ireland model (under which the findings are enforceable in the last analysis in the County Court) should be adopted.[127] Likewise, the government rejected a suggestion from the Select Committee which oversees the Parliamentary Commissioner that it should take on the task of policing implementation of the Commissioners' reports, as it does with those under the 1967 Act.[128] Although the Select Committee has proved an effective parliamentary watchdog, substituting

[123] Ibid. 9–10; and see *Annual Report for 1995/96*, 8, and *Annual Report for 1994/95*, app. 9, for further groupings of multiple complaints investigated in parallel.

[124] *Annual Report for 1998/99*, 10.

[125] *Annual Report for 1995/96*, 16.

[126] Ibid. 18.

[127] Widdicombe Report, paras., 9. 68 and 9. 69. Lord Woolf made a similar recommendation in his Civil Justice Review (nn. 111 and 112 above).

Under the Commissioner of Complaints (Northern Ireland) Act 1969, s. 7, a complainant may apply to the County Court for compensation or an order for other remedial action following a finding of maladministration resulting in injustice; the court is required to act on the facts found by the Commissioner, unless the contrary is proved. The Northern Ireland Commissioner is alone among the statutory ombudsmen operating in the UK in operating within a legally enforceable regime of this kind. This arose from the perceived reluctance of some authorities in the province to deal fairly with complaints across the sectarian divide. However, the legislation attempts to preserve the independence of the Commissioner as an investigatory official by putting the onus of legal enforcement on the complainant.

[128] *The Conduct of Local Authority Business (the Government Response to the Widdicombe Committee)*, Cm. 433 (1988), para. 6.23.

to some degree for formal remedies under that scheme, it has no recognized constitutional role in relation to individual local authorities, whereas government departments are accountable to Parliament under the doctrine of ministerial responsibility. A similar recommendation in the Financial Management and Policy Review received a lukewarm reception from the government.[129]

Whatever the constitutional niceties, the political reality is that the CLA's relative lack of political clout is due in part to the absence of a watchdog like the Select Committee whose support it can enlist in shaming an unrepentant council into making redress. The original statutory scheme provided for a representative body (now abolished), comprising local-authority representatives, but this, if anything, had a restraining effect on the CLA, since it opposed increases in staffing and funding or enhanced powers for the local ombudsmen.[130] Under the revised arrangements the commissions are funded out of the Rate Support Grant in England and Wales. However, attempts have been made to preserve a measure of external accountability and expertise by requirements for the commissions' annual reports to be sent to local authority representatives and for the minister to appoint non-investigatory commissioners to advise on efficiency and good practice. The only use to date of this provision has been to add the Parliamentary Ombudsman to the membership of the CLA, but the government has accepted the case for advisory commissioners as a means of strengthening the accountability of the CLA.[131]

## The Role of Councillors

The CLA was originally conceived of as assisting 'members of local authorities to protect the rights and interests of members of the public vis-à-vis the authority', and was presented as a means of strengthening local democracy.[132] Several features of the original scheme point to sensitivity about the place of the CLA as regards elected members: the creation of the (now defunct) representative body, the exemption for policy decisions not

[129] *Government Response* (n. 113 above), 5–6. The review argued (at the CLA's own suggestion) that a link with the Select Committee would strengthen public accountability. It also pointed out that MPs currently use parliamentary debates to air constituents' grievances about individual councils, despite the lack of responsibility, and that the issue really turns on the powers and procedure adopted by the Committee, rather than on the principle as such: n. 76, esp. 22–3.

[130] The representative body was abolished in 1989, following the recommendations of the Widdicombe Committee (n. 114 above), which had pointed to the inconsistency of local authority representatives playing a part in deciding the budget of an office established to investigate their own failings: Widdicombe Report, 223.

[131] *Government Response* (n. 113 above), 5–6.

[132] Chipperfield, op. cit., 17, citing the notes on clauses for the Local Government Bill 1974 and the Second Reading Debate (HC Debs., vol. 864, col. 35 (12 Nov. 1973)).

involving maladministration, the lack of a final sanction, and the requirement that complaints come via a councillor, except where a councillor refused to forward a complaint.

The removal of the councillor filter in the 1988 Act[133] followed regular comment by the local ombudsmen drawing attention to the large numbers of complaints being received directly from the public. Various procedural stratagems were adopted to prevent complainants who mistakenly came direct to the CLA from being deterred by referral back to a councillor. The government rejected an earlier proposal for direct access made by the CLA in 1980. It was the arguments of the Widdicombe Committee which finally prevailed. Widdicombe pointed to widespread support, even among councillors, for direct access. It argued also that reluctance to implement the proposal due to a comparison between councillors and the filtering role of MPs under the Parliamentary Commissioner Act 1967 was misconceived; it ignored differences in function between the two types of representative, notably the fact that a councillor is legally a member of the body against whom the complaint is brought.[134]

This dual function of members as part of the 'executive' and as 'citizens' troubleshooter' can create obvious conflicts in the handling of complaints, where the councillor's political interests in maintaining working relations, supporting a particular policy, or avoiding public criticism of the authority may prevail over resolution of a grievance held by an individual elector.[135] Theoretically, the presence of opposition councillors (for whom these factors will weigh less heavily or may be positive incentives to take up a case) ought to counterbalance this tendency. However, this in turn presupposes a degree of political sophistication in the person making the complaint in recognizing the value of approaching a minority councillor. Moreover, it seems likely that other factors come into play—that members of the public are more likely to approach *their* councillor (i.e. for the ward in which they live), who may be from the majority party and may be reluctant, if unwilling to refer a complaint, to pass it on to another councillor representing a different ward, who might be prepared to do so. In any event, majority party councillors may have greater influence in bringing about an informal settlement in the early stages of a complaint. These criticisms may in future be less applicable following the creation of overview and scrutiny committees as part of the executive structure reforms.[136]

An added complication is that it may be a councillor's own action which is the cause of complaint. One situation in which this occurs fairly

133 LGA 1988, s. 29 and sched. 3 (amending LGA 1974, s. 26).

134 See Loughlin, op. cit., 101. The MP filter is now to be removed also: Parliamentary Commissioner (Amendment) Bill 1999–2000.

135 Cf. the comments of Lord Denning MR in *R v LCA for North and East Area of England ex p. Bradford MCC*, [1979] QB 287, 310.

136 See pp. 234–6 below.

frequently is where, in the course of participating in a decision to which a complainant subsequently objects, a councillor fails to declare a financial or personal interest in the outcome.[137] A failure to follow the National Code is treated as prima facie evidence of maladministration. Although the investigation, report, and recommendations (if any) will be against the authority, there is now also a statutory duty to name in the report any councillor found to have breached the code.[138] Conventionally, individuals (whether the complainant, officers, or councillors) are referred to anonymously in CLA reports, because of sensitivity about privacy and reputation, and so as to secure full cooperation from all involved. This practice also underlines the corporate responsibility of the council as a whole for any maladministration. The practice of naming councillors is a deliberate break with this approach in order to bring public pressure to bear on individual elected members. Not surprisingly, it has led to challenge by way of judicial review. In one case a councillor so named unsuccessfully argued that the Commissioner had failed to take account of the overriding need for a councillor's constituents to be represented when criticizing his decision not to declare a personal interest in a decision on a proposed road scheme (his son's house was on a road affected by four out of five possible routes under discussion).[139] In a second case, Liverpool

[137] At present failure to declare financial interests is also a criminal offence (see ss. 94–8, LGA 1972), and non-declaration of interests may otherwise vitiate a council decision: Cross and Bailey, *Local Government Law*, paras. 4–26ff. Sedley J has endorsed the practice of a councillor withdrawing altogether from the room while a matter in which he or she has an interest is under discussion, while recognizing that it is not a strict legal requirement: *R v SS for the Environment ex p. Kirkstall Valley Campaign Ltd.*, [1996] 3 All ER 304.

The Committee on Standards in Public Life (the Nolan Committee), in its Third Report, *Standards of Conduct in Local Goverment in England, Scotland and Wales*, Cm. 3702 (1997), recommended major reforms of the ethical framework for councillors and officers which have been largely accepted by the government (White Paper, *Modern Local Government: In Touch with the People*, Cm. 4014 (1998), ch. 6). It proposed that each council should promote its own code based on a statutory model, to be enforced by a local Standards Committee with power to investigate and discipline the councillor, subject to an appeal to an external Local Government Tribunal, which would have the power to disqualify a councillor from office. Failure to declare a pecuniary interest would cease to be a criminal offence. The Local Government Act 2000, Part III, largely follows these proposals, with some changes of terminology. Sections 49–51 provide for the drawing up of model and local codes of conduct to be binding on members (s. 52). Sections 53 and 54 govern the composition and powers of local Standards Committees with advisory, training, and monitoring functions and including an external element in the membership. The national framework involves the creation of a Standards Board and Ethical Standards Officers, who will have investigatory powers similar to the ombudsman's (ss. 62–5) but also the power to suspend councillors, subject to review by an Adjudication Panel (ss. 75–80). And see *Local Leadership, Local Choice*, Cm. 4298 (1999), ch. 4.

[138] LGA 1974, s. 30(3A). The LCA has published guidance: *Members' Interests (Advice on Complying with the National Code of Local Government Conduct)* (London, 1994). The Nolan Committee (preceding note) suggested that the ombudsman should no longer issue advice on councillors' conduct.

[139] *R v Commissioner for Local Administration ex p. Blakey*, unreported decision of 7 Mar. 1994, QBD.

City Council failed in its attempt to show that the ombudsman's finding of maladministration arising from the council's approval of a planning application to extend Liverpool Football Club's ground, Anfield, was unreasonable; the Commissioner had perceived breaches of the code in the failure of several councillors to withdraw although they were club season ticket holders, and found that the decision as a whole was heavily, and perhaps decisively, influenced by party political loyalty.[140]

The role of councillors remains problematic: prior to removal of the councillor filter the Widdicombe Committee found that only one-third of complaints made by members of the public (not formal complaints to the ombudsman) came via a councillor. Most were made to an officer.[141] This confirms the results of a study carried out by researchers at Sheffield University in the mid-1980s which suggested a figure of 27 per cent: the same study found that where the department concerned failed to give the complainant a satisfactory answer, an approach to an MP was four times as likely as an approach to a councillor.[142] One way in which councillors can be more centrally involved is through internal complaints mechanisms, and it is to these that the discussion now turns.

### Internal Resolution of Complaints

The Sheffield study found that it was then uncommon for complaints to be handled internally by the involvement of councillors in formal committees or sub-committees. Indeed, it is unclear whether to do so would be always a positive benefit, since the cause of the complaint may often be action or inaction by a particular councillor or policies approved by the ruling group of members. The principal argument for authority-wide internal complaint mechanisms rests upon independence in handling the complaint.[143] A majority of local authorities do already have a centralized system of tracking complaints to the Local Ombudsman through the chief executive's office, and it is probable that this brings pressure to bear upon departments to resolve complaints informally. The Sheffield study found that fewer than half of councils at that time operated internal complaints processes, and that most of those which did so did not generally publicize

[140] *R v LCA ex p. Liverpool CC*, [1999] 3 All ER 85. It is noteworthy that the government's proposals for reform of executive structures (pp. 230–2 below) single out regulatory and licensing decisions like planning applications and enforcement as unsuitable for determination under the new executive arrangements (including one-party 'cabinets') and suggest that they should remain the responsibility of the whole council or one of its committees: *Local Leadership, Local Choice* (1999), paras. 3.10 and 3.23.

[141] See Widdicombe Report, iii. 54.

[142] See Birkinshaw and Lewis, op. cit., 159.

[143] In addition there may be a case, along the lines of a Chipperfield recommendation discussed below, for systematic outside involvement in complaints processes.

these. Only a third of councils had adopted an earlier code of practice from the CLA on complaints procedures. The Sheffield study argued that most complaints should be resolved at departmental level, but that authorities should also appoint a complaints officer (located centrally within the chief executive's staff) to intervene and monitor the handling of complaints, with a complaints committee of councillors before which the complainant would have a right to a personal hearing and with powers to call for an in-depth examination of the issues. A number of local authorities have now also taken the initiative of establishing their own internal ombudsmen, with independent powers of investigation.

Discussion of internal complaints procedures has also revolved around the possible beneficial effects in informing the policy-making process. Birkinshaw and Lewis argue that they assist policy-making, through regular review of complaints.[144] However, Crawford suggests that internal resolution of complaints by an authority-wide procedure may result in inconsistencies, where policy is thrown over in individual cases because of the circumstances of the particular complaint.[145] The complaints mechanism may have a narrower focus (on the individual complainant), whereas the service committee taking the original decision will have been in a position to balance a variety of interests, especially those of third parties.

Crawford also notes the danger of conflict between a service department and the complaints officer or committee in internal arrangements. This is an objection only to certain types of internal complaints procedure in which there is power to override the substance of the original decision affecting the complainant, but not to those concerned with redressing defects in the original procedure. Moreover, a power to override in exceptional circumstances is not necessarily a bad thing—even conventional administrative law doctrine recognizes the need to allow some flexibility in self-made policies to allow for exceptional circumstances[146]—provided it does not simply occur merely *because* the complainant is determined or articulate. It can be argued also that if policies are to be set aside exceptionally in this way, it is preferable that the responsibility lies with elected members of the council, who are accountable for their decisions, rather than for it to occur at the dictate of an outside official.

The introduction of effective mechanisms for the internal handling of complaints has been a long-standing concern of the CLA.[147] Earlier reports commended particular authorities for good practice in this respect.[148] The

[144] See Birkinshaw and Lewis, op. cit., 160–1.

[145] Crawford, op. cit., 251–2.

[146] *R v Port of London Authority ex p. Kynoch*, [1919] 1 K.B. 176; *British Oxygen v Board of Trade*, [1971] AC 610.

[147] Described as one of the Commission's 'supporting objectives': *Annual Report for 1994/95*, 3.

[148] The *Annual Report for 1990/91*, 5, commended Derby City Council, Bedfordshire County Council, and Harlow District Council for creating internal ombudsmen; however,

rise in complaints systems of this kind has led to a change in the Commission's own practice in handling complaints: it now applies more rigorously the statutory bar under section 26(5) for declining jurisdiction where a grievance has not been raised internally with the authority.[149] One of the LCA's first codes of practice and guidance issued under the extended powers of the 1989 Act was *Devising a Complaints System* (1992). The code is a voluntary one, but the LCA has suggested that a failure by a council to deal effectively with complaints internally could, by itself, constitute evidence of maladministration. The code stresses the need for complaints systems to be accessible, easy to use, quick to resolve issues within set time limits, objective (this may involve investigation by officers outside the department complained against), confidential, and comprehensive. The code suggests a model procedure in which investigation by an officer outside the department follows on from investigation by a named officer within the department and from initial attempts at the resolution of the complaint.

Although the code has been praised as a practical guide to the implementation of a complaints system, nevertheless Birkinshaw identifies weaknesses in three areas. First, it omits positive guidance about assistance to the complainant in making the complaint. Secondly, the independence of the complaints mechanism could be strengthened by adopting a standard authority-wide system under the aegis of the chief executive and with councillor involvement (although provision would need to be made for minority party councillors). Finally, the code does not deal with the question of publication of the outcome of the complaint; this is necessary both for reasons of public accountability and to encourage other complainants.[150] The Chipperfield review suggested that the LCA's guidance also needed strengthening by incorporating an independent external element within council complaints procedures.[151]

Suggestions that internal complaints systems might, if strengthened, replace the investigatory role of the LCA were made in the prior options review commissioned by the government, which reported in 1995. Measures to reduce the time taken in cases where formal investigations were involved featured strongly in the recommendations at the second stage. However, it should be noted that the time taken to investigate is a product not solely of the CLA's internal efficiency (indeed, a pattern of generally falling costs per complaint investigated and higher output per

the Commission has also requested that such officials be given alternative titles to avoid confusing the public or suggesting that no further remedy outside the authority exists: see *Annual Report for 1991/92*, 44.

149 *Annual Report for 1992/93*, 7, following the practice introduced by Dr Yardley; see *Annual Report for 1991/92*, 12–13.

150 See Birkinshaw, op. cit., 101–3.

151 Chipperfield, op. cit., 24.

staff member suggests that efficiency gains have been made) but also of how quickly authorities respond, the resources given to the CLA (which have been falling), and how it allocates these between straightforward and complex cases.

The Chipperfield report's suggested solution to the CLA's growing workload and lengthening queue of complainants was that internal complaints mechanisms should be seen as the primary method of grievance redress. Accordingly, it envisaged a reduction in the role of the local ombudsman: the CLA would cease to be involved in investigations and focus instead on validating and monitoring councils' own complaints mechanisms. The report therefore proposed that local authorities be placed under a statutory duty to provide their own complaints systems, with elements of both internal and external review.[152] Internal complaints procedures should be supplemented by an external person of standing and integrity as an external reviewer in each locality, acting either as an external chairman of any review panel or as a single Adjudicator.[153] The advantages of a such a person over the CLA were said to be that, because of the local connection, the council would be more committed to dealing successfully with complaints, local citizens would have ready access, and a working relationship of trust would be built up with local politicians and chief officers. More store was set by cooperation and the integrity of the individual chosen than in formal guarantees of independent appointment, or powers to obtain information.[154] The risk that the adjudicator might become too close to the authority was not even mentioned in the report.

The monitoring body's role under this scheme would have been to validate the complaints system of each council against the statutory criteria. Refusal of the appropriate certificate by this body would have put the council concerned in default of its duty to maintain a complaints system.

[152] It can be argued that an embryonic statutory duty already exists in the requirement that every council appoint a 'monitoring officer', who is legally obliged to report to the council action or inaction likely to result in either unlawfulness or injustice through maladministration, or failure to follow a code of recommended practice. Local Government and Housing Act 1989, s. 5 (implementing Cm. 433, para. 5.9); see further Ch. 8.

[153] Chipperfield, op. cit., 25–6. This followed an earlier proposal from the Citizen's Charter Unit for Local Lay Adjudicators. The CLA endorsed the idea of settling disputes close to the source but argued: 'consideration of a case by a lay adjudicator should not be a prerequisite for referral or pre-empt referral to the Ombudsman, emphasis should be placed on the role of lay adjudicators as advisers to complainants, and it should be a standing instruction to lay adjudicators that, where speedy resolution of a grievance appears unlikely, they should advise complainants about the role of the Ombudsman' (CLA, *Annual Report for 1991/92*, 6). See also comments in Select Committee on the Parliamentary Commissioner for Administration, *Second Report for 1991/92: The Implications of the Citizen's Charter for the Work of the Parliamentary Commissioner*, HC 158 (1991–2), paras. 8 and 9.

[154] 'Adequate resources', 'full cooperation, including disclosure of papers, from any officers of the authority', and 'an undertaking to implement—except in very exceptional circumstances—any recommendations' are listed as criteria of any such system: Chipperfield, op. cit., 27.

In addition, the monitoring body would hear allegations that the complaints system had not worked properly in individual instances, with a power to order a rehearing of the complaint and compensation for time and trouble taken (but not, however, to resolve the complaint).

Arguably, the proposed roles of both the local adjudicator and the central body were muddled. In places the report suggested that, as well as carrying out investigation of complaints, the adjudicator might act as a local reviewer of the operation of complaints procedures in detailed spheres, such as the statutory complaints systems for social services functions. The central body's task seemed more onerous than Chipperfield recognized—a thorough annual inspection of the complaints systems of every local authority would presumably involve auditing complaints randomly or across a cross-section of functions, and reviewing the handling of individual complaints would have been nearly as time-consuming as an investigation proper. It is difficult to imagine many complainants having the determination to pursue their complaints to the local adjudicator, to the central body, and thereafter back to the internal adjudicator. Overall, the proposed procedure would have added considerable complexity for relatively modest advantage.

The preference for local complaints systems incorporating an external element was also supported by arguments about local democracy, and especially the role of local councillors. Although the report recognized the difficulties which led to removal of the councillor filter, it underplayed their significance. Somewhat inconsistently, it acknowledged the seminal change in public attitudes brought about by consumerism and yet continued to hark back to an imagined golden era in which councillors effectively acted as complaints chasers. This showed little understanding of the effect that the politicized environment of most local authorities has on councillors' capacity or willingness to take up individual grievances.[155]

The government rejected the proposal for introduction of local adjudicators on the grounds that there was still a need for an independent investigatory body, and that to impose on councils a new general duty to maintain an internal complaints system would be unduly rigid.[156] Nevertheless, the Commission has shown increasing interest in formalizing the interrelationship of complaints to it and internal procedures, as a way of pruning and prioritizing its own workload. It has recently conducted a study (the 'Ultimate Rung Pilot Study'[157]) of the effects of requir-

[155] Cf. the Widdicombe Committee, which stressed the desirability of internal settlement of complaints, but argued that referral through a councillor was 'neither a necessary nor a very direct way of achieving this': n. 114 above, para. 9.66.

[156] *Government Response* (n. 76), 3 and 4.

[157] *Annual Report for 1998/99*, 5. About 25% of councils in England participated. The CLA has decided in a modified form: Annual Report for 1999/2000, 5–6 to adopt the scheme.

ing complainants to exhaust councils' own complaints mechanisms before it commences an investigation.

The debate about the respective merits of internal and external systems of handling complaints is symptomatic of important underlying issues concerning the nature of local democracy. This can be illustrated by a key passage taken from the Chipperfield report:

> There is no way in which the current function of the CLA can be seen as to help councillors. The individual councillor not only has lost the right to filter, but he is not even asked for his views. The CLA sees its role as investigating and making judgement without necessarily taking account of the Councillor's views. In other words ... the CLA works to remove responsibility and authority from local authorities and councillors. This derogation from local democratic control ... can be justified only on the grounds that it is more desirable or convenient to right injustices in local authorities by imposing an outside authority than it is to make local democratic procedures work more effectively by giving them both a statutory basis and providing the motivation that only full responsibility can give. It can scarcely be justified on the grounds that local democracy is not of sufficient importance, or perhaps sufficiently trusted, to have the power and authority which would go with the right and duty to deal with injustices caused by its own maladministration.

This discussion of the democratic credentials of complaints systems takes us back to where we began.

## CONCLUSION

In this chapter we have seen the different interpretations given to consumerism within local democracy. At various points a tension between this movement and representative democracy through elected councillors has been identified. Hence, consumerist initiatives in education have been criticized by some commentators as undermining local democratic control. This is not surprising, since the avowed purpose of these reforms was to compensate for the perceived unresponsiveness of council bureaucracies to the needs and wishes of the users of local services. A less generous line of criticism sees consumerism as an attempt to increase the control of central government by imposing national standards or by creating a direct relationship between users of local services and national bodies.[158]

This line of criticism, however, fails to address Mill's insight, examined in Chapter 1, that there is a national interest in some services administered locally. Local authorities both govern *and* administer local services, and the distinction implies acceptable variations in the degree of discretion which they enjoy between different fields. Initiatives like the National

[158] I. Loveland 'Local Government', in R. Blackburn and R. Plant (eds.), *Constitutional Reform* (London, 1999).

Curriculum reflect the national interest in the successful delivery of a basic standard of service by all councils. Moreover, for all their inadequacies, measurements like performance indicators have demonstrated that local variations in services are often not the product of conscious local democratic decisions at all but have arisen by default. Properly used, these initiatives have the potential to improve local democracy by empowering local politicians and increasing transparency and accountability.

Nevertheless, consumerism offers an incomplete theory of local government. Even where there are identifiable individuals who receive public services the idea of consumer accountability is a seriously incomplete statement of their relationship to the local authority. Three clear reasons for this can be identified.

First, most local government functions concerning individuals are a complex mixture of rights, duties, and discretions. For example, parents owe duties in law to ensure that their children attend school or receive some equivalent form of education.[159] Social workers have long described those towards whom they have statutory functions as 'clients' in order to emphasize duties of confidentiality and professionalism, but this cannot obscure the involuntary context in which much of such contact occurs. The root difficulty in such cases is in emphasizing aspects of the relationship which are subsidiary to the compulsion which provides the context for the meeting of citizen and governmental official: describing people as consumers rings hollow when they have no choice about using the 'service' in question. At the most extreme, to describe those questioned or arrested by the police in terms of a customer–provider relationship would give a seriously misleading picture,[160] although, naturally, such people should be entitled to information, courtesy, and so on, as well as to their specific legal rights as suspects.

Secondly, frequently the council is required to balance individual rights against community interests: the rights of service users are not absolute. A straightforward illustration is the way in which physical constraints on the size and location of a school, infant class sizes, and selection policies may inhibit parental choice.[161] Thirdly, consumer-oriented rights disguise the fact that political choices may often have to be made between the interests of different groups of public service users, for example, between highway users and school users in the location of a school crossing, and so on. For all these reasons consumerism is incapable of providing a complete theory of government (whether locally or centrally) and is best understood as a difference of emphasis.

[159] Education Act 1996, s. 7.

[160] It is more applicable where the police are dealing with the public as victims of crime or as potential witnesses.

[161] These are relevant factors under the Schools Standards and Framework Act 1998, ss. 86 and 93 and sched. 23.

Part III

# Political Leadership and Decision-Making

# 6

# *Party Groups, Councillors, and the Law*

## INTRODUCTION

Perhaps surprisingly, little attention has been directed to the legal implications of the 'internal' politics of local authorities, notwithstanding that it is precisely because each local authority is a political institution that central–local tensions may arise. The organization of party groups is part of the legal *sub rosa* of local government. Although judges occasionally refer to the inevitability of party politics on the rare occasions when it does become legally visible, more commonly this factor lurks in the background but unmentioned. This chapter aims to redress the balance by focusing explicitly on the legal position of the party political group and its place within the 'internal' politics of local government.

First, a brief historical survey. Suspicion of highly organized party caucuses within local government is often associated with the rise of radical municipal socialism during the 1980s. However, a degree of party organization is much older. Perhaps the earliest example is that of Joseph Chamberlain's Birmingham Liberal Association, the extent of whose electoral organization in 1868 in proposing a programme of municipal collectivism made it a target of suspicion.[1] The earliest documented example of party group *meetings* seems to be the adoption of the practice by the Liberal–Labour Progressive Party in the London County Council in 1890.[2]

While it is generally accepted that in the 1970s and 1980s local government became more 'politicized', many of the features of this process had been present long before; the contrast with earlier periods is probably in the intensity of party politics and political conflict, rather than the emergence of a wholly new phenomenon. An analysis by Gyford, Leach, and Game suggests that the process can be seen in five overlapping stages stretching back to the introduction of modern local government in the nineteenth century.[3] The first phase (immediately following the introduction of the 1835 reforms) in which labels such as Tories, Whigs, Conservatives, Liberals, Radical, Chartists, Improvers, and Economizers overlapped and varied according to local circumstances (a period of

[1] J. Gyford, S. Leach, and C. Game, *The Changing Politics of Local Government* (London, 1989), 9.

[2] K. Young, 'Party Politics in Local Government: An Historical Perspective', in Widdicombe Report, research vol. iv (London, 1986), 81–105.

[3] See Gyford et al., op. cit., 6–20.

*diversity*) gave way by the 1860s to a period of *crystallization*, which by the 1870s had produced clear divisions at local level between Conservatives and Liberals. The later emergence of the Labour Party as a local electoral force produced a *realignment* in which many Liberals and Conservatives formed an anti-socialist coalition under various labels. The period following the Second World War was one of *nationalization*, in which the influence of the central party machines spread to local government, but also one of relative stability and consensus in which administrators and professional groups dominated the decision-making process, rather than elected politicians. The roots of the period of *reappraisal*, with its overt politicization, can be traced back to the systematic reforms of local government implemented in the period 1972–4. This period was characterized by several trends: a strengthening of party politics in local government (one symptom was the replacement of many 'Independent' councillors with those of an overt Conservative affiliation); a reassertion of political control over officers and administrators (perhaps traceable to a disillusionment with the technocracy of the 1960s which was, among other things, seen as responsible for the social disaster of high-rise housing); and formalization of the party structure within local government (for example, in relation to party groups). This period, of course, also produced a polarization both between and within the two main political parties, reflecting developments on the national political scene post-1979.

It was events during this last phase which gave rise to the establishment of the Widdicombe Committee.[4] The major themes of the Committee's report were the prevalence of politics in local government and the failure of the existing legal structure to accommodate it. Widdicombe found that some 85 per cent of councillors were elected under a party political label and that 84 per cent of councils were under the control of one party or a coalition of parties.[5] Despite this reality, local government law largely leaves party politics behind at the ballot box. Elsewhere it is regarded as

[4] The terms of reference were: 'To enquire into practice and procedures governing the conduct of local authority business in Great Britain, with particular reference to: the rights and responsibilities of elected members; the respective roles of elected members and officers; the need to clarify the limits and conditions governing discretionary spending by local authorities and to make any necessary recommendations for strengthening the democratic process': see *The Conduct of Local Authority Business*, Cmnd. 9797 (1986), 17.

On the establishment of the Committee, see: Gyford et al., op. cit., 276ff.; on the report: Loughlin, (1987) 50 MLR 64; McAuslan, [1987] PL 154; R. Rhodes, 'The Reform of Local Government: Revival of an Industry', 65 Public Administration 193; and S. Leach, 'Strengthening Local Democracy? The Government's Response to Widdicombe', ch. 6 in J. Stewart and G. Stoker, *The Future of Local Government* (Basingstoke, 1989).

[5] Cmnd. 9797 (1986), paras. 2.37–40. There still remains, however, a minority of councils where formal groupings do not exist and where councillors do not stand at all under party affiliations. Widdicombe's findings on the extent of political influence and processes were broadly confirmed in a follow-up study: K. Young and M. Davies, *The Politics of Local Government Since Widdicombe* (York, 1990).

an 'alien presence'.[6] As we have seen in Chapter 2, local authorities are statutory corporations. Elections are the method by which the members of the corporation are chosen. From the corporate nature of local government follow the ultra vires doctrine and the prescribed method for decision-making by the authority: by a majority vote of councillors attending a meeting. The Act permits delegation by councillors of their functions and powers to smaller groups (committees or sub-committees) or to officers of the council.[7] What this model obscures is that individual councillors (especially committee chairmen) may wield much more power than their single (or casting) vote would suggest, that officers may be the proponents of policy rather than the elected members, or may serve the majority group rather than the council as a whole, and, most important of all, that the system may be dominated at all points by highly organized groups of councillors, voting *en bloc* in accordance with a pre-arranged strategy.

As we shall see, the Widdicombe report led to some safeguards being put into place such as the abolition of 'twin-tracking', the imposition of political restrictions on officers, and political balance requirements on committees. Other recommendations were not implemented, such as recognition of the de facto power of committee chair-holders and the proposal that party groups be recognized for policy development, but were not to take decisions in the name of the council. These were an affirmation of political realities and a healthy attempt to accommodate them within the legal structures. Instead, the matters were left in an uneasy compromise where some notorious abuses were outlawed, but the the law's only positive concern with party groups was to ensure proportionate representation on council committees.

One notable respect in which the political landscape has changed since the Widdicombe report is the growth of local authorities in which there is no overall political control (so-called 'hung' or 'balanced' councils). In the early 1980s the growth of 'hung' councils was due to the rise of the then SDP. After a period in which the number declined, coinciding with a revival in Conservative electoral fortunes, the collapse of the Conservative local vote in 1990s produced a similar situation. The implications of 'hung' councils are discussed at several points in this chapter and the next.

Although the account which follows deals with many of the attempts to suppress malpractice associated with party groups in local government, it is worth emphasizing some of their positive attributes also.[8] The first is a degree of organization, coordination, and predictability in political decision-making. This follows from the extent to which groups are disciplined through use of the party whip: a phenomenon which varies between the

[6] Widdicombe Report, para. 4.17.

[7] LGA 1972, s. 101. See pp. 208–10 below.

[8] Cf. C. Copus, 'The Party Group: A Barrier to Democratic Renewal', (1999) 25 LGS 76, 80.

parties and also between different local authorities. Effective political control may provide a clear sense of direction to a council's policies, enhance the accountability of the authority by making councillors, rather than officers, not just legally but factually responsible for policy-making and implementation, and so give the electorate a clear choice of local policies. The party group may also allow councillors to debate policy in a 'safe' forum and allow for the development of a holistic, corporate approach to issues facing the council.

The disadvantages of such groups are associated with the secrecy which shrouds their deliberations: group discussions may also be without the benefit of officer advice[9] and may exclude persons who have a statutory right to be consulted or to object to a proposed policy, for example, in the planning realm. Defenders of this system argue that policy formulation within a political process cannot be fully carried out in public, and that provided the formal and public meetings of the council and its committees give adequate opportunity for minority parties to criticize the policy proposed, then democratic legitimacy has been observed. However, the operation of groups presents a misleading picture to the public of where responsibility lies for the council's decisions. It is this aspect above all which has led to the present government's proposals (discussed in Chapter 7) to legitimize political executives. However, we cannot appreciate their significance (or potential limitations) except against the background of a critical account of the current position.

The structure of party groups and their relationships with each other vary according to local political circumstances, but each of the main national political parties does have standing arrangements to govern the position of its local councillors.[10] These ensure loyalty to the group and public cohesion, and concern issues such as group voting, the party whip, speaking and voting in debates, and group disciplinary procedures. Historically, the most formal arrangements have been those of Labour groups, with the Conservative and Liberal Democrat approaches described as more flexible. Councillors of all parties agree to accept the standing orders before being nominated for office. Whatever the contractual status of these arrangements, in practice they exert a powerful influence. Councillors' first loyalty is to the group rather than to the electorate, and the majority party group is the most important deliberative forum in most councils.[11]

[9] See p. 252 below *re* officer attendance at political group meetings.

[10] For a detailed account, see C. Copus, 'The Party Political Group: Model Standing Orders and a Disciplined Approach to Local Representation', (1999) 25 LGS 17. Note, however, that revision of model standing orders will inevitably follow the introduction of new executive structures: the Labour Party, for instance, has approved 3 alternate sets for use with each of the new executive models.

[11] In the past the involvement of non-councillors in party group meetings was a significant issue also for Labour groups. In the 1980s party members who were not councillors could be

Two matters in which the role of the group is crucial should be mentioned at this point. Committee chairmen will be effectively chosen in party-dominated councils through a vote at the majority group meeting; often the Leader of the group may have considerable influence in the choice.[12] Allocation of individual councillors to committees will be carried out effectively by the group in consultation with the individuals concerned (who are generally invited to express preferences to the group about the committees they wish to serve on). These preferences will then be considered, commonly by a smaller group of senior members of the party group, before being submitted for approval to the full group.[13]

The discussion which follows assesses the legal implications of party groups from three perspectives: first, the relationship of the group to the Council as a whole; secondly, the position of the individual councillor; thirdly, relationships between political groups, especially in 'hung' or 'balanced' councils. The relationship of the group and the public as regards local election manifestos and political advertising has already been discussed in Chapter 3.

## THE GROUP AND THE COUNCIL

As already noted, whereas de jure the executive power of a local authority is vested corporately in all the councillors, de facto it is vested in a majority party group, where one exists. The Widdicombe Committee found that the frequency of group meetings was in many cases determined by the need to decide upon group tactics prior to the council meeting.[14]

Consequently, in many cases the formal and effectual decisions of the council and of committees and sub-committees may amount to little more than a confirmation of those previously arrived at in a private group meeting. Despite this danger, the law makes a (somewhat artificial) distinction between the group and the council at a number of points.

involved in drawing up the local manifesto, at group meetings, and in decisions about nomination for positions (such as committee chair-holders) within the Council, or within the group (such as Leader or Secretary). This relationship with non-councillors caused stress, especially in authorities such as Liverpool during the 1980s, where the majority group on the council was in effect bound by the decisions of the local district party (resulting in subsequent criticism during an internal Labour inquiry into the running of the Liverpool District Council Labour Party): see Gyford et al., op. cit., 162–7. An arrangement under which a group of councillors acted on instruction from the local party would almost certainly be unlawful (see *R v Waltham Forest Borough Council ex p. Baxter*, [1988] 2 WLR 257; and p. 196 below) on the principle that the councillors concerned would no longer be exercising their legal discretion.

[12] See Gyford et al., op. cit., 192.

[13] Ibid. 191–2; and see the discussion of the political balance requirements (p. 194 below).

[14] Widdicombe, research vol. i, Cmnd. 9798 (1986), 25 and 82. The extent of group cohesion in voting at meetings is considered below.

The gulf between the deliberations of a party group and the formal decisions of the council has been underlined in cases where an attempt has been made to impugn the council's decision because of some factor relating to the group's motivation. The tendency of the courts has been to refuse to lift the corporate veil so as to impute to the council the activities or motives of the majority group. For example, in *Armagh District Council v Fair Employment Agency for Northern Ireland*[15] an appeal against a finding of religious discrimination by the council contrary to the Fair Employment (Northern Ireland) Act 1976 was upheld by the Northern Ireland Court of Appeal on the grounds that an agreement in a party group by the majority (Unionist) councillors to support the job application of a Protestant candidate did not amount to a discriminatory 'arrangement'[16] made by an employer. Lord Lowry LCJ, giving the leading judgment, argued that to hold otherwise was to confuse the group with the council: it was the council which was the 'employer' but the council had not made the agreement.[17] Similarly, in *Pickwell v Camden London Borough Council*[18] an action brought by a district auditor for a declaration failed. The auditor argued that a local pay settlement reached by the council with NUPE following a decision to negotiate taken in the majority (Labour) party group was 'contrary to law' as being excessive. Forbes J pointed out that a major obstacle to the district auditor's case was that the pay settlement had been approved by the council, and that a different motivation might be imputed to the council's decision than to the group's:

> It should not be thought, of course, when virtually all local authorities operate on the principle that the councillors owing allegiance to one political party or another meet in advance of council meetings to discuss policy questions, that a decision by a controlling party group can always be followed in Council without considering afresh whatever matters are relevant; the fact that a decision has been taken in party group to do something which is unlawful does not alter its legality.[19]

In another case it was held that the discussion of a proposed development in a political meeting of the majority group of councillors did not prevent the council as a whole from subsequently considering the application fairly.[20] Woolf J found that a political predisposition towards granting planning permission did not amount to bias in the treatment of the application:

> I would have thought it was almost inevitable, now that party politics play so large a part in local government, that the majority group on a council would decide on

[15] [1984] IRLR 234.

[16] Fair Employment (Northern Ireland) Act 1976, s. 17(a)(i).

[17] The complainant had failed, at first instance, to show that the actual refusal to offer employment by the council was discriminatory, and therefore was left to rely on the discriminatory 'arrangement' argument.

[18] [1983] 1 QB 962.

[19] Ibid. 996.

[20] *R v Amber Valley DC ex p. Jackson*, [1984] 3 All ER 501.

the party line in respect of the proposal. If this was to be regarded as disqualifying the district council from dealing with the planning application, then if that disqualification is to be avoided the members of the planning committee at any rate will have to adopt standards of conduct which I suspect will be almost impossible to achieve in practice.[21]

He emphasized the need for the matter to be dealt with on its planning merits, but was unwilling to infer any impropriety in the councillors' behaviour. This pragmatic approach has much to commend it; planning, like other functions, has been entrusted to bodies representing the local community which are inherently political; the courts should only interfere when there is evidence that party politics prevents proper consideration of the relevant considerations. However, one aspect of the background to the litigation leaves a nagging doubt: the party group meeting at which policy was determined was that of the *county* Labour group; it involved members of the Labour-controlled County Council (who were separately found to have breached the rules on natural justice in their handling of the planning aspects of the application[22]) and non-councillors. There was a danger in this instance of the district councillors being bound to implement policies by the vote of a party group whose composition did not strictly reflect their own responsibility to the electorate.

Although the effect of these decisions is to maintain a distinction between the de jure and the de facto seats of executive power in a local authority,[23] there are limited exceptions where the line has been blurred. In some instances litigation has been brought effectively to challenge the council's decision against named members of the majority group,[24] without any objection that the wrong defendant has been chosen. It has also been held that the actions of individual councillors in causing a local authority to be in contempt of court may make the councillors themselves liable in contempt.[25] This principle appears, however, to be based on

[21] Ibid. 509.

[22] See *Steeples v Derbyshire CC*, [1984] 3 All ER 468, in which the involvement of the County Council as landowner through a development contract for the same project ( a major theme park) was held to have produced a conflict of interest, leading to a breach of natural justice. In *ex p. Jackson* Woolf J distinguished the position of the county and district councils because of the absence of a contractual or financial interest in the development on the part of the latter: [1984] 3 All ER 501, 508.

[23] See also *ex p. Baxter*, text at n. 65ff. below.

[24] See: *Ettridge v Morrell*, (1986) 85 LGR 100 and *Barrs v Bethell*, [1982] Ch. 294, where the council was also joined as a defendant. Both cases were argued on the point of whether the proceedings against the council were public or private in nature.

[25] *R v London Borough of Poplar* (No.2), [1922] KB 95; but see *Webster v Southwark LBC*, [1983] 1 QB 698 (in which the Poplar case was not cited): 2 councillors, constituting a sub-committee, failing to act in accordance with a declaration against the council were not in contempt since the declaration was not a coercive order of the court.

simple efficacy; if it were not so, the court would have no effective means of enforcing its orders against a corporation.[26]

A more notable exception was the ruling of the High Court in the *Westminster* case that the Leader of the council (Dame Shirley Porter) and her deputy were guilty of wilful misconduct in steering the Conservative group's 'designated sales' (or 'homes for votes') policy to adoption for electoral advantage.[27] The court at first instance refused to allow the appellants to shelter behind the distinction in law between their motives and those of other members of the Conservative group or of the council. Applying a commonsense understanding they had 'caused' the policy to be adopted by others, through the party whip and the group, which resulted in loss to the council. However, the Court of Appeal allowed their appeals on different grounds,[28] and the judges took a less high-minded attitude to party group politics. For Kennedy LJ,

> In local, as in national politics, many if not most decisions carry an electoral price tag, and all politicians are aware of it. In most cases they cannot seriously be expected to disregard it, but they know that if the action which they take is to withstand scrutiny (to be 'judge-proof') there must be sound local government reasons, not just excuses. . . .

Schiemann LJ put it more strongly still:

> It is legitimate for councillors to desire that their party should win the next election. Our political system works on the basis that they desire that because they think that the policies to which their party is wedded are in the public interest and will require years to be achieved. There is nothing disgraceful or unlawful in councillors having that desire. For this court to hold otherwise would depart from our theory of democracy and current reality.

The 'unreality' of eliminating electoral calculation was demonstrated by an example given at a later point in his judgment:

> For a council to decide to lower council house rents with a view to pleasing council house tenants or to decide to lower rates with a view to be pleasing ratepayers

[26] However, *In the matter of an application by David Somerville Cook and others* (No. 2) (unreported judgment of Hutton J sitting in the Northern Ireland High Court, Queen's Bench Division, 30 Apr. 1986) a fine of £25,000 for contempt of court was imposed on the Belfast City Council following its non-compliance with an earlier order of the Court of Appeal ([1986] 1 NIJB 43) to recommence the holding of council and committee meetings suspended in protest at the Anglo-Irish Agreement. In recognizing that the responsibility was really that of the majority Unionist group of councillors, the judge commented: 'In my opinion this is a case in which the legal concept that a city council is separate and distinct from its councillors creates a situation of some artificiality. . .' Hutton J recognized that contempt proceedings could have been brought against the majority group councillors personally if the applicants (themselves Alliance councillors) had chosen to do so.

[27] *Porter and Others v Magill*, (1998) 96 LGR 157, QBD; for discssion of other aspects see pp. 124–7 above.

[28] *Porter v Magill*, [2000] 2 WLR 1420.

is not illegal provided these decisions involve no other element of illegality such as not providing for a balanced budget. These voter-pleasing decisions are lawful in my judgment even if one of the motivating factors in the minds of the councillors who vote for them is the desire to be re-elected and the consciousness that their wards contain a significant number of electors of the category which the relevant decision is designed to benefit.

Since the operation of party group meetings might be thought to make the council's meetings a mere formality, one response might be to confer lawful power upon the majority group. Attempts to acknowledge the reality of political decision-making by bringing the group's deliberations into the formal council arena have, however, proved legally problematic. In *R v Sheffield City Council ex p. Chadwick*,[29] Woolf J held that there was no power to delegate to a sub-committee of the Council the working out of a policy which a group of councillors, rather than the council as a whole, might wish to adopt. The facts were that the policy committee of the Council had a number of sub-committees, each comprising different single-party groups of councillors, and where officers' advice upon the possible implementation of group policy by the council could be discussed. In one of these, the Budget Sub-Committee, the majority (Labour) group's policy concerning the setting of the rate for the coming financial year was under discussion. The leader of the Liberal opposition group on the council was refused access to the meetings and papers of the Budget Sub-Committee, and then applied for judicial review of that refusal. Woolf J held[30] that since the councillor had a 'need to know' he was entitled to the information and to attend. The council had wrongly taken into account political considerations in refusing access to the sub-committee, because it had given to the sub-committee a party-political task which could not lawfully be delegated to it.[31] The fact that other party groups had the same facilities, that the minutes of the sub-committee went to the Policy Committee, and that the purpose was to enable policy to be formulated with the benefit of officer advice (rather than in group meetings without it),[32] did not prevent the delegation being held ultra vires. The effect of *ex p. Chadwick* was to drive party group policy formulation away from the formal structures of the council. The decision did not of itself prevent the use of one-party committees and sub-committees to implement the previously agreed policies of the council as a whole. One-party committees are now prohibited under explicit legislation, requiring political balance,[33] and so it is not legally necessary to rely

[29] (1985) 84 LGR 563.

[30] Following *ex p. Gamper*; see n. 40 below.

[31] See esp. *ex p. Chadwick* (n. 29 above), 571–2.

[32] All these points were made in an affidavit submitted by Cllr. David Blunkett (leader of the Labour group), who argued that the sub-committee's arrangement made for more open decision-making overall; see ibid. pp. 569–70.

[33] See pp. 194–5 below.

on *Chadwick* to restrain their operation. However, should any of the experimental models proposed, under which the group is permitted to act as a legal executive for the council,[34] be adopted, *Chadwick* suggests that explicit statutory authorization would be necessary; a simple exception to the political balance requirements would not be sufficient.

No mechanism exists for excluding opposition members from the full council meeting as such, but prior to 1989 they could be excluded from deliberations in effect by the delegation of functions under section 101 of the Local Government Act 1972 to committees or sub-committees comprising solely majority group members.[35] The law treated the political composition of council committees as a matter for the council itself, and so allowed for the unhindered operation of political factors below the level of legal visibility. This was in keeping with the general non-recognition of party politics as an important consideration. Consequently, one-party committees were held to be lawful under section 101.[36] Despite this, the Widdicombe Committee found the practice less widespread than might have been expected. In authorities under majority party control, some 76 per cent had no one-party committees and 63 per cent had no one-party sub-committees.[37] Even those authorities which did have one-party committees generally had only one such committee or sub-committee, usually the policy and resources committee. Research indicated, though, that it was much more common for the majority group to take chairmanship of and a majority on all committees and sub-committees.[38] These phenomena were probably due to a common understanding and exercise of self-restraint on the part of the major parties. However, it was also clear that, even before the introduction of the political balance requirements, in legal

[34] See p. 230 below, on delegation.

[35] The law now requires committees and sub-committees to reflect the political balance of the full council: p. 194 below.

[36] *R v Rushmoor BC ex p. Crawford*, *The Times*, 28 Nov. 1981, a decision which Forbes J reached 'with regret'. However, he found the council's decision to be contrary to standing orders which did not permit the suspending of committee members. The council had suspended members of the Labour group from the planning committee because of their refusal to apologize for or disassociate themselves from comments by a Labour councillor that a development application had been handled unlawfully by the ruling Conservative group. Perhaps surprisingly, Forbes J held that suspension as a form of punishment for party political reasons was not unreasonable in itself. It follows that if the standing orders had allowed for suspension, the council would in his view have acted lawfully (on the law at that time), despite the dominant political motive of the Conservative majority. However, suspension of opposition councillors for political reasons has been declared unlawful in a series of cases from Northern Ireland. See: *In Re McAnulty's Application*, [1985] NI 37 (suspension of People's Democracy Party councillor from Belfast City Council until he withdrew remark offensive to Unionist majority group unlawful); *In Re French and Other Applications*, [1985] NI 310 (exclusion by Unionist majority of Sinn Fein councillors until making a declaration renouncing violence ultra vires); *Re Curran and McCann's Application*, [1985] NI 261 (delegation of all council business to a committee comprising all councillors except members of Sinn Fein).

[37] Widdicombe Report, research vol. i, 34.

[38] Ibid. 33–4.

terms there was little advantage for a majority group in totally excluding the opposition from a committee or sub-committee. The confidentiality of one-party committees was breached by the entitlements of opposition members to information and to attend as observers, even though not formally members of the committee. Such rights arise under the statutory rights for councillors to inspect documents in the possession or under the control of the council, relating to business to be transacted at a meeting,[39] and even where those statutory rights can be lawfully excluded, a councillor may still have entitlements under the common law because of the 'need to know' with respect to his or her public duties.[40]

Although the Widdicombe Committee considered that the council as a whole rather than the majority party should continue to be the forum in which, as a matter of law, decisions are taken,[41] it nevertheless recommended some adjustment of the position of party groups. It suggested, for instance, a statutory requirement to adopt standing orders to allocate committee and sub-committee places according to the political balance of the council as a whole.[42] However, realizing that the effect might be to drive de facto decision-making outside the council, the Committee also recommended that deliberative committees (those with *no* decision-making powers) should be exempt from the requirement and also removed from the ambit of the public's and councillors' rights to attend and to have access to documents.[43] The result, if implemented, would have been that while decision-making by local authorities was subject to stronger safeguards, party groups would have been able to formulate their policy in council committees with the benefit of officer advice, if they so chose.[44] The committee justified this apparently backward step pragmatically:

[39] This right is subject to narrower exclusions than those applying to the general public: s. 100F of the LGA 1972, inserted by s. 1 of the 1985 Act. Furthermore, the rights of the public to attend committee and sub-committee meetings and to have access to documents relating to them granted by the Local Government (Access to Information) Act 1985 will apply in the absence of a resolution excluding the public reciting a category of 'exempt information' under schedule 12A of the Act. Confidentiality due to political considerations is not in itself one of the permissible reasons; see further Ch. 3.

[40] Held to give entitlements both to documents and to attend a one-party sub-committee of which the councillor was not a member in: *R v Hackney London Borough Council ex p. Gamper*, [1985] 1 WLR 1229 and *R v Sheffield City Council ex p. Chadwick* (see n.29 above).

[41] Widdicombe Report, paras. 5.30–5.

[42] Ibid., paras 5.46–5.45. Cf. the basis for apportionment of seats on joint authorities under the LGA 1985, s. 33.

[43] Ibid., paras. 5.63–71.

[44] The committee recognized, however, that policy formulation by groups would also continue outside the formal council structure (para. 4.37). It recommended that the Chief Executive should have a statutory role as referee to ensure balance between groups (ibid. paras. 6.154 and 6.155). Widdicombe also considered and rejected various models for shifting altogether the legal responsibility for decisions from the whole council to the majority group: see ibid. paras. 5.14ff.

It is a simple reality, which no legislation can alter, that politicians will develop policy options in confidence before presenting their final choice for public decision. We do not think this unreasonable. If the law prevents them from conducting such discussions in private in formal committees, then they will conduct them less formally elsewhere.[45]

This modest attempt to adjust the legal structures to accommodate the political reality of group decisions fell victim to the Conservative government's suspicion of local politics. The government's response argued for retaining the separation between group and council. It therefore proposed that groups of leading members from the majority party should retain their informal status, but that officers' contractual conditions should be amended to clear up any doubts about the legality of officer advice to such meetings.[46] Later proposals for liberalizing one-party committees on an experimental basis from a Department of the Environment working party met an equally sceptical fate.[47] As we see, however, in Chapter 7, the present government's proposals for political executives will allow for the creation of one-party cabinets in the context of introducing an executive/scrutiny division among councillors.

One legislative outcome from Widdicombe was the introduction of political balance requirements for all committees, whether deliberative or advisory. These require membership of its committees and sub-committees to be reviewed where a council is divided into political groups.[48] One-party committees are forbidden, but the majority party must be given a majority of seats on committees; beyond this, so far as practicable, strict proportionality should be attained in the overall division of committee places and, thereafter, in the allocation to each particular committee.[49] The test for the existence of a political group under the regulations is a notice delivered to the council's 'proper officer' signed by two or more councillors stating that they wish to be so regarded, and giving the name of the

[45] Ibid., para. 5.63.

[46] *Government Response to The Conduct of Local Authority Business*, Cmnd. 9797 (1986), para. 2.17.

[47] See p. 228 below.

[48] LGHA, s. 15. Regulations also require a council to review the political composition of its committees annually (timed to follow the May local government elections) and after changes in the composition of the political groups on the council: The Local Government (Committees and Political Groups) Regulations 1990, SI 1553/1990, para. 17.

One important exception to the political balance requirements is the position of area committees and sub-committees; provided the committee covers no more than two-fifths of the authority's area or population and all the members are the relevant elected ward representatives, the committee may operate on a one-party basis: reg. 16 A (introduced by the Local Government (Committees and Political Groups) (Amendment) Regulations 1991, SI 1991/1398); see further discussion of neighbourhood and area committees, p. 215 below.

[49] LGHA 1989, s. 15(5).

group and its leader.[50] A similar notice signed by the majority of the group can effect changes either to the leadership or to the group by expelling a member.[51] The leader of the group is recognized under these provisions as having standing to express the wishes of the group (but may be overruled by the majority of members in the event of conflict),[52] and to nominate members for committee vacancies allocated to the group under the statutory formula.[53] One consequence of these reforms is that the group now formally controls the allocation of individual councillors to committees, rather than the council.

An apparent attempt to circumvent the political balance requirements by use of a 'working party' comprising solely majority group councillors and officers to 'consider', 'review', and 'report' on homelessness issues to a council's housing committee received a strong rebuke from Sedley J in the High Court.[54] After finding that this homelessness board had been behaving as though it were a committee with delegated powers (something which was plainly ultra vires), he described it as a 'usurpation of power'.[55] The council had made attempts to conceal the 'policies' operated by the board. The access to information provisions only apply to committees and sub-committees[56] and the Board was neither; referring to the secrecy surrounding its activities, the judge characterized it as 'government by stealth, the antithesis of democracy and openness. . . . .'.[57]

## THE GROUP AND THE COUNCILLOR

Most rights and duties in local government law are conferred upon councillors collectively in the guise of the corporation. There are a few isolated instances such as rights of access to documents[58] and the rules requiring the declaration of pecuniary interests which deal with councillors as individuals.[59] The political group, however, receives no statutory recognition apart from the question of the distribution of committee places. The consequence is that whereas the relationship between the individual councillor and the council is recognized in a minor way so as to prevent abuses on either side, the relationship between the councillor and the group is largely unregulated.

[50] The Local Government (Committees and Political Groups) Regulations 1990, SI 1553 (1990), para. 8.

[51] Ibid., paras. 8(5) and 10 (d), respectively.

[52] Ibid., para. 13.

[53] Ibid., para. 14.

[54] *R v LB of Tower Hamlets ex p. Khalique*, (1994) 26 HLR 517; see also p. 210 below.

[55] Ibid. 526.

[56] Ch. 3 above.

[57] *R v LB of Tower Hamlets ex p. Khalique*, (1994) 26 HLR 517, 525.

[58] See pp. 221–4 below.

[59] Ss. 94–8 LGA 1972.

The chief issue is to what extent the individual may be compelled to follow the party line. The Widdicombe Committee found that some 37 per cent of party groups always voted together in council meetings whereas 11 per cent did so in committee. However, these figures mask the stronger group cohesion of Labour Party groups (59 per cent of such always voted together in council) as opposed to Conservative groups (where the corresponding figure was 23 per cent). The committee also found that 49 per cent of Labour groups never departed from the decision previously agreed in group whereas this was true of only 9 per cent of Conservative groups.[60] The conclusion that Labour Party groups appear much more cohesive than other parties is also borne out in the national arrangements the major parties make for their groups in local authorities.[61] The Widdicombe Committee raised three areas of concern in relation to these standing orders and the extent to which these are adhered to in practice: the relationship of party groups to the local political party, the attendance of non-councillors at group meetings, and the disclosure of councillors' pecuniary interests at group meetings. In all these cases it concluded that legislation was not apt, but that the parties themselves should enforce stricter standards.[62] Interestingly, although the committee recognized that councillors are 'not free-standing individuals',[63] it did not regard the intrusion of *group* discipline as a matter of concern. So far as discipline of recalcitrant councillors by the *local party* was concerned, the committee rejected as impracticable the suggestion of a specific legal prohibition of the practice of the local party mandating the party group of councillors.[64]

The Court of Appeal considered the implications of group voting in *R v Waltham Forest Borough Council ex p. Baxter*.[65] The case involved a challenge by way of judicial review to the rate set by the council on the grounds that six or seven councillors who had unsuccessfully opposed the scale of increase adopted in the majority party group meeting subsequently voted in favour of it in the council meeting. The controlling Labour group on the council had held a meeting prior to the relevant council meeting and there agreed by a majority (the six or seven voting against) to support a rate increase of between 56 and 62 per cent. The whip system in operation under the Standing Orders for Labour Groups on local authorities required members of the group to refrain from speaking or voting against the group at the council meeting unless a matter had been left to a free vote. The making of the rate was not a free vote. The appellants contended that in voting for the rate increase the six or seven councillors had abdi-

[60] Widdicombe Report, research vol. i: *The Political Organisation of Local Authorities*, Cmnd. 9798 (1986), 27–31.

[61] See Copus, 'The Party Political Group'.

[62] Widdicombe Report, para. 6.79.

[63] Ibid., para. 6.60.

[64] Ibid., para. 6.72.

[65] [1988] 2 WLR 257.

cated their responsibility and toed the party line. This amounted, it was alleged, to fettering their discretion.

The Court of Appeal unanimously rejected the argument both on evidence as to why the individual councillors concerned voted as they did[66] and on the general basis that the existence of party whips did not invalidate the council decision-making. To hold otherwise would, as Sir John Donaldson MR recognized, be to fly in the face of procedures in general use throughout the country (the court received in evidence extracts from the Widdicombe report).[67] This shows a realistic preparedness to accept party-political activity in local government. In Sir John Donaldson's view the party whip in question was unobjectionable because the ultimate[68] sanction for failing to adhere to the group standing orders was withdrawal of the party whip, which would not prevent the councillor continuing as an independent. On the other hand, a requirement that a councillor resign his seat if he wished to oppose the party group, in making him 'a mere delegate of the majority of the group', would have been objectionable in his view.[69] The court made it plain that each individual councillor had 'a personal and individual duty to consider the issues involved and to reach his own decision whether to vote for or against the resolution or to abstain' (Sir John Donaldson MR):[70] Russell LJ put it like this:

> Party loyalty, party unanimity, party policy were all relevant considerations for the individual councillor. The vote becomes unlawful only when the councillor allows these considerations or any other outside influence so to dominate as to exclude other considerations which are required for a balanced judgment. If, by blindly toeing the party line, the councillor deprives himself of any real choice or the exercise of any real discretion, then his vote can be impugned and any resolution supported by his vote potentially flawed.

In similar vein Sir John Donaldson MR[71] and Stocker LJ[72] both spoke repeatedly of an individual councillor fettering *his* discretion. Stocker LJ went further and referred to the fiduciary relationship between the *councillor* and the ratepayers.[73] This emphasis upon the decision of each individual councillor seems questionable in that as individuals no statutory discretion is conferred upon councillors as such.

We are in an area here where it is difficult for the law to intervene, since only exceptionally will there be clear evidence on which to found a

[66] See the judgment of Sir John Donaldson MR, ibid. 262–3.

[67] Ibid. 261.

[68] In practice there was evidence that in Waltham less serious sanctions would be invoked first. In *McIntosh v McGowan*, *The Times*, Law Report, 21 Jan. 1987, the Court of Appeal declined to restrain a local authority party group acting under the Labour Party model standing orders from disciplining a councillor in respect of his actions during a period when the group whip had been withdrawn from him.

[69] Ibid.

[70] Ibid. 259.

[71] Ibid. 260E and F and 261D.

[72] Ibid. 264F and H and 265B.

[73] Ibid. 264.

challenge in view of the secretiveness of party groups in the first place. Bearing this in mind, other approaches deserve consideration. In Scotland the McIntosh Commission has recommended that the political parties should review their advice to local parties on the application of the party whip to council business, so as to ensure that it is not applied inappropriately or indiscriminately. It suggests that councils should incorporate in their standing orders rules to the effect that where whipping is applied in council business it should be declared at the commencement of the relevant discussions and minuted for public information and record.[74] This would be a significant aid to transparency and accountability.

Use of the party whip also raises the issue of group discipline for those who break ranks. Disputes between individual councillors and the group may lead to irretrievable breakdown where the councillor is unable to adhere to group policy. The question of removing the councillor from a committee and appointing someone more amenable may then arise. Here again we confront the legal distinction between the group and the council, since it is formally the council which allocates councillors to committees. To what extent can a majority party use these mechanisms to penalize a non-compliant member? The standing orders of the major parties provide for withdrawal of the party whip for disciplinary reasons, although it would seem that only in the Labour Party could this lead to inability to stand for a re-election as a party candidate.[75]

The legal consequences were considered in *R v Greenwich LBC ex p. Lovelace*,[76] where the Labour whip was withdrawn from a councillor (and member of the Housing Committee) after public disagreement with the majority group. Subsequently at a Housing Committee meeting this councillor voted with seven other Labour members against an increase in homelessness rents which had been introduced as one of a number of budgetary measures to enable the authority to avoid charge-capping, defeating the motion. Following a recommendation from the Labour group, the eight were removed from the committee by a decision of the full council, and the committee was reconstituted without them. An application for judicial review of the council's decision to remove them was unsuccessful.

The Court of Appeal adopted a pragmatic approach: since local authorities were organized on party lines, they were entitled to take measures falling short of 'punishment' of a councillor. The removal was to enable the controlling group to give effect to policy, not an improper exercise of the council's powers. The applicant argued that in law councillors were representatives and not delegates. The dicta in the GLC case on the status of manifestos were cited to this effect, as was the declaration of office,

[74] *Report of the Commission on Local Government and the Scottish Parliament*, June 1999, paras. 123 and 124; for further aspects of the report, see p. 29 above.

[75] Copus, 'The Party Political Group', 21.

[76] [1991] 1 WLR 506, CA.

which requires councillors to fulfil their duties according to the best of their judgment and ability.[77] After considering the national model standing orders for Labour groups, Neill LJ found that party constraints were 'inevitable' and that group discipline did not amount to impermissible punishment meted out by the authority.[78] Staughton LJ seemed to approve the representative theory approach[79] (and even quoted Burke's speech to the electors of Bristol in his judgment,) but said that party discipline did not cross the line.[80] He maintained a distinction between the actions of the council and of the group.[81]The case arose before the introduction of the rules on apportionment of committee places according to political balance, which provide a procedure for notifying officers that an individual councillor is no longer to be regarded as part of a group, and adjusting the distribution of places accordingly.[82] These provisions give a meaure of underpinning for the reasoning in *Lovelace*.

The position is somewhat different where the council appoints members to outside bodies, where, depending on the statutory scheme in question, the councillor may be insulated from pressure by threat of removal. In *R v ILEA ex p Brunyate*[83] the removal of two LEA-appointed governors from a school governing body when they refused to give an undertaking to vote in accordance with LEA policy was held unlawful. The Divisional Court had initially held that the LEA was entitled to have a policy and to seek to implement it. However, this ruling was reversed on appeal. The House of Lords found that the LEA had usurped the function of the members of the governing body by the dismissal, since the governors had the right and duty to function independently. The decision may have been an attempt to de-politicize school governance: the governors in question were minority Conservative group members (the authority had a further eight appointed governors from the controlling Labour group, out of a total of twenty-one), and the issue in question was the politically sensitive one of whether the school should seek grant-maintained status or become a City Technology College. In principle, however, the same argument for independent judgment should hold sway to prevent removal of dissentient majority group councillors in similar situations.

77 LGA 1972, s. 83(1).
78 [1991] 1 WLR at 520.
79 Ibid. 522.
80 Ibid. 523.
81 In *R v Brent LBC ex p. Gladbaum*, (1989) 88 lGR 627, the removal of Labour councillors from committees following disagreement with the majority group was held unlawful on the narrower procedural grounds that the decision had been incorrectly delegated to the council's Policy Committee.
82 See p. 195 above.
83 [1989] 1 WLR 542. See also: *R v Brent LBC ex p. Assegai*, *The Times*, 18 June 1987 (dismissal of governor contravened natural justice); *R v Lambeth LBC ex p. Parker*, *The Times*, 1 Mar. 1983 (no power to rescind the appointment of a representative on the Community Health Council to reflect the changing political composition of the local authority); *R v Peak Park Joint Board*, (1976) 74 LGR 376.

### INTER-GROUP RELATIONS

If the non-recognition of the party political group has been one of the defining features of local government until recently, the relationships between such groups have to an even greater extent been left unregulated by the law. Prior to the Widdicombe Report it was common for the standing orders of councils to confer some degree of recognition on the political organization of the authority and its committees. The position of political Leader of the council was commonly recognized, in addition to that of Mayor or Lord Mayor, by the conferrment of special powers. Standing orders might also make provision for the tabling and answering of formal questions on a pattern not dissimilar to that employed in Parliament. Where they existed, standing orders of this kind could be legally enforceable (provided they did not conflict with some other statutory provision), but there was no requirement to adopt such procedures. In addition, as the Widdicombe Committee found,[84] in about 30 per cent of authorities standing orders were supplemented by local arrangements, understandings, or conventions operating between the parties. Conventions of this kind had usually been implicit rather than explicit. The committee commended, however, the approach of Cheshire County Council in committing its inter-party conventions to writing. Discussion of the nature and use of conventions appears later in this chapter. The emergence of a large number of 'hung' councils in many areas following the surge of electoral support for the Alliance parties in the mid-1980s focused practical attention on these inter-party arrangements. In some cases they have been tested to breaking-point, as the cases below demonstrate. In order to understand the legal issues raised, it is appropriate first to set the political context.

#### Party Groups in Hung Councils

Where a council is 'hung' this has major implications for all aspects of its work, including policy-making, the composition and operation of committees, the position of committee chair-holders, and the role played by officers. There are implications also for the control of political groups and, especially, the relationships between them. However, it is simplistic to treat all councils on which there is no overall control alike, since each is a distinctive political environment, subject to its own local factors, personalities, and traditions. Simple arithmetic means that there can be a substantial variety also. Where one party has captured exactly half of the seats on the council it may, if it chooses to use the mayor's casting vote, behave

[84] N. 2 above, para. 5.109.

in effect as a majority administration, although unforeseen events (such as the absence of a single councillor through illness) will make for a degree of unpredictability. Majority 'knife-edge' rule of this kind was adopted in the example of Bradford in 1987–8, described below. However, in other examples a 'knife-edge' administration has abstained from use of the casting vote and (in effect) behaved as a minority administration.[85]

It is more common for a third (smallest) party to hold the balance of power between the two larger political groups on the council. Where this occurs, several possibilities present themselves. The largest political group may attempt to form a minority administration, two of the groups may enter into some form of coalition to provide a working majority, or there maybe no formal outcome. Since executive authority rests in law with the council as a whole, rather than with a controlling group of councillors, there is no strict requirement for a clear administration to emerge, although there are political and administrative advantages in this. Stewart and Leach have argued that a party group has essentially four options in a newly 'hung' council in discussions about the formation of its administration: pressing for a minority administration which will enjoy a working majority on all committees; agreeing to a shared distribution of chairs of committees in cooperation with other parties; avoiding such formal arrangements but working on an ad hoc basis; and acting as a party of opposition, by eschewing a share in the administration. Which of these options a party group follows will depend upon its assessment of the probability of achieving its political objectives, maintaining its political distinctiveness, improving its electoral prospects in the future, and enjoying real status or power under the preferred arrangement.[86] The most common outcome in practice has been the formation of a minority administration, where one party takes the chair and vice-chair of the committees and takes the lead in proposing policy.

In addition to local factors, however, national guidance from the major political parties to their local party groups must also be considered as an influence. This is especially the case with the Labour Party NEC Guidelines on Hung Councils, which discourage Labour groups from sharing chairs of committees or entering into other formal pacts or arrangements with non-Labour party groups.[87] By contrast, the Liberal Democrats are positively encouraged to share power, although no equivalent formal guidelines exist. In the case of the Conservative Party, matters are left largely to the local party, with no formal advice being issued nationally. (However, Leach and Stewart did find evidence of local Conservative constituency parties exercising influence on Conservative

[85] See S. Leach and J. Stewart, *The Politics of Hung Authorities* (Basingstoke, 1992), 11–12.
[86] Ibid. 25–7.
[87] Ibid. 51–5.

groups of councillors to give up chairmanship of committees where they were unable to implement Conservative policies effectively.)[88]

The provisions introduced after Widdicombe for political balance on committees were made with the experience of 'hung' councils in mind, which explains the level of detail in which they deal with the question of distribution of seats. Where committee membership is tied between two major parties the question of the chair-holder's position may become crucial, since to retain the practice (common in majority administrations) of a chairman's casting vote in effect will give the party holding the committee chairs the majority,[89] despite the proportional distribution of seats. A range of alternative procedural devices has been adopted to deal with this difficulty in a number of councils; for example, a right for any three committee members (including at least one representative from the two opposition parties) to refer an agenda item to the full council, or abolition of the chair's casting vote, and a rule providing for automatic referral to the council meeting where no majority exists.

The major parties differ significantly among themselves over attitudes to committee membership in 'hung' authorities. It is typical for Labour groups to attempt to ensure a working majority on committees as a precondition of forming a minority administration. Conservative groups, on the other hand, have been prepared to do so without such a precondition. In keeping with their preoccupation with proportional representation, Liberal Democrats tend to insist that committees should precisely reflect the balance of power on the council itself. The changes in rules concerning the composition of the committees which were introduced in 1989 have the effect of making the Liberal Democrat position a legal requirement.[90] No such legal rule governs who should take control of the chairs of committees, and in practice this has often proved to be a vital consideration in the effectiveness of party-political strategy in 'hung' councils. However, some 'hung' councils have operated committees either without a chair-holder or on an ad hoc basis, with the chair-holder elected at the beginning of each meeting.[91] The study of policy-making in 'hung' councils found that the consequence of no one party having a majority was that the process of decision-making came closer in fact to that expressed in the law, namely, the taking of decisions by the full council and its committees, rather than in the party group meeting. The debate in committee and council meetings was no longer a formality proceeding on predetermined

[88] See S. Leach and J. Stewart, *The Politics of Hung Authorities* (Basingstoke, 1992), 58–9, and see p. 204 below.

[89] See discussion of the casting vote in the *Bradford* cases, p. 204 below.

[90] See generally Leach and Stewart, op. cit., 83–6, who describe the practice of insisting on a majority on committees as a mistaken carrying over into 'hung' council politics attitudes derived from majority party politics.

[91] Ibid. 111.

lines, as it often was where one party was in a clear majority, but became genuinely influential in framing the ultimate decision. Similarly, Leach and Stewart found that in a number of 'hung' authorities decision-making became more open, with greater public participation, because no one party had more to lose by the introduction of such policies.[92]

## Conventions in Inter-group Relations

The role of convention within local government has been somewhat neglected, perhaps inevitably, because of the statutory nature of the subject. Moreover, writers on political and constitutional conventions have traditionally drawn their illustrations from the conventions binding the Crown, and have looked only occasionally to conventions within other political systems, such as those in the European Community, elsewhere in the Commonwealth, or in the United States.[93] As with the debates in the wider constitutional literature about the nature of conventions, a number of problems arise concerning the legal status of local government conventions. One obvious difficulty is that since each local authority is a distinctive mini-political system, literally tens of thousands of such conventions await discovery by the serious explorer. As with all conventions in whatever political system, evidence of the practice and certainty about its scope are problematic, although the Widdicombe Committee's proposal that local conventions should be committed to written form where matters are not covered formally in standing orders would alleviate this difficulty.[94] The interaction of local conventions with statutes is a difficult area. Applying first principles, one would expect that statutory provisions would take priority and, indeed, that a decision based on convention could be attacked if it conflicted with a statute under the doctrine preventing the fettering of discretion. However, where statutory provisions allow a genuine discretion, potentially the doctrine of legitimate expectations could be employed to enforce local conventions. A development along these lines would represent a novel challenge to the orthodox position that constitutional conventions may be legally recognized but not legally enforced.

The issue arose controversially in cases brought following the election of a hung council in Bradford in 1988. The Conservative group took control of the authority, relying, in order to implement its decisions, upon the casting vote of the Lord Mayor (a Conservative councillor). Without the Lord Mayor's casting vote (meaning, in this sense, a second vote) there were equal number of Conservative councillors on the one hand and Labour and Alliance councillors on the other. Notwithstanding the

[92] Ibid. 141. [93] See e.g. C. Munro, *Constitutional Studies* (London, 1987), ch. 3.
[94] Widdicombe Report, research vol. iv, paras. 5.129 and 5.130.

precariousness of its position, the Conservative group embarked upon a radical programme of contracting-out of services and the introduction of other measures motivated by market rationality. Two such resolutions of the council, passed with the casting vote of the Lord Mayor, were unsuccessfully challenged in the courts.

There had been a tradition in Bradford of rotating the office of Lord Mayor between the different political parties of the council, and formerly this had been the subject of several agreements between the parties dating back to 1922 (although the council in its present form was a creation of the 1972 reforms). When the Lord Mayor whose actions gave rise to the challenges was sworn into office, the Opposition political parties supported him (it was normal for the election of the Lord Mayor to be unopposed), with the proviso that he should act 'non-politically'. Notwithstanding this long practice, the Court of Appeal felt unable to infer from the convention (if such it was) that there was a duty upon the Lord Mayor to act impartially when exercising his casting vote at a meeting of the council.[95] The court distinguished between the actions of the chairman of a meeting in calling speakers and regulating the business (which were to be done impartially) and the chairman's role on substantive issues. In the case of the latter, the legislation[96] did not suggest any limitation on the use of the statutory casting vote. Indeed, tracing the history of the provision back to the 1835 legislative code, it appeared that the casting vote had been introduced precisely for the purpose of breaking possible deadlock in local authority meetings. Therefore, the applicant's argument that the casting vote should always be exercised impartially to preserve the status quo (and hence against a change in policy where there was no strict legal duty to reach a decision), or where no 'true majority' existed, failed.

In a related attack on a different resolution from the same meeting, the High Court rejected an analogy between the position of the Lord Mayor and the Speaker of the House of Commons.[97] An argument that the convention governing the choice of Lord Mayor could create a legitimate expectation of political impartiality which was legally enforceable was also rejected. On the facts, however, this appeared to turn more upon the diffuseness of the convention and the applicant's lack of a recognizable legal interest in it,[98] than upon the issue of principle.

The Widdicombe Committee argued that written conventions might operate alongside extended standing orders[99] and cover the detailed basis

[95] *R v Bradford MBC ex parte Corris*, [1989] 3 All ER 140.

[96] Para. 39(2), sched. 12 of LGA 1972.

[97] *R v Bradford MBC ex parte Wilson*, [1989] 3 All ER 140.

[98] He was the resident of an old people's home affected by the council resolution.

[99] The Widdicombe Committee recommended the introduction of statutory requirements to include certain matters in standing orders, where they affected the relations between political groups, or between councillors and officers. These included the composition of

on which committee places were apportioned, contact between councillors and officers (especially the relationship between committee chairman and chief officers), the responsibility for agenda, the rights of councillors to obtain information and advice from officers, arrangements for informal working groups or informal briefings, the attendance of officers at party groups, the allocation of support services to councillors, and the status of staff attached to political groups or individual councillors. Although these conventions would be non-statutory, they might nevertheless be taken into account by the local ombudsman in considering whether maladministration had occurred.[100] A growth of written conventions of this type might help to overcome disputes over the existence or content of conventions of the kind which occurred in Bradford. A study in 1989 found that some two-thirds of hung county councils had published conventions, although their use was less common in districts, perhaps because of less willingness to cooperate between the parties in such councils.[101] Conventions of this kind often cover the issues of apportioning committee places, councillor contact with officers (including contact between chairholders and chief officers, the setting of agenda and rights to obtain information and advice from officers, and briefing), the attendance of officers at group meetings, and the allocation of support services to councillors. However, such documents tend to occupy a symbolic place in decision-making: if it is possible for the parties in the council to agree upon written conventions, then the informal working relationship is probably good enough for them not to be necessary. Leach and Stewart found relatively little formal use of conventions where they had been agreed.[102] This is an example of the need for cooperative decision in hung councils necessitating inter-group relationships to be relatively formalized and predictable. Where, however, there is a majority administration, frequently they feel no need for agreements of this kind.

## CONCLUSION

The growth and use of conventions illustrates a broader point about political activity within political systems and legal regulation. There seems to be an irreconcilable tension between political decision-making and the extent to which a political system is rule-governed. The Widdicombe

deliberative committees to reflect the political balance of the whole council, the taking of urgent decisions by committee chairman, the asking of questions at council meetings, and the setting aside of a period for minority party business at council meetings (the local government equivalent of the Westminster practice of Opposition or Supply Days) and the appointment of staff: Widdicombe Report, research vol. iv, paras. 5.112–26.

[100] Ibid., paras. 5.128–30. [101] Leach and Stewart, op. cit., 174. [102] Ibid. 175.

Committee recognized the reality that politics can never be fully open to public view and partisan scrutiny, and that politicians at whatever level will inevitably try to formulate policies in less public places. Justifiable though the public interests in open and accountable local government are, if they take insufficient account of this tendency, the result is to drive political decision-making into fora outside the council where there is an increased risk of abuse and corruption. The approach of the law to party groups examined in this chapter is symptomatic of this approach; for too long it was relegated to the status of sex in earlier times—something done in the dark and not to be discussed in public.

An approach which celebrated the validity of party politics as the corollary of representative democracy in local government would look quite different. The validity of majority party control would be legally recognized. Instead of legal fictions about the responsibility of councillors as a whole for decision-making, there would be a package of accountability mechanisms by which minority councillors could call the majority administration to account openly and in public for what it had legitimately decided in private. However, any such approach would require a radical rethinking of the decision-making processes of local government. As we shall see in the next chapter, radical proposals of precisely this kind are now being implemented.

# 7

# *Executive Structures*

This chapter first discusses the legal principles of delegation, which form the backcloth to any council's decision-making structure, and the ways in which this legal framework facilitates or constrains political activity. It then moves on to discussion of the strains imposed on this model by three significant recent developments. The first two—an administrative divide between the purchaser and provider imposed following compulsory competitive tendering (CCT), and the use of area or neighbourhood committees and service provision—are in operation according to differing patterns in a number of local authorities. The third, the implications of an authority becoming 'hung' (not under the overall control of one political party), affects approximately one-third of all councils. The traditional organizational structure of local authorities into service committees has been described as outdated and confusing, in failing formally to acknowledge the power which a core of councillors enjoy in practice and in failing to give worthwhile or rewarding roles to the remainder. Later in the chapter we shall consider the Labour government's antidote, which is the introduction of new forms of executive structures under the Local Government Act 2000. These all involve the separation of a political executive from the remainder of the authority. One of these models, the introduction of directly elected mayors, is now widely championed as a means of reinvigorating local democracy.

## COMMITTEES AND DELEGATION

Traditionally, local government has been characterized as government by committee. Each council will usually have an elaborate hierarchy of decision-making committees meeting on a regular cycle and building, like a pyramid, to the full council meeting which may occur every six or eight weeks (less frequently in the counties). Under this regime less important issues are delegated to officers. The law provides the general framework for delegation and referral of decisions, and the local arrangements will be contained in decisions of the council and in its Standing Orders. Until recently, this committee structure would have closely mirrored the service delivery departments of the council in question, usually with an overarching Policy and Resources committee, comprising the chair-holders of other committees or other leading councillors.

Within bureaucracies there are strong organizational imperatives favouring the delegation of decision-making: specialism, time-saving, division of labour, bringing decisions 'nearer' to those affected or to those with the necessary knowledge to inform the decision-making process, and so on. The local government variant of delegation is unusual, however, because of its use of committees of councillors (the political and legally responsible actors of the corporation) in frequently quite low-level decisions. The advantages claimed for this form of committee hierarchy are that it saves time for the majority of councillors, and allows them to develop specialism and interest in a particular area of policy and to supervise the work of the council's officers in that field.

However, a hard-and-fast line between policy and administration is difficult to draw, and this raises difficult questions about the respective attributes of elected members and professionally qualified officer groups. In practice, it is quite common for councillors to be formally involved (if only as a route of 'appeal' against the decision of an officer) not only in the detailed working out of 'policy' but also in its application to individual cases, for example, decisions on the allocation of housing grants, council tenancies, or school places. To some extent this is inevitable, since detailed policy is often developed through consideration of individual cases. In other fields there may be a statutory requirement that, because of the contentious nature of the decisions, elected members be seen to be responsible, rather than the paid employees of the council. Even where councillor involvement is not a statutory requirement it may be felt necessary for the transparency and accountability of the political process. Leaving aside these instances, though, it is a long-standing criticism that councillors are too closely involved in too much routine administration, which has been delegated to committees while it more appropriately belongs with officers. As long ago as 1967 the Maud Report warned of the danger that 'members are misled into believing that they are controlling and directing the authority when often they are only deliberating on things which are unimportant and taking decisions on matters which do not merit their attention'.[1]

The legal regime for delegation is permissive. Section 101 of the Local Government Act 1972 allows a council to arrange for the discharge of its business by committees, sub-committees, and officers, and allows delegation by such committees to sub-committees and to officers. Local authorities may empower committees to consider business in one of two ways. The first, delegation proper, vests the committee with the power to decide and dispose of the business: the committee stands in the place of the council.[2]

[1] *Report of the Committee of Management of Local Government* (London, 1967).

[2] e.g. it was held in *Batteley v Finsbury BC*, (1958) 56 LGR 165, that a committee acting within its delegated powers had validly bound the council to a contract.

The second is referral. Where powers are referred to committees, the committee's decision is not final and will be subject to confirmation or reconsideration by the full council. Committees may themselves delegate or refer business in the same way to sub-committees, with a corresponding effect on their own position. Whichever format is used, commonly the decisions of the sub-committee or committee will be reported to the full or parent committee (in the case of sub-committees) and to the meeting of the full council. In the case of delegation proper, the report will be for information only, whereas with referred decisions it will be for ratification. However, recognizing the practical advantages of referred committee powers, the law permits their ratification to be quite cursory; it need not involve a full re-examination of the issues by the parent committee or full council.[3] The distinction between delegated and referred powers is not watertight, because the standing orders of the council may provide for reopening of debate on delegated powers at a higher level also.

The introduction in 1972 of a general power to delegate to officers was an innovation designed to supersede a number of specific powers which formerly existed in disparate statutory schemes, and to encourage a clearer division of labour between officers, dealing with administration, and members, dealing with policy. In some special cases delegation is more restricted and the general provisions do not apply, presumably to ensure that councillors as a whole are responsible for deciding upon business.[4] No power existed until recently to delegate matters to an individual councillor (the legislation was interpreted to forbid a 'committee' of one[5]) since councillors only possessed legal capacity as members of the corporation collectively; although proposals for a 'lead member' system of delegation have been implemented under the reform of executive structures discussed below. The rationale for permitting delegation to a single officer but forbidding it to a single councillor was explained in terms of the officer's duty to act non-politically in the interests of the whole council.[6] Nevertheless, political influence could be retained in practice by delegation to an officer

[3] *Goddard v Minister of Housing and LG*, [1958] 1 WLR 1151. The use of a sub-committee to hear representations or evidence relating to a decision to be taken by the parent committee may, however, breach the rules of natural justice, if it deprives those affected of making representations to the decision-makers: *R v Chester CC ex p. Quietlynn*, (1984) 83 LGR 308.

[4] See e.g. *R v Birmingham CC ex p. NUPE*, (1984) 13 ILJ 177 (invalid delegation of education decision by education committee to officer; s. 101 did not enlarge on the powers of sub-delegation of specified statutory committees).

[5] *R v SSE ex p. Hillingdon LBC*, [1986] 2 All ER 273 (affirming decision of Woolf J [1986] 1 WLR 192). See also *R v SS for Education and Science ex p. Birmingham CC*, (1984) 83 LGR 79 (unlawful for committee to leave to chairman date of school closure, but council not permitted to rely on own illegality in later challenging decision after change of policy). See also: M. Jones, '"Chairman's Action": The Courts, the Local Ombudsman and the Widdicombe Committee', [1987] JPL 612, 615ff. who notes a number of ombudsman's reports critical of 'Chairman's action'.

[6] Woolf J in *Hillingdon* (n. 5 above), 816.

in consultation with the chair-holder of a committee.[7] This somewhat blurs the distinction between officers and members implicit in the legislation (officers may not be members of committees[8]), as does another common practice—the use of working parties comprising both members and officers—although groups of this kind are (formally) only permitted to act in an advisory capacity and cannot enjoy delegated authority.[9]

Councils are also permitted to delegate to other local authorities, and the use of this power for the transfer of the delivery of statutory functions under 'agency' agreements is widespread. In practice such agreements allow for the most effective and economical means to be adopted for the solution of local problems without slavish regard to some overall statutory framework for the division of functions between tiers of local government nationally. For example, aspects of highway powers closely connected with district council functions have commonly been governed by such agreements in urban areas, notwithstanding the overall responsibility of the county council. Whatever the practical convenience of such forms of intra-authority delegation, the effect on accountability to the public is less beneficial. Ultimate legal responsibility remains that of the council entrusted by statute with the function, but the public may be understandably confused about the lines of accountability when the visible delivery of the service is by a different local authority.

Similar points can be made about the use of joint committees (comprising members from two or more local authorities), which is also a permissible form of delegation under the Act.[10] Here, depending upon the composition of the committee, a council may find itself effectively and

[7] But see pp. 225–6 below.

[8] LGA 1972, s. 104 (1).

[9] See *R v Eden DC ex p. Moffatt*, *The Times*, 24 Nov. 1988, CA, where it was held that a Council could establish a working party of this kind under s. 111 LGA 1972 and that in principle a councillor might have a common law need to attend, but that on the facts the right had been correctly denied. Nourse LJ, partially dissenting, rejected the view of the trial judge and Croom-Johnson and Buckley LJJ that to allow the councillor to attend might inhibit frankness; the need to know should not be overridden by 'vague generalities and the sensitivities of those who might feel more comfortable if he was excluded'. He stressed also that a right to attend did not give a right to participate, and that members of the council have stronger reasons to attend than members of the public.

Judicial opinion differs on the correct approach to the deliberations of such working parties. In *R v Warwickshire DC ex p. Bailey*, [1991] COD 284, Simon Brown J found that a working party comprising 9 councillors who were members of the Education Committee and one teacher was not required under the legislation to be open to the public. Although this body could have been equally constituted as a committee, its status was to be decided according to the council's subjective intention; since, according to this, the working party was advisory only, there was no unlawfulness in excluding the public. This contrasts with the approach of Sedley J in *R v LB of Tower Hamlets ex p. Khalique*, (1994) 26 HLR 517, who examined notes summarizing the discussion of the council's Homelessness Board before deciding that it was behaving (unlawfully) as a committee in effect.

[10] Joint committees should be distinguished from joint boards, which require specific statutory authority and, although comprising councillors co-opted from the relevant local authorities, enjoy a separate corporate existence from any of the councils concerned. Joint

legally bound by a decision which it delegated to the committee, but which its representatives voted against. This is especially likely to occur where party group politics prevail at the joint committee level and one authority is under different political control from the remainder. Clearly, if joint committees are not to become an impediment to the political responsibility of the elected representatives of the member councils, great care must be given in drafting their composition and terms of reference.

In addition to the general requirements, delegation and referral are governed also by the standing orders of the individual local authority. Standing Orders form a type of local constitution establishing the remit of the various committees of the council and detailing matters routinely delegated to committees, sub-committees, and officers. Standing Orders are approved by the council.[11] The result is that every minute decision about local administration should be vested with authority because there can be traced a valid chain of delegation linking the person or group which took the decision to a statutory power of the council as a whole. If the chain is incomplete or the decision-maker (whether a committee or an officer) acts beyond the scope of the power delegated, this will render the decision challengeable by judicial review,[12] notwithstanding that it is within the lawful powers of the council.[13]

The same provisions govern delegation and referral of issues by a council to its officers. In the absence of explicit limitations on delegation to officers, the courts have been reluctant to infer them[14] and have generally taken a common-sense approach to the chain of delegation of decision-making within council departments.[15] In one case Schiemann J stated that

boards are open to the criticism that there is no direct electoral accountability for their decisions: the councillors concerned make decisions as members of the relevant board, not as members of the nominating council.

[11] Made under the LGA 1972, s. 106. Note, however, that in some cases legislation prescribes the content of Standing Orders, e.g. requiring political balance on committees: p. 194 above.

[12] However, some decisions where delegation is incomplete may be capable of ratification by the Council after the event: see A. Arden, J. Manning, and S. Collins, *Local Government Constitutional and Administrative Law* (London, 1999), 231–2.

[13] A number of matters are not delegable to committees. The level of Council Tax can only be set by the full council. The High Court set aside the removal of a councillor from a committee because the decision had been incorrectly delegated to the council's Policy Committee, whereas it should have been reserved for the council as a whole: *R v Brent London Borough Council ex p. Gladbaum*, (1989) 88 LGR 627.

[14] Refusing to imply a requirement that an investigating officer's report must be considered by councillors before a decision is made on whether to issue an order that a house was unfit: *R v Cardiff CC ex p. Cross*, (1983) 45 P&CR 156.

[15] Where a committee minute delegated the decision to issue planning enforcement notices to the chief officer, the Court of Appeal held that the administrative task of completing the notices was a matter properly delegated to more junior staff and the notices were presumed to be validly issued until the contrary was shown: *Fitzpatrick v SSE and Epping Forest DC*, [1988] JPL 564.

in the absence of evidence of wrongdoing the court would not investigate the internal organization of the department and would assume that the officer writing a letter had the authority of his superior to do so.[16] These decisions are to be applauded: the contrary outcome would have led the courts into bureaucratic detail without any obvious gains in the quality of decision-making, since local authorities could easily have avoided allegations of improper delegation by resorting to widely drawn standing orders. It is still open to councillors who wish to ensure the personal attention of the chief officer expressly to stipulate for it in the delegation. Matters would be different, however, where there was no attempt by the council to delegate the function to an officer at all. Hence, in one instance the purported exercise by an officer of power to serve a statutory housing notice was held to be invalid by the Court of Appeal on the grounds that all such questions had been delegated by the council to a sub-committee but no further.[17] While, generally, the common-sense approach of the courts to delegation mirrors their treatment of decisions by civil servants at central government level,[18] this aspect does not. A power conferred upon the Secretary of State will be deemed to be validly exercised by a civil servant in the minister's name unless there is evidence of a contrary intention (that is, not to delegate).[19] The difference in approach is hard to justify in terms of political responsibility; indeed, the greater importance of many central government decisions would suggest the contrary—that the law should ensure that they are more tightly under political control. It is, however, consistent with greater judicial deference to the actions of central government in general and a reluctance to inquire into departmental arrangements in the absence of a formal provision like section 101 providing for transparent delegation.

This section has described the legal framework of delegation underlying the traditional administrative arrangements within local government. We shall return later in the chapter to consider the implications of this model for 'back-bench' councillors and for the political elites—the Leader of the council and committee chair-holders—operating within many councils. Dissatisfaction over the gap between their apparent and real roles underlies the current programme for reform of executive structures, also analysed later. First, however, it is appropriate to discuss three other developments that have caused councils to develop alternative, innovative structures for decision-making. The first and third, the effects of elec-

[16] *R v LB of Southwark ex p. Bannerman*, (1990) 22 HLR 459.

[17] *Webb v Ipswich BC*, (1989) 21 HLR 325. See also *Fowler v SSE and Devon CC*, (1992) 64 P & CR 16, holding that where an officer is charged with gathering information, the council retains the power of decision and no delegation has taken place.

[18] *Carltona v Minister of Works*, [1943] 2 All ER 560. For a recent study see: M. Freedland, 'The Rule Against Delegation and the Carltona Doctrine in an Agency Context', [1996] PL 19.

[19] *R v Skinner*, [1968] 2 QB 700; *Re Golden Chemicals*, [1976] Ch. 300.

toral stalemate where no party has a majority and the creation of a purchaser/provider divide under CCT, resulted from external forces which compelled councils to adapt. The second, experimentation with neighbourhood governance, has been freely embraced by some councils seeking a more direct way to represent their communities.

## DECISION-MAKING IN 'HUNG' COUNCILS

In the mid-1980s, with increased electoral support for the then SDP and the Liberals, it became common for local authorities to be 'hung'—that is, not under the overall control of any one political party. This has remained a constant feature of local government ever since. Such authorities are often compelled to adopt new decision-making procedures. The rules established under the 1989 Act for political balance on committees[20] were made with the experience of hung councils in mind, which accounts for the detail in which they deal with the distribution of seats. Apart from increased representation on committees, the demands of a party which attains a blocking minority often include equal rights to information and briefing by officers for party spokespeople on all committees (rather than merely the chairman or vice-chairman being briefed), all-party involvement in the handling of urgent decisions (rather than decisions being delegated to officers solely in consultation with committee chairmen), and the adoption of written procedures or conventions.[21]

In councils where there is no overall control, the role of chair (or Mayor) of the council, the position of the council Leader, and chair-holders of committees all undergo change from that where there is majority party control. One tendency is for the chair of the council to become a more procedurally based office than formerly. The role of Leader may be transformed; indeed, where there is no overall control the notion of a Leader is contradictory. Most significant of all is the change in the role of committee chairholder. In practice power tends to devolve on the party spokespeople on the relevant committee, among whom the task of chairing the meeting may rotate. Where committee membership is tied between two major parties the question of the chair-holder's position may become crucial, since to retain the practice (common in majority administrations) of a chairman's casting vote will effectively give the majority to the party holding the committee chairs, despite the proportional distribution of seats. Councils have adopted a range of alternative procedural devices to deal with this difficulty; for example, a right for any three committee members

[20] See pp. 194–5 above.

[21] S. Leach and J. Stewart, *The Politics of Hung Authorities* (Basingstoke, 1992), 148.

(including at least one representative from the two opposition parties) to refer an agenda item to the full council, or abolition of the chair's casting vote and a rule providing for automatic referral to the council meeting where no majority exists in committee.

The principle of equal access to information for all parties prior to committee meetings tends to work without favouritism where there is no overall administration. However, where one party forms a minority administration, the chair-holder will retain a degree of control, particularly over agenda items, which is the residue of the power of the chairman in a majority administration. Briefings of spokespeople may either take place jointly or individually with officers. Individual briefings can cause problems of confidentiality for officers and may be symptomatic of a lack of trust between the parties. In some hung councils, however, party groups which see their role as being one of opposition have consciously withdrawn from such arrangements so as not to be compromised in their later public criticism by the earlier sharing of privileged information.

Another common procedural development is a search for less visible places in which the parties can discuss policy jointly. Accordingly, there has been an increase in use of councillor–officer working parties in hung authorities,[22] often meeting in private, and in regular meetings between the leaders and deputies of the major parties, sometimes initiated by the Chief Executive. However, Leach and Stewart report that this is only rarely used to agree on solutions to contentious issues behind closed doors because few Labour Party or Liberal Democrat groups are prepared to tolerate being circumvented in this way by their leaders.[23]

Lack of stable political control also increases the unpredictability of decision-making in hung councils. It is common, therefore, to attempt to prevent the taking of controversial decisions by committees due to opportunism (for example, the absence of an individual councillor) by adopting the practice of 'substitution'. 'Substitutes' are councillors of the same party label as the absent councillor who are, under standing orders, deemed members of the committee and who may attend and vote where a councillor from the group is unavoidably absent. This enables party group discipline on committees to be retained even in the unpredictable circumstances caused by a lack of overall control.[24] Also common has been the growth of 'requisitioning procedures'.[25] These allow for a group of councillors to refer a matter decided by the committee to the full council,

[22] About half of all hung counties investigated by Leach and Stewart reported an increase in the use of working parties and panels. One of the most developed systems was where each committee appointed a representative panel of the three party spokespeople to take urgent decisions between meetings and which officers could consult informally over future committee items. This is a clear example of a cross-party group being used to fulfil the role traditionally undertaken by a chair-holder of a committee in a majority administration: ibid. 170.

[23] Ibid. 168.

[24] Ibid. 161.

[25] Ibid. 172–3.

overriding the delegated authority of the committee. They may be designed, depending on the number of councillors who may trigger the procedure, either to allow the smallest party to operate it or to prevent them from doing so without support of members from other groups. The latter approach can be used to marginalize a third party, especially where two parties have been accustomed to alternating in office.

## NEIGHBOURHOOD GOVERNANCE[26]

One of the most interesting experiments in administrating local government in recent years has been the introduction in a number of authorities of a neighbourhood- or area-based approach to the provision of services and decision-making. Some neighbourhood initiatives have been driven by consumerism, for example the provision of 'one-stop shops'—neighbourhood service offices where all council enquiries can be dealt with, whether they relate to housing, Council Tax, planning, or whatever. Such developments can occur without any reorganization of the council's services or decision-making structure. However, the most interesting developments, discussed below, do involve attempts to reorganize decision-making in this way.

The essence of area or neighbourhood *committees* is that they are organized by reference to geographical communities rather than professional disciplines. The impetus came largely from (Liberal-inspired) community politics, although some other authorities have experimented with this model also. The advantages claimed are that decision-making is brought nearer to local communities and that there is more opportunity to reflect local opinion, rather than authority-wide solutions to problems. Where committees meet in the locality there is also the possibility of greater public interest and involvement in their deliberations.

To some extent these advantages will depend upon the degree of local autonomy enjoyed by the area committees under whatever arrangement is chosen. The public may quickly lose interest in area committees enjoying fewer discretionary powers. Naturally, a balance exists between those decisions that can be devolved to area committees and those which are reserved for a strategic, authority-wide policy. This problem has the potential for political conflict because the electoral geography of an authority will often result in areas under different (minority) party political control.

[26] For reviews of experiments across a number of councils, see D. Burns, R. Hambleton, and P. Hoggett, *The Politics of Decentralisation: Revitalising Local Democracy* (London, 1994); M. Geddes, *Extending Democratic Practice in Local Government* (London, 1996), 16–17.

Area committees and sub-committees are an important exception to the legal requirements of political balance; provided the committee covers no more than two-fifths of the authority's area or population and all the members are the relevant elected ward representatives, the committee may operate on a one-party basis.[27] This provision acknowledges the validity of experiments in decentralization. It is also an isolated recognition of the importance of the connection between councillors and the ward they represent; even where council administration is not organized on an area basis, councillors commonly act as 'ward champions' in dealing with officers and in contributing to committee discussions. However, it should also be noted that the area committee exception has the potential for imposing a form of political apartheid, since the distribution of party places on a council will often follow a clear geographical pattern, according to the nature and social composition of each ward, and the minority party councillors may be concentrated in a small number of wards. If area committees with substantial powers are in use, minority group councillors may achieve more real power in relation to decisions affecting their own wards, but at the cost of a net loss of influence and participation in the council's decision-making generally.

Freedom to pursue a distinctive political programme in such minority-controlled areas may be contentious. In one model, that used in Kingston-upon-Thames, not only are the majority of service-related decisions delegated to area committees, but the committees also have control of a (population-based) share of the council's budget. In practice much of the budget is committed to statutory functions, but nevertheless it has been estimated that the discretionary part amounts to some 10 per cent. Experience of these arrangements suggests that they produce much greater councillor interest in the detail of budgetary control, because members are able to make real local decisions involving local expenditure, and that area committees attract much greater public interest than service-based arrangements. There is also some evidence from the London borough of Tower Hamlets, where neighbourhoods were introduced following the 1986 election, of an increased turnout in subsequent local elections.

Neighbourhood governance does, however, have its limitations. A number of key decisions, for example, setting the level of Council Tax, are required by law to be dealt with by the authority as a whole. There is also the practical danger that a narrow area of member focus may atomize decisions, resulting in the loss of a broader, strategic view of the authority's policies. If area politics were to come of age, there would presumably

[27] Introduced by the Local Government (Committees and Political Groups) (Amendment) Regulations 1991, SI No. 1398.

be a risk of inter-area conflict in the politics of a council over such matters as budget allocation, but there is no evidence yet of this occurring. It has also been argued that, important as local representation is, it may be too narrow, and that a council should also reflect other forms of community interest, such as social background and race.[28]

## THE STRUCTURAL IMPACT OF COMPULSORY COMPETITIVE TENDERING[29]

The introduction of CCT under the Local Government Act 1988 had a major impact upon the organization and administration of local authorities. The effect of the legislation was to require councils that wished to continue to provide services in-house to establish financially free-standing Direct Service Organizations (DSOs). Work within designated areas could only be placed with such DSOs if it was first offered by competitive tender to private-sector contractors. Although there was no statutory obligation to accept the lowest tender and work could be retained in-house by a DSO even if the tender was higher than a private-sector competitor, the duty to treat part of its workforce at arm's length required councils clearly to separate service regulation (the 'client' role) and service provision (the 'contractor' or 'provider' role).[30]

This client/contractor divide has had a major impact upon the organization of local authority departments and upon the way in which local government officers and members see their respective roles. This effect is likely to survive despite the formal abolition of a legal requirement to market-test stipulated work, following the introduction of the 'Best Value' regime.[31] It casts some council officers on the 'client' side in the role of quality control managers: they need to develop new skills of inspection and monitoring of the contractor's work and even imposing penalties. Others, on the contractor side, become in effect commercial operators. Members involved in running or overseeing DSO boards were similarly transformed from public representatives to directors of a commercial enterprise. Arguably, it was not permissible for the same councillors to be involved on both the client and the contractor sides. For some critics the

[28] See J. Stewart, 'Recent Experience of Extending Devolution and Democracy in Local Government', in *Extending Devolution and Democracy in Local Government* (Kingston, 1996), 19.

[29] Discussion here is solely of the structural implications of CCT. Other aspects, including the legislative requirements for letting contracts and for combating alleged anti-competitive practices, are dealt with in Ch. 10.

[30] B. Griffiths, 'Client and Contractor Roles in a Changing Local Government Environment', (1989) 4 J. of Local Economy 177; Audit Commission, *Occasional Paper No. 7: Preparing for Competition* (London, 1989). For a particularly valuable treatment, see P. Vincent-Jones, 'The Limits of Near-Contractual Governance: Local Authority Trading Under CCT', (1994) 21 J. of Law & S. 214.

[31] LGA 1999, s. 21, provides for the abolition of CCT.

client/contractor divide risks undermining a holistic approach to local services, with 'contractor' departments concerned only to (minimally) attain performance standards, or the 'client' side being perceived as an unnecessary intermediary between a DSO and its ultimate customers, service users, or recipients.[32] Such criticism may, however, depend on a somewhat rose-tinted view of the past, which underplays the potential for inter-departmental rivalry in service-based arrangements.

Compulsory competitive tendering fitted uneasily within a committee structure based on service committees for two main reasons. First, the most effective organization of a direct labour or direct service organization often transects conventional service groupings of officers and their corresponding political structures. The chief officer–chairman model of responsibility may conflict with the management structure of the DSO or DLO. This is related to the second difficulty—the commercial, quasi-autonomous role of DSOs and DLOs, which may require a high degree of political independence, or at least separateness, from other council activities, because of the need for commercial confidentiality. In some authorities the client/contractor split has also radically affected the traditional organization of officers into departments, responsible to service committees. Some authorities have adopted a tripartite departmental structure of client services, contractor services (in smaller authorities this may be under a unified DSO), and central services (for instance, legal and financial advice).[33]

While it may be possible to segregate officer groups of the council to separate client and contractor roles, it is more difficult at the councillor level within a legal structure that emphasizes that councillors as a whole have responsibility for all decisions taken in the name of the council. One solution was to involve councillors in separate committees overseeing the 'client' and 'provider' roles.[34] However, at some (higher) level there would be a conflict of interest between councillors' responsibilities for the 'client' and 'provider' sides. This conflict could be avoided by delegating fully the respective decisions to different committees, but to do so would place the individual councillors on these committees in the artificial position of politically representing only a part of the overall interests of the

[32] Griffiths, op. cit., 179. Vincent-Jones, op. cit., 217, suggests that a unified public authority ethos may become replaced by the emergence of a series of 'private' interests reflecting fragmented semi-independent business units.

[33] K. Walsh, *Competitive Tendering for Local Authority Services: Initial Experiences* (London, 1991), para. 9.20.

[34] e.g. if a local authority has established a Leisure Committee and a DLO Committee respectively, the councillors concerned may each play a different role in considering whether the Council's workforce should bid (and at what tender price) for a contract to maintain local parks; other councillors will be involved in considering whether the bid should be accepted, in comparison with other tenders.

council on the issue, while remaining legally responsible for all aspects. CCT was not alone in raising such difficulties: similar problems may arise wherever a council acts in the dual capacity as property owner or service provider and regulatory authority, for example, granting planning permission for land which it owns,[35] or in conducting a health inspection of a council catering facility. Councillors were left in an ambivalent position in relation to DSOs. If the function of the DSO was solely to produce a commercial return and fulfil a contractual obligation, the scope for member influence appeared to be minimal, and this was confirmed by evidence of decreasing member involvement—a process of de-politicization of local service provision.[36] In terms of committee organization, most local authorities responded to CCT by establishing distinct DSO boards, apart from the normal service committees. Active member involvement on these boards was for the most part a matter of preparing for compulsory tendering and working through the tender process; thereafter there was a tendency to delegate matters to officers. Consequently, CCT had the result of partially reversing the trend towards full-time councillors which came to the fore in the 1970s and 1980s. In some authorities councillors were formally debarred by standing orders from bridging the 'client' and 'contractor' roles at committee level,[37] leading to unease that there was a realm of activity conducted in the name of the authority to which councillors were denied access on commercial grounds.[38]

The managers of DSOs inevitably desired a degree of commercial independence, for example, freedom to purchase goods and services from outside the council, or to seek business from other clients, by tendering 'cross-border' for other local authority work. When work is awarded in-house there is the same potential for contractual disputes between the DSO and the client as if a private contractor had been employed, even though there may be no formal contract to symbolize the arrangements. New methods of internal arbitration and dispute resolution have emerged as a result.[39] In some respects DSOs were cast in the role of clients as regards other council officers, such as professional advisers like accountants and lawyers, with the result that their services were provided to DSOs on a pattern more nearly reflecting private-sector professional arrangements. This might include billing for work done or the use of

[35] On which see *R v Amber Valley DC ex p. Jackson*, [1984] 3 All ER 501; *Steeples v Derbyshire CC*, [1984] 3 All ER 468 (discussed at pp. 188–9 above)

[36] See K. Walsh and H. Davies, *Competition and Service: The Impact of the Local Government act 1988* (London, 1993), 25.

[37] Walsh, op. cit., para. 9.27.

[38] Ibid., para. 9.27

[39] Vincent-Jones, op. cit., 224–5. See also P. Vincent-Jones, 'The Limits of Contractual Order in Public Sector Transacting', (1994) 14 Legal Studies 364; P. Vincent-Jones 'Responsive Law and Governance in Public Services Provision: A Future for the Local Contracting State', (1998) 61 MLR 362

'Service Level Agreements'.[40] These arrangements could give rise to professional conflicts of interest, for example, if both 'client' and 'contractor' sides sought legal advice on potential liability for failing performance.

A number of these difficulties arose because the legal relationship between a DSO and its council was cramped by the lack of a distinct legal identity for the DSO. In law the DSO had no separate corporate legal identity apart from the authority: as Freedland puts it, the relationship involved 'a double legal fiction, whereby a non-corporation is deemed to enter into a non-contract',[41] and it is therefore ultimately governed by public law doctrine. Nevertheless, Vincent-Jones has pointed to the emergence of a number of features of 'near-contractual' relations in planning and monitoring service provision; for example, more detailed specification of the service to be delivered, increased emphasis on monitoring, and use of penalties against DSOs.[42]

The internal contractualization of local government also has implications for local service users. Freedland has pointed out that conceiving governmental issues in contractual terms can give rise to the danger that the contractual doctrine of privity may be employed to restrict the public law concept of standing to those within the contractual nexus, so as to exclude the citizen, voter, or service user.[43] However, Fredman and Morris argue that there is a case for extending the burgeoning judicial review of contractual decisions to provide the ultimate consumers of the service with legal remedies, and that internal quasi-contracts (such as 'framework' agreements or successful DSO tenders) may create a legally recognizable legitimate expectation among service recipients and users.[44] From a different perspective, the Audit Commission urged that CCT should be regarded as a three-way relationship in which consumers are included in consultation about service requirements and have a significant role in monitoring performance.[45]

[40] These regulate relations between central services and DSOs, containing a description of the service provided, an indication of service standards, and the basis for charging and possible penalties. Walsh, op. cit., paras. 10.14 ff.

[41] M. Freedland, 'Government by Contract and Public Law', [1994] PL 86; and see I. Harden, *The Contracting State* (Buckingham, 1992), 50.

[42] The Limits of Near-Contractual Governance'. However, he also points to the inherent limitations in this form of governance and to the extent to which the government and the Audit Commission have worked from a stylized and unreal model of contractual relations in the business world in introducing CCT and assessing its impact.

[43] Freedland, op. cit., 99–100.

[44] S. Fredman and G. Morris, 'The Costs of Exclusivity: Public and Private Re-examined', [1994] PL 69, 79.

[45] Audit Commission, *Realising the Benefits of Competition: The Client Role for Contracted Services* (London, 1993), paras. 52–4; Vincent-Jones, ''The Limits of Near-Contractual Governance', 229. A follow-up study found that in 6 out of 9 activities subject to CCT examined, fewer than half of authorities had consulted service consumers on requirements and standards and fewer than 20% reported on monitoring to consumers: Audit Commission, *Making Markets: A Review of the Audits of The Client Role for Contracted Services* (London, 1995), 5 and 12.

Having reviewed the strains on the traditional model from the developments of hung authorities, neighbourhood governance, and CCT, we can now turn to some of the other implications and their limitations. In approaching the creation of the new political executives, involving a division among councillors between the executive and scrutiny roles, we first consider the ways in which the traditional model has treated these two groups—backbench councillors and members of the political elite. As we shall see, it is because of dissatisfaction with their current legal status that the movement towards reform has taken hold.

## 'BACKBENCH' COUNCILLORS[46]

The committee system has traditionally been organized in most local authorities to reflect departmental officer groupings according to specialized statutory functions: housing, planning, education, social services, highways, leisure, and so on. With the advent of full-time committee chair-holders, these service-based committees began to mirror patterns of minister–permanent secretary responsibility in Whitehall, with a combination of chief officer and chairman responsibility to the relevant service committee. The number of committee posts to be filled in most councils is such that each councillor will generally be a member of more than one committee, and so in one sense 'backbenchers' do not exist. The lack of a separation in local government law between the executive and the council as a whole, however, leaves the full council meeting in an anomalous position. The legal authority of a committee derives only from delegation by the councillors as a whole. Non-committee councillors are left, therefore, in the position of having vestigial responsibility for decisions but with little practical opportunity to influence them, except, perhaps, if they are members of the majority group, through group meetings outside the formal structure.[47] Consequently, their legal rights to information assume some significance and this is an issue which will, if anything, be more important under the new executive models, introducing a formal political executive.

Under the common law, as members of a corporation, councillors are entitled to any information in the council's possession necessary for them to discharge their legal responsibilities—the 'need to know' test.[48] The standard adopted is whether access to the documents is reasonably

[46] See also P. Birkinshaw, *Freedom of Information: The Law, the Practice and the Ideal* (2nd edn., London, 1996), 136–9.

[47] Some councils have sought to bring clearer accountability for holders of committee chairs through introduction of a formal 'question time' at the full council meeting.

[48] *R v Barnes B.C. ex p. Conlan*, [1938] 3 All ER 226.

necessary in order to be informed of matters to enable the proper discharge of work as a councillor.[49] Action motivated by private interest[50] or mere curiosity will not suffice. On this basis, the Court of Appeal has upheld the refusal to supply to a councillor the unabridged version of an earlier, contentious report to the relevant committee, since it contained material based on rumour which was possibly defamatory and which at this later stage was not relevant to the committee's work.[51] Under the test, members of a committee will automatically be able to demonstrate a 'need to know' in relation to the committee's work. The House of Lords has also held that a councillor who is not a member of the committee may still be able to demonstrate a 'need to know', based on the council's residual responsibility. On the facts of this case 'the need to know' overrode any confidentiality in the information, which related to the personal details of prospective adoption parents.[52] Prior to the Local Government and Housing Act 1989, the law allowed the use of one-party committees provided that their function related to the disposal of the business of the council as a whole and not merely the formulation of 'group' policy.[53] However, opposition councillors could invoke 'the need to know' principle either to attend the meetings of such committees or to have access to their papers.[54] The distinction may once again become important as one-party executives emerge under the new reforms.

The common law test can be criticized for its weak recognition of councillors' interests. It has been stated, for example, that a councillor does not have 'a roving commission' over a council's papers.[55] There are complex and conflicting interests to be balanced, not least the privacy of users and recipients of council services. Nevertheless, the common law approach arguably puts the onus the wrong way around by requiring democratically elected representatives, with legal responsibility for a layer of government, to *prove* their interest before being allowed access to information gathered on behalf of the public. The 'need to know' test can too easily be used to reinforce a political culture of secrecy within a local authority or can result in employees, whose legal position is supposedly subordinate to councillors, becoming the privileged gatekeepers of access to information. These tendencies are if anything strengthened by another facet of the

[49] Ibid. 230, per Humphreys J, where it is expressly linked to a councillor's 'common law duty to keep himself informed of all matters necessary to enable him to properly discharge his duty as a councillor'.

[50] *R v Hampstead BC ex p. Woodward*, (1917) 15 LGR 309.

[51] *R v Lancashire CC ex p. Hook*, [1980] QB 603.

[52] *R v Birmingham City Council ex p. O*, [1983] 1 AC 578. Cf. the ombudsman's power of investigation in adoption cases: *Re a Subpoena (Adoption: Commissioner for Local Administration)*, [1996] 2 FLR 629.

[53] *R v Sheffield CC ex p. Chadwick*, (1985) 84 LGR 563; see further Ch. 6.

[54] *Ex p. Chadwick*; and *R v Hackney LBC ex p. Gamper*, [1985] 1 WLR 1229; see p. 191 above.

[55] *R v Southwold Corp., ex p. Wrighton*, (1907) 97 LT 431, 431–2, per Lord Alverston CJ.

approach, which is to treat decisions over access to information as comparable to other local authority decisions, and therefore only invalid if based on *Wednesbury* unreasonableness.[56] In making the council as a whole the arbiter over disputes of this kind and subject to such a weak standard of review, little attention has been paid to the political realities of majority party control of local authorities. Information is an essential tool in political accountability and criticism: control of it is a dangerous weapon to grant to those who have most to lose from disclosure.

The common law 'need to know' test has been added to by amendments under the Local Government (Access to Information) Act 1985. In addition to the rights that members of the public have under the legislation,[57] councillors are given extended rights, to any document in the possession of the council or under its control relating to any business to be transacted at a council, committee, or sub-committee meeting.[58] The provision makes no distinction between councillors who are members of the relevant committee and those who are not. Furthermore, the exemptions, which may be applied to requests by councillors, are narrower than those applicable to the public at large. Where councillors are involved, exemptions may not be claimed for financial details of third persons, the identity of tenderers, or proposed expenditure by the authority (ensuring that members have access to details of the council's commercial activities), or for information about proposed statutory notices and orders.[59] An attempt is made to depoliticize refusals of access of information to councillors by requiring the council to designate an officer as the 'proper officer' with responsibility for determining whether the exception is applicable. However, since the remaining exemptions are discretionary rather than mandatory, there exists the possibility of political instruction to the officer concerned, depending on the arrangements adopted for discharge of this important function under the council's standing orders.

Where the document to which the councillor is seeking access relates to a meeting, these statutory rights are stronger than those under the common law since they do not depend on whether the councillor is a member of the committee concerned, nor on establishing a 'need to know'.

[56] See e.g. *ex p. Hook* (n. 51 above, upholding refusal of access on this basis), R *v Eden District Council ex p. Moffat*, (n. 9 above, need to know outweighed by the danger of inhibiting frankness of discussion), and *ex p. O* (n. 52 above, refusal to prevent disclosure to councillor since it was not *Wednesbury* unreasonable).

[57] S. 100 F(5) of the LGA 1972 states that the rights for members are supplementary to rights existing apart from the section, i.e. to the common law 'need to know' principle, to the rights members of the public enjoy under the Act (pp. 81–5 above), and under other provisions (e.g. the right to inspect documents of account: LGA 1972, s. 228(3)).

[58] S. 100F(1) LGA 1972. This is wider than the public's rights, which are to 'background papers' only and are parasitic on public rights of access to agenda, reports, and minutes: see Ch. 3.

[59] S. 100F(2) and sched. 12 A, LGA 1972.

However, the common law right remains useful where a statutory exception is invoked, since the statutory rights are supplementary to those at common law,[60] and the common law rights are not subject to exceptions. Hence, in some circumstances, the common law right may in effect be used to override the exemptions. For example, although one of the permissible exemptions concerns information relating to adoption, care, fostering or education of any particular child,[61] the case of *R v Birmingham CC ex p. O*,[62] in which a councillor's 'need to know' such information about a proposed adoption was upheld by the courts, could still be decided in the same way, notwithstanding the legislative changes. If a councillor is seeking access to a document *unrelated* to a meeting the statutory rights will not apply, and the issue continues to be governed by the common law.[63]

From considering the position of backbench councillors, discussion now moves to the extent to which the current legal regime recognizes the position of a political elite within authorities.

## POLITICAL LEADERSHIP

A second difficulty with the conventional model is its lack of legal recognition for committee chair-holders and for the political leader of the council. The legal model suggests that all councillors are of equal importance because of their formal contribution to decision-making within the corporation and equality of voting rights. However, the de facto influence of certain councillors belies this. To some extent a concentration of power of this kind has been officially encouraged by official reports advocating the adoption of a businesslike management board, with a policy team of councillors, often comprising the chair-holders of programme committees. Inevitably, within the politicized structure of local authorities operating under a whip system, this group come to be regarded as a cabinet. Their de facto authority may be recognized by officers and third parties who take their instructions to represent the will of the council as a whole.

The law has wavered between rejection and acceptance of these political realities. Thus, it has leaned against recognition of the de facto power of individual members who are committee chair-holders in refusing to sanction delegation to them[64] and by penalizing improper pressure which may be brought to bear by powerful politicians on officers.[65] However,

[60] S. 100F(5), LGA 1972.

[61] Sched. 12 A, para. 6, LGA 1972.

[62] N .52 above.

[63] The same may be true of a working party which is not formally a committee or sub-committee of the council: see *R v Eden DC ex p. Moffatt*, *The Times*, 24 Nov. 1988, CA (see further, n. 9 above).

[64] No committee of one: see n. 5 above.

[65] See *R v Port Talbot BC ex p. Jones*, [1988] 2 All ER 207.

where an individual councillor has purported to speak on behalf of a council in stating its position and probable action affecting outsiders, the council has sometimes been (adversely) credited with the motives of the councillor concerned.[66] In one case Scott J rejected as excessively legalistic the idea that the Leader of a county council had no authority to speak for the council; the judge treated the question as a matter of fact and found that in meetings with a developer in which the Leader represented the council he could be treated as speaking for it, but in giving a radio interview following a committee meeting he was speaking only for himself.[67] Similarly, the judgments in defamation actions brought by the Leader of Derbyshire County Council and the council itself show a preparedness to acknowledge that the reputation of a council may be closely bound up with that of its governing party or leading politicians within that party.[68] In exceptional circumstances the courts have also allowed a leader to sue his own council in a representative capacity as a means of having a decision set aside which had been discovered to be tainted by impropriety.[69]

In practice chief officers frequently have a close working relationship with the leader of the council and committee chair-holders, but this too is fraught with legal ambiguity.[70] It is relatively common for council standing orders to provide for the dispatch of urgent business, otherwise normally delegated to a committee, by a chief officer 'in consultation' with the chair-holder of the relevant committee. This formula is adopted to provide a degree of political consultation over urgent decisions where formal collective member involvement is impracticable, without falling foul of the absence of statutory power for delegation to a single councillor.[71] The

[66] See esp. *Wheeler v Leicester CC*, [1985] AC 1054, where the House of Lords used accounts of the meetings involving prominent councillors with the rugby club to determine that the council had acted improperly in determining the club's licence to use a training-ground.

[67] *KLF (UK) v Derbyshire CC, The Times*, 21 Aug. 1984.

[68] *Derbyshire CC v Times Newspapers*, [1993] AC 534, 550, where Lord Keith of Kinkel gives this as a reason for denying that the council has an independent reputation of its own which is capable of protection through defamation: see further Ch. 3; see also *Bookbinder v Tebbit*, [1992] 1 QB 770, CA—a further action of libel brought by the same councillor in relation to an allegation of squandering public money through action of the council.

[69] *R v Bassetlaw DC, ex p. Oxby, The Times*, 18 Dec. 1997, CA (application to have a planning permission issued as a result of bias declared invalid); see also *R v Port Talbot BC ex p. Jones*, [1988] 2 All ER 207, 215 per Nolan J.

[70] There are suggestions, e.g. in the case law, that other members may have rights of access to a Leader's meetings: *R v Hyndburn BC ex p. Strak* (unreported judgment of Woolf J as to costs in an application brought by an excluded Alliance councillor: QBD, 17 Dec. 1985). However, these are premissed on the assumption that the meetings in question were deliberative (rather than consultative), in which case they would be unlawful under the present law for lack of political balance.

[71] It is not necessary, however, that any decision delegating the power should be phrased in terms of consultation. In one case a standing order which allowed chief officers to deal with urgent business between committee meetings with the 'approval' of the mayor or relevant committee chairman or sub-committee chairman was upheld. The standing order required the officer effectively to have reached a decision that urgency required action before

procedure is, however, open to legal criticism on the ground that section 101 does not explicitly provide for delegation to an officer and councillor (s) jointly.[72] By giving the decision to the officer, political neutrality may be formally respected, in a way which action by a single politician (rather than, as on a committee, by a cross-section of political opinion) would not. However, the exact nature of the consultation is likely to depend on the political culture of the individual council and the personalities and relevant standing within the political microsystem of the chief officer and councillor concerned. Where the officer's political position (in a broad sense) is subordinate, the consultation may take the form of an irresistible suggestion made by the councillor, or a right of veto over proposals made by the officer. The auditor's report into the Designated Sales Policy of Westminster City Council provides clear evidence of how hard it may be for individual officers to withstand pressure from overbearing leading members.[73] The courts have also shown themselves alive to this danger. In one instance a decision to allocate a council tenancy which had been formally delegated to the council's Housing Officer in consultation with the chairman and vice-chairman of the Housing Committee, was set aside because of evidence (from the officer) that to all intents and purposes he had acted under dictation from the members to take a decision he would not otherwise have reached. The case dramatically illustrates the potential for political abuse in such arrangements—the decision in question was to allocate a vacant council house to a sitting councillor in disregard of the council's other housing priorities, so that she could retain the necessary statutory residence connection with the authority.[74] A variation on this practice which has been adopted in hung councils should also be noted—delegation to an officer in consultation with a panel of the parties' spokespeople committee, or for this group itself to constitute an 'urgency' sub-committee with delegated powers. This development is to be welcomed as dispersing the concentration of power in chief officers and chairholders.

This tension, between the formal legal position where each elected councillor is equal and the political reality of the powerful position of leading councillors, is a further symptom of the general non-recognition of the executive in local government.

The Widdicombe Committee suggested that the law should be brought nearer to practice by the introduction of a power to delegate urgent deci-

approaching the relevant councillor, so that in practice the decision was not that of the councillor alone—the major instigator and executor of the action was the officer: *Fraser v SSE ex p. RB of Kensington and Chelsea*, (1987) 56 P & CR 386.

[72] M. Purdue, E. Young, and J. Rowan-Robertson, *Planning Law and Procedure* (London, 1989), 20.

[73] See p. 267 below.

[74] *R v Port Talbot BC ex p. Jones*, [1988] 2 All ER 207.

sions to committee chair-holders.[75] In the event the government chose not to implement this proposal. More radical proposals, for a 'lead member' system, later emerged as one of a series of options from a Department of the Environment Working Party.[76]

We turn now to proposals to bring the legal position nearer to the political realities by creating a legally distinct political executive.

## A POLITICAL EXECUTIVE?

It is perhaps misleading to argue that local government suffers from the lack of a separation powers, because, strictly, local authorities do not have a significant function equivalent to legislation; and the notion of a separation of powers is poorly reflected anyway within the British parliamentary tradition. Nevertheless, understood as a point about the lack of distinctive institutions responsible for policy formulation, implementation, and scrutiny, the point has some force. The existing fusion of these functions is said to be confusing, to obscure and distort public debate and lines of accountability, to be secretive, and to divert councillors into time- and energy-consuming management, rather than employing them in representation and scrutiny roles.[77] A DoE consultation paper published in 1993 suggested that the committee system was ill-adapted to the new styles of public management then being introduced by compulsion (in the case of competitive tendering) or by experimentation in local government.[78] A number of proposals have been made for a clear legal separation between the executive and the assembly (scrutiny function) to remedy these defects. The advantages of such executive models are said to include the following: 'they provide clear political direction for the authority; make clear where accountability lies; provide a more efficient, quicker and coordinated decision-making process; and provide a confidential forum for the ruling group to test the range of policy options with its official advisers.'[79] The advantage for non-executive councillors of the political

[75] Widdicombe Report, paras. 5.72–8. It felt that a power of this kind would be of practical use for cases in which it was impossible to obtain political balance on a small 'urgency' panel of councillors, or where delegation to an officer was inappropriate. However, under these proposals safeguards against abuse would have been incorporated: it would have been for the chief executive to certify that the threshold of urgency had been reached, and every use of the powers would be subject to report to the next meeting of the committee or sub-committee concerned.

[76] N. 84 below.

[77] e.g. CLD, *Taking Charge: The Rebirth of Local Democracy* (London, 1995), chs. 3 and 4.

[78] *Community Leadership and Representation: Unlocking the Potential* (London, 1993).

[79] Ibid., para. 5.22. Very similar justifications were put forward by the Labour Government: *Modernising Local Government: Local Democracy and Community Leadership* (London, 1998), ch. 5; *Modern Local Government: In Touch with the People*, Cm. 4014 (1998), ch. 3.

executive is said to be that they will be freed from routine committee work in order to take on a stronger role in scrutinizing the execution of council policy and acting as constituency and consumer champions. The disadvantage is a decrease in the formal right to make a contribution to policy formulation.

A variety of proposals for reform of the administration of local authorities along these lines has been made. A recommendation under the Major government that new statutory powers be granted to allow the Secretary of State to authorize new styles of local governance on a monitored basis[80] was reportedly shelved after ministerial opposition to the notion of 'Trust Councils', but was later revived by the Labour Party and a House of Lords select committee.[81] The Working Party concluded that the 1989 Act framework was overly restrictive because of its failure to legitimize a majority controlling group as the de facto executive, although the need for political safeguards was, nevertheless, accepted.[82] The Widdicombe Committee's recommendation of single-party advisory committees (discussed in Chapter 6) was resurrected, with a suggestion that the rules on political balance and on access to information be amended to allow private deliberations, with the benefit of officer advice.[83] This was envisaged as a non-executive committee. However, the Working Party also went considerably further than Widdicombe in considering possible models for political executives. Each of these involved political control being exercised by one or more people, either directly elected or appointed from the council. Each of the possible models (four were discussed in the Working Party report[84]) had different implications for the ruling group, for backbench councillors, and officers.

[80] The DoE Working Party report, *Community Leadership and Representation: Unlocking the Potential* (1993), 7–8 and 55–6, proposed statutory powers under which the Secretary of State would be able to authorize local experiments within a framework of agreed standing orders, subject to review by an advisory panel appointed by the minister and drawn from the DoE, local authority associations, the Audit Commission, and the Local Government Management Board. A similar proposal was made in the Labour Party policy document *Renewing Democracy, Rebuilding Communities* (London, 1995), 4 and 14 (subject to the consent of local people).

[81] *House of Lords Select Committee on Relations Between Central and Local Government, 'Rebuilding Trust'*, HL (1995–6) 97, para. 3.30; in its response (Cm. 3464 (1996), para. 41) the (Conservative) government accepted the recommendation and undertook to bring forward legislation to allow experiments with internal organization in 1997–8.

[82] DoE Working Party op. cit., 34.

[83] Ibid. 36–7.

[84] Under the Single-Party Executive Committee, the council would decide upon the extent of delegation within standing orders: within this field a committee comprising majority group councillors would have authority to take decisions in the name of the council; in other areas it would act in an advisory capacity. Retained decisions could equally be taken by the full council (e.g. approval of the budget) or delegated to other committees. Under the Lead Member system, responsibility for particular areas of executive policy would be delegated by the full council to named councillors such as the chair-holders of service committees, who together would constitute a non-executive committee. This would legitimize the de

Following its election to office Labour signalled its intention to reform the political management of local authorities in a flurry of consultative and White Papers. In February 1998 the Consultative Paper *Modernising Local Government: Local Democracy and Community Leadership* was published, which declared the committee system to be 'inefficient and opaque' and 'designed over a century ago for a bygone age'.[85] It signalled an intention to separate the executive and representational roles of councillors in the interests of clarity, accountability, and transparency. At the same time a private peer's Bill was introduced in the House of Lords by Lord Hunt, the Chairman of the Select Committee on Central–Local Relations, which would have created a regime for licensing various experimental forms of local administration.[86] Despite professed government support for the Bill, time was not found for it to pass through the parliamentary timetable. Ministerial enthusiasm for directly elected mayors had been flagged in the consultative paper. By the time a White Paper was issued in July 1998 the proposals had crystallized into three models: a directly elected mayor with cabinet, a cabinet and leader, and a directly elected mayor with council manager.[87] The detail of these proposals was provided in a further White Paper and accompanying draft Bill, published for consultative purposes in April 1999.[88] The proposals were examined in depth by a Joint Committee of both Houses of Parliament in a report to which the government responded[89] before bringing forward the final version of the new arrangements in the Local Government Bill 1999/2000.

facto power of chair-holders of committees, but under the control of the council as a whole and without further enhancing the executive powers of a majority group. In a Cabinet System the feature of individual councillor responsibility was retained, but delegated from an executive committee rather than the council: this committee (the cabinet) would be collectively responsible to the council for policy.

A significant difference between the Lead Member and Cabinet Systems was the formalization of a local equivalent to the Westminster convention of collective responsibility: the executive committee would take on the role of setting a policy agenda for lead members, and resolving differences among such members or departments. The position of backbench councillors would be weaker, although powers to 'call in' or reverse executive decisions could be retained. The Strong Political Executive model involved a formal legal separation of the political executive from the council. The primary role for the council would be scrutiny of executive decisions after the event, although it might also have powers to reverse executive decisions or to dismiss the executive.

85 Para. 5.1.

86 Local Government (Experimental Arrangements) Bill 1998. Under the Bill experiments would have been approved for up to 8 years by the Secretary of State, following consultation with the Local Government Association and the Audit Commission. See C. Crawford, 'Trusting Experiments', (1998) 1 JLGL 8.

87 *Modern Local Government: In Touch with the People*, Cm. 4014 (1998), ch. 3.

88 Local Leadership Local Choice, Cmnd. (1999); Local Government (Organisation and Standards) Bill.

89 *Report of the Joint Committee on the Draft Local Government (the Organisation and Standards) Bill*, HL 102-I, HC 542-I (1998–9); *Government Response to the Report of the Joint Committee on the Draft Local Government (the Organisation and Standards) Bill*, Cm. 4529 (1999).

The arguments for change are based on the need for effective and visible leadership. The case for change does not apply equally, however, to all council functions: the White Paper proposed that planning and regulatory decisions should remain subject to the current regime, presumably on the basis that these are somehow less 'political' than other functions.[90] It can be argued that the political executive exists informally anyway in the UK and that the new models merely give it legal recognition and introduce controls. The White Paper argued also that the split will lead to more effective scrutiny: as backbench councillors are freed from unproductive involvement in deliberative committees, where they exercise little real power or influence on policy, they will be able to take on new roles. The White Paper stated that the effect would be to free them for more work in representing their constituents and engaging in scrutiny of the executive, while still retaining a share in the policy and budgetary decisions of the council.[91]

## THE NEW EXECUTIVE STRUCTURES[92]

Under new legislation a council must adopt one of the prescribed forms of executive.[93] There are three basic models: a directly elected mayor who appoints an executive of two or more councillors (the 'mayor and executive' model); a council leader, elected by the full council, who then either appoints an executive drawn from the council or heads an executive appointed by and drawn from the council (the 'Cabinet' model); and a directly elected mayor, with an officer of the authority, appointed by the council, as a council manager (the 'Mayor and Council Manager' model).

Each local authority is required to draw up, to consult the public about, and to notify the Secretary of State of its proposed executive arrangements.[94] These proposals must set out the form of executive that the authority intends to adopt, the functions for which the executive will be

[90] And see *R v Amber Valley DC ex p. Jackson*, [1984] 3 All ER 501, and *R v CLA ex p. Liverpool CC*, [1999] 3 All ER 85; pp. 173–4 and 188–9 above.

[91] N. 87 above, para. 3.13.

[92] L. Pratchett, 'Introduction: Defining Democratic Renewal', (1999) 25 (4) LGS 1. For surveys by the Local Government Association reporting the proposals of a large number of authorities in advance of the legislation see: LGA, *Leading the Agenda: Case Studies of New Political Management Arrangements* (London, 1999); *Leading the Agenda No. 2: Further Case Studies of New Political Management Arrangements* (London, 1999).

[93] LGA 2000, s. 11. Much of the detail of the three schemes is to be found in DETR, *Local Government Bill: Consultative Drafts for Proposed Guidance and Regulations on New Constitutions for Councils* (London, Jan. 2000) (hereafter *Guidance*).

[94] S. 25. Changes to executive arrangements must be implemented (including holding any referendum and mayoral election) by June 2002. It is expected that proposals will have at least been submitted to the Secretary of State by June 2001. See *Guidance*, para. 2.22.

responsible, the overview and scrutiny committee(s) to be established, a timetable, and details of any transitional arrangements. A (binding) local referendum must be held if the authority proposes that there will be an elected mayor (ie. under the 'Mayor and Executive' or 'Mayor and Council manager' model).[95] This is a duty which applies once only, but a council may also decide later to invoke a similar procedure to change its executive arrangements.[96] These procedures contain safeguards for elected mayors, to prevent them being bypassed or abolished in the event of conflict;[97] there may include a referendum vote in favour before the council can change to a different form of executive.[98] A review may also be triggered by petition of electors in an area[99] under provisions made by the Secretary of State requiring a referendum to be held.[100] (The original proposal for an automatic referendum under a petition signed by 5% of electors was abandoned at a late stage.) In all cases, however, once a referendum has been held further referendums cannot take place for a period of five years.[101]

The effect is that the Cabinet model can be implemented without a referendum. This is unfortunate, because cabinets are perceived to be the most closed form of the new local constitutions and the nearest to the present conditions prevailing in most local authorities. It also appears to be the option most favoured by councillors, judging from the declared intentions of local authorities to date. In these circumstances the range of safeguards built into the legislation and guidance to ensure that genuine public consultation[102] is carried out in an even-handed way by the council, and the ministerial powers to step in and require a referendum to be held, will be important.

All three models involve a split between the functions of the executive and council as a whole.[103] Two further innovative features are common to what are likely to be the most popular of these two models (the Mayor and Executive model and the Cabinet model). Firstly, the executive and any committee of the executive can be drawn from one party only: they are exempt from the statutory political balance requirements.[104] Secondly, in

[95] S. 27(1). [96] S. 30. [97] S. 30(2)(b).
[98] S. 30(2). [99] Under regulations made by the Secretary of State under s. 34.
[100] S. 35. [101] S. 45(1).

[102] See *Guidance*, para. 2.8, and see the restrictions on publicity by councils both in referendum campaigns and in mayoral elections: ibid., paras. 3.23 and 4.27ff. and the duties to seek to maximize electoral turnout: para. 4.11.

[103] In all cases the Secretary of State prescribes which decisions must be taken by the authority and which can be subject to executive arrangements: ibid., s. 13(3). The council decides which of the latter group are to be taken by the executive in its case (see definition of 'executive arrangements' in s. 10) subject to the overriding power of the Secretary of State to prescribe *circumstances* in which the authority rather than the executive must decide: s. 13(6).

[104] Ibid., s. 24. The political balance requirements, nevertheless, will apply to the oversight and scrutiny committees.

addition to the existing legally permitted types of delegation, it will be permissible to delegate functions to a single councillor who is a member of the executive (and for that councillor to further delegate to an officer).[105]

These arrangements were criticized as being unduly restrictive in forcing all local authorities into patterns designed to deal with the inefficiencies and abuses of urban, politicized councils.[106] Some flexibility is available in the facility for approval of other arrangements by the Secretary of State.[107] This may be particularly appropriate, for example, for those few rural areas where there are no party groups but where the authority does not wish to adopt the Mayor and Council Manager model. At a late stage the government gave way on its earlier insistence that any arrangements approved should involve a political executive, rather than a simple slimming down of the existing committee structure and greater delegation to officers.[108] Some small authorities (non-unitary district councils with a population of less than 85,000) will be permitted to operate 'alternative arrangements' under regulations (see sections 31, 32 and 33), provided these incorporate mechanisms for the review and scrutiny of council decisions. Calls for a (fourth) 'Leader and Council Manager' model to be introduced were rejected on the grounds that this would confer too much power on a single individual who had not been directly elected to that role (unlike elected mayors). However, the government suggested that it would look sympathetically at proposals for a very small executive of as few as three members operating with a council manager, in cases of councils without a political tradition.[109] Under the draft guidelines accompanying the legislation, flexibility has been shown also in accommodating authorities who wish to continue, or to adopt, a decentralized structure based on area committees, provided that these committees operate within a context of 'a systematic scheme of delegations and clear limits to those delegations in terms of functions and budgets' intended to ensure 'clear corporate accountability for executive functions'.[110]

105 Ss. 14–16. However, under the Mayor and Executive model (s. 14), the mayor retains control in arranging delegation in the first place, and he or she is able to prohibit further delegation by executive, the member of the executive, or committee. Under the leader and cabinet model, the council may either give the leader a similar right to distribute responsibilities and to retain a veto (s.15(4)) or delegate directly to the various members of the executive (s. 15(3)).

106 The joint committee were concerned for the position of hung authorities and those with no tradition of party politics: *Report of the Joint Committee on the Draft Local Government (the Organisation and Standards) Bill*, HL 102-I, HC 542-I (1998–9), para. 42.

107 Under regulations made under ss. 11(5) and (6) and 12.

108 Government Response to the *Report of the Joint Committee on the Draft Local Government (the Organisation and Standards) Bill*, Cm. 4529 (1999), paras. 2.5–9.

109 Ibid., paras. 2.16–18.

110 Ibid., para. 2.11. Potential conflicts of interest arising from the overlapping membership of area committees acting under delegated executive powers and a council's overview

**Cabinets:[111] The Leader and Executive Model**

Under the Cabinet model, the Leader will be chosen by councillors[112] and will be removable by them without reference to the electorate. The council may either give the Leader the ability to decide on the size and responsibilities of the cabinet (the so-called 'strong Leader') or may choose to do so itself by delegation of the various portfolios (the 'weak Leader').[113]

The procedures by which the Leader or any member of the cabinet can be removed are left to each council to determine under its standing orders; a 'strong' Leader might have the power to dismiss other members of the Cabinet, whereas a 'weak' one would not. These procedures will obviously be of importance when control of the council changes or if there is a power struggle within the majority party group. The introduction of cabinets at the same time as a system of annual elections[114] could have related, unforeseen results. The new electoral process will result in councils changing hands politically more frequently. However, bearing in mind that in many councils membership of the cabinet will be a full-time, salaried position, it may be difficult to find councillors prepared to volunteer for what could be a short and insecure political career.[115]

Although the creation of cabinets might be seen as a move towards a Westminster style of politics for local government, it has been argued that generally the Leaders of councils are less powerful than their central-government equivalents, and that local party groups are, correspondingly, more powerful in controlling their Leaders than are backbench MPs.[116] According to another commentator, the Leader and Cabinet model is the option most likely to be chosen since it 'represents the formalization of already existing group-dominated political processes'.[117] Except in hung authorities, where the election of the Leader may become a semi-transparent process, it is likely that normally the leadership and membership of the cabinet will be decided behind closed doors in the group meeting of the majority party and then presented to the council meeting for endorsement. This power of the party group to choose and dismiss the executive will enable it to control the cabinet and ensure that they carry out the group's policies.

and scrutiny committees will be handled by barring such members from scrutiny of decisions in which they were involved in the first place.

[111] S. Leach, 'Introducing Cabinets into British Local Government', (1999) 52(1) Parl. Affs. 77.

[112] S. 11(3) (a) provides for an election by the council.

[113] Ss.15 (4) and (3) respectively. See *Guidance*, ch. 9.

[114] See p. 15 above.

[115] Leach, op. cit., 84.

[116] Ibid. 78.

[117] C. Copus, 'The Party Group: A Barrier to Democratic Renewal', (1999) 25(4) LGS 76, 89–90.

It can be argued that these changes undervalue the virtues of the committee system, especially its transparency: decisions are generally made following advance notice through a published agenda and on the basis of an open report, by a body which includes political opponents and after a process which is open to the public.[118] There is the fear that any move to political executives will carry the risk of excluding backbench councillors and the public from decision-making and increase the possibility of abuse of power and corruption. It may seem remarkable that in the short period since the 1989 legislation implementing the Widdicombe report of 1986 that the law has come full circle back to single-party decision-making. Particularly ominous from this viewpoint is the high number of authorities opting for the Cabinet model: this in effect allows for a lawful form of one-party government and for suspension of the safeguards put in place in the 1980s. This line of criticism, however, perhaps overlooks the safeguards for ethical standards which are also put in place under the Act[119] and underplays the introduction of Overview and Scrutiny Committees, to which discussion now moves.

## Overview and Scrutiny Committees

Provisions for overview and scrutiny committees must be included in all executive arrangements.[120] Overview and scrutiny committees are described as a 'key element' of the new constitutions and as the 'main way by which the executive is held to account for the discharge of executive functions'.[121] The purpose of these committees will be twofold: first, to scrutinize the discharge of executive functions and, secondly, a policy role in making reports and recommendations to the authority or the executive about the discharge of their functions and on matters which affect the authority's area or inhabitants.[122] Linked with this is a strong duty favouring accountability and openness in the requirement that all members of the executive record decisions which they have taken and make available these decisions and the reasons for them (responsibility for this aspect will lie with the 'proper officer'). [123]

118 Peter Keith-Lucas, 'Two Cheers for the Committee System', unpublished paper to the Law Society's Local Government Group Annual Weekend School, Durham, Apr. 1999.

119 See p. 173 above.

120 The Secretary of State has power to make regulations about the operation and functions of overview and scrutiny committees which must be included within an authority's executive arrangements, and to issue binding guidance: ibid., s. 38.

121 *Guidance*, para. 6.3.

122 S. 21(2).

123 Ss. 22(3)–(5).

It is envisaged that scrutiny may take the form either of 'calling in' decisions before they are made or reviewing them, either individually or as part of an examination by the committee of the effectiveness of an overall policy. The government counsels, however, sparing use of the 'call-in' power, as it may detract from any efficiency gains of the new structures.[124] 'Call-in' could be limited by requiring the agreement of a certain number of committee members, or rationed by capping the number of decisions a committee may look at in a particular week or month, or by restricting the jurisdiction to items over a certain expenditure threshold. These will be matters left to each authority in designing its own constitution. The power to 'call in' decisions is not intended to supplant the responsibility of the executive in implementing the council's policy: at the most, the overview and scrutiny committee might be able to refer the matter for a debate in the full council meeting. Overview and scrutiny committees will have the power to require members of the executive and officers to attend and answer questions (and there will be a corresponding duty on them to do so) and to invite other people.[125] The government clearly envisages that reviews of policy should be carried out by overview and scrutiny committees in a way which will allow the committee to investigate the impact of the policy on users of council services and other partners of the council in delivering them. There will be a natural link between such reviews and community planning and performance review under the 'Best Value' regime.[126] If this process is to be effective the executive will need to be responsive in amending its policy following review by the overview and scrutiny committees: by comparison, while the thoroughness of parliamentary select committees' investigation is often praised, all too frequently their conclusions are ignored by government.

The division between executive and scrutiny councillors is based on a parliamentary select committee model. Separation from the executive is enforced by a provision preventing overview and scrutiny committees from including members of the executive.[127] Where a member of the committee has been involved in a decision delegated by the executive to an area committee, he or she will have to stand down and take no part in the subsequent scrutiny of that decision.[128] However, as in Parliament itself, the ideal may be marred by party allegiances. The scrutiny committees will have a majority of councillors who are from the same party as the executive.[129]

[124] Guidance, paras. 6.17ff. [125] S. 21(13) and (14). [126] S. 21(5) and see pp. 339–40.

[127] S. 21(9). In view of this, and since the governing party is to take a majority of seats on the oversight of scrutiny committees, the number of councillors involved in these committees will constrain the possible size of an executive.

[128] *Guidance*, para. 6.12.

[129] Overview and scrutiny committees will be subject to the political balance requirements (pp. 194–5 above). Consequently, where an authority has area committees these will only be able to engage in oversight and scrutiny if they are politically balanced.

Moreover, while formal checks may operate within the council machinery, such as a duty to record reasons for decisions, these do not prevent the executive from using party group meetings outside that framework to influence the scrutiny councillors. Without reform of the party group system to prevent this type of behind-the-scenes pulling of strings, the division of councillors into executive and scrutiny groups may only serve to consolidate and legitimize the position of invisible party oligarchies. One critic has argued that the democratic renewal programme is over-reliant on structural reforms and fails to address the position of party groups and considerations of political culture, especially the loyalty of councillors to their groups and their preference for discussing policy behind closed doors.[130] The dilemma is, however, that traditionally political parties have been regarded as separate, private entities. They have only recently become subject to legal registration, and to legislation governing political funding and restricting their role in election and referendum campaigns.[131] Self-regulation through amendment of the various parties' standing orders for local party groups looks more likely than legislative intervention as a means of promoting good practice.[132] The government has welcomed a proposal that where scrutiny committees are whipped, this should be declared openly, but has suggested that the adoption of a duty to do so would be for councils and the political parties rather than for legislation.[133]

[130] Copus, op. cit., 88–9.

[131] Registration of Political Parties Act 1998, introduced for the purpose of implementing the new voting systems for devolved government and in European Parliament elections, and the Political Parties Elections and Referendums Bill 1999/2000, cl. 20 of which extends to candidates representing a political party in a local government election.

[132] In 1999 the Labour Party announced a review of its party group procedures. New model Standing Orders have been promulgated for each of the three types of reformed executive structure. Each of them prohibits the whipping of group members in a decision of an overview and scrutiny committee. In a speech to the Labour Party Conference on 27 Sept. 1999 the Local Government Minister, Hilary Armstrong, promised that Labour groups on overview and scrutiny committees would not be whipped, and challenged other political parties to make the same commitment.

[133] *Government Response to the Report of the Joint Committee on the Draft Local Government (Organisation and Standards) Bill*, Cm. 4529 (1999), paras. 2.93–5; *Guidance*, para. 6.47.

[134] See H. Elcock, 'Leading People: Some Issues of Local Government Leadership in Britain and America', (1995) 21(4) Local Govt. Studs. 546; G. Stoker, 'The Reform of the Institutions of Local Representative Democracy: Is There a Role for the Mayor–Council Model?' (London, 1996); G. Stoker and H. Wolman, 'Drawing Lessons from US Experience: An Elected Mayor for British Local Government', (1992) 70(2) Public Administration 241; A. Norton, *International Handbook of Local and Regional Government* (Aldershot, 1994); M. Parkinson and D. Judd, *Leadership and Urban Regeneration* (London, 1990).

**Elected Mayors**[134]

A directly elected mayor is a feature of many foreign systems of local government, especially urban authorities in the US, France, Italy, and Germany. Michael Heseltine, during his period as Secretary of State for the Environment, was the first Westminster politician to show an interest in introducing directly elected mayors to Britain.[135] The public seemed, on the whole, keener on the suggestion than were councillors.[136] Following its adoption by the Commission for Local Democracy,[137] the idea received some interest from the Labour Party, which showed qualified enthusiasm for local experiments where these were supported by local people.[138] After Labour's election victory a consultation paper was published in July 1997,[139] which canvassed the elected mayor option for the proposed new London Authority, followed by a White Paper in March 1998[140] in which it was a firm proposal. In a referendum held in Greater London on 7 May 1998 a majority of those voting supported the White Paper's proposals. Legislation was introduced to give effect to these proposals and, following the passage of the Greater London Authority Act 1999, elections were held in May 2000 for Britain's first elected mayor.

In relation to councils outside London, in its 1998 White Paper[141] the government proposed an elected mayor as one of the three models for political executives which it would make available to councils as part of its modernization agenda. The 1999 White Paper proposed that councils be placed under a duty to consult local people about the form of government they wished to see, with an elected mayor as one of the options, together with the possibility of a referendum being triggered to put the elected

[135] However, the DoE consultation paper *The Internal Management of Local Authorities in England* (1991), published during his period of office, while exploring different possible models of political executive, did not consider elected mayors.

[136] J. Percy-Smith, *Discussing Democracy: The Response to 'Taking Charge: The Rebirth of Local Democracy'* (London, 1996), found 50% of respondents questioned against the Commission for Local Democracy proposal for an elected mayor, with 39% in favour, 10% neither in favour nor against, and 2% undecided. However, the respondents were predominantly councillors and officers, with a vested stake in the current arrangements. A 1995 survey of public opinion found a large gap between the public (70% of whom supported direct elections for the leader of the council) and councillors (of whom only 16% supported a directly elected mayor): see W. Miller and M. Dickson, *Local Governance and Local Citizenship* (Glasgow, 1996), cited in Stoker, op. cit., 19.

[137] Commission for Local Democracy, *Taking Charge: The Rebirth of Local Democracy* (London, 1995), ch. 4.

[138] Labour Party, *Renewing Democracy, Rebuilding Communities* (London, 1995), 4. The policy paper on London argued for a strategic authority for London, but merely invited views about whether there should be a directly elected mayor: Labour Party, A *Voice for London* (London, 1996), 8.

[139] *New Leadership for London* (1997).

[140] *A Mayor and Assembly for London*, Cm. 3897 (1998).

[141] *Modern Local Government: In Touch With the People,* Cm. 4014 (1998), ch. 3.

mayor option to the electorate, even where this was not the council's preferred choice.[142] The Local Government Act 2000 gives effect to these proposals. It does not, however, specify in detail the division of powers between the mayor, the executive, and the council: these matters will be addressed in the regulations approving model Standing Orders for use by councils.

The advocates of a directly elected mayor claim that the office has several advantages. The Commission for Local Democracy (CLD) argued that a separation of the executive (comprising a directly elected mayor or leader and the council's staff) from the elected assembly of councillors would bring about a potential increase in public knowledge about and participation in local government, an alignment of formal and informal accountability, a weakening of party dominance, and the release of individual councillors to fulfil their representative role. Introduction of the office in British local government would arguably be a less radical change than it might appear, since in reality key individual politicians already exercise dominance within the group system—in practice the Leader of a Council often enjoys this effective power, and the mayoralty is a purely titular office. With an elected mayor, instead of the leadership of the group being settled as a private political question by the party, it would become a question directly for the electorate.[143]

Public interest in local democracy might also be fostered, as at the national level, by a form of presidential politics. Advocates also argue that a high-profile position of this kind might attract into local government a different calibre of local representative. Experience of the campaign to elect a Mayor for London in 1999–2000 would seem to bear this out: the candidates who proposed themselves for selection by their parties included three former government ministers (Frank Dobson, Glenda Jackson, and Steven Norris), a former Leader of the Greater London Council (Ken Livingstone), and a former Deputy Chairman of the Conservative Party (Jeffrey Archer).

The Commission for Local Democracy argued that elected mayors would be highly visible figureheads capable of representing their communities at national level in discussion with central government and other local authorities, and in Europe. The increasingly competitive environment in which local authorities bid against each other to host international events, or for European or domestic funding (for example, from the Regional Fund or the City Challenge scheme), may require new local government institutions to meet new challenges. Certainly, the elected mayors of major conurbations would enjoy greater personal power than most

142 *Local Leadership, Local Choice*, Cm. 4298 (1999), ch. 2.

143 The CLD cited a survey giving 72% public support to the idea of a directly elected council leader: *Taking Charge*, 23.

junior (and some Cabinet) ministers. Whether power and visibility of this kind would be accompanied by an increase in public accountability is the key issue. This depends in part on the balance of formal powers between the mayor and the elected council. Under the CLD proposals the main tasks of the mayor were to prepare a budget and an annual policy review for approval by the council and to respond to council scrutiny of the executive, to oversee the implementation of council policies by the officers, to exercise the formal powers of the council, and to represent the council externally.[144]

There are some disadvantages, however, arising from enhancing still further the power of individual politicians. The creation of the office calls into question the function of other locally elected politicians, particularly where it is superimposed on existing structures, rather than, as in London, part of a design for a wholly new authority. Placing further power in the hands of one person could be an invitation to abuse, unless it is counterbalanced by other management reforms. British portents from local authorities where strong political leadership has cowed officers into submission and into agreement with policies at best questionable and at worst illegal, like Liverpool and Westminster in the 1980s, are not encouraging. It is significant that the government's proposals rejected calls that elected mayors should be subject to 'recall' (i.e. removal from office), preferring instead to trust the balance of political mechanisms which it was creating to subject the mayor to scrutiny and embarrassment, possibly culminating in resignation in extreme cases. It was argued that a power of removal by a special majority of the council would encourage confrontational politics, and that removal by public petition would be unworkable and would, in any event, be unprecedented for an elected office in the UK.[145]

Any proposed reform must also be considered in the context of changes to the electoral system (of both the cycle and method of elections), and against the background of additional powers to obtain information and of scrutiny for non-executive councillors, especially if the objective is (as in the CLD proposals) a weakening of party control.[146] Although elected mayors may give local politics a higher profile, the change also involves a loss of opportunities for participation by other councillors and the people they represent, with the risk that the executive may be less responsive to the electorate, except every four years, when re-election looms. The question of domination of officers is more difficult, especially if the mayor's powers extend to the hiring and firing of senior staff, who would supply

144 Ibid. 21.

145 *Government Response to the Report of the Joint Committee on the Draft Local Government (Organisation and Standards) Bill*, Cm. 4529 (1999), paras. 2.30–5.

146 The CLD proposals (n. 137, 21) envisage the introduction of proportional representation, which would presumably increase the number of hung councils.

policy and managerial advice. In this context there might be a case for specific procedures for officers to alert the council to the mayor's actions and concurrent protections against victimization for doing so, in addition to those applying normally to council staff.[147]

The White Paper envisaged two distinct executive models involving an elected mayor: a directly elected Mayor with Cabinet, and a directly elected Mayor and Council Manager.[148] In the Mayor with Cabinet model the elected mayor would be responsible for providing political leadership, proposing the policy framework and a budget of the council, and taking executive decisions within that framework. The policy framework and budget would be subject to agreement by the full council; councillors outside the cabinet would be able to propose amendments to the budget as well as new or changed policies for the council. The Mayor would appoint members of the Cabinet from the ranks of councillors, and they would be responsible for implementing the policies of the council under powers delegated to them as a group or as individuals. The Mayor would also have available a personal political policy adviser, paid for by the council. The executive and the full council would have to agree on the appointment of a chief executive and of chief officers.

The office of mayor would be less powerful in the second model, that of the directly elected Mayor and Council Manager.[149] This envisages a clear split between the Mayor, who would be responsible for overall political leadership and proposing the broad policy framework of the council, and the Council Manager, who would be appointed by the council[150] and have a central role in developing and implementing policy and the budget under the guidance of the Mayor. The Council Manager would be a powerful figure working within the agreed policy framework without the need for further approval by the council of the means by which policies are to be executed, and with extensive powers of delegation.[151] The council would retain overall responsibility for approving the policy framework and deciding on a budget, with councillors outside the executive able to propose amendments to each. Either the Council Manager or the council might be responsible for appointing chief officers. In either of the mayoral models, officers would be responsible both for implementing the council's policies and for providing support for non-executive councillors, and accounting to them for the executive's actions.

These arrangements are simply two from a number of possible alternative schemes which could be devised for the allocation of powers between an elected mayor and the council or assembly, depending on what objec-

[147] See pp. 268–73 below.

[148] And see ss. 14 and 16 LGA 2000.

[149] Council managers operate in the local government structure of New Zealand and of some parts of the USA.

[150] S. 11(4) (b) LGA 2000.

[151] *Local Leadership, Local Choice*, para. 3.54.

tives are in mind. In a survey prior to the current debate Stoker characterized three alternative models of mayoral system which could be designed: Open, Partisan, and Leadership.[152] The Open system is based on a conscious splitting of powers, both to initiate proposals and of scrutiny, between the assembly and the mayor; the objective is to create a working tension between the institutions which drives the actors into public (hence 'Open') negotiation and compromise. By contrast, the Partisan approach assumes the continuation into the new arrangements of strong party-political allegiances between the assembly and the mayor (who would come from the same party), thus providing stable and effective (but more closed) government. The Leadership model similarly vests the power of initiative predominantly in the mayor, with the assembly having fewer checking powers than in the Open model, but with a different electoral cycle for choosing the two institutions and a greater likelihood of different political control.

Either of the models proposed by the government has the potential to create a new set of tensions between two separately elected parts of the council, each pursuing their own agenda. The timing and method of elections proposed for the mayor increase the probability that the mayor could be from a different party from that of the council as a whole and, perhaps, of the remainder of the executive in those cases where it is the council rather than the mayor which chooses the other members. Mayors will be chosen under the 'supplementary vote' system[153] to serve a four-year term of office.[154] In the councils most likely to opt for the model (metropolitan districts and unitary authorities) the mayoral election must be timed to take place in the year in the four-year cycle when other elections of councillors are not occurring.[155]

The White Paper proposed that while non-executive councillors should be able to propose policy, the mayor would have a right to veto, or at least to delay, such proposals, so ensuring that policy differences between the two would receive public attention.[156] It was envisaged that the mayor would have a week within which to exercise the veto by writing to the

[152] Stoker, op. cit., 29–34.

[153] LGA 2000, s. 42 and sched. 2. This is a limited form of Alternative Vote system in which voters list their first and second preferences from among the candidates. A candidate receiving a majority of first-preference votes is elected. Failing this, the 2 candidates who achieved the greatest number of first-preference votes have redistributed to them the second-preference votes of all the other candidates (who are eliminated) and the candidate who then has the highest number of votes overall is elected. If there are fewer than 3 candidates a simple majority system is used instead.

[154] S. 39(6) LGA 2000.

[155] S. 41 gives the Secretary of State power to make regulations concerning the timing of elections. See *Guidance*, para. 5.4; other authorities can choose which year elections will normally be held in.

[156] *Local Leadership, Local Choice*, paras. 3.66–70.

council's monitoring officer, giving reasons. The council would be able to override the mayor's veto at its next full meeting either by simple majority or by a majority specified in the council's constitution. The government argued that the mechanism for resolving disagreements over the budget would be one of the key indicators of the relative strengths of the executive mayor and the council, and that this should be primarily a matter for local choice at the time of adopting one of the executive models.[157] The last word could be left with the full council, which would have the right to override any veto by the mayor of its amendments to his or her budget, or a specified majority might be required at a later council meeting.[158] Overall, the form proposed by the government in the Mayor and Cabinet model comes nearest to the Open Model, in that a clear policy/scrutiny split is envisaged, but concessions have been made to the Leadership model by preserving the ability of non-executive councillors to initiate policy proposals, because of concerns about their powerlessness. The Mayor and Council Manager executive is nearer again to the leadership model.

The 1999 White Paper made a clear link between directly elected mayors and the new emphasis on partnership working as part of the new role of councils as 'community leaders':

> the executive must be outward looking and engage with those it serves, not inwardly focused. In the new forms of local governance, an executive would shape the agenda, but would do so in the light of the views of the community, other local stakeholders, including potential partners, and the recommendations of councillors outside the executive. An elected mayor would be ideally placed to make these links.[159]

One possible model for an elected mayor and executive is that contained in the Greater London Authority Act 1999.[160] This provides for separate elections of the Mayor and an Assembly (who together constitute the Authority), to be held at the same time every four years.[161] The Mayor is

[157] Ibid. 3.72–77. Under the Mayor and Council Manager model, responsibility for approval of the budget would be that of the Council and mechanisms for resolving disputes would be less necessary: ibid., para. 3.78.

[158] Cf. Greater London Authority Act 1999, sched. 6, para. 8(4), specifying that the Assembly can only amend the budget by a two-thirds majority. While it does not intend to prescribe uniform procedures for dealing with conflicts, the government's intention is that all council constitutions will contain such procedures: *Government Response to the Report of the Joint Committee on the Draft Local Government (Organisation and Standards) Bill*, Cm. 4529 (1999), paras. 2.101–3. The proposed guidance suggested that as a minimum these should allow a specified time within which the executive would be able to require the council to reconsider its policy resolutions so that there could be an open debate: *Guidance*, paras. 14.28ff.

[159] *Local Leadership, Local Choice*, para. 3.32.

[160] Introduced following proposals in the White Paper, *A Mayor and Assembly for London*, Cm 3897 (1998) and approved in a referendum of electors in London held in May 1998. See M. Supperstone and T. Pitt-Payne, 'The Greater London Authority Bill', [1999] PL 581.

[161] GLA Act ss. 1 and 2 and sched.1

elected under the supplementary vote system which, if there are three or more candidates, allows voters to express a first and second preference among the candidates. (If there are fewer than three candidates, the 'first past the post' voting system is applied.) If no candidate achieves more than 50 per cent of first preferences, all but the top two candidates are eliminated and the second preferences of those who voted for the eliminated candidates are redistributed, with whoever receives most votes being elected. The Assembly comprises twenty-five members, of whom fourteen represent constituencies and eleven are chosen for London-wide seats, according to the Additional Member system, using the electoral strengths of the respective political parties.[162] The principal purposes of the Authority are to promote economic development and wealth creation, social development, and improvement of the environment in Greater London.[163] Other provisions in Part II of the Act require the Mayor to develop and present strategic plans in specified fields and give the Authority the power to investigate and question the Mayor on progress.

The Mayor will be the most visible face of the new Authority and will be the main source of initiatives in policy affecting London as a whole, as well as being responsible for coordinating the contributions of other agencies and bodies across the capital. As well as running new transport and economic development bodies,[164] the Mayor will work closely with (and make appointments to) the new Metropolitan Police Authority and London Fire and Emergency Planning Authority, and will be responsible for setting the overall framework for the development of London, within which borough councils will deal with planning. He or she will also have a coordinating role in improving the environment and air quality in London, in other environmental issues such as waste and noise, and in encouraging local initiatives. The Mayor will have a small personal office[165] and will be able to exercise most of the functions of the Authority and to delegate responsibility in turn to the Deputy Mayor, Transport for London, and the London Development Agency.[166] The Mayor is to

[162] There will be no by-elections under this system: any vacancies to constituencies will remain unfilled until the next election; vacancies for London-wide seats will be filled from the party list of candidates at the previous election.

[163] S. 30(2) GLA Act.

[164] The London Development Agency is the Regional Development Agency for London and the GLA may have transferred to it powers under the Regional Development Agencies Act 1998 by the Secretary of State: p. 25 above.

[165] Under the provisions of s. 67(1)(a), the Mayor will be able to appoint 2 political advisers. They will be personal appointments made by the Mayor alone for his or her term of office, and the posts will be exempt from open competition. The Mayor will also be able to appoint not more than 10 other members of staff—section 67(1)(b). All other staff will be appointed by the assembly or under powers delegated from it under the provisions of section 67(2).

[166] S. 38. Section 49 provides for the appointment of a Deputy Mayor from among the assembly members, who will also be a member of the Metropolitan Police Authority and will

prepare a series of strategies to deal with various matters: transport, economic development and regeneration, spatial development, biodiversity, municipal waste management, air quality, ambient noise, and culture.[167] The process also involves consideration of national targets and wide duties of consultation with the Assembly and the functional bodies, each London borough council, and other organizations or individuals he or she considers it appropriate to consult, including those from designated categories. A requirement to publicize the strategies also applies.[168]

The Assembly is required to keep the Mayor's exercise of statutory functions under review.[169] It has power to investigate, and prepare reports about, any actions and decisions of the Mayor, any actions and decisions by any member of the Authority's staff, matters relating to the principal purposes, matters in relation to which statutory functions are exercisable by the Mayor, or any other matters which the Assembly considers to be of importance to Greater London. The Assembly as a whole (the power is not exercisable by a committee or individual Assembly member) may submit proposals to the Mayor, which he or she is required to make a formal response to.[170]

Assembly members are paid, full-time politicians. In addition to the work of the Assembly and its committees, they also sit on a number of the London-wide authorities, boards, and bodies. The Mayor appoints Assembly members to the new police and fire authorities for London, and hence will be able to influence them indirectly. The Assembly can also agree or suggest changes to the Mayor's overall budget and plans, and agree proposals for raising revenue. It exercises oversight over the performance of the functional bodies for transport and economic development, and of the police and fire authorities. It also has power to consider any other issues that it believes are important to Londoners.

The Assembly may delegate any of its functions to a committee or subcommittee, or to a single Assembly member, or member of staff of the Authority.[171] The allocation of appointments to committees must reflect

become acting mayor if the Mayor resigns, dies, is disqualified, or is temporarily unable to act; the Deputy Mayor cannot, however, be the Chair or Deputy Chair of the assembly. The Mayor may dismiss the Deputy Mayor at any time.

[167] Respectively, GLA Act ss. 142, 306, 334, 352, 353, 362, 370, and 376. Under s. 41, in preparing, reviewing, or amending the strategies, the Mayor must have regard to various specified matters. These include: consistency with national policy and any international obligations notified by the Secretary of State; the principal purposes of the Authority and the implications for the health of people in London and the achievement of sustainable development in the UK; the resources available to implement each strategy; and the desirability of promoting and encouraging the safe use for transportation of the River Thames.

[168] S. 43. [169] S.59. [170] S. 60.

[171] S. 54. Staff appointments delegated to a named individual, however, may only be delegated to a member of the staff of the Authority appointed by the Assembly.

the strength of different political groups in the Assembly as a whole.[172] The Assembly retains the power to act notwithstanding any delegation of its functions. The Assembly, its committees, and sub-committees are required to hold meetings in public, give public notice of meetings, and make documents publicly available.[173] However, 'background papers' which would disclose advice to the Mayor are exempt from disclosure.

Several mechanisms exist to ensure the accountability of the Mayor and Assembly. The Mayor is required to make a report to the Assembly at least three clear working days prior to each of its monthly meetings, detailing the significant decisions taken, with reasons, and responses to any formal proposals made by the Assembly.[174] The Mayor will attend the Assembly's meetings to answer questions, but is not obliged to disclose advice received from the staff of the Authority or from functional bodies or their staff.[175] Similarly, although the Assembly has powers to summon such people, they are not obliged to disclose advice given to the Mayor. This is a move towards treating such officers more in the mould of civil servants than has been customary with local government officers (similar restrictions apply to civil service evidence to parliamentary select committees) and follows, perhaps inevitably, from the formal recognition of a distinct political executive. The Assembly meetings, the Mayor's reports, the text of questions and answers, and the minutes of the meetings will be open or available to the public, subject to the exceptions for confidential and other exempt material set out in Part V(A) of the Local Government Act 1972. The Mayor is required to prepare an Annual Report assessing progress on implementing strategies, including the achievement of any targets and giving any information which the Assembly has asked to be included before the beginning of the relevant year. The report is to be followed by an annual 'State of London' debate.[176] In addition, a 'People's Question Time' must be held twice-yearly.[177]

Overall, the Act creates a powerful new office with few formal restraints on its powers. The Mayor and the Assembly will have to work together, but although the latter has strong powers to review the work of the Mayor, whether it can block initiatives or policies will depend on the precise electoral mathematics: the necessary two-thirds veto by the Assembly is

[172] Ss. 57 and 58.

[173] Pt. VA of the Local Government Act 1972 (ss. 100A–K and sched. 12A).

[174] S. 45.

[175] Ss. 61–5 deal with the attendance of witnesses at Assembly meetings and production of documents. Apart from senior staff of the Authority and the four functional bodies (Transport for London, the London Development Agency, the Metropolitan Police Authority, and the London Fire and Emergency Planning Authority), these include the chairman and board members of one of the functional bodies (or anyone who has been within the preceding three years), former contractors and grant-holders (within the preceding three years) and their staff, and members and former members of the Assembly: ss. 61 (2)–(5).

[176] S.47.

[177] S.48.

unlikely to be obtainable in practice, especially within an Assembly elected at the same time as the Mayor. The Mayor, therefore, has the upper hand. Significantly, attempts by the Liberal Democrats to amend the legislation to give a power to the Assembly to 'impeach' the Mayor were rejected by the government.[178]

## CONCLUSION

One commentator on the new executive arrangements has suggested that they fly in the face of the three cherished local government nostrums: the legal equality of all councillors, the council meeting as the supreme decision-making body, and the power of party groups.[179] The discussion in this chapter and the previous one of the position of the party group, of backbench members, and of council leaders and committee chair-holders has shown the mythical quality of the first two of these commonly accepted ideas, because of the reality of the third. The reforms of executive structures instituted by the Labour government are to be applauded if they succeed in bringing the law closer to the existing political reality in many councils and so, as has been claimed, aid clarity and accountability.

The argument that the roles both of backbench councillors and of the political elite should be strengthened by more clearly separating them appears compelling. Whether the reforms also succeed in bringing openness and accountability will depend in part, however, on the legal apparatus of scrutiny, especially the powers of the new overview and scrutiny committees and the duty upon the executive to record its decisions and the reasons for them. The arrangements both for these committees and for the institutional division of powers between elected mayors and their councils attempt to create a working tension within institutions in the hope of generating public interest in local democracy and producing greater openness. Whether this succeeds may ultimately depend on factors beyond the reach of the law and, especially, on whether the political parties genuinely work to change the political culture and climate within which the new legal regime will operate.

178 Cf. refusal to incorporate a 'recall' in the elected mayor proposals under the LGA 2000: p. 239 above.

179 Leach, op. cit., 79.

# 8

# *Officers and Politics*

## INTRODUCTION

Although there are approximately 2 million full and part-time employees in local government, many are in professional groups which are unconcerned with the formulation and implementation of local policy (for example, teachers, social workers, police, and fire officers). The working lives of these groups are so heavily regulated by national legislative and administrative guidelines, with little possibility for local discretion, that they may be regarded as a part of local administration rather than local government. For example, teachers work under national conditions of service, enjoy rights and duties under universally applicable legislation, and teach (in state schools) according to a National Curriculum prescribed by law.[1] Only about 20 per cent of local employees are employed in the administrative, professional, and technical grades normally referred to as local government 'officers', and only 0.3 per cent are chief officers. Among blue-collar groups there was a steady decline after 1979, attributable mainly to contracting out.[2]

In this chapter the role of officers is considered first from the perspective of the representative democratic model of local politics. This discussion proceeds from the view of officers as neutral, professional servants of the whole council to consider points which have caused tension due to the increasing politicization of local government: relations with councillors, the appointment of officers, political restrictions on officers' activities and 'twin tracking', and the use of political advisers. The new legal duties imposed on officers (including those requiring statutory disclosure of information, or 'whistle-blowing') are evaluated in turn. The chapter then turns to questions of reform. The introduction of compulsory competitive

[1] See on national conditions of service, and employment rights and duties of teachers: School Teachers' Pay and Conditions Act 1991, s. 1, which set up a review body, publishing annual documents entitled 'School Teachers' Pay and Conditions Documents'. These are given effect to by statutory instrument under s. 2 of the Act. National Curriculum: Education Act 1996, ss. 352–7 (as amended).

[2] Comparison of figures for 1979 and 1993 showed a total loss of 138,000 jobs (nearly 90,000 of them manual), with fewer than 10% of the 1979 total employees engaged in transport, about 54% in cleaning and refuse disposal and collection, 61% in construction, and 86% in leisure and tourism. Figures are taken from: T. Byrne, *Local Government in Britain* (6th edn., Harmondsworth, 1994), 249–51; DoE, *Annual Report for 1996*, Cm. 3207 (1996), 137; K. Escott and D. Whitfield, *The Gender Impact of CCT in Local Government* (Manchester, 1995), 15–17.

tendering (CCT) had novel implications for the role of officers, raising fundamental questions quite different from these debates grounded on a liberal view.[3] Arguably, the effect was a sharp move towards a 'new neutrality' view, this time based upon officers as commercial managers. Finally, the implications of the new executive structures of councils for officers are discussed.[4]

## NEUTRALITY AND COMMITMENT

Two contrasting approaches can be taken to the politics of local government officers. At one pole, rooted in liberal-democratic notions of privacy and of freedom of belief and association, any restraint on (or indeed inquiry into) the political activities of officers can be seen as impermissible. This view makes a clear separation between the private views of the individual and the public function they perform. The other view, grounded in a different variant of the same democratic theory, argues that officers should be committed to the policies of the democratically elected local representatives, the councillors. Two kinds of commitment might be envisaged. The first is a preparedness to use all professional and technical expertise in the implementation of councillors' agreed policies (the 'weak commitment' view); this is not markedly different from the 'neutrality' view, except that it may be argued that an officer's personal convictions and extramural behaviour may become appropriate topics of inquiry and control where they suggest an inability to give the necessary allegiance. A second version of the commitment view seeks officers who are personally committed to the programme of the council. This 'strong' version of officer commitment has not, until recent times, been a prominent feature of British local government, and legislation contains some controls designed to combat potential abuses which may arise from it. In describing the legal and administrative arrangements governing officers in this chapter we are concerned mainly with tensions between the 'neutrality' and the 'weak commitment' views.[5]

Both these views of officers rest, as in the case of the Civil Service, on the feasibility of a division of policy (the preserve of councillors) from administration and implementation of policy (the domain of officers). A distinction of this kind is a central feature, whether the officers are seen as serving the council as a whole or are required to implement the policies of the

[3] The structural implications have been introduced in Ch. 7 and other implications will be addressed in Ch. 10.

[4] See Ch. 7.

[5] Cf. the Widdicombe Report, writing in 1986 of 'the structural ambiguities in the role of officers which are inherent in the present statutory framework': para. 6.140.

majority group. However, such a division has obvious difficulties, not least because the process of policy formulation is critically dependent on accurate advice about the council's current position, and the options open to it which must, in turn, come from officers. While exhorting councillors to abstain from routine management, the Widdicombe Committee recognized that it was unrealistic to exclude councillors from management policy issues, especially where the form of delivery of service was itself a matter of key political belief, as, for example, with privatization or decentralization of services.[6]

Officers need a strong and continuous commitment to local democracy in order to offer advice dispassionately and with no regard to departmental advantage. Furthermore, in the politicized atmosphere of local government which has prevailed since the 1980s, councillors have increasingly looked not merely for neutral, technical competence in implementing council policy, but also for active enthusiasm and ideological assent from officers. In the remainder of this section, the extent to which law and practice embody the 'neutrality' view is first discussed, and then the political strains on that view are considered.

The neutrality view argues that officers should be politically neutral in the performance of their duties. They serve the entire council, rather than the controlling political group. A number of functions given to officers in local government law reinforce this view, especially those which make officers the custodians of the public's or of members' rights under the access to information provisions,[7] and the functions of financial and monitoring officers.[8] This view requires a high commitment to the continuity of the local democratic process from those who work within it, and clear ability to subscribe to, and to make in practice, the necessary mental feat of separating private views from public duties. Recognizing that officers are, in effect, part of the permanent administration of the council, they should do nothing to undermine councillors' or the public's confidence in their ability to serve a different political party. It also calls for trust and restraint on behalf of local politicians in not seeking to use officers for partisan purposes.[9]

There is, however, a danger (as with the Civil Service) that in espousing a 'neutral/technical' view of the best local policies officers may

[6] Ibid., para. 6.83. [7] As under in the duties of the 'proper officer': p. 85 above.

[8] See further p. 269 below and Ch. 4.

[9] Even prior to specific legislation governing officers' activities (discussed below) the courts had held that some restrictions may be imposed on the political purposes which a council allows its staff to engage in, through judicial control of the council's power as an employer. Hence, a decision by ILEA to release one officer to a joint organization representing trade unions could be justified by implied power to promote good industrial relations, but in the same case a decision of the GLC to give 7 staff paid leave to campaign against abolition of the council was unlawful: *R v GLC ex p. Westminster CC*, *The Times*, 27 Dec. 1984; see also *Meek v Lothian Regional Council*, 1980 SLT 6.

unconsciously impose an unrecognized political agenda of their own, and may become the permanent government unchanging behind the 'store front' politicians. Moreover, there are some significant differences in the relations of appointed officers and elected politicians between local and central government,[10] which, if anything, tend towards enhancing officer dominance. Senior local government officers have received technical, professional training, whereas their equivalents in central government are more likely to be generalists. Councillors, on the other hand, are more likely to be part-time, whereas their central government counterparts, ministers, are full-time, and often have non-career civil servants as personal advisers.[11] However, local councillors do enjoy greater access to council officers than backbench MPs have to civil servants. Contact of this kind is partly institutionalized through committees, but also occurs frequently and informally as councillors pursue constituents' problems in the town hall.

The view of officers as technical experts serving a council of elected amateurs led during the 1960s and 1970s to a pattern of management and organization along quasi-commercial lines. These developments were encouraged by two official inquiries into local government organization. The Maud Committee, which reported in 1967,[12] favoured organization based upon a model drawn from the private sector, the creation of a management board of senior councillors.[13] Set against what was perceived as a decline in the standard of councillors, the report reaffirmed the pragmatic case for local *administration*, but, perhaps because its focus was local government officers, it placed less emphasis on delivery through a locally democratic mechanism. The Bains report, timed to coincide with the structural reorganization of local government in 1972,[14] recommended a pattern of organization which was widely adopted in the new authorities: a powerful Chief Executive and management team of chief officers advising a Policy and Resources committee of leading councillors. This pattern was designed to imitate a commercial board of directors, rather than the traditional organization of local authorities on the basis of service-related committees. In practice, though, in most authorities it was merely superimposed upon the traditional committee structure. Consequently, many of

[10] These comparisons are taken from, J. Kingdom, *Local Government and Politics* (Hemel Hempstead, 1991), ch. 10.

[11] Councillors may be paid, not only in the sense of receiving attendance allowances but also in terms of qualifying for special responsibility allowances.

[12] *Report of the Committee on the Management of Local Government* (London, 1967). This followed a model implemented by Newcastle City Council when it appointed Frank Harris as chief executive from the Ford Motor Company in 1965.

[13] Kingdom, op. cit., 163.

[14] *The New Local Authorities; Management and Structure* (London, 1972), esp. paras. 4.14, 5.9, 5.13, 5.38, and 5.42.

the new chief executives became *departmentless* powerbrokers attempting to reconcile the needs of senior councillors and service department chief officers.[15] More radical change has come instead as a result of the purchaser/provider split necessitated by the implementation of CCT.[16] The Bains model emphasized officer power and expertise, leaving the majority of councillors outside the magic circle of power of the committee chairholders. However, by creating central Policy and Resource committees, often with enhanced powers under Standing Orders, it also created the potential for more direct political control of officers by leading majority group councillors to the exclusion of other parties and 'backbench' members of the majority group.

The 'neutrality' view is reflected in the general legal duty of officers to serve the whole council and not solely the controlling political party. Legislation reflected this by permitting delegation of decisions to individual officers,[17] but not to individual members.[18] In this respect the law failed to acknowledge the close working relationship which often existed between the chief officer of a service department and the chairman of the relevant service committee, which could at times be equivalent to that between a Permanent Secretary and a minister at central government level. The Widdicombe Committee, for instance, found evidence that chief executives had much more frequent contact with the leaders of majority groups than with those of minority groups, and the role they played in relation to each generally differed; 'advising' the former, while 'informing' the latter.[19] In practice, this legal non-recognition was often overcome by delegating decisions to an officer 'in consultation' with the chairman. This was an untidy approach which invited abuse. The danger was illustrated in one case in which the power of the Housing Officer to grant council house tenancies in consultation with the Chairman and Vice-chairman of the Housing Committee was used to allocate a three-bedroom council house, contrary to the council's normal policy, to a single councillor. The High Court found that because of the political pressure brought to bear on the Housing Officer, the decision was effectively taken under dictation from the committee Chairman, and was therefore unlawful.[20]

[15] However, under the Local Government and Housing Act 1989, s. 4, each council must now designate a head of the paid service with responsibility for reporting on the staffing and organization of the authority as a whole; this may be the Chief Executive.

[16] See p. 217.

[17] LGA 1972, s. 101.

[18] *R v SS for Education and Science ex p. Birmingham CC*, (1984) 83 LGR 79; *R v SS for Environment ex p. Hillingdon LBC*, [1986] 1 All ER 967. but see *KLF (UK) v Derbyshire CC, The Times*, 21 Aug. 1984. The position is, however, changing under LGA 2000, ss. 12–14; see further p. 209 above.

[19] Widdicombe Report, para. 6.137.

[20] *R v Port Talbot Borough Council ex p. Jones*, [1988] 2 All ER 207.

Research for the Widdicombe Committee indicated a growing (but minority) practice of chief officers attending political group meetings.[21] The 'purple book' contains a prohibition on this in the case of junior officers.[22] However, where chief officers are concerned, the rule is 'without prejudice to any arrangements to the contrary which may be made in agreement with any officer and which includes adequate safeguards to preserve the political neutrality of the officer in relation to the affairs of the council'.[23] Such arrangements may include attending for the purpose of giving information or advice but withdrawing before any debate of political tactics, and informing other political groups that the officer is advising in group and offering equal briefing terms.[24]

One unusual situation in which officer neutrality and commitment may come into conflict is where an officer is called upon to give evidence of his or her own professional opinion, rather than the council's agreed policy. This problem most commonly arises at planning inquiries: if the council has resolved to refuse planning permission or to take enforcement action against the advice received from its professional planning officers,[25] those officers will be put in an uncomfortable position if asked (as invariably they will be) their opinion in the context of a subsequent appeal. Judicial comments tend to emphasize the neutrality approach: the planning officer is under a duty to state his or her professional opinion even where it conflicts with the council's position.[26]

With the politicization of local government the notion of officer neutrality came under increasing stress. The reasons mirror those for the alleged politicization of the civil service: the decrease in respect for administrators, the breakdown of the postwar political consensus leading to the emergence of more radical political styles of left, right, and (importantly at this level) Liberal. This new breed of local politician wanted to effect changes, often in the way local services were delivered (thus directly impinging on 'administration'), and refused to accept the view that this was the exclusive domain of the professional officer. A degree of commitment to policy changes was increasingly demanded from council employees.

[21] J. Gyford, S. Leach, and C. Game, *The Changing Politics of Local Government* (London, 1989), 131–2 and 204–6.

[22] National Joint Council for Local Authorities Administrative, Professional, Technical and Clerical Services (APT&C), *Scheme of Conditions of Service*, para. 70(c).

[23] Joint Negotiating Committee for Chief Officers of Local Authorities, *Constitution, Salaries, Conditions of Service*, para. 37.

[24] Gyford et al., op. cit., 205–6.

[25] The advice will be publicly available because of the application of the Local Government (Access to Information) Act 1985 (see Ch. 3).

[26] *Accountancy Tuition Centre v Secretary of State for the Environment*, [1977] JPL 792, cited by M. Purdue, E. Young, and J. Rowan-Robinson, *Planning Law and Procedure* (London, 1989), 544.

The breakdown in central–local relations from 1979 until the mid-1990s also cast officers in the role of pitting their wits against the then prevailing Conservative administrations in central government: an exercise which required from officers an even more sophisticated conception of liberal democracy if it was not to become confused with opposition to Conservative policies as such. In effect local government employees were asked to play a role more analogous to the function of an accountant or tax lawyer, looking for loopholes in legal restraint imposed by central government[27]—not the predominant reason why people commonly enter public-sector employment.

Against this background of 'politicization', the recommendations of the Widdicombe Committee concerning officers were designed to enable senior officers to balance their three roles of professional managers of service departments, advisers to the authority, and arbitrators in disputes between political groups.[28] While the first of these roles was subject to dramatic change due to the introduction of CCT, it is the second and third which create most possible conflicts within the political realm. In many respects Widdicombe accepted a mixture of the 'weak commitment' and 'neutrality' views. On the one hand, it endorsed the legitimacy of local politics, with consequent implications for the officers' role, but it also wanted appropriate safeguards for minority parties. The discussion which follows considers the recommendations and changes made,[29] first, concerning the appointment and dismissal of officers and secondly, political activity by officers.

## APPOINTMENT AND DISMISSAL OF OFFICERS

The theoretical discretion that local authorities have in employing staff is broad. Legislation speaks of officers being employed on such 'reasonable terms and conditions' as the Council 'think fit'.[30] However, in practice the

[27] For a discussion of resistance to legislation by local government in a different area, see D. Cooper, 'Defiance and Non-compliance: Religious Education and the Implementation Problem', (1995) 48 Current Legal Problems 253.

[28] Widdicombe Report, paras 6.125 ff.

[29] See also: G. Ganz, 'The Depoliticisation of Local Authorities: The Local Government and Housing Act 1989, Part I', [1990] PL 224; J. Greenwood, 'Facilitating Officer/Councillor Relationships: Meeting the Post-Widdicombe Challenge', (1990) LGS 77.

[30] LGA 1972, s. 112; this replaced earlier legislation protecting named statutory officials from dismissal except with ministerial consent or by a two-thirds majority of councillors voting on a motion of which prior notice had been given: Widdicombe Report, para. 6.125. Only a handful of designated posts are now required to exist. S. 112(4) LGA 1972 preserves the duty to appoint: chief education officers, chief officers and other members of fire brigades, agricultural analysts and deputy agricultural analysts, and directors of social services. In addition, local authorities must secure that one of their officers has responsibility for the administration of their financial affairs (LGA 1972, s. 151), designate one of their officers as the 'head of the paid service' (LGHA 1989, s. 4), and designate one of their officers as 'monitoring officer' (ibid., s. 5).

terms and conditions of local government officers are constrained both by the courts[31] and, more importantly, by national collective agreements.[32] In law a local authority is free to depart from the nationally agreed terms, since the courts have held that the national agreements are no more than guidance to councils of the level of reasonable remuneration in the exercise of their discretion under section 112;[33] under conventional administrative law principles it would be an unlawful fetter of its discretion for a local authority to bind itself unconditionally to accept the recommendations of the non-statutory joint negotiating committees. As locally negotiated pay becomes a more prominent feature of the public-sector landscape, this flexibility is likely to become increasingly important. Hitherto, the scope for variation between local authorities has been mainly over the organization and number of employees devoted to a particular function (reflecting local priorities) and, to a more limited degree, the gradings attached to a particular posts. However, the possibility of contracting-out discharge of some functions has produced increased variety of service provision and patterns of employment.

No equivalent exists at local level to the Civil Service Commission[34] to ensure the appointment and promotion of staff purely on merit, rather than on political or other grounds. In practice local authorities vary considerably in the degree to which appointments are delegated purely to senior officers without councillor involvement. The Widdicombe Committee favoured a requirement that all appointments below Principal Officer level should be made by other officers and not by councillors.[35] This proposal has not been implemented. However, there is now a statutory requirement that appointments should be made on merit.[36] This has the effect of adding to statutory categories of discrimination on grounds of

[31] In *Roberts v Hopwood*, [1925] AC 578, the House of Lords treated pay as an ultra vires gift, because the Council had set it without regard to prevailing market conditions and out of a desire to act as a model employer; but see *Pickwell v Camden LBC*, [1983] QB 962 (refusal to intervene in pay settlement above national levels) and *Newbold and Another v Leicester City Council, The Times*, 20 Aug. 1999, CA. See further, Ch. 4.

[32] The more important are APT&C (the so-called 'Purple Book') and various Whitley Council agreements; see Byrne, op. cit., 252–6; S. Fredman and G. Morris, *The State as Employer* (London, 1989), ch. 5.

[33] *Carr v District Auditor for No. 1 Audit District (Alston-with-Garrigill)*, (1952) 50 LGR 538, 545 per Slade J.

[34] A proposal of this kind was considered and rejected by the Widdicombe Committee because of the need on grounds of local variation for councils to retain the power to appoint their own staff: para. 6.189. Mallaby Committee (*Report of the Committee on Staffing of Local Government* (London, 1967), para. 419.

[35] Widdicombe Report, para. 6.163.

[36] LGHA 1989, s. 7. Appointment of chief officers is governed by advertising and interviewing requirements under prescribed Standing Orders: Local Authorities (Standing Orders) Regulations 1993, SI 202 (1993), sched. 1, pt. I, paras. 1–3.

sex, race,[37] disability, and (in Northern Ireland) religion, but without providing an equivalent framework of remedies for other types of discrimination. In addition, many councils have also adopted equal-opportunity policies going wider than the statutory grounds of discrimination and covering issues such as religious views (in Great Britain, where no legislation exists on this issue) and sexual orientation. The combined effect may be to give a disappointed job applicant remedies in public law either to have the council's action declared ultra vires for failure to respect the merit principle or for the council's failure to honour legitimate expectations created as a result of a voluntarily adopted policy.

The Widdicombe Committee's recommendation that a code of conduct be established to govern the appointment of senior officers to allow for open competition and to reduce political patronage has been followed in a somewhat modified form.[38] Where appointments are not made by officers alone, councils are required to have standing orders providing for the shortlisting and appointment processes to be undertaken by a committee reflecting the political composition of councillors so that a cross-section of political opinion is involved;[39] the same applies to the disciplining and dismissal of staff. The statutory Code of Conduct advises councillors involved in the appointment of staff: 'the only question you should consider is which candidate would best serve the whole council. You should not let your political or personal preference influence your judgement.'[40]

The task of ensuring that these procedures are correctly followed will fall upon the authority's monitoring officer, who is required to report on whether the requirements have been met in relation to every politically restricted post (including whether matters have been considered which ought not to be taken into account). In the event of the monitoring officer finding an infringement of legislation or of the Code, the authority is obliged to consider the report before proceeding with the appointment, dismissal, and so on.[41]

[37] Minor exceptions exist for Genuine Occupation Qualifications and, where there is recognized shortage of applicants from a particular racial group, facilitatory moves stopping short of positive discrimination may be permissible: Sex Discrimination Act 1975, s. 7, and Race Relations Act 1976, ss. 7(2) and 35. Political assistants (LGHA 1989, s. 9) are an exception permitted on grounds of political views: see p. 256 below.

[38] Widdicombe Report, para. 6.204. This would have required also the involvement of an outside assessor in the appointment of the Chief Executive.

[39] LGH 1989, s. 8. This is stronger than the Widdicombe Committee's recommendation of a statutory code of conduct backed by enforcement through enlargement of the ombudsman's jurisdiction over maladministration in staff appointments: paras. 6.189 and 199.

[40] National Code of Local Government Conduct, para. 25 (DoE Circular 8/90), promulgated under LGHA 1989, s. 31; revised arrangement for a model code of conduct for members apply under s. 50 LGA 2000.

[41] This is the combined effect of ss. 8(3)(c) and (d) and 5(5) and (6) of the LGHA 1989; see discussion of monitoring officer below.

The position of the chief executive is pivotal, in view of the specific statutory responsibilities of the head of the council's paid service,[42] which may bring him or her into open disagreement with the majority group of councillors. The Widdicombe Committee recognized that there was sometimes a justifiable need for authorities to dispense with the services of senior staff, whether for serious political incompatibility or incompetence, subject to the normal principles of unfair dismissal. However, it wished to provide protections against political victimization by giving the chief executive exclusive right to initiate dismissal of other staff and by requiring a two-thirds majority of all councillors before a resolution could be passed dismissing the chief executive (an attempt to prevent the post being in the gift of any one political group).[43] In fact, neither proposal has been included in the legislation. The protection for the head of the paid service requires the referral of any proposed disciplinary action (other than suspension for up to two months on full pay) to an independent person, either agreed between the council and the officer or, failing agreement, appointed by the Secretary of State. The designated independent person has powers to investigate and make recommendations; the council is forbidden to take disciplinary action except 'in accordance' with any such recommendation.[44] This is intended as effective protection from victimization for the chief executive's statutory duties of whistle-blowing.[45]

The appointment of council officers as political advisers[46] represents a departure from the neutrality view, significant in principle but subject to stringent statutory restrictions and limited in scale. The Widdicombe Committee found that there had been a growing trend by all political parties to appoint political advisers at the local government level, mirroring to some extent similar moves in central government— the use of political advisers to advise ministers and to supplement or counterbalance civil service advice has been common since the 1960s. Widdicombe saw such

[42] LGHA 1989, s. 4. In debates on the legislation it was assumed that the chief executive would often also be the monitoring officer: Standing Committee G, 7 Mar. 1989, col. 242 (cited by Ganz, op. cit., 233).

[43] Widdicombe Report, paras, 6.125 and 6. 203.

[44] The Local Authorities (Standing Orders) Regulations 1993, SI 202/1993, Pt. II and sched. 1, pt. I, para. 4. Specifically excluded from the definition of disciplinary action is failure to renew a fixed-term contract—a significant omission in view of the growing trend to advertise such senior posts on a fixed-term basis. The government seems to have undergone a change of heart. In its response to Widdicombe it had previously accepted the argument that special safeguards, especially against dismissal, would undermine trust between leading members of the authority and the chief executive: *The Conduct of Local Authority Business: The Government Response to the Report of the Widdicombe Committee of Inquiry*, Cm. 433 (1988), para. 5.46.

[45] However, in authorities where the roles of monitoring officer and head of paid service are in different hands, there may seem to be a gap in the protection for the monitoring officer. See further p. 269 below.

[46] See Ganz, op. cit., 234ff.

moves at the local level as a healthy experiment which, provided abuses were prevented, could help to prevent the politicization of local officers in general—a type of weak inoculation against the main virus. The government initially rejected this approach,[47] but subsequently modified its stance in the resulting legislation, which allowed for the appointment of political advisers within strict limits.[48]

The legislation requires a balanced approach: no more than three such posts may be created in total by the council, any one group may only be assigned one adviser, and if the facility is used it must be offered to every party with more than 10 per cent of the council's seats.[49] The appointment of a political adviser is a departure from the normal rules already described.[50] Although the appointment should still be made on merit as between qualified candidates, there is no bar on considering the political view of the appointee. Moreover, the choice of appointee is made by the political group to whom the adviser will be assigned, and not by officers or by a committee representative of the council as a whole. Obviously, in order to carry out their duties, political advisers need freedom from the restrictions on political activities applicable to other officers enjoying contact with councillors or with the public. Political advisers appointed under these provisions cannot have delegated to them powers from the council.[51] This clearly differentiates the role of political advisers from that of officers generally.

## OFFICERS' POLITICAL ACTIVITIES: POLITICALLY RESTRICTED POSTS

The freedom to participate in political activity is one of the marks of a liberal democracy. However, the danger of such participation by those who are themselves involved in the political process as employees is also commonly recognized. This can result in a blurring of roles between elected and appointed personnel, an erosion of institutional checks and balances, and a dilution of accountability to the electorate.

One solution is to require political commitment from government employees. Although this pattern is used in some parts of European local government, it involves the possible dangers of political patronage and restriction of the rights of those whose political views are at variance with the employing authority. Apart from the recent innovation as regards political assistants, the UK tradition has been to presume neutrality. At

[47] Cm. 433 (1986), para. 5.32.

[48] LGHA 1989, s. 9.

[49] Standing orders must be adopted which incorporate these terms: LGHA, s. 9 (5)–(7). Where only one group has more than 10% of seats, there must be 2 appointments, the second adviser being assigned to the next largest group.

[50] See p. 254 above.

[51] LGHA, s. 9(8).

central government level civil servants have long been subject to restrictions on their political activities: they are divided into three categories—with junior staff unrestricted, a large intermediary category (where specific permission may be obtained for political activity), and a politically restricted group.[52] In local government there were no such established rules, except a long-standing disqualification which prevented officers from becoming members of their own authorities and vice versa.[53] This can be attributed to the need to preserve separate roles and accountability for each group.

The invocation of the law to buttress the presumption of neutrality is relatively recent. As with the Civil Service, it takes the form of restrictions on the public political activity of some categories of local government employees, by designation of certain posts as 'politically restricted'.[54] Politically restricted posts are defined by seniority and salary level[55] but also include posts which involve giving regular advice to the council or its committees, or statements to the media on behalf of the authority.[56] This allows a small degree of discretion in designating such posts, subject to judicial review,[57] and to appeal to the Adjudicator appointed under the Act. The Adjudicator must grant an exemption from the restrictions if satisfied that the duties of the post (whatever the salary level) do not in fact involve giving advice or making statements on behalf of the council.[58] The government has argued that the cumulative effect of these provisions is that it is the nature of the post, rather than the salary level, which is the

[52] The initial scheme was introduced in the White Paper, *The Political Activities of Civil Servants*, Cmd. 8783 (1953), and amended following the report of the Armitage Committee, *Committee on the Political Activities of Civil Servants*, Cmnd. 7057 (1978). See now *Civil Service Pay and Conditions of Service Code*.

[53] LGA 1972, s. 80(1)(a) disqualifies an employee from standing as a councillor in the same authority (on which see *Boyd v Easington RDC*, [1963] 3 All ER 747; *Lamb v Jeffries*, [1956] 1 All ER 317); see also s. 104(1) (disqualification from membership of committees) and s. 80(2) (disqualification of employees of joint boards from service on constituent authorities). Councillors have long been prevented from taking up paid office with the authority (this extends for 12 months from the date of ceasing membership of the authority): LGA 1972, s. 116. The provision has been held to be breached even where pay is waived for the period of the disqualification: *AG v Ulverston UDC*, [1944] 1 All ER 475.

[54] Strictly there is no intermediate category, but note the role of the Adjudicator.

[55] Linked to the local government officers' standard scale (APT&C, pt. 44) with the consequence that it is automatically adjusted with annual pay negotiations. The Widdicombe Committee had recommended that the restrictions should apply to all on the Principal Officer grade (para. 6.217, summarizing paras. 6.211–15), however, not all councils use this scale, and so the government adopted a salary-related base instead.

[56] LGHA 1989, ss. 2(2) and (3).

[57] In *Darroch v Strathclyde Regional Council*, (1993) SLT 1111, it was held that judicial review would run to the council's decision to designate the post of a Deputy Electoral Registration Officer as 'politically restricted' under the Act.

[58] S. 3(4). Chief officer posts may not, however, be exempted. The adjudicator may also require a council to include a post in its restricted list on his or her own initiative if it appears that the legislation applies to it: s. 3(2)(b).

decisive criterion of whether a post is politically restricted. It has been estimated that approximately 40,000 local government employees fall within the salary qualification and a further 7,000 are potentially subject to restriction because of the nature of their duties.[59] In total, 2 per cent of local government employees are affected. Of some 1,374 applications for exemption received by the Adjudicator betwen November 1989 and January 1995, 1,176 were granted.[60]

One critic of the restrictions has argued for a more rigorous approach to whether restrictions are necessary in particular posts. Professor Gillian Morris argues that since restrictions are inappropriate where the provision of local services is privatized, the designation of a post as 'politically restricted' should be tested against whether the performance of the duties could be contracted out.[61] Equally, she advocates the strengthening of the rights of officers to challenge these decisions before an independent statutory appellate Board analogous to the Civil Service Appeals Board or to the Standards Boards which have been newly created for councillors.[62]

Where a post is so designated, the holder is disqualified from standing for Parliament and conditions are implied into the contract of employment preventing him or her from taking part in other political activities specified by regulations. Regulations have been made[63] which cover various activities which publicly promote or oppose any political party or 'a point of view identifiable as the view of one political party and not of another'. Prohibited activities include speaking or publishing material with the apparent intention of affecting public support for a political party. Interviews with the press or media are included. Similarly prohibited are speaking and publishing (irrespective of the content) where the impression is likely to be created that the publication was authorized by a political party. Unlike the equivalent restrictions on the Civil Service, no distinction is made between involvement in national and local politics.

A wide test is to be applied in considering an officer's intention under the regulations:

> whether the appointee referred to a political party or to persons identified with a political party, or whether anything said by him or the relevant work promotes or opposes a point of view identifiable as the view of one political party and not of another; and
>
> (b) where the appointee spoke or the work was published as part of a campaign, the effect which the campaign appears designed to achieve.[64]

[59] Argument by the UK government in *Ahmed v UK* (n. 74 below).
[60] Ibid.
[61] [1998] PL at 32–3.
[62] [1999] PL at 217.
[63] See the Local Government Officers (Political Restrictions) Regulations, SI 851 (1990), made under LGHA 1989, s. 1(5) and (6).
[64] Para. 4 of the regulations.

There is an obvious similarity with the reach and drafting of the restrictions on political advertising by councils.[65]

Less visible activities such as membership of a political party or taking part (without public speaking) in a public demonstration or march in support of a political cause are not prohibited. If a wide reading is taken of the regulations, actions such as displaying a candidate's election poster, holding a placard at a demonstration, or signing a public petition are at least of doubtful legality. The regulations are a substantial incursion into the political freedoms of the largest single group of public-sector employees and, unsurprisingly, they have been attacked for interference with civil liberties—a topic to which we shall return shortly.

The provisions also prohibit 'twin-tracking'—the holding of a political office with one authority while in the employment of another.[66] Although in theory twin-tracking posed no threat to the political neutrality of the officer in the employing authority, it required remarkable mental gymnastics by the individuals concerned to keep these roles separate. The task was made more complex by the dual structure of local government, since involvement as a councillor at county or district level would inevitably bring contact through the local party with councillors of the employing authority. In metropolitan districts, which after 1985 became unitary authorities, the organization of local parties in the conurbations would involve the same dangers of contact between neighbouring areas. Moreover, there was some evidence of abuse by a small number of councillors who were in effect full-time politicians but nominally drawing a salary from their employing authority, a practice which might be informally condoned where the two (often neighbouring authorities) were under the same political control.[67] Following the Widdicombe report, 'twin-tracking' was outlawed in the 1989 legislation[68] as one of a number of conditions which apply to the holders of 'politically restricted' posts.[69] This is in addition to the earlier restrictions, with the result that an officer (at whatever level) is debarred from becoming a councillor of the same authority and, if in a politically restricted post, in any other council also.

The political restriction regulations have been unsuccessfully challenged before the courts, both domestically and in Strasbourg. In *National and Local Government Officers Association v SSE*,[70] they were attacked as an

[65] See pp. 74–8 above.

[66] See n. 53 above for the position in the officer's own authority.

[67] For examples see Ganz, op. cit., 226–7.

[68] See Widdicombe Report, paras. 6.29ff.

[69] LGHA 1989, s. 1(1). Such officers are also debarred from becoming an MP. See House of Commons (Disqualification) Act 1975, sched. 1; definition of politically restricted post in s. 2 LGHA 1989.

[70] *The Times*, 2 Dec. 1992, CA (affirming an unreported judgment of Hutchinson J in *R v Secretary of State for the Environment ex p. NALGO*, 20 Dec. 1991, QBD).

infringement of freedom of speech. It was argued that the regulations went beyond the scope of the power in the 1989 Act, that they violated an earlier undertaking to respect legitimate trade union activities, and that the minister had paid insufficient regard to Article 10 of the European Convention on Human Rights. All these arguments failed. The Court of Appeal also rejected arguments that the restrictions were disproportionate to the objective of maintaining neutrality. In the court's view the regulations did no more than restrict activities by senior local government officers which, judged by an objective standard, affected public support for a particular political party.

In view of the earlier House of Lords' decision in *Brind*[71] that ministers were not bound to consider the Convention as a matter of domestic law when exercising statutory powers, the Convention argument at that time was doomed in the domestic courts. Following implementation of the Human Rights Act 1998, both the Secretary of State in drafting or revising the regulations and local authorities in applying them would, as 'public authorities' under section 6 of that Act, be bound not to act in violation of the officers' Convention rights (unless this was clearly required by the 1989 Act itself). Even leaving aside the issue of domestic enforceability of the Convention on Human Rights, however, it is unclear whether restrictions of this kind do infringe the Convention.

In a line of cases concerned with political restrictions from Germany, the Convention organs had earlier adopted a mixed approach to denial of employment on political grounds in the public service—a more severe form of impediment.[72] However, there was some potential comfort for local government officers in the most recent of these,[73] in which the European Court of Human Rights found that the dismissal of a teacher in Lower Saxony violated Articles 10 (protecting freedom of speech) and 11 (protecting freedom of association) of the Convention. In keeping with the German Basic Law the teacher had been required to swear loyalty to the Constitution, including the principle of a 'democracy capable of defending itself'. Under federal and Lower Saxony law this required public officials to renounce membership of unconstitutional political parties. It was well established that the DKP (German Communist Party), of which the applicant was an active member, fell into this category. The Court found that although member states enjoyed a margin of appreciation in relation to restrictions on rights under Articles 10 and 11, and protection for

[71] *R v SS for Home Affairs ex parte Brind*, [1991] 1 AC 696. *Brind* was decided while the *Nalgo* case was pending.

[72] *Kosiek v Germany*, (1987) 9 EHRR 328; *Glasenapp v Germany*, (1987) 9 EHRR 25. For discussion see: L. Lustgarten and I. Leigh, *In from the Cold: National Security and Parliamentary Democracy* (Oxford, 1994), 144–52.

[73] *Vogt v Germany*, (1995) 21 EHRR 205.

constitutional reasons was a legitimate aim, the dismissal was a disproportionate means of doing so. The applicant had been dismissed for having publicly campaigned for the party, especially standing as a candidate in elections for the parliament in the Land. It is this aspect of the ruling which seemed most relevant to the UK restrictions on political activities, since this was in effect penalization of public political activity per se. Moreover, the case against such restrictions on public officials' rights was stronger in the UK, both because of the absence of a concept of militant constitutionalism (which had quite specific historical roots in Germany) and because the range of political opinion reached by the restrictions extended to mainstream UK political parties. On this basis there seemed to be scope for attacking the political restriction regulations in an application under the Convention. It was against this background that a challenge was mounted at Strasbourg to the restrictions on UK local government officers.

When the case reached the European Court of Human Rights, it found no breach of Articles 10 or 11 (protecting freedom of speech and of association, respectively).[74] The Court found that some local government officers were as entitled as the remainder of the population to the right of free speech under Article 10 and that the regulations were a restriction on this right.[75] It found, however, that the regulations fell within the permitted limitations to the Articles: they were 'prescribed by law',[76] in pursuit of the legitimate aim of protecting the rights of others to effective political democracy, and were 'necessary in a democratic society'. In order to satisfy the last test the Court applied its normal standard of whether there was a 'pressing social need', and considered whether the regulations were a disproportionate restriction, granted the legitimate aim. Whereas the Commission had found the restrictions disproportionate, the Court accepted that members of a council and of the public were entitled to expect political neutrality from local government officers under the British tradition of local government, and that both the groups of officers targeted and the forms of activity restricted fell within the 'margin of appreciation' allowed to a member state under the Convention. The findings of the Widdicombe Committee particularly influenced the Court in holding that the UK had acted within its discretion under the Convention. Three judges

[74] *Ahmed v UK* (65/1997/849/1056), Judgment of the European Court of Human Rights, 2 Sept. 1998, (2000) 29 EHRR 1. The analysis of the Article 11 issue followed that of Article 10; a claim that the restrictions violated Article 3 of Protocol No. 1 to the Convention (the right to free elections) was also rejected. For more detailed analysis see G. Morris, 'The Political Activities of Local Government Workers and the ECHR', [1999] PL 122; H. Cullen, 'Freedom of Association as a Political Right', (1999) EL Rev., HR/30, 36–9; the Commission's opinion in the same case is discussed in G. Morris, 'Local Government Workers and Rights of Political Participation: Time for a Change?', [1998] PL 25.

[75] Paras. 41 and 42.

[76] The applicants' argument that the regulations were too uncertain to meet this standard failed: ibid., paras. 43–8.

dissented from the majority view: they noted that, unlike Article 11, Article 10 did not explicitly authorize restrictions on public employees, that comparable restrictions on local government employees had not been found necessary elsewhere in Europe, and that the restrictions were broad in their effect on those to whom they applied.[77]

The majority opinion in *Ahmed* can be criticized for going considerably further than the previous cases from Germany in which the court has considered the concept of 'militant constitutionalism'. This has been invoked previously to bar from state employment members of 'extreme' political parties.[78] In *Ahmed* the court rejected the argument that the protection of effective democracy could only be invoked as a reason for limitation of free speech rights where there was a threat to the stability of the constitutional or political order. In its view this undervalued the importance of local democratic institutions and their proper functioning as an aspect of the European public order.[79] It is clear from the majority judgment, however, that if a state took a different view of officer politics (for example, by requiring officer loyalty to the local party in power), this too could probably justify restrictions on Convention rights.[80]

The incorporation of the European Convention into UK law under the Human Rights Act 1998 will probably bring added protections for public-sector workers generally, since all public authorities are under a new legal duty not to act in contravention of a person's Convention rights.[81] This provision in itself should be sufficient to undo the reasoning which marginalized the Convention in the *Brind* and the *Nalgo* cases. The fact, however, of the adverse Strasbourg ruling in *Ahmed* probably closes the door to any domestic challenge to the political restrictions regulations. Theoretically it would be possible for a UK court—which, unlike Strasbourg, is not bound by the 'margin of appreciation' doctrine to 'take account' of the Convention case law and then interpret the Act—to give

[77] Joint Dissenting Opinion of Judges Spielmann, Pekkanen, and Van Dijk.

[78] Nn. 72 and 73 above. However, as regards Art. 11, Cullen (op. cit. at 38) distinguishes *Vogt* from *Ahmed*, arguing that in the former simple membership of a political party was restricted, in the latter it was active membership, and so the restriction was less onerous.

[79] Para. 52, citing also the European Charter of Local Self-Government (see p. 30 above).

[80] Only one judge (Concurring Opinion of Judge De Meyer) would have gone further and held that restrictions on the political activities of officers were not merely legitimate but also necessary. He demurred from the implication of the majority that a more general restriction would not have been acceptable.

[81] Human Rights Act 1998, s. 6. It is clear that local authorities are 'pure' public authorities for the purpose of this provision, all of whose actions are subject to challenge for violation of a person's Convention rights: K. Ewing, 'The Human Rights Act and Labour Law', (1998) 27 Ind. LJ 275, 284–6; G. Morris, 'The Human Rights Act and the Public/Private Divide in Employment Law', (1998) 27 Ind. LJ 293. There may be an argument, however, about whether these rights should be enforced by judical review or by a private action in an Employment Tribunal: see Morris, op. cit., 300.

additional protection to officers' rights above that in the European Court of Human Rights. However, it would be optimistic to pin much hope on such an outcome.

## OFFICERS AND STANDARDS

In this discussion of officer standards we will focus mainly on standards in relation to political action of councillors, as this is the aspect most relevant to the overall emphasis of this book. However, it is worth emphasizing that this is merely an aspect of the wider issue of ethical behaviour by council officers. Like councillors, officers are required to declare financial interests that they have in contracts or proposed contracts entered into by the council, and failure to do so is a criminal offence.[82] Officers also have wider duties not to behave in a way giving rise to a suspicion of improper motives or inconsistently with their official duties under the standard conditions of service[83] and under the Code of Conduct issued by the Local Government Management Board (this extends the duty to declare interests to non-financial ones). The necessity of maintaining public confidence in officer impartiality means that the law covers conduct considerably wider than criminal corruption. A local government officer was, like a councillor, subject to possible surcharge for ultra vires expenditure, but this power has now been abolished.[84] The Widdicombe Committee proposed that the analogy with councillors should be pursued further by introducing disqualification from the public office of Chief Executive where an officer acted unlawfully and the court was not satisfied that he or she acted reasonably in the belief that the action was authorized.[85] However, this proposal has not been implemented.

The Committee on Standards in Public Life concluded that it was unnecessary to establish a national code of conduct for officers similar to that applying to councillors.[86] Nevertheless, they were concerned that offi-

[82] LGA, 1972, s. 117. This provision, together with the Public Bodies Corrupt Practices Act 1889 and the Prevention of Corruption Acts 1906–16, criminalizes the acceptance of bribes by council officers. See: Salmon Commission, *Report of the Royal Commission on Standards in Public Life* 1974–6, Cmnd. 6524 (1976); A. Doig, *Corruption and Misconduct in Contemporary British Politics* (Harmondsworth, 1984); A. Doig, 'Continuing Cause for Concern? Probity in Local Government', (1995) 21(1) Local Government Studies 99, discussing cases in Lambeth and West Wiltshire.

[83] APT&C, *Scheme of Conditions of Service*, para. 70; Joint Negotiating Committee for Chief Officers of Local Authorities, *Constitution, Salaries, Conditions of Service*, paras. 34 and 35.

[84] See Ch. 4.

[85] Widdicombe Report, para. 9.107.

[86] Committee on Standards in Public Life, Third Report, *Standards of Conduct in Local Government in England, Scotland and Wales*, Cm. 3702-I (1997), recommendations 19–22. Codes of conduct for officers were, however, recommended to deal with the registration and declaration of interests by officers.

cer–member relationships could cause difficulties if they were either too close or combative. They therefore recommended that councils should be required to adopt a formal protocol for dealing with officer–member relations. The committee stressed the importance of the head of paid service and the monitoring and finance officers in ensuring propriety: it recommended that the government consider extending to them protections against disciplinary action which currently only apply to chief executives. The committee was also concerned that staff should have clear avenues open for whistle-blowing to raise concerns confidentially (the committee argued that its proposed Standards Committee might be a suitable internal investigatory forum) and, where necessary, outside the authority itself.[87] Possible conflicts of interest arising from movements of staff when council services were privatized should also be covered by specific terms in the contracts of employment of the relevant officers.[88] The government, however, has taken powers for the Secretary of State to promulgate a Code to apply to officers and to be incorporated into their contracts of employment.[89]

The most reliable source of concern about malpractice and corruption in local government comes from the work of the charity Public Concern at Work (PCAW).[90] Statistics from people seeking advice or help from PCAW show that local authorities are prominent among the institutions or sectors raising public concern, the most common cause for contacting PCAW being financial malpractice, followed by workplace safety, and public safety generally. A report by PCAW recognized that the increasing number of contracts awarded for work external to a council under the CCT regime[91] had given many new opportunities for fraud and corruption.[92] PCAW emphasized the need for the whole council, and especially the councillors, to create an environment in which fraud and corruption are tackled. It particularly stressed the need for elected members to follow appropriately established procedures for dealing with the placing of contracts.

[87] Ibid., recommendation 26. It proposed that staff of bodies contracting with the authority should also be able to use these procedures (recommendation 32).

[88] Ibid., recommendation 33.

[89] LGA 2000, s. 82; see further: *Modern Local Government: In Touch with the People*, Cm. 4014 (1998), paras. 6.38 and 39. The restrictions on political activities (pp. 258–60 above) will be contained in the Code (ibid., paras. S.2.47–5.2.59), as well as continuing under the 1989 Act.

[90] Whose aim is to help ensure that concerns about serious malpractice in the workplace are raised and addressed. I am grateful to them for the details that follow.

[91] See Ch. 10.

[92] Examples given include the case of a council manager who demanded money from contractors in order to retain them on a tendering list and an unhealthily close relationship between the officer placing urgent contracts in the education department of a county council and one contractor. Public Concern at Work, *Local Government: Blowing the Whistle on Fraud and Corruption* (London, 1994). See also: M. Wilson, 'Contracting Corruption', (1991) 17(3) Local Government Studies 2.

The same report identified a substantial gap between the (relatively low) levels of fraud—which are mainly housing benefit frauds perpetrated by outsiders on councils—and public perception and concern about corruption in local government,[93] which suggests that councils have a long way to go in creating public confidence.

Rather than suggesting specific legislative reforms, the PCAW report emphasized internal reforms such as better communication, training, and management.

It did, however, advocate the introduction of a statutory duty for Chief Financial Officers to report to the council regularly on the level of fraud and corruption and on countermeasures,[94] as a way of giving these questions a high political priority. Likewise, the Audit Commission has recommended that auditors should comment on such arrangements in their management letters. PCAW's view was that the role of finance officers should also be better publicized within councils so that employees who are reluctant to raise such questions with their own managers are encouraged to contact an independent official. This would help establish a climate which fosters a preventative attitude towards fraud by processes which are open and easy to use.

Quite apart from financial corruption, it is common in other fields (especially the police) to speak of 'noble cause corruption'—the breaking or bending of rules not for personal advantage but for some disinterested motive, for example, fabrication of evidence to ensure the conviction of a suspect believed to be guilty. In local government the equivalent behaviour is most likely to occur because of collusion by officers with, or pressure from, the majority group or leading politicians. It may take the form of concealment of information to avoid political embarrassment, tailoring or distorting professional advice to the wishes of the majority, or, at the extreme, deception and assisting in the improper or illegal policies which councillors have adopted for party-political reasons.

A textbook catalogue of these abuses can be found in the report of the auditor into the Designated Sales policy of Westminster City

[93] Market research found that 28% of people questioned were very concerned and a further 35% were quite concerned about fraud and corruption in local government. Only 1 in 12 expressed positive confidence in local government probity. Even among the small group (1000 people throughout the United Kingdom) questioned, 1 in 20 claimed to have direct experience of fraud or corruption in local government: PCAW, *Local Government*, 34. The apparently low level of actual fraud is confirmed in a study by the Audit Commission which suggested an annual figure of some £25 million for local-government fraud. Although this is trivial when compared with an estimated annual £9 billion in the UK as a whole, it nevertheless amounted to an estimated 54,000 reported instances each year. The Audit Commission concluded that 'probity in local government was generally in good order especially with regard to honesty of staff': *Protecting the Public Purse* (London, 1993), 1.

[94] Ibid. 10.

Council.[95] The auditor found that some senior officers had assisted leading members of the Conservative group of the council in devising and implementing the tainted policy. It was intended to secure an electoral advantage by changing the social composition of eight key (electorally marginal) wards prior to the 1990 local election through sale of council-owned property, thus increasing the number of owner-occupiers. The role of these officers extended to preparing committee reports designed to disguise the true objective of the policy; indeed, the auditor found that it was the Chief Housing Officer who had proposed the deception in the first place since he was aware that a simple policy focused on the eight wards would have been transparently unlawful.[96] Officers neglected their duty to serve the whole council and became preoccupied instead with the unlawful objective of promoting the electoral advantage of the ruling Conservative group.

The report brushed aside the argument that since officers did not vote for the policy, they were not responsible for it. It emphasized instead the administrative reality of decision-making: that members adopted the policy on officer advice which, in turn, fell below the standard of impartial and objective professional opinion and failed to provide members with the information they required in order to reach a reasonably informed decision.[97] The auditor found that a group of more junior officers who played a lesser role were not guilty of wilful misconduct. Nevertheless, and despite their fear of reprisals and the indifference and collusion of their superiors, he criticized their failure to speak up against improper action of which they were aware. His conclusions are worth quoting in full:

> It was [his] duty to give such candid advice, however unpalatable, unwelcome or politically damaging to leading Members it might be, regardless of any possible threat to [his] own employment and irrespective of any failure by other officers of the Council to act properly.[98]
>
> . . . . a local authority officer is under a duty not merely to refrain from doing those things which may not be done in the proper discharge of a local authority's functions but also to ensure, so far as he/she reasonably can, that the local authority complies with the law and does not act unlawfully. Such duty may require an officer to disclose the misconduct or suspected misconduct of other Members or officers of which he/she becomes aware. In such circumstances, an officer has a duty to 'speak up' and do what else he/she reasonably can to protect the public from such misconduct and any consequences it may have had or has had.[99]

[95] Westminster City Council, Audit of Accounts 1987/8 to 1994/5, *Designated Sales, Decisions and Statement of Reasons on the Section 19 and/or Section 20 Objection in Relation to Individual Respondents*, vol. 3(B) (Officers) (May 1996). For other aspects see Ch. 4.

[96] *Designated Sales* report, para. 2312.

[97] Ibid., paras. 2314, 2315, 2677, 2776, 2990.

[98] Ibid., para. 2812.

[99] Ibid., para. 3075; and see paras. 3141, 3173.

While these are irreproachable aspirations, it is questionable whether they do not ask too much of officers who were, at least until recently, given only fairly flimsy legal protection in return. On the auditor's own findings the regime was plainly insufficiently robust to withstand the prevailing atmosphere in Westminster: a climate of fear among officers, deliberate attempts to conceal unlawful policies, and the collusion of higher officers in the illegality. Since the period of those events, the late 1980s, the legal regime has been strengthened, both through the imposition of additional statutory duties to expose wrongdoing and recently through protection from victimization for 'whistle-blowers'. We turn now to consider the scope of those duties and protections.

## WHISTLE-BLOWING[100]

The tension between the 'neutrality' and the 'weak commitment' approaches described earlier is at its most acute where the officer concerned has reason to believe a course of action proposed by the majority group of the council may be unlawful.[101] In a number of older decisions the courts made clear that if a local government officer faces a choice between acting unlawfully and disobeying the orders of the council, he or she should choose the latter. Thus, in one case in which a Town Clerk had withheld information from the council on the instructions of a leading Alderman, the judge argued that he should have disobeyed and looked to public opinion for protection.[102] This decision was given in 1944, at a time when the officer would not have had the additional protection available today of unfair dismissal legislation. However, it also pre-dates the politi-

[100] For discussion of whistle-blowing, see: Y. Cripps, *The Legal Implications of Disclosure in the Public Interest* (2nd edn., London, 1994); D. Lewis, 'Whistleblowers and Job Security', (1995) 58 MLR 208; N. Rose, 'Whistleblowing: Time for a Change?', NLJ, 27 Jan. 1995, 113; G. Dehn and N. Rose, 'The Case for the Public Interest Disclosure Bill', [1996] PL 235; J. Gobert and M. Punch, 'Whistleblowers, the Public Interest and the Public Interest Disclosure Act 1998', (2000) 63 MLR 25. See also L. Vickers, 'Whistleblowing in the Public Sector and the ECHR', [1997] PL 594, discussing the possible application of Art. 10 of the European Convention on Human Rights, which protects freedom of expression.

[101] See also S. Fredman and G. Morris, *The State as Employer: Labour Law in the Public Services* (London, 1989), 212–14.

[102] 'the question must at once arise as to whether it is not his duty forthwith to resign his office, or at any rate to do what he thinks is his duty and to await the consequences. This is not so dangerous or heroic a course as it may seem. The integrity of public affairs is such that publicity may be safely relied upon to secure protection for anyone in the position in which the town clerk was said to have been placed.' *Re Hurle-Hobbs ex p. Riley and Another* (unreported, 1944), cited in R. Jones, *Local Government Audit Law* (2nd edn., London, 1985), 353–4; the courts have taken a similar view of the predicament of a council treasurer who is asked to authorize unlawful expenditure: *R v Saunders*, (1854) 3 E and B 763, and *A-G v De Winton*, [1906] 2 Ch. 106 (holding that a treasurer's fiduciary relationship to the burgesses was not abrogated by the orders of the council).

cization of local government by the Muncipal Left and the New Right in the 1980s and the emergence of a breed of powerful full-time councillors. Whatever the theory, the pressures brought to bear on officers, in Westminster for example, not to speak out suggest the need for more stringent safeguards than blind trust in 'the integrity of public affairs'.

The statutory creation of the post of Monitoring Officer—an officer designated and required to report possible ultra vires action—is a response to this problem, unique within British government. The local government monitoring officer is more than a recognized 'whistle-blower', however. The officer is required to advise the council if it appears to him or her that any proposal, decision, or omission by the council or its committees will give rise to a contravention of any enactment, rule of law, or statutory Code of Practice, or to maladministration or injustice within the ombudsman's jurisdiction.[103] The council or the committee concerned are then disabled from taking the relevant decision until the report has been discussed, which must occur within twenty-one days.[104] Councillors are not required by these provisions to follow the recommendations of the report, but, having been put on notice in this way, they may become personally liable for wilful misconduct if they proceed in the face of an adverse report to take a decision which is subsequently found to be ultra vires. The lack of discretion acts in a curious way for the Monitoring Officer's protection, since it can be used against powerful councillors threatening disciplinary action. However, although the council's Head of Paid Service is protected from victimization,[105] the Monitoring Officer is not and, where the two offices are separated, is in a legally exposed position. The government has accepted a recommendation from the Nolan Committee that this loophole should be closed.[106] UNISON, the union representing 800,000 local government officers, argued that the provisions had been little used, perhaps because the environment in local government offered too many opportunities for members to 'settle scores' against whistle-blowing officers.[107]

Similar duties are imposed on the authority's Chief Financial Officer to report decisions involving unlawful expenditure or likely to result in loss to the council, and concerning illegal items of account.[108] However, the government sought to guard against the danger that in curbing political 'abuse' it might simply encourage officer domination: the legislation provides that the posts of monitoring officer and chief finance officer cannot

[103] LGHA 1989, s. 5(2). A copy must be sent to every councillor. In preparing the report the monitoring officer must consult with the head of the authority's paid service and with the chief financial officer: s. 5(3).

[104] Ibid., s. 5(5).

[105] See p. 256 below.

[106] *Modern Local Government: In Touch with The People*, Cm. 4014 (1988), para. 6.41.

[107] Telephone interview with Owen Davies, UNISON, 11 Oct. 1996.

[108] Local Government Finance Act 1988, s. 115 (and see Ch. 4).

be combined,[109] preventing the creation of one all-powerful Chief Executive.

In the absence of specific protections, local government officers asked to act unethically were, until recently, forced to rely on general exemptions. In the last analysis an officer who loses his or her job for action in reporting, or refusing to participate, in illegality, fraud, or corruption may have a claim for unfair dismissal.[110] This is precisely what happened in the case of an accountant dismissed by Hackney Borough Council for raising concerns about suspected fraud (at the councillor's request) with the chair-holder of the relevant committee and with his trade union.[111] The Industrial Tribunal which heard his claim found that he had contributed to his own dismissal by passing on documents containing his suspicions about another officer in what they described as 'a highly irresponsible and unprofessional way', rather than raising them through the 'proper channel of communication' with management. The tribunal reduced his award of compensation by 50 per cent because of this action. The Employment Appeal Tribunal took a different view and found that he did not contribute to his dismissal, especially in view of the facts that it was the officer's duty as an accountant to uncover corruption, that the councillor had requested the documents, and that the matter had been raised with the union to obtain their advice in view of the failure to resolve matters otherwise. Welcome as the Employment Appeal Tribunal's approach is, it is unclear whether it would still apply if circumstances had been different, for example, an officer with no financial expertise raising an issue at his or

[109] LGHA 1989, s. 5(1), and see Kingdom, op. cit., 168.

[110] Employment Rights Act 1996, ss. 98 and 111. This requires an employer first to demonstrate a potentially fair reason for dismissal, after which an Employment Tribunal will assess whether the dismissal is fair or unfair. Breach of an express or implied duty of confidentiality owed to an employer might fall within s. 98, either in its own right or because it vitiates the possibility of future trust between the employee and employer. In addition, in limited circumstances falling outside the scope of unfair dismissal (e.g. employees who cannot satisfy the qualifying period) an action for wrongful dismissal may lie: see Cripps, op. cit., ch. 12. Quite apart from this, such duties may be direct enforceable in breach of confidence, subject to a public interest defence.

The Purple Book contains an express term requiring confidentiality: para. 72 states that an officer may only make public the proceedings of any committee meeting or the contents of any document 'if required by law or expressly authorised to do so'. 'Required by law' would cover situations in which the officer is required to report to the whole council (in the case of the monitoring or financial officer), or required to give evidence to a court, or information to the district auditor or to the local ombudsman, or to a member of the public under the Local Government (Access to Information) Act 1985. However, the enforceability of this condition in the cases of some other disclosures by officers is debatable. The law recognizes the public interest in the disclosure of wrongdoing through the principle that there is no confidence in iniquity. An injunction will only be issued to restrain publication in breach of confidence against a public servant or former public servant where it is the public interest on the balance of convenience to do so: *AG v Guardian Newspapers* (No. 2), [1988] 3 WLR 776. Disclosures by employees to regulators are generally lawful: *Re A Company*, [1989] IRLR 477.

[111] *Cornelius v LB of Hackney*, LEXIS, 18 Jan. 1996, EAT.

her own initiative with a minority group councillor. The existence of a recognized route (through the finance or monitoring officer) might lead to such action being found to be inappropriate.[112]

Officers standing up against proposed unlawful decisions previously lacked formal protection against victimization.[113] One case reported by PCAW shows the dangers of collusion between powerful politicians and senior officers. When an official refused to accommodate the expressed preferences of the Leader of the council in the conduct of transactions involving the sale of land and raised concerns about this pressure with the Chief Executive (who was also the Monitoring Officer), he was suspended within a week and the council brought forward plans to contract out the work of his department.[114] There was no formal protection either against more informal or minor penalties or deterrents which might be applied to an officer who appears to be 'uncooperative' in situations like these, such as deteriorating work conditions or loss of promotion prospects.

New legislation may remedy this, at least in part. General protection against victimization or unfair dismissal of officers for 'whistle-blowing' came into force in July 1999 under the Public Interest Disclosure Act 1998.[115] The protection applies only to disclosures made by the employee on certain matters, and there are preconditions concerning the circumstances of the disclosure which must be satisfied also, which vary according to whom it is made. Disclosures are protected if they tend to relate to criminal offences, breaches of legal obligations (not only public duties but also breaches of contract and negligence), and dangers to health and safety or to the environment.[116] Additionally, a disclosure about any attempt to cover up any of these matters will attract protection.

An officer who makes the disclosure within the council will be protected if he or she has an 'honest and reasonable suspicion' that the misconduct has happened, or is likely to.[117] Power is given under the legislation for regulators to be 'prescribed', in which case a disclosure to them will be

[112] Likewise, a voluntary code of conduct drawn up by the Local Government Management Board provides for routes for employees to raise deficiency in the provision of the service, impropriety, or breach of procedure 'through agreed procedures . . . [to] the appropriate level of management': Lewis, op. cit., 211.

[113] Specific protections existed, however, against victimization for reporting suspected discrimination under the Race Relations Act 1976, s. 2 (but see the narrow interpretation in *Kirby v Manpower Services Commission*, [1980] ICR 420, where it was held that a demotion was not discriminatory under this section, because the employer would have responded in the same way to any employee divulging confidential information) and under the Sex Discrimination Act 1975, s. 4, and for reporting of health and safety concerns under the Employment Rights Act 1996, s. 100 (dealing specifically with dismissal for doing so).

[114] PCAW, op. cit., 42.

[115] The protections extend also to contractors and their employees: Employment Rights Act 1996, s. 43K.

[116] Ibid., s. 43B.

[117] Ibid., s. 43C.

protected provided (in addition to the internal test) that the officer acts in good faith and 'reasonably believes' that the information disclosed and allegations made are 'substantially true'.[118] It is likely that the financial regulatory and health and safety bodies will be designated under these provisions; it is unclear whether the local ombudsman or the auditor will be.

In keeping with the policy of the legislation of encouraging internal resolution of disclosures, more onerous conditions have to be met before a wider disclosure (such as to the press) will qualify for protection. Here it is necessary not merely for there to be good faith and belief in the truth of the disclosure but also that it is not made for personal gain, that it should be reasonable in all the circumstances, and that alternative avenues for dealing with the allegation were not open or have been exhausted.[119] A variety of factors is relevant in addressing the reasonableness of external disclosures: the person to whom the disclosure is made, the seriousness of the issue and whether it is continuing or likely to recur, whether the disclosure involves breach of any duty of confidentiality owed to a third person, and the response of the employer or regulator to a previous disclosure.[120] Employers are encouraged to create clear internal procedures for whistle-blowing, because the presence of these will be material in assessing the reasonableness of the employee's action, whether or not he or she used them.[121]

Quite apart from these routes for exposing wrongdoing, officers are, of course, required to cooperate with an ombudsman's or auditor's investigations, and for them to refuse to do so (or for anyone else to attempt to prevent them doing so) would be a criminal offence.[122] Failure by an officer to advise against an unlawful course of conduct could previously result in the officer being surcharged if the auditor found this to constitute wilful misconduct.[123] The direct legal responsibilities imposed upon officers under these provisions suggest a level of distrust of the efficacy of representative democracy, in contrast to the judge's remarks in the *Hurl-Hobbs* case quoted earlier.[124] The clear message is that responsibility of officers to councillors and, thereafter, of councillors to the electorate is too diffuse as a safeguard against abuse and illegality. This stands in stark

[118] Employment Rights Act 1996, s. 43F.

[119] Ibid, s. 43G. Subs. (2) provides that the employee must reasonably believe that he or she would be victimized if the issues were raised internally or with a prescribed regulator, or that there was no prescribed regulator and he or she reasonably believed evidence would be concealed or destroyed.

[120] Ibid., s. 43G(3). However, disclosures of 'exceptionally serious failures' may be protected notwithstanding: s. 43H.

[121] Ibid., s. 43(G)(f).

[122] See respectively LGA 1974, s. 29(8), and LGFA 1982, s. 16(4).

[123] See Ch. 4.

[124] See p. 268 above.

contrast to the attitude expressed at central government level, where ministers are the only constitutionally recognized channel of communication between the government, Parliament, and the public, and where information emanating from civil servants is subject to both ministerial approval and control. The difference in approach between central and local government employees follows in part from the greater restrictions on representative democracy imposed on councillors (who are much more likely than ministers to be found to have acted unlawfully) by the ultra vires doctrine,[125] and this in turn affects officers' positions and responsibilities.

## CONCLUSION

In this chapter we have surveyed the legal responses to the politicization of local government, which challenged the neutral position of officers, serving the council as a whole. These have been two-pronged: a minor concession in the creation of political assistants, but a substantial strengthening of the legal regime through restrictions on officers' political activities. Related protections against political pressures have been introduced to compel disclosure of impropriety (the roles of the 'financial' and 'monitoring' officers), and in other cases officers may benefit from more general whistle-blowing protection. In the tension between the 'neutrality' and 'weak commitment' views identified earlier,[126] it seems that the 'neutrality' view is legally dominant, whatever the difficulties that may cause for individuals employed in highly political environments. This tension looks set to continue as a feature of local government employment in the new structures.

For officers, the clear implication of a political executive model might appear to be a reversal of the present legal position, where officers serve the council as a whole but a tiny minority can be attached to political groups. The majority of officers would be employed in the name of the council but would serve the executive—their role and status would be analogous to civil servants in effect. Perhaps surprisingly, then, the government has argued that the traditional approach towards officer neutrality will be equally applicable when the new arrangements for separate political executives are introduced under the Local Government Act 2000.[127] All staff will continue to be contractually employed by the

[125] See Ch. 2.

[126] See pp. 230ff. above.

[127] *Modern Local Government: In Touch with the People*, para. 3.65. *Local Leadership, Local Choice* (1999), para. 3.82.

council, rather than under separate arrangements with the executive.[128] The 1998 White Paper envisaged that a small number of officers might have specific roles supporting the new Mayor, Leader, or Cabinet (depending on the model adopted in a particular authority) or backbench councillors serving on overview and scrutiny committees. However 'the great majority' would act in a dual capacity: 'They will be responsible to the political executive through their line management with statutory duties to account for their actions to the council in its scrutiny role.'[129] The draft guidance published by the Department of Environment Transport and Regions is not prescriptive and stipulates only broad principles by which a council should arrange its officers' support. These include the need for 'effective and proper' officer support for overview and scrutiny, and mechanisms for 'resolving potential conflicts of interests for officers brought about by the executive/scrutiny separation of roles'.[130] The government recognized that where the same officers were supporting both sides, conflict could arise, because the executive's decision subject to scrutiny in the overview and scrutiny committees would often be based on the advice of the officers concerned. Nevertheless, it did not believe that a formal separation of officer support was necessary (and it would be impracticable in smaller councils), although some councils might choose to take this route;[131] the legislative scheme would neither forbid nor require it.[132]

The government has made a virtue of this non-interventionist approach by invoking local discretion. However, it can also be characterized as complacent. In the worst-case scenario, the majority group on a council will be able to starve the overview and scrutiny committees of the effective levels of staffing support needed to carry out their functions, and staff will be wary of doing anything which might be seen publicly to undermine the position and policies of the ruling executive. For those who are prepared to speak out, the legislation adds few additional protections against reprisals.[133] Ultimately, it may be the possibility that the new electoral

[128] This contrasts with the conclusions of the 1993 DoE Working Party on the effect of possible reform of the internal management of local authorities on officers: *Community Leadership and Representation: Unlocking the Potential* (London, 1993); see further Ch. 7, n. 84. The Working Party proposed that under its Strong Political Executive model the formal separation between executive and scrutiny councillors would be mirrored by a separation in the officer corps: each group would have separate contractual arrangements, councillors on either side of the divide would have powers of delegation to officers, and the relationship between the officer groups would need to be legally formalized (para. 5.76).

[129] Ibid., para. 3.65.

[130] DETR, *Local Government Bill Draft Guidance New Constitutions* (London, 2000), para. 14.46.

[131] In these cases regular staff exchanges between the two sides would be desirable.

[132] Ibid., paras. 14.50 and 14.51.

[133] Although the protections from suspension or dismissal of Chief Executives without the involvement of an independent person (p. 256 above) are to be extended to the chief

arrangements could produce more frequent changes of political control in many councils which may strengthen officer neutrality: officers will be unwilling to be too closely aligned to a political executive whose grip on power may be short-lived.

financial officer and to the monitoring officer: *Guidance*, paras. 14.41 and 14.42. The 1993 Working Party argued the need for formal protections for officers. It recognized there could be acute conflict in the case of the Chief Executive who would act as 'cabinet secretary to the executive; as chief executive in carrying out the executive policy; and as chief officer to the council' (ibid., para. 5.53). One possible solution was the creation of a statutory role of clerk, on whom the present functions in relation to councillors' rights and of monitoring might be conferred. In practice, though, this appointment would require more formal insulation from the remainder of the council's service than simple secondment would allow.

The Working Party also argued that it should be made clear that in the case of powers delegated to a single councillor, the lead member would have ultimate power in deciding how to implement the council's policies, balanced against formal protection for an officer to place contradictory advice before the council or a committee (ibid., para. 5.56.) Officers would have the final word over what information behind a lead member's decision to release to the council as a whole. On this point, note the suggestion that officers' factual advice to the executive should normally be published: *Local Leadership, Local Choice*, paras. 3.62 and 3.63.

Part IV

# The Council in the Community

# 9

# *The Politics of Local Contracts*

## TWO DIFFERENT APPROACHES

The importance of the contractual position of local government is difficult to overestimate. One of the defining features of corporate status is the ability to enter contracts which bind the authority as a distinct legal entity. This process is fundamental to the employment of staff,[1] buying or renting land, and the purchase of all materials necessary to perform any of the council's functions (whether discretionary or mandatory) which involve positive action. Without contractual capacity local authorities would be reduced to regulatory bodies, and even then they would need to employ a core of staff to carry out inspections, serve statutory notices, and bring proceedings. The contractual power of local authorities is, therefore, necessarily bound up with questions about the proper domain of the council, and political controversy about this question spills over into the relevant legal doctrine.

The contracting, purchasing, and employing power of local authorities has long been a political battleground. Whereas the Left has seen in the use of the power to purchase labour, supplies, and materials the opportunity to achieve secondary social goals, the Right has argued that such transactions should be governed by strict market principles of value for money and of efficiency.

This division of opinion dates back at least to the 1920s when a key component of 'Poplarism'[2] was the use of local-government employment to pay 'fair' wages, even if considerably in excess of the market rate.[3] In more recent times contract compliance became a method of promoting equal-opportunity policies, particularly those beyond the strict reach of the council's domain, by ensuring that contractors employed by the council met defined employment standards. It is now, however, severely constrained by both domestic legislation and European law. The Right, on the other hand, introduced a number of measures designed to open local government markets to outside competition through compulsory competitive

[1] The general principles discussed in this chapter are applicable to employment, but the position of officers is discussed in more detail in Ch. 8.

[2] B. Keith-Lucas, 'Poplarism', [1962] PL 52; N. Branson, *Poplarism, 1919–25: George Lansbury and the Councillors' Revolt* (London, 1979); G. W. Jones, 'Herbert Morrison and Poplarism', [1973] PL 11; P. Fennell, 'Roberts v. Hopwood; the Rule Against Socialism', (1986) 13 J. of Law and Society 401.

[3] Declared ultra vires in *Roberts v Hopwood*, [1925] AC 578 (see p. 290 below).

tendering (CCT). This process began with relatively autonomous council function such as building and repair works often put out to private contractors, but was later extended to refuse disposal, catering, and, more recently, to traditionally pivotal parts of the local officer domain, such as legal services.[4] (CCT and its replacement, Best Value, are discussed further in Chapter 10 in the context of relations between the council and the community.) In practice the picture has been further complicated by the close working association between many Labour councillors and public-sector trade unions, and the similar affiliation of many Conservative councillors with local business interests.

The central questions to be addressed in this section are whether contracts made by local authorities should be governed by contractual or by public law principles and how each approach accommodates the political nature of local authorities. According to classical contractual principles,[5] the law's concern is to establish the necessary criteria for entering the contract, not the motive for doing so, or the adequacy of the bargain. A refusal to enter a contract is not generally actionable. It is the interests of the contracting parties which are of legal significance, not those of third parties; the doctrine of privity can be used to rule out such interests.

Under the rigid application of a contractual model councils would be treated as full legal actors, but, following from their independent contractual capacity, the interests of their current councillors, electors, taxpayers, or service users (if their relationship to the authority is not itself contractual) would be subordinated to the question of contractual liability. Hence the courts have held that contracts entered into by a local authority are unaffected by a change in political control of the authority.[6] On the other hand, to treat local authority contracts under public law doctrine is to recognize that contractual capacity is a legal fiction, created to enable councils to attain political objectives, but subject none the less to the general principles governing their capacity.

Two distinct but commingled lines of legal tradition are significant here. The first is the ultra vires doctrine: the ability to contract is always secondary to the achievement of some other statutory objective, and hence the problem arises of how any contract is affected if the purpose for which it was entered into is beyond the powers of the council or if it involves a

[4] A programme of contracting-out of this kind by the newly elected Conservative council in Bradford led to legal challenges when it was approved through repeated use of the mayor's casting vote: *R v Bradford CC ex p. Corris*, [1990] 2 WLR 247, and *R v Bradford CC ex p. Wilson*, [1990] 2 WLR 255 (and see p. 204 above).

[5] This will be familiar territory for legal readers. For an introductory account of the basic principles see P. Atiyah, *An Introduction to the Law of Contract* (5th edn., Oxford, 1995).

[6] *Storer v Manchester CC*, [1974] 1 WLR 1403; *Verrall v Great Yarmouth BC*, [1981] QB 202: see p. 282 below.

misuse of power. The second is the rule against fettering discretion by entering contracts which will unlawfully prevent the future exercise of discretion by a local authority.

The difference between the public law and contract approaches is not merely an arcane boundary dispute about which kind of law and which procedure is to apply, although at the remedial level it can raise such questions.[7] It is about the standards which are to be applied to the use of state power and property. Daintith has argued, in a similar context concerning central government, that it concerns the difference between imperium (i.e. government by use of coercive rules) and dominium (implementation of policy through use of property).[8] Some commentators have coined the term 'the contract state'[9] to describe a perceived shift towards the use of dominium. However, where local government is concerned, the courts have been antipathetic to the notion of dominium, as we shall see. This hostility is in some respects less readily understandable than the criticisms which can be made of the similar use of contractual largesse by central government. For, whereas policy may be pursued by central government as an alternative to legislation at the central level, with a corresponding deficit in terms of democratic approval and legitimacy, this is less likely in local government. Local authorities' decision-making processes are such that any such policy must be open and subject to clear democratic approval, control, and delegation.[10] However, it may be argued that local authorities should be restrained from playing at politics or law enforcement outside the areas strictly delegated to them under legislation, and this may account for some judicial hostility.

The public law and contractual approaches do not equate symmetrically with political divisions of opinion about the use of contractual power. Nevertheless, there are some obvious similarities. For instance, the contractual approach likens the position of local authorities directly to that of private individuals and companies in their legal dealings: it treats the corporation in the same way as any other contractor. It should be noted, however, that the Right approach to council contracts went considerably

[7] See P. Craig, *Administrative Law* (3rd edn., London, 1994), 552–91. This point has a substantial history which it is not necessary to explore here, but for the most recent judicial pronouncements concerning contractual arrangements see: *Doyle v Northumbria Probation Committee*, [1991] 4 All ER 249; *Roy v Kensington and Chelsea and Westminster Family Practice Committee*, [1992] 1 All ER 705; *Mercury Communications Limited v Director-General of Telecommunications*, [1996] 1 All ER 575.

[8] T. Daintith, 'Regulation by Contract: The New Prerogative', (1979) 32 CLP 41; and see T. Daintith, 'The Techniques of Government', in J. Jowell and D. Oliver (eds.), *The Changing Constitution* (3rd edn., Oxford, 1994).

[9] I. Harden and N. Lewis, *The Noble Lie: The British Constitution and the Rule of Law* (London, 1986), 177–8; I. Harden, *The Contracting State* (Buckingham, 1992); P. Birkinshaw, I. Harden, and N. Lewis, *Government by Moonlight* (London, 1990); M. Freedland, 'Government by Contract and Public Law', [1994] PL 86.

[10] Ch. 7.

beyond the classical contractual approach. Whereas the contractual approach leaves market rationality as a private question of motive between the parties (indeed, traditionally contract law has not been concerned with the adequacy of the consideration or how good a bargain has been struck), during the 1980s the Right imposed explicit statutory duties on councils to behave in an 'economic' fashion (e.g. CCT). The public law approach recognizes that political considerations may modify what would otherwise be legally enforceable contracts. Paradoxically, however, in practice the public law approach has been used to 'rescue' local authorities from uneconomic bargains, i.e. to reinforce market rationality,[11] as well as to impose procedural standards on local authorities in their contractual dealings.

In comparing these approaches, we may first notice some contexts where the application of contractual principles proceeds in the same way as in private law, with the result that the political nature of one of the contracting bodies is in effect ignored. Thus, in *Storer v Manchester City Council*[12] an incoming Labour administration was held to be contractually bound by the agreements reached by its Conservative predecessor to sell to tenants their council houses. The issue was approached as a straightforward matter solely on contract-law principles.[13] Similarly, another Labour-controlled local authority was not allowed to renege on a booking of a hall for a political meeting,[14] when the Court of Appeal granted an order of specific performance to enforce the booking for a National Front conference, approved when the council was under different political control. Cumming-Bruce LJ said that it was insufficient to enable the council to avoid the contract that the majority group 'take a different view of the pros and cons of the bargain from the view taken by their predecessors on the Council who made the contract'.[15] Political inconvenience or inappropriateness is deemed irrelevant to the issue of whether a legally binding contract has been concluded.[16]

Conversely, in some contexts local authority contracts may be regarded as governed by the straightforward application of public law principles, leading to the conclusion that an ultra vires contract will be void. This is arrived at by extension of the normal consequences of the ultra vires con-

[11] *Roberts v Hopwood* (n. 3 above).

[12] [1974] 1 WLR 1403; distinguished on contractual grounds in *Gibson v Manchester City Council*, [1979] 1 WLR 294. Older authorities establish that a council will be bound by a contract that turns out to be a poor bargain: see *New Windsor Corp. v Stowell*, [1884] 27 CLD 665; *MMI Ltd. v Pontefract Corp.*, [1917] 116 LT 671.

[13] Cf. *R v Hammersmith and Fulham LBC ex p. Beddowes*, [1987] 2 WLR 263, discussed below, where the fettering discretion principle was unsuccessfully invoked.

[14] *Verrall v Great Yarmouth BC*, [1981] QB 202.

[15] Ibid. 222.

[16] There is, however, depending on the interpretation of the fettering discretion cases (p. 292 below), a possible exception to this where a public body is deemed incapable of entering into some kinds of politically limiting contracts.

cept to contract. Since local authorities are artificial and subordinate legal entities, their contractual power is itself subject to legal limitation. The application of this rule to local authorities is simply a corollary of the nineteenth-century doctrine of the limited capacity of corporate bodies generally.[17] As originally formulated, the rule means that a corporation should not be able either to extend[18] or curtail its powers by contract. The first aspect has been especially important where local authorities have attempted to use agreements as an alternative to statutory coercion, especially in the case of planning agreements.[19] The second aspect leads to the rule against fettering discretion, discussed below.

The rule can be seen as a means of protecting the financial interests of local taxpayers.[20] Historically, the ultra vires contract rule operated harshly in its effect on those dealing commercially with local authorities, since in many cases it put them at risk of losing by the council's unlawful action.[21] Consequently, it put the onus on those dealing with a local authority to inquire into the legality of the council's action—a subject on which the council and its professional advisers were generally more qualified to reach a conclusion.

The contracting power is merely ancillary to the achievement of other statutory objectives conferred on local authorities: they are not trading entities in their own right[22] and hence the contracting power will be

[17] *Ashbury Railway Carriage and Iron Co. v Riche*, (1875) LR 7 HL 633. See pp. 38–41 above. Historically the rule did not apply to local authorities created by royal charter, which were deemed to have all the powers of a natural person: *Payne v Brecon Corp.*, [1858] 3 H & N 572. In practice, though, statutory controls over the finances of local authorities were used to inhibit this contractual freedom: *A-G v Newcastle Corp. and North Eastern Railway Company*, [1889] 23 QBD 492, *A-G v Manchester Corp.*, [1906] 1 Ch. 643; *A-G v Leeds Corp.*, [1929] 2 Ch. 291. Since all local authorities are now statutory corporations, this distinction based on the source of the council's powers has now disappeared: see *Hazzell v Hammersmith and Fulham LBC*, [1991] 1 All ER 545, 563–6 per Lord Templeman (London borough incorporated by royal charter had no powers statute to enter contracts for interest swap transactions). The only residue is that some authorities retain the designation 'Royal' in their titles. See further Ch. 2.

[18] This is also the justification that estoppel will not apply to local authorities: *Rhyl UDC v Rhyl Amusements Ltd*, [1959] 1 All ER 257.

[19] See e.g. *Windsor and Maidenhead RBC v Brandrose*, [1983] 1 WLR 509. The legality and desirability of planning agreements has generated a substantial literature: P. Healey, H. Purdue, and F. Ennis, *Gains From Planning? Dealing With the Impact of Development* (York, 1993).

[20] Indeed, one commentator bases her justification for judicial review of governmental procurement decisions generally on the need to hold to account those receiving public money: S. Arrowsmith, *Government Procurement and Judicial Review* (Toronto, 1988), 112.

[21] The consequence of a contract being declared ultra vires is that it is regarded as void ab initio and loss will lie where it falls. Hence a council which has obtained services ultra vires may be able to avoid paying for them. However, the principles of restitution may fill the gap (see n. 27 below) and see now, Local Government (Contracts) Act 1997, p. 298 below.

[22] Indeed, trading is specifically forbidden: Local Authorities (Goods and Services) Act 1970, s. 1.

limited according to the terms of what we may call the parent power. Hence, the House of Lords has held that local authorities had no power to engage in 'interest swap' transactions on the money markets in so far as the purpose extended into speculation or trading, rather than merely managing existing debt.[23] In practice, the legal basis of many council contracts is not explicit, but the parentage is traced by coupling a general power to contract with the specific statutory duty or power in question.[24]

The effect of the ultra vires doctrine can be contractually inconvenient, since a council may have enjoyed benefits under an arrangement subsequently found to be ultra vires and may even be in a position to plead its own illegality as a reason for evading the agreement.[25] Furthermore, with some types of ultra vires contract the party dealing with the council may have no way of discovering whether the contract is an ultra vires one. Cane has criticized the fact that a local authority can in effect plead its own illegality to evade an ultra vires contract as producing a conflict of two of the underlying aims of judicial review: protecting citizens against illegal governmental actions and protecting the public and the public purse from the effects of illegality.[26] For this reason he argued that the law should distinguish in the effect of such contracts according to which party is seeking to enforce the contract, with a citizen who was unaware of the illegality able to recover at least damages under an ultra vires contract. In some instances, however, the law of restitution will operate to fill these deficiencies to allow recovery of payment under ultra vires contracts where one party has been unjustly enriched.[27] We will see later how Parliament also has attempted to remedy the commercial disadvantages of the application of the doctrine.[28]

Although the results described may appear to be straightforward applications of public law doctrine, it can be argued that the effect is to modify

[23] *Hazell v Hammersmith LBC*, [1991] 1 All ER 545. However, see the critical discussion by Loughlin (M. Loughlin, 'Innovative Financing: The Limits of Legal Instrumentalism—Pt. II', [1991] PL 568, 590 ff.), who argues that the Lords may have misinterpreted the background to some of the transactions in question. See also *Credit Suisse v Allerdale BC*, [1996] 4 All ER 129, CA.

[24] Either s. 111 LGA 1972 (pp. 46–50 above) or now s. 1(1) Local Government (Contracts) Act 1997 (p. 298 below).

[25] As in *Rhyl UDC v Rhyl Amusements Ltd*, [1959] 1 All ER 257, where a lease was held void because the council had failed to obtain a necessary ministerial consent.

[26] P. Cane, 'Do Banks Dare to Lend to Local Authorities?', (1994) 110 LQR 514, 517.

[27] See e.g. the restitutionary claims brought by banks after the *Hazell* case (n. 23 above): *Westdeutsche Landesbank Girozentrale v Islington London BC*, [1996] 2 All ER 961, HL; *Kleinwort Benson Ltd. v. Lincoln CC*, [1998] 4 All ER 513; *Kleinwort Benson Ltd v Sandwell BC*, (1993) 91 LGR 323, upheld by the CA, [1994] 4 All ER 890; and see *Kleinwort Benson Ltd v South Tyneside MBC*, [1994] 4 All ER 972; *Morgan Grenfell and Co. v Welwyn Hatfield DC*, [1995] 1 All ER 1; *Morgan Guaranty Trust Co. v Lothian Regional Council*, *The Times*, 30 Nov. 1993.

[28] See discussion of Local Government (Contracts) Act 1997: pp. 298–9 below.

each of the fundamental tenets of contract law discussed earlier. These will now be reconsidered.[29]

THE FUNDAMENTAL THINGS APPLY?

## Refusal to Contract and the Challenges to the Exercise of Contractual Power

In private law a refusal to contract is not generally actionable. A purchaser or customer can be utterly capricious in the choice of, or reasons for choosing or rejecting, a contractual partner and the law will not intervene (unless there is unlawful discrimination). A decision not to contract made by a local authority may, however, be reviewable if it is based on 'irrelevant considerations'. For this purpose the scope of relevant considerations at common law is critical. The assumptions implicit in the judicial approach can be laid bare by examining several examples. In one a boycott of a company's products by a local authority was found to be ultra vires because it was actuated in part by a desire to bring pressure on the company to sever trading links with South Africa.[30] Similarly, a decision to boycott Murdoch-owned newspapers by a library authority in order to bring pressure on the group in connection with its industrial dispute over the move of its premises from Fleet Street to Wapping was deemed unlawful.[31] The court found that this motive was irrelevant to the execution of the council's duty under section 7 of the Public Libraries and Museums Act 1964 to run a 'comprehensive and efficient library service'.[32] This line of attack does not only apply to decisions *not* to contract: a third party can

[29] The purpose here is in a sense the opposite of S. Arrowsmith, 'Government Contracts and Public Law', (1990) 10 Legal Studies 231, who argues (mainly on the basis of Crown procurement practices) that public law doctrine is insufficiently applied to public contracts because of a continuing belief that contracts are 'private' matters; see also Arrowsmith, *Government Procurement*, 10ff.; and 'Judicial Review and the Contractual Powers of Public Authorities',(1990) 106 LQR 277. See also D. Oliver, *Common Values and the Public–Private Divide* (London, 1999), 177–87, drawing parallels between contract and judicial review.

[30] *R v Lewisham LBC ex p. Shell UK Ltd*, [1988] 1 All ER 938 (contrast opposite result in Canadian case of: *Re Shell Products Ltd v City of Vancouver*, CA, (1991) 81 DLR 353).

[31] *R v Ealing London Borough Council ex p. Times Newspapers*, (1987) 85 LGR 316. Similarly, in *R v Derbyshire CC ex p. Times Supplements*, (1991) 3 Admin. LR 241, it was held that a ban on placing teaching job advertisements in the *Times Education Supplement* in reprisal for an article critical of the council's leader which appeared in the *Sunday Times* was ultra vires.

[32] 'the ban imposed by the borough councils was for an ulterior motive. It was inspired by political views which moved the borough councils to interfere in an industrial dispute. . . . I would go so far as to say that no rational local authority would for a moment have thought that such a ban was open to it to impose in discharge of its duty under to service libraries.' Per Watkins LJ, *ex p. Times Newspapers*, 329.

also challenge a decision to *enter* a contract on the grounds of irrelevant considerations.[33]

A local authority may also be under a duty to act fairly in contractual matters.[34] This is illuminated by a remarkable piece of litigation from South Wales, concerning the allegedly malicious refusal by the council to grant permission for change of use in a business lease.[35] The lease was between the council and the wife of a councillor from a minority political group (and former council leader). In the end the action failed because of the view the House of Lords took of the evidence and the inappropriateness on the facts of ordering a fresh trial. However, the Court of Appeal had held that the alleged malice of the new leader of the council towards the applicant and her husband was capable, if it tainted the vote of the majority group as a whole in voting against the change of use, of amounting to the tort of misfeasance in a public office by the council. It made no difference to the question of misfeasance whether the power was derived from statute or, as here, from a lease, since in either case the council was to exercise its powers for the public good:[36] the Court of Appeal expressly rejected the notion that a local authority was free to behave as capriciously as a private landlord in such matters.[37]

Applicants have also attempted to utilize the emerging public law of doctrine of legitimate expectation[38] to impose liability on local authorities in pre-contractual situations where no action would lie under private law.[39] In one case a council's refusal to renew a business lease was successfully quashed by this route because the court held that the council had failed to honour an earlier undertaking to enter formal negotiations for renewal.[40] However, other applications in comparable situations have

[33] See p. 289 below.

[34] Contrast the position of the Crown, which is under no duty to adopt fair pre-contractual practices: *R v Lord Chancellor ex p. Hibbert and Sanders*, [1993] LCOD 326 (discussed in D. Oliver,'The Case of the Shorthand Writers', [1993] PL 214).

[35] *Jones v Swansea City Council* (CA), [1990] 1 WLR 54; (HL) [1990] 1 WLR 1453 (and see p. 42 above).

[36] Ibid. 70–1 (per Slade LJ), 85 (Nourse LJ).

[37] Although no contractual relationship between the parties was involved, a local authority's responsibilities as landowner were considered at length in *R v Somerset CC ex p. Fewings*, [1995] 1 All ER 513 (QBD); [1995] 1 WLR 1037 (CA), where a ban on deer-hunting on local-authority land was held to be unlawful since it was deemed to fall outside the scope of the statutory provision under which the land was held (s. 120 LGA 1972). See pp. 41–5 above.

[38] See P. P. Craig, 'Legitimate Expectations: A Conceptual Analysis', (1992) 108 LQR 79; C. F. Forsyth, 'The Provenance and Protection of Legitimate Expectations', [1988] CLJ 238; G. Ganz, 'Legitimate Expectation', in C. Harlow (ed.), *Public Law and Politics* (London, 1986), 145; P. Elias, 'Legitimate Expectation and Judicial Review', in J. Jowell and D. Oliver (eds.), *New Directions in Judicial Review* (London, 1988), 37.

[39] See generally: S. Arrowsmith, 'Protecting the Interests of Bidders for Public Contracts: The Role of the Common Law', (1994) 53 CLJ 104, who argues for the development of new private law remedies to protect bidders because of the limitations on remedial relief in public law.

[40] *R v Watford BC ex p. Incorporated West Herts Golf Club*, [1990] 1 EGLR 263.

failed on the facts.[41] There is potential overlap with contractual principles here: one case (which, on the facts, would have been well outside the time limits for judicial review) concerned an administrative failure in the handling by a local authority of a tender, but proceeded instead on the basis of a collateral contract, which the court implied, to consider all tenders submitted.[42] Overall, it is too early to pronounce with certainty on the application of legitimate expectation to such decisions.

Where a contract is terminated by a council within the powers available in private law, public law may nevertheless grant the contracting party a remedy. Thus, in a famous example from the 1920s it was stated that if a council decided to dismiss all red-headed teachers the decision would be plainly unreasonable and ultra vires.[43] In a more recent case a council's decision was held to be ultra vires when it revoked a rugby club's licence (an unprotected form of property interest) to use a training-ground because of the failure of the club to give a clear condemnation of the participation by some of its players in a 'rebel' tour of South Africa: the council's opposition to apartheid was found to be irrelevant to the administration of the land under the Open Spaces Act 1906, and the House of Lords characterized the council's action as punishing the club for views which were not unlawful.[44] In another instance it was held that a local authority was bound to observe the rules of natural justice when revoking a (contractual) licence for street trading.[45]

The consequence of these decisions is that where local authority contracts are concerned, the motive for refusing to contract is subject to legal scrutiny. A partial explanation for these judgments lies in a judicial

[41] *R v Torbay BC ex p. Cleasby*, [1991] COD 142 (no legitimate expectation of allocation of pleasure boat franchise by rota); *R v Barnet LBC ex p. Islam*, [1991] EGCS 83 (no legitimate expectation of sale of land for mosque). It has also been held that legitimate expectations cannot operate pre-contractually to override the fiduciary duty which a council owes to local taxpayers: *R v Portsmouth CC ex p. Bonaco Builders*, unreported decision of QBD, 6 June 1995.

[42] *Blackpool and Fylde Aero Club v Blackpool BC*, [1990] 1 WLR 1195. See also *Fairclough Builders Ltd v Port Talbot BC*, decision of the Court of Appeal, 16 July 1992. However, any collateral contract may be excluded by appropriate wording in the tender documents: S. Arrowsmith, *The Law of Public and Utilities Procurement* (London, 1996), 40.

[43] *Short v Poole Corporation*, [1926] Ch. 66, 91 per Warrington LJ. However, in this decision the court upheld a decision to dismiss all married women teachers in an attempt to save money without causing undue hardship to single-income families (an interesting example of attempting to achieve a secondary social goal through a contractual decision in its own right). Even without employment protection and sex discrimination legislation, it seems unlikely that the same result could be reached today.

[44] *Wheeler v Leicester City Council*, [1985] AC 1054.

[45] *R v Wear Valley DC ex p. Binks*, [1985] 2 All ER 699. The court followed *R v Basildon BC ex p. Brown*, (1981) 79 LGR 655, in equating the trader's position to that of stallholder in a statutory market, who would have a clear public law entitlement to a hearing before revocation of the licence. However, in the latter case the Court of Appeal refused to intervene (Lord Denning dissenting) on the basis that the contract was clear and exhaustive. Dunn LJ stated that it was not the function of the court to rewrite the contract by adding public law duties to it: ibid. 674.

revulsion at what is regarded as the abuse of public power. While this may be laudable where a private individual is the victim, it is arguably unnecessary where the litigant is a multinational company and is on more than an equal economic footing with the council.

However, there are other factors at work also. The judges seem to have in the background an assumption about what criteria are relevant in exercise of contractual discretion, an implicit division between 'political' considerations which can be classified as irrelevant and 'commercial' ones which are pertinent.[46] Paradoxically, although this level of control ostensibly mirrors private-sector or commercial behaviour, as has been seen where private contracts are concerned, the law has no interest in the question of motive. A private contractor may behave from good or bad motives—they are simply irrelevant. Hence before modern anti-discrimination legislation the common law generally upheld discriminatory contractual decisions.[47] Equally, ethically or politically motivated behaviour in the private sector, for instance donations to political parties from company funds, paying higher than market rates to Third World workers, refusal to test products on animals, or refusal to invest in politically repressive regimes, are not open to legal question on contractual grounds.[48] In such cases the mechanisms of company law granting powers to shareholders are deemed sufficient safeguard of their interests. However, the local authority cases demonstrate a startling unpreparedness to trust the equivalent accountability mechanism of the franchise.[49]

Private-sector behaviour of the kind described may be motivated by non-commercial considerations, but it is also often symptomatic of a longer-term view of commercial interests which looks beyond immediate cost-saving or profit—that the company's stance may be one which attracts consumers to its products (who themselves may not behave solely as narrow-minded economically rational persons), or that it may enhance employee satisfaction or loyalty. All such considerations seem out of bounds to public bodies, on the ostensible grounds that Parliament cannot

[46] This anticipated a similar but not identical distinction introduced in legislation: LGA 1988, s. 17 (p. 302 below). Note, however, that s. 19(9) LGA preserves the common law where the non-commercial criteria test is inapplicable. A purported distinction between commercial and political contracts also runs through some of the cases on fettering discretion (see pp. 292–8 below).

[47] A. Lester and G. Bindman, *Race and Law* (Harmondsworth, 1972), 49–69.

[48] In the comparable field of charity law it has been held that charitable trustees are permitted (but are not overly compelled) to have regard to the ethical background of the charity in making investment decisions: *Harries v Church Commissioners for England*, [1992] 1 WLR 1241.

[49] In an old Canadian local government case, *Hignell v Winnipeg (City)*, [1933] 3 WWR 193, 197, MacDonald CJ explicitly relied on electoral accountability as a reason for not interfering with a contract: 'If the ratepayers are satisfied, that is all that is needed; if they are not satisfied redress is at the polls and not through the courts' (cited by Arrowsmith, *Government Procurement*, 209).

have intended them to behave in such a way, or that they are inappropriate for custodians of public money: the benefit or satisfaction that the local electorate may derive, or any approval or endorsement they may have given (or withheld) is irrelevant. In other words, in purportedly following a private model of contract-making the courts have, paradoxically, imposed a more onerous regime on local authorities than that applicable to private contractors.

### Third-party challenges

Generally, only parties to a contract have legal interests arising under it. The doctrine of privity of contract prevents actions brought by third parties. Public law, however, allows non-contracting parties to challenge a decision to award a local authority contract, in a sense circumventing the doctrine of privity of contract. For instance, in one case the court granted an injunction to prevent a local authority from engaging advertising agencies to conduct a political campaign on the basis that such expenditure would be unlawful.[50] Such challenges may also arise as a consequence of a duty to behave fairly and to follow procedural rules for the making of contracts, whether contained in statute or in the council's own standing orders.[51] Under the erstwhile CCT regime various statutory provisions enabled the Secretary of State, the Audit Commission, or a disappointed tenderer to challenge a decision.[52]

The principles are illustrated in a case in which a council house tenancy was set aside as ultra vires. The house had been allocated preferentially for reasons unrelated to the operation of the council's housing waiting-list, namely a desire for the tenant to retain her connection as a councillor with the ward in which the house was situated and to have accommodation in which to receive her constituents.[53] Similarly, a stranger to an unlawful

[50] *R v Greater London Council ex p. Westminster City Council*, *The Times*, 22 Jan. 1985.

[51] *R v Hereford Corp. ex parte Harrower*, [1970] 1 WLR 1424 (although part of the decision turned upon the locus standi of the applicants as ratepayers and not as potential contractors, this pre-dates the post-1977 relaxation of standing and would not now be of importance). See also *N.W. Leicestershire DC v East Midlands Housing Association*, [1981] 1 WLR 1396; *Mass Energy Ltd v Birmingham CC*, unreported decision of the Court of Appeal, 3 Sept. 1993 (unsuccessful tenderer permitted to challenge award of contract to another private company since procedure for waste disposal contracts was governed by Environmental Protection Act 1990 and was, therefore, a public law issue).

[52] See pp. 317–19 below. However, these applied only to third parties and did not require fairness in the treatment of the council's own workforce in deciding whether to execute work through it or through an outside contractor: *R v Walsall BC ex p. Yapp*, *The Times*, 6 Aug. 1993.

[53] *R v Port Talbot BC ex p. Jones*, [1988] 2 All ER 207; there were also procedural improprieties in the way in which the decision was taken, under the excessive influence of the Housing Committee chairman (see further p. 224 above). The action was brought by the new leader of council against the authority but was unopposed by the council (who indeed supported it). This seems a circuitous but transparent device for avoiding the tenancy, to which

planning agreement was able to prevent a local authority from following it and, thereby, determining a planning application to his detriment.[54]

### Questioning the bargain

In private law the value of consideration given is not questionable by the courts. Since the law pays no attention to the motive for entering into a contract, there is no stipulation that the parties behave in an 'economically rational' way. In public law, however, the courts have sometimes allowed challenges where it is alleged that a local authority has made an excessive price increase for a service provided to a private individual with whom it is in a contractual relationship: this has normally been arrived at by construction of the statutory scheme within which the power to make the charge arises.[55] In the past such claims were often brought as public law challenges to the council's policy decision, but the issue may also arise by way of defence to non-payment in private law proceedings.[56]

Conversely, in several instances a challenge has been brought on the basis that a council has been or would be acting ultra vires by contracting on unfavourable terms. Some early decisions hold that a council is bound by a contract in the same way as a private individual, and it is no reason to invoke the ultra vires doctrine that it turns out to be a bad bargain.[57] However, it may be significant that it was the council itself which was attempting to plead ultra vires as a reason for non-performance. Later cases have involved challenges brought by third parties, and the courts have shown greater preparedness to use the doctrine.

In the well-known case of *Roberts v Hopwood*[58] the House of Lords held that the then unprecedented novelties of a council paying its manual

the authority may have been driven by the understanding at that time of the law on procedural exclusivity (n. 7 above).

54 *Stringer v Minister of Housing*, [1971] 1 All ER 65.

55 e.g. a line of cases concerning the setting of council house rents. In *Belcher v Reading Corp.*, [1950] Ch. 380, 391, it was said that the council had to balance the interests of its ratepayers and tenants in setting rent levels. However, in *Luby v Newcastle-under-Lyme Corp.*, [1965] 1 QB 214, it was held that a council was entitled to have regard to a social policy in devising a differential rent structure. The courts have subsequently limited this discretion. *Backhouse v Lambeth LBC*, (1972) 116 SJ 802 (rent increase of £18,000 per week on an (unoccupied) council house set aside as irrational and a transparent sham devised to evade statutory controls). And see *R v. Secretary of State for Health and Social Security ex p. Sheffield CC*, [1985] HLR 6.

See also: *R v Birmingham CC ex p. Dredger* QBD, *The Times*, 28 Jan. 1993, where an excessive increase in the rent of a market stall was held ultra vires; *R v Camden LBC ex p. Cran*, (1996) 94 LGR 8 (successful challenge to order designating parking fees because of irrelevant matters taken into account).

56 *Wandsworth LBC v Winder*, [1985] AC 461 (and see cases referred to in n. 7 above).

57 *New Windsor Corporation v Stovell*, [1884] 27 Ch. D. 665; *Municipal Mutual Insurance Ltd v. Pontefract Corp.*, [1917] 116 LT 671.

58 [1925] AC 578.

workers what it considered to be a 'fair' wage and paying employees the same wage regardless of their sex were ultra vires. The council had raised wages substantially while prices were rising, but later voted to maintain them at existing levels despite the deflationary effect of general price and wage decreases in 1921–2. The court held that since by the council's own evidence it did not feel bound to follow either wage or price decreases in setting wage levels, the payments amounted to a gift (i.e. they were not a reflection of work performed) and were ultra vires; or, as Lord Atkinson intemperately put it, 'furthering Feminist goals and Socialist philanthropy with other people's money'.[59] Alternatively, the apparently unfettered discretion to pay such wages as the council thought fit had to be construed subject to an implied condition of reasonableness, and subject to a fiduciary duty owed to ratepayers.[60] Beneath a thin veneer of legalism the judicial espousal of market economics could scarcely have been more obvious.

While later judges have been more circumspect in their political criticism, the fiduciary principle of breach of trust has been applied in two further instances to strike down the proposed implementation of 'uneconomic' contractual arrangements in the field of subsidized public transport.[61] However, when what was regarded as a generous pay settlement in favour of municipal workers was challenged in the early 1980s, the courts refused to intervene.[62]

Although most of the instances in the case law are of challenges brought by other public officials or bodies enjoying distinct powers or adversely affected,[63] there seems no reason in principle why any person having sufficient interest (for instance a council taxpayer, elector, or pressure group, or a disappointed tenderer) could not also mount such a challenge. Once it is accepted that some kinds of poor bargain may be beyond the powers of a local authority, equally there appears no reason in principle why a council should be unable to raise the matter in defence[64] to escape from such an agreement. By comparison, in the private sector no one is in a similar position to question such a bargain.

[59] Ibid. 591 and 595.

[60] See further Ch. 4.

[61] *Prescott v Birmingham Corp.*, [1955] Ch. 210; *Bromley LBC v Greater London Council*, [1983] 1 AC 768. For the purpose of this discussion it is immaterial whether the legal action took the form of a direct attack on the individual contracts (each of which, since it involved a single journey, was purely nominal) or on the decision to implement a policy of subsidization of the fares.

[62] *Pickwell v Camden LBC*, [1983] QB 962. See, however, the setting aside of voluntary redundancy payments on different grounds in *Allsop v North Tyneside MBC*, [1991] RVR 104.

[63] In *Bromley LBC v Greater London Council*, [1983] AC 768, the challenge was brought by another local authority affected by the consequential financial effects of the decision, because the implementation of it required a supplementary rate precept.

[64] In *R v Portsmouth CC ex p. Bonaco Builders*, unreported decision of QBD, 6 June 1995, Keane J accepted that the council could consider the duty *pre-contractually* when considering bids for building maintenance work, so as to take account of redundancy payments which would follow to its own staff if a bid from an outside contractor were accepted.

Once again in these cases the courts can be seen employing a contradictory model of private sector behaviour—private-sector employers are assumed to pay only market rates of pay and minimal redundancy terms. While this may be true of some private-sector commercial behaviour, other undertakings grow profitably despite or because of their reputation for treating their staff better than the minimum pay or conditions demanded by the market. It is as though the courts had set out to impose on local government the worst features only of private-sector employment practice.

## The Fettering Doctrine

The practical effect of a contract may be open to question if it acts to fetter the statutory discretion of the local authority. It is here that the conflict between the application of contractual and public approaches becomes most acute.

Contracts are intended to create legally enforceable arrangements, and hence will limit the subsequent behaviour of the parties. Generally, a party to a contract may not rely upon his or her own conduct as a reason for rendering performance of the contract impossible (i.e. the doctrine of frustration of contract does not include self-induced circumstances). Conversely, one party will not be permitted to sue the other for breach of contract if the first party's action was the substantial cause of the non-performance. This doctrine is of particular relevance to public bodies because of the difficulties of 'two-hattedness', i.e. the regulatory powers of the authority may come into conflict with its contractual obligations.

While the principle that a contract should not be able to override a statutory duty is supportable as giving primacy to an obligation over a discretion,[65] the case for striking down a contract which inhibits the exercise of a statutory discretion is more questionable. The difficulty is that since the origin of a local authority's contractual power is itself a statutory discretion, what is involved is giving priority to one discretion over another (with the attendant risk of displacing a political value judgment in favour of a judicial one) or of subordinating the present exercise of discretion in favour of the future exercise of discretion.[66] The subject is complex, but for present purposes several of the problems can be illustrated sufficiently by

[65] Although cases of a local authority purporting to bind itself in a field governed by a statutory duty (rather than a discretion) are often cited as applications of the fettering doctrine (e.g. *Stringer v Minister of Housing and Local Government*, [1971] 1 WLR 204), they should be treated separately.

[66] Mitchell attributes the fettering doctrine to an overarching principle requiring the preservation of governmental effectiveness: J. Mitchell, *The Contracts of Public Authorities* (London, 1954), ch. 1.

concentrating on a single decision, with only passing reference to the wilder fringe.[67]

In the case under discussion[68] the question of fettering arose in an extreme form, since it concerned a contract concluded only hours before the controlling political group on the council changed as a result of an election. The contract was one with a property developer for the sale of a council housing estate for development for owner-occupation. Although the contract entered into only transferred the ownership in part of the estate, it also contained covenants which prevented the council moving new tenants into the remainder, so that, eventually, it too would become available for redevelopment. It was a matter of dispute whether these covenants had been inserted at the developer's insistence to make the first phase of the scheme viable, or to perpetuate the owner-occupation policy of the Conservative majority group by tying the hands of any future Labour administration.[69]

The three judges in the Court of Appeal were finely divided on whether the contract was void for fettering the discretion of the council, although they held by a majority that it did not. Fox LJ found that the purpose of the scheme was the provision of housing accommodation (albeit through owner-occupation) and therefore found that it was within the council's powers—the question of a fetter on the housing responsibility did not arise, since the agreement was a means of performing the responsibility. Kerr LJ dissented because he took the view that the dominant motive of the council was to make the policy irrevocable in the event of a change in political control.[70] Buckley LJ recognized that this desire had played a part but held that the dominant motivation had been a lawful one.[71]

Behind this range of views lay a comparable division of opinion over the relative importance of the present and future political autonomy of the Council. Kerr LJ's view was that

> policies are liable to be reviewed as a result of events or political changes or both. They should remain open to review under our democratic institutions, save to the extent that an immediate policy decision renders it reasonably necessary to fetter future policy decisions.[72]

Contrast the view of Sir Denys Buckley:

[67] Fuller discussion of the doctrine can be found in: S. Arrowsmith, *Civil Liability and Public Authorities* (Winteringham, 1992), 72–9; P. Rogerson, 'On the Fettering of Public Powers', [1971] PL 288; Mitchell, op. cit., 57–64; C. Turpin, *Government Contracts* (Harmondsworth, 1972), 19–24; P. Hogg, *Liability of the Crown* (2nd edn., Toronto, 1989), 169–72; see P. Craig, *Administrative Law* (3rd edn., London, 1994), 699–703.

[68] *R v Hammersmith and Fulham LBC ex p. Beddowes*, [1987] 2 WLR 263.

[69] The Labour group (then in opposition) had made attempts to dissuade the developers from proceeding: ibid. 269.

[70] Ibid. 283–4.

[71] Ibid. 285.

[72] Ibid. 284.

if a statutory authority acting in good faith in the proper and reasonable exercise of its statutory powers undertakes some binding obligation, the fact that such obligation may thereafter preclude the authority from exercising some other statutory power, or from exercising its statutory powers in some other way, cannot constitute an impermissible fetter on its powers. Any other view would itself involve a fetter on the authority's capacity to exercise its powers properly and reasonably as it thinks fit from time to time.[73]

Although in some of the case law it is suggested that a contract will be ultra vires wherever it might prevent the future exercise of any statutory discretion by the authority,[74] this is an erroneous view and unsupportable in principle.[75] Pure conflicts of discretion have most often arisen in relation to the different uses to which land may be put, since it is here that alternative courses of action are most clearly mutually exclusive; for instance, the grant of a right of way will prevent the erection of buildings,[76] a site cannot be used both as an airport and as a housing estate,[77] and so on. It has been pointed out that the doctrine cannot prevent a council from agreeing (contractually) to exercise one discretion simply because of an inconsistency with the simultaneous exercise of some other statutory discretion: otherwise, where discretions overlap neither could be exercised because each would impede the other, with the result that the council would enjoy less power than the legislature intended.[78] The practice of the courts shows that the doctrine is of much more limited scope. Professor Arrowsmith argues that it properly only applies where a clash between a contract is reasonably foreseeable rather than a mere theoretical possibility, and even in this category it has not always been applied.[79]

Several factors confine the doctrine more narrowly than a bald statement would suggest. If the supposedly fettering agreement lacks an apparent statutory basis it would be invalid, without the need to consider

[73] Ibid. 285–6.

[74] This is stated in *Ayr Harbour Trustees v Oswald*, (1883) 8 App. Cas. 623. However, it is disputable whether that case properly involved the doctrine at all. It concerned the consistency with a private statute granting powers of compulsory purchase and development of a right of way (for the vendor's use) in the deed conveying the land in question. Since both the purchase and the inclusion of the right of way were against the vendor's wishes, it is questionable whether this is really an instance of fettering by contract. It seems likely that the House of Lords was hostile to the inclusion of the covenant as a self-serving attempt by the trustees to reduce the compensation payable under the statute. The Ayr Harbour ratio seems to have been applied unequivocally in only one decision: *York Corp. v Henry Leatham and Sons*, [1924] 1 Ch. 557. It was interpreted more narrowly in *Stourcliffe Estates Co. Ltd v Bournemouth Corp.*, [1910] 2 Ch. 12, and *Birkdale District Electricity Supply Co. v Corp. of Southport*, [1926] AC 355 (also doubting *York Corp. v Henry Leatham and Sons*).

[75] See P. Rogerson, 'On the Fettering of Public Powers', [1971] PL 288.

[76] As in the *Ayr Harbour* case (n. 74 above).

[77] See *Dowty Boulton Paul Ltd v Wolverhampton Corporation*, [1971] 1 WLR 204.

[78] Per Devlin LJ in *Blake v Hendon Corp.*, [1962] 1 QB 283, 301.

[79] See Arrowsmith, *Civil Liability and Public Authorities*, 73.

any possible conflict with other statutory discretions. Where the basis for a contract is section 111 of the LGA 1972, that provision itself provides that it cannot be used to override other statutory limitations. It therefore dictates a statutory hierarchy of powers without recourse to the fettering doctrine.[80] Moreover, it is only the proper exercise of a discretion which must not be fettered. The exercise of a discretion for the sole purpose or dominant motive of frustrating a contract could itself be ultra vires under normal principles[81] or amount to misfeasance in a public office.[82] It seems also that the doctrine does not prevent the contract having some influence on subsequent decision-making; it merely prevents it being decisive. It has been held, therefore, that where the exercise of a discretion would involve breaking a contract, that is one of the factors which must be considered in exercising the discretion.[83]

A judge wishing to avoid the effect of the doctrine can also adopt an interpretative strategy by reading the contract or the allegedly clashing statutory discretion so as to avoid conflict. For example, the court may refuse to imply a term into the contract which it would have implied between purely private parties.[84]

A contract is perhaps more likely to be found to fetter a discretion if the discretion which is allegedly impeded is the same one under which the contract is purportedly made.[85] However, principle suggests that this should only invalidate the contract if it is clear that the legislature intended the discretion to be one continually available to the council, rather than exercisable within finite limits. There is some support for this in the case law,[86] but it does not emerge as a major consideration.

The fettering doctrine clearly raises the question whether there are circumstances in which a public body ought to be free, for political reasons, to depart from its contractual undertakings. The public interest requires a

[80] In *Allsop v N. Tyneside MBC*, [1991] RVR 104, the Court of Appeal invoked this limitation in s. 111 to declare ultra vires voluntary redundancy arrangements providing for payments in excess of those under other statutory provisions (discussed further at p. 50 above). Since the coming into force of the Local Government (Contracts) Act 1997 it is better to regard s. 1 of that Act as the source of power for contracts not explicitly authorized in other legislation.

[81] See p. 285 above.

[82] *Roncarelli v DuPlessis*, (1959) 16 DLR (2d) 689 (SCC); *Jones v Swansea CC* (p. 286 above).

[83] *R v Hillingdon Health Authority, ex parte Goodwin*, [1984] ICR 800, 809–10 per Woolf J (three months' notice requirement in doctors' contracts relevant to decision on hospital closure).

[84] *William Cory and Son v City of London*, [1951] 2 KB 476 (refusal to imply term preventing later use of power to make by-laws which would have the effect of frustrating the contract); and see *Commissioners of Crown Lands v Page*, [1960] 2 QB 274, implying an exception for the Crown's powers to a covenant for quiet enjoyment in a lease.

[85] This is the interpretation given to the *Ayr Harbour Trustees* case in the *Stourcliffe* and *Birkdale* decisions (n. 74 above).

[86] Lord Watson in the *Ayr Harbour Trustees* case (n. 74 above, 639) refers to the wording of the Act as requiring the discretion to be available 'from time to time'.

positive response, although critics have suggested that a limitation on the contractual capacity of the authority may not be the best way to achieve the objective.[87] However, any other solution would still require some demarcation of those situations where the authority may depart (if at a price) from its promises and those where it is liable to be ordered to perform them, whatever the political consequences.

A better, and principled, basis for demarcating those contracts which should be upheld and those which may be invalid as a fetter would be the public importance or type of the statutory power in question. A contrast to similar effect in the law of tort is the policy/operations distinction, which governs the tortious liability of public authorities: if the exercise of a discretion is said to fall within the policy field, liability is denied so as not to impede the performance of statutory functions.[88] With appropriate variation this approach might be adopted for use in relation to local government contracts. It is proposed that it should apply in the following way. A contract made in pursuance of an operational discretion should be ultra vires if it impedes the exercise of a policy discretion. Conversely, a contract in pursuance of a policy discretion should prevail over the exercise of an operational discretion. This leaves the situations in which the discretions are of the same type (and perhaps the same discretion in fact). If both discretions are purely operational, there seems to be no reason in public law why there should be any departure from the normal principles of contractual liability: the contract would prevail as the earlier (and intended to be binding) exercise of the discretion. If both discretions are policy ones the issue becomes more difficult, but it is suggested that the contract should not be allowed to prevail, unless there is statutory support for the view that the discretion under which the contract is made was intended to take priority. Where the same (policy) discretion is involved the issue should turn on whether the discretion was intended to be open-ended.

The crucial question is then, of course: where should the line be drawn between policy and operational powers? Here we return to first principles: the only objective of having different principles to govern public contracts

[87] Accordingly, Mitchell, (op. cit., 60 and 65) argues that the rule is more credibly explained as a method by which valid contracts may be overridden. Likewise, Hogg has suggested that rather than approaching the issue as one of contractual capacity (leading to the conclusion that the contract is void) it would be better to approach the question as a matter of discretion in the grant of judicial remedies i.e. specific performance would not be awarded where it would fetter the discretion of a local authority, but damages might remain an appropriate remedy: see especially Hogg (op. cit., 171–2) and P. Hogg, 'The Doctrine of Executive Necessity in the Law of Contract', (1970) 44 ALJ 154. This approach has been applied in: *Dowty Boulton Paul v Wolverhampton Corporation*, [1971] 1 WLR 204 (refusal to grant specific performance) and *Dowty Boulton Paul v Wolverhampton Corporation (No. 2)*, [1973] 2 All ER 491 (refusal of judicial review).

[88] See P. Craig, *Administrative Law* (3rd edn., 1994, London), 621–32; see also the comments of Lord Browne-Wilkinson in *X (Minors) v Bedfordshire* CC, [1995] 3 WLR 152, 170–3.

is that state institutions are different from private individuals in their contractual dealings, and that the exercise of government must be protected in the public interest in a way which requires that the interests of the community take precedence over bilateral contractual interests. The designation of a discretion as a 'policy' one should depend on whether the power is one not conventionally exercised by private persons and companies.[89] The label 'operational' would mark the overlap between the powers of local government and those of private individuals: where discretion is statutory solely because local authorities are artificial legal entities and therefore require an explicit legal basis for what other persons enjoy as 'natural' powers.

Adopting a distinction on these lines would reinforce the important jurisprudential point that many powers enjoyed by local authorities are indistinguishable from those enjoyed by private persons, except for the source of the power, which happens (I use the word advisedly) to be statutory. That the power is derived from statute is insufficient by itself to justify a difference in treatment, in view of the fact that the only reason why that is the source is because of the legal fiction of corporate status. A distinction on these lines would reinforce the point that what the fettering doctrine requires in the case of local government is the comparison of two statutory discretions (the one under which the ostensible contract is made and that purportedly impeded), which must be ranked to see which should take priority.

In this section we have seen several ways in which the application of the ultra vires rule in effect displaces normal contractual principles.

One consequence is to give the private contractor a set of remedies additional to those applicable if the contract had been between private parties.[90] In a context where local authorities are increasingly enjoined to act commercially and competitively, this appears to be an anomalous benefit gratuitously conferred on the other contracting party. Interestingly, in some legislative contexts it has been recognized that public law remedies are capable of being used by commercial undertakings against local authorities to further their own private commercial interests, contrary to the public interest. For this very reason the Local Government (Access to Information) Act 1985 allows a council to protect details of contracts it proposes to enter from disclosure:[91] allowing a tenderer access to information of this kind would considerably impede the council's negotiating position.

[89] There is some similarity with the test propounded by Wade to distinguish a true prerogative power: H. Wade, 'Prerogative and Procedure in Public Law', (1985) LQR 180. However, in *Jones v Swansea CC*, [1990] 1 WLR 54, 70 (per Slade LJ) the Court of Appeal refused to adopt a similar distinction.

[90] This is not the place for an extended discussion of remedies: see P. Craig, *Administrative Law* (3rd edn., London, 1994), Pt. 3.

[91] Sched. 1, Pt. 1, paras. 8 and 9; Ch. 3 above.

Similarly, commercial decisions are exempted from the jurisdiction of the ombudsman.[92] These provisions, in part, also protect the commercial confidentiality of those dealing with the council, thus reinforcing the competitiveness of the process in the interests both of the authority and of its contractors.

We conclude this extended treatment of the ways in which local contracts can be ultra vires and the implications with a brief treatment of the legislative attempts to ameliorate the position.

## Reform

The commercial disadvantages of the application of ultra vires to local authority contracts became all too apparent during the 1990s. Legislative attempts to restore commercial confidence to those contracting with councils were made following a series of high-profile decisions in which financial institutions lost money due to contracts being held ultra vires by the courts. The Local Government (Contracts) Act 1997 is designed to provide reassurance through a scheme of 'certified' contracts.

The key provision (section 2(1)) provides that a 'certified' contract shall 'have effect as if the local authority had power to enter into it'.[93] This does not prevent it being determined either on judicial review or as part of the audit process that the contract is ultra vires (these are exempted under section 5). It does, however, give protection to contractors from authorities pleading their own illegality in defence to private law proceedings to enforce the contract. In judicial review and audit proceedings a new test is introduced: the court may decide that an otherwise ultra vires contract is to be treated as lawful in exercising its discretion, having regard 'to the likely consequences for the financial position of local authority, and for the provision of services to the public, of a decision that the contract should not have effect'.[94] This test is an explicit recognition of the disruption and administrative inconvenience which can be caused by a finding that a local authority has contracted unlawfully. Moreover, even where a 'certified' contract is found to be ultra vires, any break clause which it contains will nevertheless stand.[95] This allows the parties to stipulate in advance for the possibility that the contract might be found to be unlawful, and so allows potential contractors to limit their risk.

[92] LGA 1974, s. 26(7) and sched. 5, para. 3. See Ch. 5.

[93] The certificate must be given within 6 weeks of the contract being entered into and must refer explicitly to the purported statutory basis on which the council is relying in making the contract: ss. 2(5) and 3(2)(d).

[94] S. 5(3).

[95] S. 6. Where the contract does not contain a break clause of this kind the contract is not to be treated as void from the start, merely from the date of the court's determination: s. 7.

The Act treats the symptoms, not the causes: plainly it does nothing to change the application of the ultra vires principle from the council's side by giving greater freedom to contract. Section 1(1) of the Act makes it explicit that wherever other statutes confer or impose functions on local authorities they include an implied power to contract with other people for the provision of assets or services for discharge of those functions. It is doubtful if this adds much, however, to the ancillary power already present under section 111 of the Local Government Act 1972.[96] Curiously, one restriction under the Act leaves firmly in place the problem identified in the *Allerdale* case. 'Certified' contracts must be between the authority and another person providing services to the authority or in connection with the discharge of its functions.[97] Financial guarantees can be 'certified' contracts provided they are 'in connection with' such a contract.[98] Where, however, as in *Allerdale*, the contract that they are connected with is not between the contractor and the council but rather with a company which the council has established, it would seem that there is no certified contract involved, and that the protection of the Act does not apply.[99]

The discussion now moves to another area of legislative incursion where it is clearer, if anything, than in the earlier treatment of the common law that local authorities have been subjected to an artificially constructed version of private-sector behaviour— controls on contract compliance.

## CONTRACT COMPLIANCE: THE PURSUIT OF SECONDARY SOCIAL GOALS THROUGH CONTRACT

Several different approaches can be taken towards the achievement of secondary social objectives through contracts awarded by local authorities.[100] The most restrictive view is that all such contracts are ultra vires, if the secondary purpose lacks an explicit statutory basis. At the opposite extreme, these contracts might be permitted unless expressly forbidden by statute, since councillors act as public representatives and are politically accountable for their contractual decisions. A middle position would be to uphold such contracts provided the secondary objective falls within a policy field which is itself delegated to the local authority. This approach would, for instance, uphold agreements providing planning gain (even without an express statutory provision) but strike down contractual decisions on questions such as the implementation of a nuclear-free zone.

[96] See, though, C. Emery, *Administrative Law: Legal Challenges to Official Action* (London, 1999), 238, who argues that the effect is to make contracting a statutory function in its own right.

[97] S. 4(3). [98] S. 4(4). [99] Emery, op. cit., 246–7.

[100] Arrowsmith, *Government Procurement*, ch. 12, discussing the Canadian case law.

None of these positions is without major difficulties as far as British local government is concerned. The first approach neglects the fact that the power to enter contracts is itself a statutory power, and one expressed in very general terms: accordingly this position involves a judicial decision that the contractual power should in effect be subordinated to other statutory provisions. The reasons for doing so are unclear, but arguably are based on a view which denies councils autonomy. Conversely, the second position may be said to overstate the efficacy of political accountability mechanisms in view of the imperfect nature of local democracy.[101] It also ignores the possibility that the council may act to a potential (disappointed) contractor's detriment in a way which may lack an explicit legal basis, thus violating one of the most commonly claimed justifications for judicial review—protection of the individual from unwarranted exercise of power by a public body.

The strand of case law suggesting that contractual decisions should not be used as a form of 'punishment' imposed on those of whose views the council disapproves clearly invokes this objection.[102] However, the characterization of the local authority action as 'punishment' of the other party's views is itself contentious, and gains much of its force from regarding the council as acting legislatively or judicially rather than commercially in allocating contracts. For example, some of the judicial rhetoric in the House of Lords' judgment in *Wheeler*, which characterized the withdrawal of the licence as punishment for exercising the right of free speech, loses all credibility if one regards the case as being about the use of property.[103] It is debatable also whether standards of due process which might be relevant to issues of criminal liability should apply in view of the lesser stigma of 'blacklisting'.[104]

The argument that a council should be free to pursue a policy delegated to it within its recognized sphere of competence by contractual means appears superficially attractive on constitutional grounds. It recognizes the political autonomy of the authority within a limited area, and respects the legislative grant of powers to the council. However, in practice difficulties are likely to occur particularly at the boundaries of institutional competence, for instance where another layer of government is responsible for other aspects of the policy field, and if the use of the contractual

[101] See Ch. 1.

[102] See p. 285 above. *Wheeler v Leicester City Council*, [1985] AC 1085; *R v Ealing LBC ex p. Times Newspapers*, (1987) 85 LGR 316; *R v Lewisham BC ex p. Shell UK Ltd*, [1988] 1 All ER 938; and see *Jones v Swansea City Council*, [1990] 1 WLR 54 (on misfeasance in public office).

[103] Esp. at 1080, per Lord Templeman. See A. Hutchinson and M. Jones, 'Wheeler-Dealing: An Essay on Law, Politics and Speech', (1988) 15(3) J. of Law and Soc. 263, esp. 275.

[104] S. Arrowsmith, 'Public Procurement as an Instrument of Policy and the Impact of Market Liberalisation', (1995) 111 LQR 235, 247.

power apparently conflicts with any limitations in the grant of power.[105] Furthermore, councils are permitted to spend up to a specified sum per capita on objects for the benefit of their inhabitants not expressly provided for in other provisions.[106] There is the possibility that this power might be used as an adjunct to contracts to fund a social premium (for instance paying a higher price in return for community benefit)[107] outside a recognized delegated policy field, provided it were done without conflicting with other provisions.

Arrowsmith argues that the purpose of a doctrine of limited contractual power in municipal law is to ensure that municipal funds should only be expended for properly authorized purposes.[108] Whatever the merits of this argument in general,[109] she concedes that this may be insufficient justification for preventing a council from pursuing a secondary objective through contractual means where no additional expenditure is involved[110] or even money may be saved.[111] Moreover, this view involves reading into general statutory provisions authorizing contracts an implied limitation on the use of public funds, and one—curiously, in view of its supposed predominance—which is unstated on the face of legislation. Nevertheless, as we have seen, in effect the courts have restrained local authorities from making uneconomic contracts on just such grounds in some instances.[112]

To suggest that commercial considerations should always be linked to social ones is to argue that contract compliance and economy, efficiency, and competitiveness are locked in a zero-sum game. However, as Morris points out, contract compliance can be justified on commercial grounds;[113] he argues that it fosters genuine competition between contractors, rather than economy based merely on undercutting a business rival's labour costs, and that it promotes long-term commercial considerations because

[105] In practice this will often arise as a question of construction of the limits of section 111 of the LGA 1972, which allows authorities to do anything which is calculated to facilitate or which is conducive or incidental to its functions, provided they do not transgress express limitations in the relevant provision. See Ch. 2.

[106] LGA 1972, s. 137; see Ch. 2.

[107] The principle of apportioning expenditure related to s. 137 projects has been recognized in *Leicester City Council v District Auditor for Leicester*, (1989) 29 RVR 162.

[108] Arrowsmith, *Government Procurement*, 112.

[109] It seems to ignore the specialized procedures available through the auditor to control the use of money by local government (Ch. 4). These make it unnecessary for private individuals also to be able to challenge contractual decisions for public financial reasons.

[110] Arrowsmith, *Government Procurement*, 213.

[111] As in the *Ealing* case (n. 102 above), through the cancellation of library subscriptions to periodicals produced by a publisher involved in an industrial dispute.

[112] See pp. 290–2 above.

[113] P. Morris, 'Legal Regulation of Contract Compliance: An Anglo-American Comparison', (1990) 19 Anglo-American LR 87, 89–90. In addition, EC law will prohibit contract compliance in some situations: S. Arrowsmith, 'Public Procurement as an Instrument of Policy and the Impact of Market Liberalisation'.

it is consistent with management by setting objectives and raising employee morale (in the United States business has supported it on this basis).

In Britain contract compliance was made unlawful under section 17 of the Local Government Act 1988[114] (subject to a minor exception for promotion of race discrimination policy[115]). The provision covers both the actual award of a contract and pre-contractual arrangements, such as the drawing up of a list of tenderers. Local authorities are prohibited from acting on factors deemed to be 'non-commercial': these include[116] employment and training conditions of the contractor's or subcontractor's workforce,[117] a contractor's involvement in 'irrelevant' fields of government policy,[118] the political or industrial affiliations of contractors,[119] the geographical location of the contractor's interests, the involvement of the contractor in industrial disputes, or the making or withholding of support by the contractor to institutions to which the authority gives or withholds support. Morris has criticized this list for over-inclusiveness, since the effect of prohibiting consideration of matters such as a contractor's training arrangements or affiliation to a trade association is to rule out matters directly touching on commercial competence.[120]

A contractor is entitled to be informed of adverse contractual decisions, together (on request) with the reasons for them.[121] Contractors alleging a breach of these provisions may be entitled both to remedies in public law and to damages for the expenses involved in abortive tendering.[122]

Brief mention should also be made of the position under EC law governing public procurement. Even without the 1988 Act provisions, it can be argued that the achievement of social objectives through procurement decisions is contrary to EC law, because it may conflict either with provi-

[114] For a full discussion of this provision, see Morris, op. cit., 103–20, and S. Arrowsmith, *The Law of Public and Utilities Procurement* (London, 1996), ch. 16.

[115] LGA 1988, s. 18(2) allows contract compliance for promotion of racial equality by local authorities; applied in *R v London Borough of Islington ex p. Building Employers Federation*, [1989] IRLR 382; cf. elimination of religious discrimination in Northern Ireland: Fair Employment (Northern Ireland) Act 1989, ss. 25–6 and 41. However, contract compliance to promote other non-discrimination policies—even those under-pinned by legislation (e.g. Sex Discrimination Act 1975 and Disability Discrimination 1995)—is unlawful; see the *Building Employers Federation* case on sex discrimination.

[116] S. 17(5).

[117] In *R v London Borough of Islington ex p. Building Employers Federation*, [1989] IRLR 382, clauses requiring a contractor to comply with the Sex Discrimination Act 1975 and the Race Relations Act 1976 were attacked under this provision. Those relating to sex discrimination were held to be in breach as they interfered in the contractor's relationship with its employees. Those relating to racial discrimination were saved by s. 18(2).

[118] i.e. concerning defence or foreign policy: LGA 1988, s. 17(8).

[119] Cf., however, *R v Barnet LBC ex p. Johnson*, (1991) 89 LGR 581, where a prohibition by a local authority in the conditions governing the use of a park on any political activity was held to be meaningless (see p. 78 above).

[120] Morris, op. cit., 107, 114. [121] LGA 1988, s. 20. [122] Ibid., s. 19(7) and (8).

sions in the Treaties or with Directives governing the award of public contracts.[123] EC law will become a more significant source of constraint if in future the present statutory limitations are relaxed to allow councils to incorporate terms requiring contractors to implement equal-opportunities policies or employ local people.[124]

The Labour government has taken powers to relax the list of 'non-commercial' criteria by way of ministerial order as part of the move towards 'best value'.[125] This may be done either in relation to 'best value' authorities as a whole, or selectively, as part of the 'Beacon Council' programme,[126] or in relation to specific functions.

## CONCLUSION

It is often suggested that the principles of contractual liability apply to public bodies in the same way as to private persons. This is intended as an affirmation of the view propounded by the constitutional writer Dicey that to subject public authorities to ordinary principles of legal liability upholds the 'Rule of Law'.[127] Thus, it used to be commonplace to assert that England had no distinct law of public contracts,[128] with the possible exception of the rule against fettering discretion. For some writers this was a cause of concern, although for differing reasons. Nearly fifty years ago, Mitchell argued that the lack of a distinct law of public contracts caused injustice because it treated the state and the individual as equals; instead,

[123] See Case 31/87, *Gebroeders Beentjes BV v Netherlands*, [1988] ECR 4365 (requirement that contractors should provide work for long-term unemployed capable of breaching Directive 71/305 if it favoured tenderers from the awarding state). See also *General Building and Maintenance plc v Greenwich LBC*, (1994) 92 LGR 21 (health and safety requirement not in conflict with regulations implementing EC law); *R v Secretary of State for the Environment ex p. Harrow LBC*, QBD, 12 Jan. 1996 (refusal of judicial review of minister's decision that Council would be in breach of regulations by stipulating in housing management contracts that contractors should be UK Housing Associations capable of accepting later transfer of housing stock). See generally: S. Arrowsmith, 'Public Procurement as an Instrument of Public Policy', (1995) 111 LQR 235; A. Arden, J. Manning, and S. Collins, *Local Government Constitutional and Administrative Law* (London, 1999), paras. 7.5.41 ff. The Government has promulgated the following regulations: Public Works Contracts Regulations 1991, SI 1991/2680 , Public Supply Contracts Regulations 1995, SI 1995/201, and Public Services Contracts Regulations 1993, SI 1993/3228, to give effect to the relevant EC directives.

[124] Proposed by Labour Party, *Renewing Democracy, Rebuilding Communities* (London, 1995), 8. A series of recommendations proposing a return to contract compliance as a way of implementing equal opportunity policies was made in K. Escott and D. Whitfield, *The Gender Impact of CCT in Local Government (Equal Opportunities Commission, Research Discussion Paper No. 12)* (Manchester, 1995), ch. 11.

[125] LGA 1999, s. 19. For further discussion of 'best value', see p. 321 below.

[126] See p. 58 above.

[127] For discussion and criticism see further S. Arrowsmith, *Government Procurement and Judicial Review* (Toronto, 1988), 10 ff.

[128] Unlike France: see Mitchell, op. cit.

he advocated that contract law should recognize the strengths and weaknesses of the state through the imposition of added burdens and extra privileges.[129] Arrowsmith, writing over three decades later during which the courts had appropriated the power of judicial review as never before, lamented what she saw as the incomplete application of public law principles to the power of procurement of the state.[130] However, there is a danger that by treating local government and central government contracting power together, commentators may pay insufficient attention to the constitutional differences between the two sectors, especially the limited and subordinate position of the former.

From the survey in this chapter, it should now be apparent that the consequence of applying public law principles to local government contracts has been the creation of a distinctive body of public contract law, which modifies each of the core tenets of contract doctrine applicable where both parties are private individuals. Most elements of this scheme are now in place, if of recent origin, although some, like the effect of legitimate expectations, may develop further. With the exception of the fettering doctrine, they all operate to the detriment of the local authority. Paradoxically, much of this has been achieved by implicit comparison with patterns of private sector or 'commercial' behaviour.

We have seen that both at common law and under statute there is considerable hostility to the use of the contracting power of local government as dominium: corporate status is quite a limited fiction and the normal political processes are not trusted to regulate the contractual activities of local authorities. Instead a series of (mostly) procedural controls have been imposed. Unlike the rules governing contract formation in the private sector, these rules are generally constricting, not empowering. Although purportedly using models derived from private-sector behaviour, in fact the courts and Parliament have used a quite limited vision of commercial behaviour which always has the effect of constraining local authorities by subjecting them to an additional layer of control to those applicable in the private sector. On occasion this control has extended beyond procedural control to substantive issues, for instance, the substance of a bargain. It is hard to avoid the conclusion that the notion of commercial behaviour imposed on local government has in fact been a cover for a level of public control of public contracts, i.e. a distinctive law of public contracts travelling in disguise.

[129] Mitchell, op. cit., 243–4.

[130] See references in n. 29 above. However, in her most recent book, *The Law of Public and Utilities Procurement*, Arrowsmith refers to the procurement rules as the 'special "public law" on procurement' (9).

# 10

# *Local Government, Business, and Partnership*

## INTRODUCTION

The purpose of this chapter is to consider what might be called the 'external relations' of local authorities—their place in the wider community. This involves examining the relationship of councils both with the private sector (local businesses) and with other public bodies (such as local quangos) and the voluntary sector. Twenty-five years ago this might not have merited much more than a few paragraphs. However in the intervening period a fundamental shift has occurred, due to several developments.

First, the privatization policies of the Thatcher administrations, implemented in local government through Compulsory Competitive Tendering (CCT), were premissed on a radical reappraisal of the role and competence of the public sector which has had a lasting impact, although its more coercive and ideological aspects have now been lifted. The same government's distrust of local authorities led to the channelling of public service provision through alternate local public bodies (such as Training and Enterprise Councils, Housing Associations, the now defunct Urban Development Corporations, and Grant-Maintained schools) and through the voluntary sector under grants direct from central government. Apart from creating a complex web of local actors with fragmented powers, loyalties, and resources, this trend also resulted in a shift in modes of regulation, away from reliance solely on legislation imposing powers and duties and towards the use of legal devices associated with the private sector: contracts, partnerships, and joint ventures. Use of these, especially partnerships and joint companies, is explored below. These legal forms have been used not merely to mediate relations with the centre but also as a means of offsetting the fragmentary effect: hence the slogan of the Blair government calling for 'joined-up' or collaborative government. It is necessary to examine, then, the legal powers for reassembling the local state, especially new powers of partnership under the Local Government Act 2000.

We shall explore the legal context of 'external relations', on two levels: first, in relation to service provision (CCT and 'Best Value') and secondly, at the level of organizational cooperation between the voluntary sector and councils and in the notions of partnership and community leadership. Before attempting to unpack this jigsaw and to put it back together again, it is helpful to explore the underlying implications for the role of councils.

## THE ENABLING COUNCIL

Few terms applied to local authorities have been so widely used in recent years as the concept of the 'enabling council'. One undoubted reason for the appeal of the idea is its capacity to convey different aspirations about the role of local authorities.[1] For these purposes we can distinguish between what may be described as the narrow version of the 'enabling council' espoused by the New Right, the focus of which was on changing the mode of service provision through use of contracting-out, and broader, communitarian versions which stress the council's role in facilitating the initiatives of other actors in the public, voluntary, and private sectors within its locality, and acting as a representative advocate for its area, regardless of its responsibility to provide specific statutory services.

The narrow version was essentially concerned with changing the mode of service delivery, so that the council itself was no longer in the role of being directly responsible for service provision and moved instead towards regulating (especially through use of contract) service delivery. In its purest or most doctrinaire form it was espoused famously by one Secretary of State (Nicholas Ridley) as the council which 'meet once a year to award contracts, have lunch and go away again for another year'.[2] However, in reality no local authority, not even Conservative boroughs like Westminster which embraced contracting out enthusiastically, came near to so completely divesting itself of the provision of public services. Although this version of 'enabling' required a considerable reorientation and involved the introduction of compulsory competitive tendering to force reluctant councils to adopt it, it was fundamentally about the mode of service delivery rather than the council's wider role. Enthusiasm for market mechanisms has accompanied this approach. The focus was largely upon the tripartite relationship between the authority, the contractor/provider, and the service user (although the needs of the latter received inadequate recognition).

The broader version is epitomized in the work of Professor John Stewart.[3] Stewart argues for the role of councils as community government, focusing on the needs and problems of their communities and with the capacity to respond flexibly to these. This has many implications, some of which have been pursued in earlier chapters, especially as regards the

[1] See R. Brooke, 'The Enabling Authority: Practical Consequences', (1989) 15 LGS 55; A. Cochrane, *Whatever Happened to Local Government?* (Buckingham, 1993), ch. 4.

[2] Speech by the Secretary of State for the Environment (Nicholas Ridley) 7 Oct. 1986. N. Ridley, *The Local Right: Enabling Not Providing* (London, 1988).

[3] See esp. J. Stewart and G. Stoker (eds.), *Local Government in the 1990s* (Basingstoke, 1995), ch. 14.

powers and structure of councils. One central issue concerns the degree of discretion which such a council requires:

> As the community governing itself, the local authority is entitled to take actions that are sought by that community. It need not search for specific powers, because the powers derive from the concept of local government itself. Because the local authority is the community governing itself, it is or can be concerned with any needs or problems faced in the community, and not merely the services it provides directly. The identity of the authority does not derive from the services provided, but from the community.[4]

This implies a holistic approach—the focus is not on a series of services (however provided) but on community representation and advocacy; moreover, it works directly against the recent trend towards the fragmentation of the local state into a series of single-function agencies. The role for councils envisaged by Stewart requires a broader discretion than that allowed traditionally under the ultra vires doctrine, and so he argues for a power of general competence for local authorities.[5] To some extent there is an overlap with the narrow version of enabling, in that the wide version is equally sceptical of the traditional assumption that the council itself should provide services. 'The Authority seeks to provide services not *to* the public but *for* the public *with* the public.'[6]

A key feature of Stewart's vision is the experimental nature of community government. In this he is the lineal descendant of Mill.[7] However, Stewart argues that the need for local authorities to have the capacity to experiment and adapt themselves flexibly is greater now than ever, because of the uncertainties of current employment, economic, social, and environmental conditions. In this situation the need is for councils with a high capacity both for learning and for adaptation. In common with a number of other writers, Stewart is enthusiastic about the experimental approach to local government adopted in recent decades in Scandinavia.

If community government is to play a full role in bringing together the needs of the whole locality, it also requires additional powers to inquire into and to consult other bodies acting within its area in the private, voluntary, and public sectors. It is assumed that the council will employ the full range of methods of governing: direct service provision, use of its own resources, and employment and contractual practices to bring change in the local economy, legislative or quasi-legislative control,[8] disseminating information and advice to local organizations and coordinating their responses to local problems, and acting to involve service users in decisions. One clear implication would be a requirement to relax current

[4] Ibid. 252. [5] Ibid. 251 and Ch. 2 above. [6] Ibid. 254. [7] See Ch. 1.

[8] Stewart envisages that councils may enjoy enhanced discretion over e.g. the penalties in relation to particular offences to reflect local needs.

restrictions on the use of contractual conditions to achieve social goals.[9] The organization of such community government is unlikely to be focused on traditional service committee lines: Stewart emphasizes new developments such as those involving local-authority companies, new partnership organizations between the public and private sectors, tenants' cooperatives and service-user consultative committees, decentralized and neighbourhood management, and consultative bodies.

Community government is descriptive in the sense that many of its elements are already present in some parts of local government. However, it is prescriptive in the sense of bringing these together and recognizing the implication that councils should enjoy considerably more discretion to respond and to experiment in meeting local aspirations. These ideas have found broad acceptance in the current government's new power to promote community well-being and in partnership powers, considered below.[10]

Two quotations from a 1998 Green Paper show the extent of the official endorsement of Stewart's vision:

> The days of the all-purpose authority that planned and delivered everything are gone. It is in partnership with others—public agencies, private companies, community groups and voluntary organisations that local government's future lies. Local authorities deliver important services but their distinctive leadership role will be to weave and knit together the contributions of the various local stakeholders.[11]

> Councils are in a unique position to take the lead in developing a vision for their locality and provide a focus for partnership in delivering that vision. But they cannot act alone. All need to work together, in conjunction with local people and with local business and the local voluntary sector, if they are to be effective in tackling the difficult cross-cutting issues and achieving the benefits that can accrue from a genuine partnership approach.[12]

This coordinating role is partly a matter of necessity because of the increasing fragmentation of the local state (commentators have resorted to the description 'local governance' in preference to 'local government'). The resulting apparent deficit of accountability where services are fragmented and delivered by non-elected bodies may be partly offset where the council is exercising 'community leadership'. Change in the role of councils should also be understood in the context of a declining faith in traditional forms of local representative democracy.[13] In these circumstances the traditional objections to public service delivery by non-elected bodies (that they lack democratic legitimacy and are not accountable to the public) increasingly ring hollow.

[9] See p. 302 above.

[10] See pp. 336–7 below.

[11] *Modernising Local Government: Local Democracy and Community Leadership* (London, Feb. 1998), para. 1.9.

[12] Ibid., para. 6.5.

[13] See pp. 13 ff above.

Before moving on to discuss the legal implications of this new vision, we begin with the narrower version of enabling, with the reforms introduced by the Conservative administrations affecting service provision, CCT, and with Labour's replacement for it, 'Best Value'.

## COMPULSORY COMPETITIVE TENDERING[14]

The shift towards 'contracting out' of public work was a significant theme of the Conservative programme of privatization. It broke the assumption that because a function was suitable for public oversight or regulation it should also be delivered by public provision. As has been seen in Chapter 7, perhaps the major lasting consequence of CCT has been the structural change which it has encouraged in local authority administration.[15] The creation of Direct Labour Organisations (DLOs) and Direct Service Organisations (DSOs) created a divide between 'client' and 'contractor' roles which has affected not only the organization of services in departments and under committees but, more radically, officer and member perceptions of their functions, and of the entire relationship of the authority to the public.[16] The account here will focus on an outline of the legalities of the process of competitive tendering,[17] on the assumptions implicit in the legislation, and on the practical effect on the contracting process.

Legal requirements to follow defined procedures in the placing of local contracts considerably pre-date CCT. However, whereas the concern in former decades was the prevention of corruption, the attempt to create a

[14] K. Walsh and H. Davies, *Competition and Service: The Impact of the Local Government Act 1988* (London, 1993). For other surveys, see K. Walsh, *Competitive Tendering for Local Authority Services: Initial Experiences* (London, 1991); J. Painter, 'Compulsory Competitive Tendering in Local Government', (1991) 69 Public Administration 191; M. Radford, 'Competition Rules: The Local Government Act 1988', (1988) 51 MLR 747; J. Greenwood and D. Wilson, 'Towards the Contract State: CCT in Local Government', (1994) 47 Parl. Affs. 405; P. Vincent-Jones, 'The Limits of Contractual Order in Public Sector Transacting', (1994) 14 LS 364. A more partisan account, which also contains valuable background material on the whole subject, can be found in R. Carnaghan and B. Bracewell-Milnes, *Testing the Market* (London, 1993) (hereafter *Testing the Market*).

[15] See also Walsh and Davies, op. cit., chs. 1–4.

[16] Freedland describes the resulting position of DSOs which successfully tender as involving 'a double legal fiction, whereby a non-corporation is deemed to enter into non-contracts': M. Freedland, 'Government by Contract and Public Law', [1994] PL 86, 89; and see P. Vincent-Jones, 'The Limits of Near-Contractual Governance: Local Authority Internal Trading Under CCT', (1994) 21 J. of Law and Society 214. Freedland also argues that the privity doctrine may be utilized against service users who stand outside the resulting contractual nexus (op. cit., 99–100).

[17] For more detailed legal accounts, see: Radford, op. cit.; S. Cirrell and J. Bennett, *Encyclopedia of Competitive Tendering*; S. Arrowsmith, *The Law of Public and Utilities Procurement* (London, 1996), chs. 12–14 and pp. 947–54; A. Arden, J. Manning, and S. Collins, *Local Government Constitutional and Administrative Law* (London, 1999), paras. 7.4.1 ff.

statutory framework by which to ensure that economy and value for money are obtained is a more recent concern. The Local Government Act 1972 required councils to adopt standing orders governing the placing of certain types of contract put out to tender from the private sector. A number of changes strengthening the Prevention of Corruption Acts and to prevent conflicts of interest were recommended by the Salmon Commission after the Poulson scandal.[18] In that ideologically distant time the association of local business and councils evoked popular images of corruption and of public projects completed late and over budget, rather than efficiency or the superiority of the private sector over public provision. Legislation was designed to deal especially with situations in which councils placed contracts for construction projects too large for them to deal with in-house. Although nothing prevented local authorities from placing the performance of routine services such as refuse collection or school catering with private contractors, in practice such work was overwhelmingly undertaken by the council's own workforce, irrespective of the political persuasion of the authority. Even before the election of the Conservative government in 1979, however, central government had expressed concern at the inefficiency of some local authority direct labour organizations, and had promised legislation to improve accountability and make them more like private contractors.[19]

Post-1979 the new element was the Conservative government's view that local services could be delivered more efficiently if subject to competition from the private sector. This was based partly on simple cost-saving and partly on the belief that council workforces were being anti-competitively protected through the enjoyment of a monopoly as the sole providers to their authorities. Accordingly, the initial legislation[20] was designed to show the council's Direct Labour Organization (DLO) as a distinct accounting unit, so that its costs could be identified. It was required formally to tender for work against private contractors for building and maintenance work. The 1980 Act required DLOs to meet a required rate of return on capital specified by government[21]—an attempt to replicate the private-sector discipline in the public sector. In practice, though, this rate of return was easily achievable, perhaps a reflection of the inappropriateness of the mechanism (DLOs tended to be labour- rather than capital-intensive) or of the low levels specified. Although it was possible for the minister to take action against DLOs that failed to meet these targets,[22]

[18] *Report of the Royal Commission on Standards in Public Life 1974–1976*, Cmnd. 6524 (1976).

[19] *Testing the Market*, 27.

[20] Local Government, Planning and Land Act 1980.

[21] Ibid., s. 16.

[22] This included, ultimately, the ability to direct that a DLO cease to undertake certain types of work: ibid., s. 17.

sanctions were applied sparingly.[23] Moreover, the scope of the legislation was limited in view of the restricted range of affected local authority functions and because it could be circumvented in practice. The government's stated position was that local authorities should generally be free to decide whether their services were best delivered through contract or by their own workforce. Subsequently its ideological attitude hardened as the privatization programme got under way and, faced with an evident lack of enthusiasm by local authorities about voluntarily putting out to tender other services, the government embraced a compulsory regime capable of extension to all local government functions (including those of the professional officer classes, for instance architects, accountants, and lawyers). It is on this legislation (the Local Government Act 1988[24]) that the account here will focus.

The initial scope of contracting out[25] was confined to the 'defined activities' named in the Act, the blue-collar tasks of household and commercial refuse collection, cleaning of buildings, street cleansing, school and welfare catering, other forms of council catering, ground maintenance and repair, and maintenance of vehicles.[26] While the Bill was in Committee, Conservative backbenchers proposed a variety of other local-government activities suitable for contracting out. However, rather than overload the tendering system in the initial stages (the defined activities were in any event phased in over a three-year period), the Secretary of State retained a general power to add to the list by statutory instrument.[27] Subsequent delegated legislation required tendering in the areas of leisure provision.[28] Environmental legislation was introduced requiring the contracting out (rather than market testing) of waste disposal,[29] so as to prevent a conflict of regulatory and commercial considerations. With the 1991 White Paper *Competing For Quality*[30] the government announced its intention to extend CCT into professional services in local government, alongside the process of market testing which was to be applied to the Civil Service. The intention was to bring about a major restructuring of the officer side of local government. Critics feared that some traditional officer groups would either diminish severely or disappear entirely, so destroying the professional ethos of the service. The minister spoke of breaking down 'the

[23] Up to the replacement of this system by different sanctions under the 1988 Act only 4 DLOs closed: *Testing the Market*, 29.

[24] See, for a more detailed critique, Radford, op. cit.

[25] Although contracting out and CCT are often used synonymously, there is the possibility that a council may contract out work (that is place a contract in the private sector) without doing so competitively (see below).

[26] LGA 1988, s. 2 and sched. 1.

[27] S. 2(3)(4).

[28] LGA 1988 (Competition in Sports and Leisure Facilities) Order 1989, SI 2488.

[29] Environmental Protection Act 1990, ss. 32 and 51.

[30] Cm. 1730 (Nov. 1991).

barriers of inertia and bureaucracy that presently protect all in-house operations'.[31]

The 1988 Act created for accounting purposes Direct Service Organizations, equivalent to DLOs in their respective domains, and subject to similar accounting provisions and duties to produce a return on capital.[32] The Act announced its objective (in the long title) as: 'An Act to secure that local and other public authorities undertake certain activities only if they can do so competitively'. In formal terms this required not so much contracting out of work as its 'market-testing': local authorities were permitted to continue to provide 'defined activities' so long as the statutory conditions were fulfilled.[33] In approaching the issue in this way the government was following the received wisdom that cost-saving in service provision was determined not so much by whether the service was provided by an in-house or a private sector operator as by the presence or absence of competition.[34] However, some commentators detected a clear bias towards private provision from the fact that if the council determined at the outset that the service was to be provided through private-sector provision, the complex scheme for ensuring competition did not apply.[35] There was an implicit assumption that competitiveness was guaranteed in the private sector but had to be explicitly enforced in the public sector. Some councils exploited this to avoid the CCT regime by 'externalizing' white-collar services, that is, selling such services to private 'host' companies.[36]

If the local authority was unable to provide the relevant service competitively within the statutory criteria, it would have in theory been ultra vires for it to continue to do so. The Audit Commission oversaw the tendering process: it was unlawful for an authority to carry out relevant work on its own behalf ('functional work') unless it had met the tendering provisions in the legislation and delegated legislation.[37] The statutory preconditions under section 7 of the 1988 Act were that the authority was complying with the detailed specification for the work, which was advertised between three and six months in advance of tender, that at least three outside tenders were invited, and that in-house bids must be in writing. In

[31] HC Debs., Standing Committee A, col. 182 (27 Oct. 1987).

[32] S. 9 required the maintenance of a separate trading account for the DSO. S. 10 required a DSO to meet its financial objective. S. 11 required it to prepare an annual report, to be sent to the auditor and the Secretary of State, which could trigger ministerial sanctions against the council.

[33] LGA 1988, s. 6(1).

[34] *Testing the Market*, 48.

[35] See e.g. Radford, op. cit., 766.

[36] K. Escott and D. Whitfield, *The Gender Impact of CCT in Local Government* (Manchester, 1995), 6; Arrowsmith, op. cit., 749–50.

[37] LGA 1988, s. 7. Equally a DSO could not undertake other work (e.g. for another authority) unless it was open to tender: s. 4(2)(4). This prevented possible avoidance of the Act by cross-placing of work by authorities with each other's DSOs.

practice, however, rather than relying simply on the principles of ultra vires, the Act provided its own regime of enforcement, especially sweeping powers for the Secretary of State to issue directions to individual local authorities (discussed below).

The legislation did not operate by crudely requiring a council to accept the lowest tender, since, however detailed the initial specification, bids commonly contain significant variations in the method of service delivery, and a variety of other factors, especially the standing and expertise of the contractor, will also be relevant. It was therefore possible for a council to accept the tender of its DSO even though it was higher than a tender from a private-sector operator;[38] conversely it might accept a higher bid from a private-sector operator over a lower one from its own DSO if clear service improvements were involved. However, councils were under a duty in reaching a decision not to 'act in a manner having the effect or intended or likely to have the effect of restricting, distorting or preventing competition'.[39]

The scope of the duty not to engage in anti-competitive practices was initially left undefined in the legislation, as it was intended to be a deterrent weapon of deliberately indeterminate aim, available against obstructive local authorities that were opposed to the spirit of the legislation.[40] A government circular claimed that 'anti-competitive behaviour is by its nature difficult to define exhaustively' and placed the onus back on local authorities to bear the requirement in mind,[41] while reassuring them that 'authorities acting in good faith have nothing to fear'.[42] Among the practices which it is claimed were used to undermine the legislation were inflating the size of the contract (so as to make it beyond the expertise, turnover, or ability of contractors), the inclusion of onerous contract conditions, the inclusion of the council's own projected redundancy costs if the contractor were successful over the life of a single contract,[43] and

[38] Circular 9/91, para. 5 asserted the Secretary of State's view that 'good and specific reasons' would be necessary for such a course of action. Later, detailed guidance for the comparison of external and internal bids was given in the Competition Regulations (SI 848, 1993).

[39] LGA 1988, s. 7(7).

[40] See Radford, op. cit., 755ff., and *Testing the Market*, 56–7.

[41] DoE Circular 19/88, paragraph 32.

[42] Ibid., para. 33: the statement was held not to create a legitimate expectation in *R v Secretary of State, ex parte Knowsley MBC*, QBD, *The Times*, 28 May 1991 (affirmed by the CA, unreported judgment, 31 July 1991). See also *R v Portsmouth CC ex p. Bonaco Builders*, unreported decision of QBD, 6 June 1995, where Keane J held that the equivalent duty not to behave anti-competitively in s. 9(4)(aaaa) of the Local Government Planning and Land Act 1980 did not give rise to a private right of action for breach of statutory duty, since this would circumvent the balanced scheme by which the council's representations were taken into account by the Secretary of State before deciding on any directions.

[43] However, the Secretary of State accepted that some such costs could be legitimately taken into account (Circular 10/93, para. 10), as did the courts (*Knowsley* and *Bonaco* cases). In addition, significant legal controversy arose concerning the liability of a successful outside tenderer to former council staff under TUPE; see p. 314 below and Arrowsmith, op. cit., 719, 723, and 728.

showing the tenders to the DSO to enable it to revise its bid (a tactic which was unlawful in any event).[44] The legislation was later amended by the introduction of a statutory power to make regulations defining anti-competitive behaviour and to give binding guidance on how to avoid it, which was used to make rules covering a number of these tactics.[45]

One specific issue of great importance in relation to the powers over 'anti-competitive' behaviour, but also contracting out generally, whether compulsory or not, is the effect of the Transfer of Undertakings Regulations (TUPE).

## TUPE[46]

The policy of contracting out local authority services (whether compulsorily or voluntarily) depends upon the assumption that private contractors can provide equivalent services more economically. It is implicit that labour costs can be saved by more 'flexible' (i.e. worse) conditions of service than those applicable to local government officers, either without diminution in the service provided to the authority or with an acceptable diminution. Some advocates of CCT underpinned their enthusiasm with Public Choice theory, a strand of New Right thinking which argues that bureaucracies have an inbuilt tendency to over-provision. In order to deliver savings, staff providing the service in-house must either be made redundant or transferred to the new contractor on markedly different conditions of service. In principle, the latter situation is no different from that of a take-over or merger of a company in a commercial context.

However, the freedom to move employees as part of the enterprise is constrained by a complex body of law, colloquially known as 'TUPE', comprising UK regulations on the transfer of undertakings,[47] designed to implement a European Directive on Acquired Rights.[48] After some initial vacillation, by both the UK government and the UK courts,[49] it became clear that TUPE would frequently apply to the transfer of local authority

[44] *Testing the Market*, 57. See *R v Avon CC ex p. Terry Adams Ltd*, *The Times*, 20 Jan. 1994 (CA) (council not entitled to distort competition by imposing regulations that only one tenderer effectively could comply with).

[45] LGA 1992, s. 9 (discussed in Arrowsmith, op. cit., 745–6).

[46] See generally B. Napier, *CCT, Market Testing and Employment Rights: The Effect of TUPE and the Acquired Rights Directive* (London, 1993); K. Ewing, 'Swimming with the Tide: Employment Protection and the Implementation of European Labour Law', (1993) 22 Ind. LJ 165, 173–6; Arrowsmith, op. cit., 636–47; Arden et al., op. cit., n. 17 above, paras. 7.9.1 ff.

[47] Transfer of Undertakings (Protection of Employment) Regulations, 1981 SI 1981 No. 1794 (now amended by Trade Union Reform and Employment Rights Act 1993, s. 33).

[48] Council Directive 77/187 (as amended by Council Directive 98/50); on the 1998 amendments, see M. Sargeant, 'Transfers of Undertaking: A New Meaning?' (1999) 25 LGS 71.

[49] The various shifts and announcements can be traced in Napier, op. cit., 4–12.

services. This has major implications for the terms on which 'contracting out' takes place.

The TUPE regulations originally contained an exclusion for undertakings 'not in the nature of a commercial undertaking'.[50] However, this was removed in 1993.[51] The government was at pains to minimize the extent of the change, claiming that it merely clarified the existing position, but commentators have pointed out the inconsistency with earlier ministerial statements that the regulations had no impact in the public sector. It seems that the government was forced to make the change under pressure of enforcement proceedings from the European Commission[52] and the threat of individual actions for compensation from individuals over failure fully to implement the Directive, both of which seemed likely to succeed in the light of earlier decisions from the European Court on the meaning of the Directive.

The case law of the European Court of Justice indicates the scope of the potential application of TUPE to contracted out public services. In the *Sophie Redmond case*[53] the Court held that where a transfer is from a body subsidized out of public funds it could fall within the Acquired Rights Directive. The *Rask*[54] decision suggests the Directive will apply to arrangements where a contractor takes over part of a larger operation and continues to use the company's staff, premises, and equipment. Although the case concerned provision of catering in a private-sector company, the comparisons with the form that much public-sector contracting out has taken are obvious. In 1992 the government was forced to concede that the Acquired Rights Directive applied to the transfer of Further Education lecturers from local authority-controlled FE colleges to independent corporations.[55]

Under the revised regulations, consultation must take place with employees before a transfer of staff is effected.[56] The European Court of Justice has held that an employee is not a piece of property to be

[50] Reg. 2(1); see also *Expro Services Ltd v Smith*, [1991] IRLR 156, and *Woodcock v Friends School*, [1987] IRLR 98.

[51] Trade Union Reform and Employment Rights Act 1993, s. 33; and see Ewing, op. cit., 174. On the correct scope of the earlier provision, see *Birch v Nuneaton and Bedworth BC and Sports and Leisure Management*, [1995] IRLR 518.

[52] Case C-382/92, *Commission v United Kingdom*, [1994] ECR I-2435.

[53] *Dr Sophie Redmond Stichting v Bartol*, [1992] IRLR 366.

[54] *Rask and Christensen v ISS Kantinservice A/S*, Case C-209/91, 12 Nov. 1992, ECJ. See also: *Schmidt v Spar- und Leihkasse der frühere Amter Bordesholm, Kiel und Cronshagen*, [1994] ECR I-1311, and *Dines v Initial Health Care Services*, [1994] IRLR 336, suggesting that the test is one of 'retention of identity'. See, however, *Case C-13/95, Ayse Süzen*, [1997] IRLR 255, proposing a test of whether there has been a transfer of significant tangible or intangible assets, or the taking over by the new employer of a major part of the workforce.

[55] Napier, op. cit., 9.

[56] Trade Union Reform and Employment Rights Act 1993, s. 33(6).

transferred at will, and has a right to decline to be transferred.[57] However, the UK legislation was designed to give minimum compliance with this principle, since although it allowed employees to register their objection, the consequence was that their employment terminated at the date of transfer and they were deemed not to have been dismissed[58] (accordingly they were not even entitled to redundancy payments). Where employment is transferred under TUPE the effect is to give *continuity* of employment—the employee continues on the same conditions with the new employer (enjoyment of the same pension rights is a particularly important issue in relation to transfers of local government officers). Continuity of employment means that time with the old employer is counted as service with the new, with important implications for the time limits under redundancy, unfair dismissal, and benefits legislation. Where employees are transferred, any attempt by the new employer to change unilaterally the conditions may amount to constructive dismissal.

These principles have been applied in cases concerning local government staff dismissed following contracting out. When members of the Borough Services Department of Eastbourne Borough Council were dismissed following a successful bid for refuse collection from a private company, the Employment Appeal Tribunal found that the Industrial Tribunal had wrongly concluded that TUPE did not apply, because a transfer of services was involved.[59] However, the application of TUPE will depend on the facts in each case—whether, in view of arrangements for staff, premises, property, and so on both before and after contracting out, there has been a transfer. The result was to generate considerable uncertainty in the process of submitting and considering tenders under CCT. Although surrounded with considerable legal complexity, these issues go to the heart of contracting out, since the whole economic justification of the policy depends on the new provider undercutting existing council costs, usually through savings in labour costs. A legal scheme which requires a private contractor to accept the transfer of council staff on existing terms and conditions, or to allow for the costs of unfair dismissal awards, changes the economic balance entirely.

If private contractors are required to accept the transfer of local authority staff on existing or comparable conditions of service (especially pension rights, which are frequently enhanced in the public sector), this will often make such tenders commercially unattractive. The Department of the Environment argued (unconvincingly) that TUPE rarely applied to

[57] This is the effect of the ECJ's judgment in *Katsikas v Angelos Kanstantinidis*, Cases C-132/91, C-138/91, and C-139/9, judgment of the Court 16 Dec. 1992.

[58] Trade Union Reform and Employment Rights Act 1993, s. 33(4).

[59] *Wren and Others v Eastbourne BC and UK Waste Control Ltd*, [1993] IRLR 425, EAT, remitting the case to the industrial tribunal.

local authority services,[60] but this view has been contradicted by the developments in the case law. Nevertheless, the Department persisted in its view that it would be anti-competitive behaviour for a council to insist that a successful bidder should employ the council's former employees or take over council assets.[61] However, this view, even if correct, could not affect any directly enforceable rights which individuals would have under the Directive.

On the other hand, a local authority which attempted to tender without making appropriate provision for TUPE could equally find itself subject to judicial review from public-sector unions.[62] The Department of Environment's advice was that tenderers should make clear in the tender documentation their assumptions about TUPE and, perhaps, submit alternative bids (and that councils should allow all tenderers to do so), and that councils could seek indemnities to cover potential liability should TUPE be found to apply. Where the council and the tenderer could not agree and the contract was awarded in-house, the Secretary of State warned councils of the need to be able to justify their approach to the TUPE question, or be found to have acted anti-competitively.[63]

**Enforcement of CCT**

A variety of enforcement mechanisms was employed to uphold the CCT regime, some at the instance of a disappointed contractor, others by the Audit Commission or the Secretary of State. The legislation operated by creating public law duties to which the council was subject in the tendering process.[64] The authority was required to notify any person excluded from an approved list of contractors, not invited to tender, whose submission of a tender was refused, or who tendered unsuccessfully. The council could be required to give reasons for these decisions.[65] Where a decision was made to award a contract to a DSO the council had to produce a statement comparing the bids.[66] The provisions enabling a contractor to take action for contractual decisions based on non-commercial criteria were also available as a remedy.[67]

Where the minister formed a prima facie view that one of the statutory preconditions[68] had not been complied with, a notice could be served

[60] Napier, op. cit. 11–12, citing *Purchasing Guide for Market Testing*, Annex A, para. 25.3.2, Oct. 1992, DoE Circular No. 1/91, 8 Mar. 1991, and various ministerial statements.

[61] DoE Circular 10/93, paras. 41–3, White Collar Guidance, paras. 61–2.

[62] Napier, op. cit., 11.

[63] Arrowsmith, op. cit., 644–7, citing the Issues Paper, 'Handling of TUPE matters in Relation to CCT', circulated by the DoE and Welsh Office to local authorities on 21 Jan. 1994.

[64] Radford, op. cit., 765 notes the disparity, compared with the contractual remedies which the council will enjoy against a contractor.

[65] S. 20.

[66] S. 12(1), (2).

[67] See p. 302 above.

[68] See p. 312 above.

requiring a detailed explanation from the authority.[69] If notwithstanding these comments the minister remained of the view that the Act had not been followed, a further notice could be served either debarring the authority from doing the work in question or imposing conditions on it doing so.[70] These powers were fairly widely used; by December 1994 preliminary (section 13) notices had been served on 366 occasions (76 relating to anti-competitive failure and 290 relating to financial failure) resulting in 127 section 14 notices (39 of which related to anti-competitive behaviour and 88 to financial failure).[71]

The courts gave little encouragement to councils to challenge the Secretary of State's powers, and tended to emphasize instead the wide discretion afforded under the statutory scheme. In two decisions the Court of Appeal refused to intervene to quash notices served by the minister after the councils had accepted substantially higher bids from their DSOs than other tenders. In the first the court upheld the minister's refusal to accept a series of accounting practices adopted by three local authorities to adjust tenders to take account of various costs which would result if the contract were awarded to a private contractor. These included apportioned staffing costs where staff could not be made redundant, loss of DSO 'profit', and losses on forced sale of redundant plant.[72] The judges made it clear that the minister's intervention was not unlawful merely because the council's view was a permissible one under the Act. It had to be shown that the minister's view was itself impermissible in the sense of involving a misconstruction of his powers. Consequently, the minister might lawfully serve a notice in respect of action, which the court or a different minister might have ignored.[73] This approach left the minister as the arbiter of whether a local authority had acted anti-competitively, and able to intervene in the circumstances where an action brought directly by a contractor against the authority would have failed because it could not be shown that the council had acted unreasonably. Furthermore, the Court of Appeal held that the minister could impose a condition requiring the tender process to be repeated, with the proviso that before the Council could accept a tender from the DSO it would require ministerial consent.

The second decision emphasized also the minister's discretion in serving notices by holding that the Act did not require less serious sanctions to be imposed in preference to notices debarring the council from undertak-

[69] LGA 1988, s.13.

[70] Ibid., s.14.

[71] DoE, *Annual Report for 1995*, paras. 4.1.66–7. In 1995 a further 56 (s. 14) Directions were issued: DoE, *Annual Report for 1996*, para. 6.70.

[72] *R v Secretary of State for the Environment ex p. Knowsley MBC and Others*, CA, unreported judgment of 31 July 1991.

[73] This is the predominant tenor of the judgments of Ralph Gibson LJ and of Legatt LJ; Parker LJ seemed to go further and to rule that some of the council's practices were in fact anti-competitive.

ing the work.[74] An argument that the minister had been improperly motivated by a desire to punish the council failed, despite a departmental press briefing (issued to coincide with a ministerial statement on the day before the announcement of the General election) in which it was stated that the council had been debarred to set an example to others. Indeed, the judgments suggested that such a motive was lawful: the contrast with the decisions prohibiting use of a local authorities contractual powers punitively[75] could not be more striking.

The results of the legislation were mixed. Three-quarters of all contracts awarded on the first phase of tendering (from August 1989) were placed with DSOs.[76] In the initial stages it appeared that whether contracts were placed with private-sector contractors depended on a variety of factors. One consideration was the level of available private-sector expertise in the field: for instance 97 per cent of school and welfare catering contracts in the first phase were placed in-house, reflecting the start-up costs and lack of expertise of the private sector in this area.[77] However, the comparable figure for cleaning contracts (for which there was an established private sector market) was only 57 per cent.[78] Political will seems to have been an important factor: 95 per cent of contracts were awarded in-house on the first phase by Labour authorities, compared to under 50 per cent by Conservative ones; overall, two-thirds of all contracts awarded to the private sector were from Conservative-controlled non-metropolitan districts.[79] Against this background, the strategic use of the Secretary of State's powers assumed some tactical significance.

The question of whether the legislation resulted in cost savings also produced a mixed response. In 1996 the Department of the Environment claimed: 'CCT has maintained or improved service standards, led to tighter specifications and a more customer-oriented approach, improved monitoring of performance and management of service organisations and produced cost savings of around 7%.'[80] However, the research by Walsh and Davies which was the basis of these claims presented a more mixed picture. Although they reported that in 64 per cent of cases costs were reduced following competitive tendering (with an average reduction of 6.5 per cent),[81] they also reported considerable difficulty in collecting and interpreting data about estimated savings. Most authorities had specified an equivalent service to that applicable before competitive tendering, so in that sense the situations were comparable. However, it was unclear how far savings were attributable to competition as such and how far to the

[74] *R v Secretary of State for the Environment ex parte London Borough of Haringey*, CA, (1994) 92 LGR 538; see also *R v SSE ex p. Bury MBC*, *The Times*, 5 Mar. 1998, CA.
[75] See pp. 285–6 above.
[76] Painter, op. cit., 196.
[77] Ibid. 199.
[78] Ibid. 199.
[79] Ibid. 201, 208.
[80] DoE, *Annual Report for 1996*, para. 6.71.
[81] Walsh and Davies, op. cit., 142, and chs. 12 and 13 generally.

general effects of the then economic recession. In addition, the level of savings varied considerably according to the type of contract. Other commentators argued that if a broader view were taken of the costs associated with CCT, taking account of the bureaucratic costs of establishing the processes, and losses to the state because of the part-time, lower-paid jobs created through privatization, the indirect costs could be two and a half times as much as the direct savings.[82]

Concerns were also raised about the discriminatory impact of CCT upon women: part-time women employees undertaking tasks such as building cleaning and schools catering emerged as major losers from the deterioration in conditions of employment following CCT.[83] Paradoxically, this occurred at precisely the time when such employees had begun to take advantage of rulings in sex discrimination law conferring a raft of equal-opportunities rights on part-time employees[84] (who are overwhelmingly women).[85]

Commentators were unable, however, to find clear evidence of an overall lowering of standards as a result of implementing the legislation, as many critics had prophesied. This absence of evidence could, though, be attributable to the qualitative nature of the judgments involved and the lack of defined standards of quality of service prior to the introduction of CCT. The clearest benefits were said to be not in the financial realm, but in monitoring the services provided. Implementing the legislation had required authorities to specify, in many instances for the first time, what level of service was expected, and to establish quality assurance systems to ensure it was being delivered, whether by an outside contractor or by a DSO. The Audit Commission concluded in 1995 that local government had generally managed CCT well in terms of letting contracts and maintaining continuity of service provision, but emphasized the importance of the 'client'-side monitoring of contracts and 'customer' involvement in the

[82] Escott and Whitfield, op. cit., 181–5, calculated total costs of £41.2 million, compared with savings of £16.4 million, arising from CCT in 39 authorities studied. However, their methodology included a number of assumptions about lost tax and NI payments and increased unemployment and other benefits resulting from the introduction of more adverse conditions of employment following CCT. This approach is also questionable in view of the later view taken of TUPE in the UK, which in many cases required a successful outside contractor to re-employ the council's workforce on the same terms as before: p. 314 above.

[83] Escott and Whitfield, op. cit.

[84] *R v SS for Employment ex p. Equal Opportunities Commission*, [1994] 1 All ER 910 (HL)

[85] See *Ratcliffe and others v North Yorkshire County Council*, [1995] 3 All ER 597 (HL); for discussion see A. Morris, 'Equal Helpings: *Ratcliffe and others v. North Yorkshire County Council*', [1995] 4 Web JCLI. However, this also impinges on private contractors by making it less easy to cut costs (e.g. in relation to holidays, pensions, sick pay, and NI payments) by employing part-time staff rather than their full-time equivalents.

setting and monitoring of standards. It acknowledged that competition in some areas was still limited.[86]

## BEST VALUE[87]

Labour came to power in 1997 committed to removing CCT. A 1995 policy document had suggested that the requirement to market-test work would be repealed and the scheme in effect reversed, so that where councils decided to put work out to tender (as they would be permitted to do) they would be under a duty to give their own workforce fair opportunity to bid.[88] This was in line with the view that councils should be free to adopt a variety of methods of service provision. The policy of Best Value developed considerably once the government was elected[89] before it was given statutory underpinning by the Local Government Act 1999. Some forty local authorities and two police authorities were selected to pilot the new approach and exempted from much of the CCT regime in advance of its formal abolition in the new legislation.

The policy is notable for reinterpreting a number of previous themes of the Conservative administration, especially the emphasis on consumer consultation and performance indicators. It also integrates them, however, in a new way through a statutory planning and performance review process, new developments in quality audit and assurance, and powers of intervention in cases of failing performance. Unlike previous initiatives, it is claimed that the policy is sensitive to local political choices about distribution of resources and service levels and to differing modes of service provision.[90] Under section 3(1) of the 1999 Act a best value authority[91]

[86] Audit Commission, *Making Markets: A Review of the Audits of the Client Role for Contracted Services* (London, 1995), updating Audit Commission, *Realising the Benefits of Competition: the Client Role for Contracted Services* (London, 1993). For critical discussion of the latter report see Vincent-Jones, op. cit.

[87] For a valuable appraisal comparing 'best value' and CCT, see P. Vincent-Jones, 'Central–Local Relations under the Local Government Act 1999: A New Consensus', (2000) 63 MLR 84; see also P. Vincent-Jones, 'Competition and Contracting in the Transition from CCT to Best Value: Towards a More Reflexive Regulation', (1999) 77 Pub. Admin. 273; P. Vincent-Jones, 'Responsive Law and Governance in Public Services Provision: A Future for the Local Contracting State', (1998) 61 MLR 362; and see the special issue of *Local Government Studies*, 'Managing Local Services: From CCT to Best Value', (1999) 25(2) LGS.

[88] Labour Party, *Renewing Democracy, Rebuilding Communities* (London, 1995), 8–9.

[89] See: Green Paper, DETR, *Modernising Local Government: Improving Local Services through Best Value* (Mar. 1998); White Paper, *Modern Local Government: In Touch with the People*, Cm. 4014, (1998), ch. 7.

[90] These aspects are considered further at pp. 339–43; the account here is concerned solely with the consequences for tendering.

[91] All local authorities are covered under s. 1 of the 1999 Act; the duty applies whether the council is providing a service directly, under a contract through a private sector operator, or

must make 'arrangements to secure continuous improvement in the way in which its functions are exercised, having regard to a combination of economy, efficiency and effectiveness'.

The Green Paper on Best Value professed to eschew ideology about the form of service delivery in favour of pragmatism.[92] While there was to be no compulsory competitive tendering, failure to market-test services might lead to a successful challenge if the council was unable to justify its decision to retain work in-house. CCT and DLOs were, therefore, abolished with effect from January 2000.[93] Although the framework does not specify how councils are to deliver services, there remains a place for competition: 'services should not be delivered directly if more efficient and effective means are available.'[94] The Green Paper suggested that market-testing would become in effect a management tool by which a council could demonstrate transparently that 'Best Value' is being obtained. To this end it was proposed to issue statutory guidance on procurement practice including a 'general presumption that services should be exposed to be to competition except where an authority is able to argue convincingly why this is inappropriate'.

Equally pragmatic are wide-ranging provisions which allow ministers to remove statutory provisions which restrict a Best Value authority's ability to fulfil its duty, or to give new powers (for example, a general to form companies through which to exercise council functions) which would facilitate the achievement of 'Best Value'.[95] This is seen as a way of encouraging experimentation in new forms of service delivery, and especially the use of partnerships with the private sector, as an alternative to contracting out.[96] Power is also given for the Secretary of State to amend the list of 'non-commercial matters' which a council may not consider in inviting tenders and awarding contracts.[97] It is intended to allow a more flexible approach, within the confines of European public procurement law, to matters affecting the workforce where contracting out or partnerships are used.

It is envisaged that authorities will conduct reviews of specified functions within the Best Value regime according to a prescribed timetable.[98] It is expected that all council services will be reviewed initially within five years. These reviews will be fundamental: ranging from questions whether the council should be undertaking the function in the first place,

in partnership with a voluntary or other public body (Green Paper, para. 3.6). The coverage is more extensive than the former CCT regime.

[92] Para. 1.6.

[93] LGA 1999, s. 21; the same provision allows for ministerial guidance to local authorities on 'best value', which authorities must have regard to.

[94] Green Paper, para. 4.16. [95] LGA 1999, s. 16. [96] Green Paper, para. 4.18.

[97] LGA 1999, s. 19, allowing for amendment of s. 17 LGA 1988 (p. 302 above).

[98] LGA 1999, s. 5(2).

and if so 'the level at which and the way in which it should be exercising the function', to objectives, performance against specified criteria, comparison with the performance of other authorities, and progress towards meeting targets for improvement.[99] Consideration of whether to 'externalize' the service will inevitably form a part of the process. For example:

> an authority which was considering how education might be provided to excluded children would begin, initially, by considering whether it ought to provide the service at all. In this case, there are certain statutory standards that the authority needs to observe in terms of the minimum level of education provided, and its further consideration under the review might result in the authority only providing the statutory minimum level of education, or something higher; and giving an indication of how the function is to be performed—e.g. by home visits or through education centres.[100]

Powers of ministerial intervention are retained, although these are to be used as a last resort.[101] The White Paper stated that intervention by ministers would only follow from 'objective triggers'[102] (for example, an ad hoc report from the Audit Commission showing continuing failing performance). Nevertheless, the powers are broad. While some ministerial interventions may be merely procedural, it is also envisaged that the power might be used to take over a specific function, or indeed to transfer it to another authority or private-sector provider.

In many respects Best Value is to be welcomed as potentially more respectful of local democracy than CCT: councils will be free to determine their own modes of service delivery and the level at which services are provided as matters of political choice, provided they can justify those decisions and show that the processes are operating effectively. Taken together with the power of community initiative, there should be greater freedom than under CCT to experiment with new modes of service delivery, especially through partnerships with other public, private, and voluntary agencies.

From relations with local businesses we turn now to a second important area of councils' 'external relations'— the voluntary sector.

[99] S. 5(4).

[100] Explanatory Notes Clauses, Local Government Bill 1998–9, para. 21.

[101] See p. 340 below.

[102] White Paper, para. 7.48. Other triggers might be Ofsted reports or other such equivalent inspections (e.g. by the Social Services Inspectorate, HM Inspectorate of Constabulary, and the Fire Inspectorate). Para. 12 of the Intervention Protocol refers also to: annual audits of financial accounts; public interest reports; reports of inquiries, ombudsman investigations, or judicial findings.

## LOCAL AUTHORITIES AND THE VOLUNTARY SECTOR

### Complementary Features

The boundary between the voluntary sector and the state (at whatever level) is controversial and contingent. In some fields the local public and voluntary sectors have overlapped, especially in social services (e.g. residential homes); education (special needs, playgroups, nurseries); housing (as social landlords, and in relief of homelessness); leisure (community groups). A number of charities have been established against a pattern of partial state provision in education, health, and social services, with the intention of supplementing what the state does not provide. However, the financial restraints of the past two decades have led to councils increasingly eliminating discretionary expenditure in these areas and providing instead the bare statutory minimum service. The delivery of social services has been particularly affected, and the courts have proved generally sympathetic to the plight of councils by turning away claims from disappointed service-users.[103] This has left voluntary organizations to fill the gap, with increasing strains on their own resources. This realignment may be efficient in the sense of discouraging overlap between council and voluntary-sector provision and encouraging complementary working. It can, however, also set up voluntary bodies as representative challengers to council policy decisions to cut services.[104] Replacing state provision with their own may also place voluntary organizations, which are charities, at the boundary of their legal powers under their trust deeds.

Local authorities and voluntary bodies have a number of similarities: they are non-profit bodies, each emphasizes user needs, each has a limited legal capacity (at least in the case of voluntary bodies enjoying charitable status), and each is financially constrained. However, there are significant differences between the two sectors. Although voluntary bodies and councils frequently each rely on outside grant funding, councils are often also in the position of distributing grants to voluntary bodies, and, obviously, local authorities have tax-raising powers where voluntary bodies rely on gifts. Accountability mechanisms are another point of contrast: councils are subject to the political accountability of elected members and financial accountability of local audit, which strictly reinforces the legally limited scope of their powers. Charities will be subject not only to a trust deed specifying their objects but also to general limitations (for example, on political activities) and to the jurisdiction of the Charity Commissioners.

[103] e.g. *R v Gloucestershire CC, ex p. Barry*, [1997] 2 All ER 1. See E. Palmer and M. Sunkin, 'Needs: Resources and Abhorrent Choices', (1998) 61 MLR 401.

[104] *R v Sefton MBC ex p. Help the Aged*, [1997] 4 All ER 532, CA.

Other voluntary bodies may be incorporated as companies by guarantee (and so subject to a Memorandum and Articles of Association) and control by directors or, if unincorporated, subject to a constitution conferring powers and duties on members and officers.

One major contrast concerns political activities. Local authorities are by nature political bodies, whereas charities are prevented from engaging in political activities. However, on closer examination this difference is more one of degree: councils are prevented from engaging in many of the same political actions forbidden in charity law, especially political advertising and campaigning using taxpayers' or trust money. The fundamental difference, however, concerns the voluntary principle—council discretion and assistance for sections of the public and users of public services are generally underpinned by a complex web of coercive powers, which voluntary bodies lack.[105]

**Access to Council Resources**

We can consider the legal modes of interaction between local authorities and voluntary bodies as being points on a spectrum, reflecting the degree of dependence or subservience, on the one hand, or independence and autonomy, on the other, of the voluntary organization. One example of subservience is where provision of services by voluntary bodies is subject to inspection or licensing by local authorities; these include inspection of playgroups and nurseries under the Children's Act 1989 and of residential care facilities under the Registered Homes Act 1984. Equally, grants of council resources and permission to use council premises (for example, for community groups) involve a high degree of subservience—that is, there is little legal constraint on the local authority's discretion.

The importance of local grant funding to the voluntary sector cannot be overemphasized, especially in urban areas. For example, one metropolitan borough alone distributed grants totalling £5.9 million from twenty-one different council budgets to 1,286 voluntary projects in its area in 1996/7.[106] Of the total, £3.67 million was council money (from the social services, community and leisure services, housing, and education budgets) and £2.3 million came from central government initiatives (including City Challenge, Mental Illness Support Grant, and Community Chest). Grants varied in size from £8 to £132,0000. Some national charities such as Age Concern and the NSPCC benefited, but so too did many purely local

[105] Although some, like the RSPCA or the NSPCC, may work closely with statutory agencies.

[106] I am grateful to the Funding Information Support Unit of Newcastle City Council for supply of the information in this paragraph. The unit gives advice and information to organizations seeking grant aid, develops and manages corporate bidding, and monitors use of grants.

bodies, such as local residents' associations, youth clubs, arts and theatre groups, ethnic minority cultural groups, and sports clubs.

The same council imposes a series of conditions upon bodies receiving grants from it, concerning information (e.g. access to accounts of the voluntary body and the supply of data on numbers of people attending events of the body, and their gender and ethnic composition), access for monitoring purposes to meetings and events organized by the sponsored body, compliance with the council's (non-statutory) equal-opportunities policy, and salary scales of staff employed by the body. In addition, the council in effect extends the restrictions on political publicity, which apply to it under the Local Government Act 1986, to the voluntary bodies which it aids. The wide range of such conditions is part of a well-recognized strategy, especially among Labour councils, to extend their reach of influence in implementing social policies beyond their immediate employees and service users. Whereas ability to do so by imposition of similar conditions in contracts was constrained by a prohibition on use of 'non-commercial' criteria,[107] grant conditions are less regulated.

Although the power of grant is largely unconstrained, administrative law may impose some minimal restrictions on its use. In *R v Liverpool CC ex p. Secretary of State for Employment*[108] it was held that a local authority which disaproved of central government policy had acted unlawfully in withdrawing grants from voluntary bodies which participated in the government's Employment Training Scheme; the withdrawal of the grant was seen as an unlawful act of punishment. Interpretation by the House of Lords of the power to make grants to voluntary bodies by the former Greater London Council, however, had the effect of increasing the dependence of these bodies upon other local authorities for annual grants.[109] The court held by a majority that the council had no power of 'forward funding': attempts by the GLC to give grants of £25 million to seventeen umbrella organizations who in turn undertook to distribute them to 900 voluntary organizations after the council's abolition were held to be ultra vires on the application of London boroughs who otherwise stood to have the GLC's balances distributed to them.

Use of council premises such as community centres, sporting facilities, and parks is often equally important to voluntary bodies, which may be unable to make the capital investment to provide their own premises or to pay commercial rates to use private-sector alternatives, where these exist. Here too, administrative law may impose constraints on the discretion of councils to give or withhold permission to use land and premises.[110] So,

[107] LGA 1988, s. 17; p. 302 above.

[108] (1988) 154 LGR 118.

[109] *Westminster CC and Others v Greater London Council*, [1986] 2 All ER 278.

[110] See discussion of *R v Somerset CC, ex p. Fewings*, [1995] 3 All ER 20, and *Wheeler v Leicester CC*, [1985] AC 1054, at pp. 41–6 above.

for example, when a local authority imposed conditions on the use of a park by a community festival which prevented any political activity by any of the voluntary bodies represented at the festival, these were held by the Court of Appeal to be meaningless and *Wednesbury* unreasonable.[111]

## PARTNERSHIPS

Having discussed the position of local authorities in their relations with business and with voluntary bodies individually, we can now move to an area of interest with regard to both. It has become increasingly common in the last two decades for councils to enter cooperative joint arrangements with both sectors. Cooperation takes place on many levels, from the coordinating role that local authorities play in bidding for external funding (for example, from the Single Regeneration Budget) to statutory cooperation and consultation between the public and voluntary sector with regard to education and social services, and use of companies and trusts as a vehicle for joint action.

This section discusses the form of these partnerships and some of the legal difficulties which have arisen. A study based on the experience of one metropolitan borough council suggests that they may vary both in geographical extent (whether region-wide, borough-wide, or in a single locality) and in objectives. The purpose may range from project management, resource acquisition (for example, to give access to grant funding), service delivery (especially with community care programmes), strategic policy, and information exchange, to community empowerment.[112] Particular problems have been encountered in forming such partnerships to do with liabilities on the transfer of staff, with treatment of the assets of the partnership, and with the ethical position and liability of officers and councillors who participate in the partnership arrangements, especially the extent to which they remain bound by the local government ethical framework.

Partnerships can take one of two basic legal forms. A separate legal entity such as a company or a trust may be created. Alternatively, a legal framework can be adopted which either allows (or requires) joint working between the council and other bodies, without creating institutions which are legally independent; these are discussed below, following the treatment of quangos. First we deal with the use of trusts and then with companies.

[111] *R v Barnet LBC ex p. Johnson*, (1991) 89 LGR 581, 590–1 per Purchas LJ; his Lordship also held that it would be lawful for the council to attach conditions to a grant to the festival prohibiting use by any political *party*, but that an extension to any organization promoting or opposing any political cause would be ultra vires.

[112] A. Johnson, 'Making A Reality of Partnership', in Local Government Information Unit, *Turning Community Leadership into Reality* (London, 1999).

**Trusts**

The use of trusts to extend council powers is subject to the normal principles of trust law. Thus, in *R v District Auditor ex p. West Yorkshire MCC*[113] a purported trust to disseminate information to fight the abolition of the council was held to be invalid since the intended beneficiaries were uncertain (or, if they were the two and half million people within the area, too numerous).

As with its use by private individuals, one advantage of the trust may be the ability to provide for the execution of the settlor's intention beyond death (political, in the case of councillors). It was precisely this point which provoked controversy in a case from Manchester, involving a dispute between the Conservative-controlled Metropolitan County Council and the Labour City Council.[114] The city council brought an action for declarations that the county council had acted beyond its powers in passing the resolutions of April 1978 to establish a trust (to which it later paid £1.12 million) for the purpose of providing free or assisted places at independent schools. It was held that the council had power to establish the trust as being incidental to or consequential on the power under section 137 of the Local Government Act 1972, and the trust was to be regarded as the means of achieving the council's legitimate end (education, notwithstanding that it was not a LEA), rather than a distinct objective in its own right. An objection to the use of the money over seven years to pay the educational costs of the children starting school in 1978 failed on the grounds that a single payment from the council within the current year was permissible, even if the trust were to use the money over a longer period. The Court of Appeal held that there was no general principle that a local authority could not enter into a commitment which would continue beyond the life of the currently elected body.[115]

The same decision raised an interesting question about the degree of control which the council had over the money in trust. The first trustees were the chairman and vice-chairman of the county council. The Court of Appeal had argued that the county council retained control over the trustees both in law and in fact. However, the House of Lords held that while the county council effectively directed the trustees, through the medium of the trust purposes, governing how the money was to be used, they did not thereafter have any legal power to exercise direct personal control over the actions of the trustees.

[113] (1985) 26 RVR 24.

[114] *Manchester City Council v Greater Manchester MCC*, Court of Appeal, (1980) 78 LGR 71; House of Lords (1980) 78 LGR 560; and see p. 51 above.

[115] But cf. *Westminster CC and Others v Greater London Council*, [1986] 2 All ER 278; see esp. the dissenting speech of Lord Bridge at 286.

## Local Authority Companies

As partnership between the public and the private and voluntary sectors began to play a significant role in the 1980s, especially in initiatives aimed at local economic development, it became increasingly common for local authorities to be involved in the formation of companies. The advantage of private corporate governance was perceived to be a more commercial and flexible style of decision-making and management, and one with which private-sector partners would be familiar. The company provides a useful vehicle for partnership because control can be shared through apportionment of company shares or directorships, according to the degree of involvement or control required. At the same time the constitution of the company (the memorandum and articles of association) could permit it to undertake projects which would be ultra vires for the local authority. Moreover, the affairs of a company are, in the name of commercial confidentiality, subject to a much less rigorous regime of public disclosure than local authorities. However, the disadvantage was a corresponding democratic deficit. Actions undertaken through a company in which councillors or officers participate would be outside the normal range of controls designed to render their actions publicly accountable: answering to council meetings, the ombudsman's jurisdiction, the auditing process, and judicial review.

Specific legislation on local authority companies has attempted to remedy some of these defects. It distinguishes between companies controlled by local authorities, those influenced by authorities, and those where the authority has a minority interest.[116] Broadly, these categories mirror the degree to which the council can influence company decisions, through use of shareholdings or appointment of directors.

Regulations restrict the use of payments by the authority to a controlled or influenced company. Further provisions apply to the terms on which influenced companies can be granted interests in land held by the authority, and to other contracts, loans, and gifts between the two. Local authority expenditure outside these regulations will be unlawful. The intention is that controlled companies should not be a vehicle for avoiding the strictures of the ultra vires rule. Such companies are also subjected to the remit of the local ombudsman, required to use auditors approved by the Audit Commission, and are under duties to allow public access to information.[117] Regulations prevent controlled or influenced companies being

[116] See Local Authorities (Companies) Order 1995, SI 849 (1995).

[117] However, where the council agrees before a given financial year not to use its powers of control and the company is operating commercially to produce a return on capital, a controlled company may be treated as an 'arm's-length company', with the consequence that the public information and grievance redress provisions will not apply.

used to circumvent other controls on the use by councils of capital finance, on councillors' entitlements to information and the prohibition of party political activity, on disqualification from public office, and on the placing of contracts. Where a council officer or member represents the authority on any of these categories of companies, arrangements must be made to enable questions to be tabled in the authority about their performance.

The stringency of this scheme (especially attributing capital receipts to the local authority) provides a powerful incentive to local authorities to bring their degree of involvement below the thresholds at which the company becomes regulated, i.e. 20 per cent shareholding or directorships in the case of 'influenced' companies. This means, however, that such companies are less useful to councils as a vehicle for community leadership, since it leaves them as junior partners.[118] Moreover, formal delegation of council business to companies of this type is not permitted (s. 101 LGA 1972). To overcome these obstacles it has been suggested that a new type of company (a Public Partnership Limited Company), based on US models, which would have an overriding duty to act to benefit the community, should be introduced specifically with public–private and public–voluntary sector cooperation in mind, which would then allow relaxation of other controls.[119]

The relationship between local authorities and companies has also been questioned in the courts when councils have sought to disown as unlawful their dealing through or with companies. An argument of this type succeeded in the *Allerdale* case, in which a local authority's loan indemnity given in respect of timeshare development by a company owned and controlled by it was held to be ultra vires.[120] The Court of Appeal held that the decision to establish the company and to give the guarantee were part of a scheme to avoid controls on local authority borrowing and therefore ultra vires, since they were undertaken for an improper purpose.

In another case a local authority established a 'deadlock' company (in which it had a 50 per cent shareholding, the other 50 per cent being owned by a company specializing in public housing finance and leasing schemes), and entered into a loan guarantee to enable the company to purchase properties which it then leased to the council to enable the provision of accommodation for homeless people. The council was found by the Court of Appeal not to be liable on the guarantee. It was ultra vires to delegate its functions as a housing authority to a partly owned company, since this was not envisaged under section 101 of the 1972 Act (authorizing delegation) nor could it be permitted under the ancillary powers rule (section 111

[118] Z. Billingham, 'Partnerships and the Legal Framework', in Local Government Information Unit, *A Framework for the Future* (London, 1997).

[119] Johnson, op. cit.

[120] *Credit Suisse v Borough of Allerdale*, [1997] QB 306, CA, esp. Neill LJ at 332–3 and Peter Gibson LJ at 345. See further pp. 48–9 above.

of the same Act), because Parliament had introduced a detailed scheme elsewhere for these matters.[121] Similarly, in *Morgan Grenfell and Co. Ltd v Sutton LBC*,[122] it was held that a guarantee to an unregistered housing association was ultra vires because section 111 could not be used to override a specific limitation on loans and indemnities in section 60 of the Housing Act 1985. Only guarantees of loans to registered associations were permitted under these provisions.

Collectively these decisions fail to advance the notion of the 'enabling authority', by inhibiting councils from financially guaranteeing the liabilities of arm's-length organizations. Each example turns on its own particular statutory context. Nevertheless, there are some lessons of general application. It is clear that the courts will not allow councils to establish companies, whatever their degree of interest in them, solely for the purpose of evading financial or legal restrictions. This means that use of companies is effectively restricted to fields in which there is specific authority to do so[123] or where the statutory context is permissive and it cannot be said that the authority has improperly delegated its statutory functions.

In response to arguments that these restraints were inhibiting councils in the community leadership role, expanded discretionary powers to enter into partnership arrangements with other local bodies, organizations, or agencies have been given by the Local Government Act 2000. These are intended to remove the present uncertainty over the legality of some of these cooperative ventures.[124] The power includes specific ability to give financial assistance, enter into arrangements or agreements, cooperate with or facilitate or co-ordinate the activities of any person, exercise on behalf of any person any functions of that person, and provide staff, goods, services, or accommodation to any person.[125]

## QUANGOS

The terminology used to describe the appointed, rather than elected, sector of governmental agencies is almost as varied and inconsistent as the

[121] *Credit Suisse v Waltham Forest LBC*, [1997] QB 362, CA, per Neill LJ at 374 and Hobhouse LJ at 379.

[122] (1996) 95 LGR 574.

[123] e.g. Housing Act 1985, s. 58; Education Act 1985, s. 2; Transport Act 1985, s. 67; LGHA 1989, s. 33; Environmental Protection Act 1990, s. 32.

[124] The 1998 Green Paper proposed a modest reform of s. 111. The purpose was twofold: to broaden so that ancillary power could be more than one step removed from the primary power (i.e. ancillary to ancillary) and to resolve doubts over use of s. 111 for cooperation and partnership activities, including participation in companies: Green Paper, para. 6.13. The second of these is followed through in ss. 2 (4) and 4 LGA 2000; the first appears to have been abandoned.

[125] LGA 2000, s. 2(4).

sector itself. The officially preferred designation is NDPBs (Non-Department Public Bodies); this is used instead of populist 'quangos' (Quasi-Autonomous Non-Governmental Organizations), a term which is laden with connotations of bureaucracy and patronage. However, the official preference is not merely a matter of linguistic practice; exclusion of agencies associated with central government departments allowed the Conservative government to claim that there had been a decline in the number of such bodies since 1979, something disputed by commentators preferring different terminology, such as EGOs (Extra-Governmental Organizations).

Definitional politics aside, there are good reasons for focusing in this discussion on the appointed nature of the bodies concerned, rather than their formal relationship with central government. This is because a number of the agencies most important at the local level enjoy, at least formally, some autonomy. In 1996 Greer and Hoggett claimed that there were then more than 4,800 local quangos with a budget of over £37 billion, with 50,000 members (more than double the number (23,000) of elected local councillors in England and Wales). The scale of the phenomenon has led some to write of a 'new magistracy', and others to refer to the quangocracy, or at least a world of 'local governance' made up of diverse agencies operating at the local level.[126]

There is considerable diversity in this sector. For example, some appointed bodies are concerned only with a single institution: former grant-maintained schools,[127] health service trusts, and Further Education Colleges are examples. However, other quangos exercise more general executive, regulatory, or advisory functions and may operate nationally, regionally, or locally; at the regional level these include bodies appointed to perform a strategic sub-national function or to coordinate matters regionally, comprising co-opted or indirectly elected members; locally they include bodies appointed by local authorities or acting in their place.[128] This diversity among quangos has implications for their relationship with local government, which is equally diverse. While some could be abolished and their functions given to directly elected councils, more thought would be required in the case of others about how they could be rendered accountable, although not directly elected.[129] Some local quan-

[126] See generally: S. Weir and W. Hall, *EGO Trip: Extra-Governmental Organisations in the UK and Their Accountability* (1994); L. Pliatsky, 'Quangos and Agencies', (1992) 70(2) Public Administration 555; J. Stewart, 'Appointed Boards and Local Government', (1995) 48(2) Parl. Affs., 226; *Report on Non-departmental Bodies*, Cmnd. 7797 (1980); A. Greer and P. Hoggett, 'Quangos and Local Governance', in L. Pratchett and D. Wilson (eds.), *Local Democracy and Local Government* (Basingstoke, 1996); J. Stewart 'Reforming the New Magistracy', ibid.

[127] Under the Schools Standard and Framework Act 1998 most grant-maintained schools became 'foundation' schools, although some became 'voluntary aided'.

[128] A. Whitehead, *Holding Quangos to Account* (London, 1995), 4–5.

[129] See J. Stewart, *Reforming the Local Appointed Boards* (London, 1996).

gos provide services to discernible customers directly; others are in the position of 'purchasing' services or coordinating other institutions or suppliers.

In a number of cases the origins of these bodies lay in a thinly disguised desire to bypass elected local government, with the objective either of cutting down 'bureaucracy', avoiding local politics, or of creating a more direct relationship between the public consumer and the supplier. For example, Urban Development Corporations were created because the normal planning process through local planning authorities was seen to be incapable of solving the problems of dereliction and industrial decay in the inner cities. The Local Government, Planning and Land Act 1980 allowed the Secretary of State to designate an area of land as an urban development area where he or she was of the opinion that it was expedient to do so in the national interest.[130] An Urban Development Corporation was then established by statutory instrument. The members were appointed by the Secretary of State, having regard to 'the desirability of securing the services of people having special knowledge of locality', and after consulting local authorities in the area.[131] The Corporation could then be vested with the powers of a local planning authority over development control within its area.[132] During their lifetime (the UDCs have now been wound up) the relationship between UDCs and local authorities was, not surprisingly, strained.

The creation of Training Enterprise Councils represented the replacement of one type of quango by another; their predecessors, the Manpower Services Commission and the Local Area Manpower Boards, had included representatives from local government, the voluntary sector, and trade unions, together with businesspeople. However, in 1988 a government White Paper suggested that the need to become competitive required private-enterprise domination of these initiatives, rather than local-authority and trade union representation. It was stressed that membership should be based upon the calibre of the individuals concerned, rather than on notions of formal local representation. Subsequently, a series of studies argued that TECs failed adequately to represent their local communities.[133] Their creation was a deliberate attempt to weaken the interest of LEAs in the field of vocational education. TECs operate as companies, and their relationship with central government is a contractual one, consistent with the commercial orientation behind their establishment.

[130] 1980 Act, s. 134.

[131] Ibid., sched. 26.

[132] See generally M. Purdue, E. Young, and J. Rowan-Robinson, *Planning Law and Procedure* (London, 1989), 430–4.

[133] See the research summarized in M. Jones, *TECs and Local Accountability: Options for Reform* (London, 1996), 1–3; Greer and Hoggett, op. cit., 163.

There was also a second motivation for forming quangos: to create a direct relationship between those providing the service and the public 'consumers', without the intervention of elected representatives. This was illustrated, for example, in the case of grant-maintained schools, in which the local authority influence was diluted and parental involvement in the governing body was increased.[134]

In view of this desire to bypass local authority control, it is not surprising that subsequent difficulties have arisen in the relationship between these bodies and local councils, and that concerns have been expressed by local government associations over their accountability. Areas of difficulty which have been highlighted include the composition and appointment of members of these bodies, their lack of openness and consultation in decision-making, the lack of rules and procedures governing conflicts between private and public interest in the actions of their members, and the lack of mechanisms by which the community can hold them to account for their decisions.

So far as appointment of members was concerned, the first report from the Committee on Standards in Public Life (the Nolan Committee) found widespread public concern about appointments; it recommended a strengthening of the principle that appointments should be made on merit, with greater advertising of vacant positions. While ministers should remain responsible for making appointments, it also suggested the creation of an independent Public Appointments Commissioner to regulate, monitor, and report on the public appointments process.[135] Further recommendations directed at ensuring probity in the actions of local unelected bodies, such as Higher and Further Education Corporations, grant-maintained schools, Training and Enterprising Councils, and Housing Associations, were contained in a second report from the Nolan Committee.[136] Although its earlier report had highlighted differences in probity mechanisms between local councils and these quangos, the second report did not propose the uniform extension of the statutory safeguards, such as the declaration of interests, which apply to councils. Instead, it championed 'best practice' on appointments and openness, and suggested greater use of codes of conduct to regulate matters such as propriety and whistle-blowing.

Moving beyond Nolan's limited brief, Painter has suggested three possible routes for strengthening accountability of local quangos: changing

[134] See P. Meredith, *Government, Schools and the Law* (London, 1992), ch. 6; see further p. 149 above. Under the Schools Standards and Framework Act 1998, LEA representation was restored to the governing bodies of former GM schools.

[135] Cm. 2850 (1995); and see Government Response, Cm. 2931 (1995).

[136] Committee on Standards in Public Life, *Standards in Public Life: Local Public Spending Bodies, Second Report of the Nolan Committee*, Cm. 3270 (1996). In its Fourth Report, in Nov. 1997, the committee expressed continuing concern over local spending bodies.

the composition of these bodies to include greater representation from local authorities, increasing formal accountability to elected local or regional bodies who would have legal powers of scrutiny, or reversing the bypass process by abolition and return of their powers to local government.[137] Stewart argues that the form of any accountability mechanisms must take account of the diversity of quangos themselves.[138] He argues that the greater the responsibility of a local body for determining local policy within its policy framework, the stronger the case for some form of democratic control. In some cases this may justify a separate directly elected body, where the functions are sufficiently freestanding (i.e. unrelated to others exercised, for example, by elected councils), and there would be sufficient electoral interest to justify such arrangements. In other instances the local council might be given direct control (for example, by majority control of the governing board) or indirect control (for example, by power to set the policy framework in which a local quango operates). However, even without control, powers could be given to local councils to enable enhanced scrutiny of local quangos: these might include statutory rights to information or to summon representatives from the body or to appoint members, falling short of a majority.

Painter pointed to a number of examples where councils have attempted to exercise strategic community leadership by creating administrative and political structures which allow for formulation of policy and monitoring of activities in the locality, whether or not the council itself is directly responsible for particular statutory functions. Lewisham, for example, has established an external relations sub-committee 'to promote positive relations with local non-elected agencies and the role of the council as a community advocate'.[139] Initiatives such as these currently lack formal statutory underpinning. Hopes that these powers might be given as part of the community leadership role, recognized in the Local Government Act 2000, have been disappointed.

The 1998 White Paper commended the establishment by councils of non-statutory local public forums, to allow for public debate and education on issues of concern; in some instances these have included giving public or private bodies the opportunity to respond to local concerns about their actions or proposals. However, these are not a statutory requirement nor clothed with powers, for example to compel the attendance of, and information or evidence from, other local actors such as quangos and privatized industries (for example, water companies).[140]

[137] C. Painter, *Local Government and the Unelected State* (London, 1996), 2–3.
[138] Stewart, 'Reforming the New Magistracy'.
[139] Painter, op. cit., 5.
[140] Green Paper, paras. 6.25–7.

## COMMUNITY PLANNING AND CONSULTATION

One of the legal mechanisms currently favoured in the vogue for 'joined-up' (or 'collaborative') government is the statutory plan. These plans serve several purposes: to make transparent the objectives of public bodies, to structure discretion, and to provide a measure for audit and performance review. They also require consultation of the public and of other stakeholders about the provision of public services, and coordination of efforts among public authorities and other service providers in tackling intractable cross-cutting social problems, especially in the areas of crime, social exclusion, and health. An early archetype of such planned cooperation was a provision requiring local authorities in formulating a community care plan to consult voluntary organizations representing the likely users of community care and their carers.[141] The position of voluntary bodies under these various existing plans, strategies, and reviews is generally fairly weak: there may be a procedural right to be consulted, but even the choice of bodies to be consulted may be within the discretion of the public authority.[142] The weak nature of these arrangements contrasts with the requirements applicable under the devolution legislation to the National Assembly of Wales, which is required to have formal arrangements for liaising with voluntary bodies.[143]

To add to what some local government practitioners describe as strangulation by plan, it is now proposed that there should be a 'Community Plan', to bring together local stakeholders to identify needs and aspirations of local communities and to improve service provision in response to those needs and aspirations.[144] It is to be developed with local people, local business, and the public and voluntary sectors. The White Paper suggested that there would be some freedom about the content of the Community Plan and the process of its preparation. Although the plan would have no direct effect, it would be considered when applications are

141 National Health Service and Community Care Act 1990, s. 46(3).

142 For recent examples see Crime and Disorder Act 1998, s. 5(3), requiring chief police officers and local authorities in devising a strategy for reduction of crime and disorder in their locality to invite participation from specified categories of bodies; Schools Standards and Framework Act 1998, s. 6. A rare example of a stronger right is the position of diocesan authorities (voluntary sector providers of church schools) where there is in effect a right of review before an Adjudicator: Education (School Organization Plans) England Regulations 1999.

143 Government of Wales Act 1998, s. 114, requires the Assembly to make a scheme setting out how it proposes in the exercise of its functions to promote the interests of relevant voluntary organizations, how it proposes to provide assistance to such organizations (and how use of any such grants etc. will be monitored), and how voluntary organizations will be consulted about the exercise of its functions relating to them.

144 *Modern Local Government: In Touch with the People* (London, July 1998), ch. 8. LGA 2000, s. 4.

made for special funding and would be a background consideration to other statutory plans which the council is required to prepare for particular services or functions.[145] The Local Government Act 2000 links these strategic plans with the power to promote the well-being of the community.[146] Councils are required, therefore, to 'prepare a strategy for promoting or improving the economic, social, and environmental well-being' of their areas (s. 4(1)). In so doing the council may consult widely and must have regard to ministerial guidance. The strategic plan is intended to provide focus for the leadership and coordinating aspects of the community leadership role. Apart from a specific power to incur expenditure, detailed powers to enter partnerships also feature prominently.[147] These, however, are illustrative only in an attempt to prevent the general power being read down by the judges.[148]

## CONCLUSION

As we have seen, legal constraints may prevent effective partnership between local authorities and other bodies in three ways. First, by limiting the range of activities undertaken to those which the council itself could lawfully engage in under the ultra vires rule. Second, by what can be termed organizational limitations. Two examples of these can be given. Section 101 of the Local Government Act 1972 only currently permits certain forms of delegation of council decision-making and functions; joint arrangements with other local authorities are permitted, but those with other bodies are not envisaged. A second illustration is the rules on local authority companies, which in some instances treat the company as a mere extension of the council itself, so neutralizing any advantage in using a company in the first place. The third constraint is financial: rules which attribute partnership capital, income, and expenditure to the council are a disincentive to participation for councils already subject to stringent controls in those areas. With the proposed reforms, however, local authorities will have much more freedom to enter these partnerships.

In this chapter we have seen how in two decades ideas of how a local authority should relate to the community around it have changed

145 A different approach is taken in the case of the new strategic authority for London, where the Greater London Authority Bill 1998/9 does not require the preparation of an overall plan. Instead there are to be a series of strategies to deal with spatial development, transport, waste management, air quality, and ambient noise.

146 See p. 59 above.

147 The power includes specific ability to give financial assistance, enter into arrangements or agreements, cooperate with, or facilitate or coordinate, the activities of any person, exercise on behalf of any person any functions of that person, and to provide staff, goods, services, or accommodation to any person: LGA 2000, s. 2(4).

148 S. 2(6).

radically. The notion of 'enabling', with an emphasis solely on the means by which services were provided, has given way to the idea of community leadership. Links with the private and voluntary sectors are fundamental to this role, but it eschews ideology about the means of delivering local services. The new emphasis on encouraging experimentation is reminiscent of Mill's justification for local government with which we began in Chapter 1. In the final chapter we will assess how the different elements of the democratic reform programme, of which community leadership is one, mesh together into an overall vision.

# 11

# *Conclusion: The New Local Government*

More than any other area of the constitution, local government has undergone constant change over the past two decades. The Labour government has initiated further changes under the Local Government Acts 1999 and 2000 as part of a ten-year programme of reform to reinvigorate local democracy. Laurence Prachett has pithily summarized the crisis of local democracy that these proposals are designed to address as involving 'electoral apathy', 'functional impotence', and 'arcane decision-making structures'.[1]

The renewal programme has three strands: a new form of accountability, the 'Best Value' regime; the reform of executive structures (including the introduction of cabinets and directly elected mayors); and new powers for councils to become 'community leaders', working in partnership with other public, private, and voluntary bodies, both under a new power to promote community well-being and under the 'Beacon Council' scheme. We have examined these developments individually at various places throughout the book. This conclusion will briefly examine the programme as a whole and assess the tensions within the various strands to evaluate the extent to which it amounts to a coherent vision for local democracy.

## NEW ACCOUNTABILITY: THE CHARACTERISTICS OF BEST VALUE

At first sight the much-trumpeted 'Best Value' would appear to have little to offer by way of democratic renewal. Instead, it appears to be part of the steady incursion of ever more sophisticated forms of audit into the public sector. Under section 3(1) of the 1999 Act a Best Value authority[2] must make 'arrangements to secure continuous improvement in the way in which its functions are exercised, having regard to a combination of economy, efficiency and effectiveness'. As we have seen in Chapter 10, it is envisaged that authorities will conduct fundamental reviews of all their functions within the Best Value regime according to a prescribed timetable over a five-year period.[3] The consultative paper emphasized that, as a

[1] L. Pratchett, 'Introduction: Defining Democratic Renewal', (1999) 25 LGS 1, 3.

[2] All local authorities are covered under s. 1 of the 1999 Act; the duty applies whether the council is providing a service directly, under a contract through a private sector operator, or in partnership with a voluntary or other public body (Department of Environment, Transport and Regions, *Modernising Local Government: Improving Local Services through Best Value* (London, 1998), para. 3.6). The coverage is more extensive than the former CCT regime.

[3] LGA 1999, s. 5(2).

duty owed both to taxpayers and to local service users, Best Value is about quality of service as well as cost.[4] The possible tension between cost and quality of services, that is between council taxpayers' and service users' interests, is left somewhat unresolved. Indeed, the consultative paper makes a virtue of this:

The government does not intend that the duty of best value should transfer decisions about cost and quality in local services from councils to the courts or auditors. . . . . It intends the council should be accountable primarily through the ballot box to local people, rather than to the Secretary of State, in their duty to obtain best value.[5]

This explains why the duty comprises not absolute obligations but rather a series of procedural arrangements providing for consultation, preparation of Local Performance Plans, performance reviews, inspection, and auditing of the whole process, with the information made available to the public at each stage. In deciding how to fulfil its duty to secure Best Value, the authority is required to consult representatives of local council taxpayers, of non-domestic ratepayers, and of users of its services, and 'persons appearing to the authority to have an interest in any area within which the authority carries out functions'.[6] It is a process and an attitude, rather than a minimum prescribed standard. This ambitious attempt to define a municipal lifestyle inevitably appears somewhat lacking in concrete content when translated into the cold statutory prose of the Local Government Act 1999.

Local Performance Plans (LPPs) are to be 'the main instruments by which best value authorities will be held accountable for delivering best value by their local communities'.[7] The plans are to be prepared for each financial year and will be both backward-looking (reviewing success in achieving previous targets and comparing the authority's performance with that of others) and forward-looking to set targets for the coming years. As performance reviews are completed, the results will be included in the LPPs and will lead to revised targets and proposed action. The form of the LPP may be subject to ministerial regulations and guidance.

The scheme envisages external review of Best Value through a tripartite arrangement of audit, inspections, and (exceptionally) ministerial interventions. Local Performance Plans are to be 'assessed' by auditors for conformity with the statutory Best Value provisions and a public report delivered.[8] In the case of failures not requiring an inspection, remedial action may be recommended. Serious deficiencies and failures in the plan

[4] Green Paper, para. 2.1.

[5] Ibid., para. 3.3.

[6] LGA 1999, s. 3(2). The council has discretion under subs. (3) to determine which bodies or persons are representative of particular groups. However, it must have regard to ministerial guidance in determining who to consult and the form of consultation: subs. (4).

[7] Green Paper, para. 25.

[8] LGA 1999, s. 7.

will lead to a recommendation of follow-up by a Best Value inspector, or (exceptionally) ministerial intervention. Authorities are under a duty to respond to the Secretary of State concerning findings of serious deficiencies in the auditor's report, and that response will automatically form part of the next performance plan.[9]

Inspections under sections 10–14 are envisaged as a way of giving implementation of Best Value added rigour. They will normally follow on in a programmatic way from the service reviews which the authority has itself carried out, but the scheme also allows for ad hoc inspections in cases of apparent serious failure and also for a ministerial power to direct an inspection. Inspections are the responsibility of the Audit Commission. Inspectors will have the normal powers of auditors, but with a right of access to premises also. Failings identified on inspection (together with the authority's response and programme of action) will feed back into the next LPP. Those which are serious may be reported to the minister for use of intervention powers.

As a result of these changes, the crowded stage of actors advising councils on their administrative practices now includes, internally, the statutory financial and monitoring officers, non-statutory complaints, and ombudsman procedures. Externally, there are government inspectorates for particular services, the Local Commissioners, and, in the Best Value regime, inspectors, the District Auditor, and the Audit Commission. Although these approach the issues from the divergent directions of maladministration and of value for money and effectiveness, there is a substantial overlap between the handling of complaints and audit in the attempts to encourage good practice by councils. This gives credence to proposals for small-scale quangocide, or at least some rationalization of roles. Martin Loughlin has proposed that there should be a unified Commission for Local Government 'to guide and support both the audit function and complaints procedures'.[10] Separate branches would be retained to undertake these functions.

It is noticeable, however, that although the Best Value regime expands the role of the Audit Commission and, to a significant measure, draws its inspiration from both consumer and financial accountability, the CLA and the Audit Commission have survived as separate institutions. Findings of maladministration may be one of the 'objective triggers' for ministerial intervention but no further attempt has been made at fusion. In view of the powers of review and inspection conferred on the Audit Commission, it would now seem anomalous to give the CLA the parallel power of investigation on its own initiative which it has requested. If the local ombudsman's 'ultimate rung' strategy is judged a success it would, however, seem

[9] S. 9.

[10] M. Loughlin, *Administrative Accountability in Local Government* (York, 1992), 153–4.

a natural development to incorporate internal complaints handling within the Best Value regime, subject to preserving a residual route for complaints which cannot be resolved internally. Likewise, much of the guidance on good administrative practice now seems to fall more naturally within Best Value.

The White Paper on Best Value stated that intervention by ministers would only follow from 'objective triggers'[11] (for example, an ad hoc report from the Audit Commission showing continuing failing performance). Nevertheless, the powers are broad. While 'default powers' are a longstanding feature of local government legislation, section 15 gives powers of ministerial intervention of a breadth and flexibility never seen before. Ironically, these have been promoted by a government anxious to repair central–local relations after two decades of rupture. While some ministerial interventions may be merely procedural, it is also envisaged that the power might be used to take over a specific function, or indeed to transfer it to another authority or private-sector provider. The scheme is a considerable broadening of similar intervention powers taken to deal with 'failing' schools.[12]

The government has, following agreement with the Local Government Association, set out the general principles intended to underpin the exercise of the Secretary of State's intervention powers in a non-legal protocol.[13] This makes it clear that councillors, officials, and contractors have the 'prime responsibility for delivering quality services'. It states that the Secretary of State will exercise intervention powers only when there is 'clear evidence' of failure, that reasons for intervention will be given, and that the authority will normally be given the opportunity to take corrective action by a specified deadline during which progress will be monitored. Where the minister or a person acting on his behalf takes over a function, the authority's progress will be reviewed so as to return that function to the control of the council 'as soon as is practicable'. Where the minister gives a direction to an authority about the exercise of a function, the direction is to be lifted 'when the Secretary of State is content that the objectives of the intervention can be met on a sustainable basis'. Whilst reserving the right to exercise his powers otherwise, the Secretary of State has indicated that he intends 'to intervene proportionately to the seriousness of the failure', and that a single procedural failure relating to best value is unlikely to trigger intervention, but that a failure of substance is more likely to do so.

What makes these powers contentious is their relationship with the local democratic process. At best they can be seen as a safety net for the

[11] White Paper, para. 7.48.

[12] See Schools Standards and Framework) Act 1998, Pt. 1.

[13] DETR, *Protocol on Intervention Powers* (London, 1999).

users of local services, when elected representatives and perhaps even the electorate itself (armed with information about poor performance from Best Value audits) have failed to act decisively to produce positive change in the management of an authority. However, there is a danger that they could be used to short-circuit electoral accountability in pursuit of some centrally imposed standard of performance against which a council is deemed to be under-achieving. The consultative paper, however, denied any such ambitions, claiming that the primary method of accountability would remain the ballot box.[14]

In many respects Best Value is to be welcomed as potentially more respectful of local democracy than CCT: councils will be free to determine their own modes of service delivery and the level at which services are provided as a matter of political choice, provided they can justify those decisions and show that the processes are operating effectively. Whether the regime becomes more a set of procedural hurdles and elaborate paper exercises which councils will become adept at satisfying will depend in large part on how interventionist auditors, inspectors, and ministers are in using the exceptional powers granted under the scheme. Certainly, the machinery is in place for a government with a different agenda for local government to move it further in the direction of local administration.

This, however, does not appear to be the present intention, and Best Value should be understood as part of the overall package of reform which includes the power of community initiative and the creation of new executive structures. Taken together with the power of community initiative, there should be greater freedom than under CCT to experiment with new modes of service delivery, especially through partnerships with other public, private, and voluntary agencies. The new executive structures may also be particularly adapted to the Best Value regime. If the reforms splitting the executive and scrutiny functions succeed in creating a genuine climate of positive political management, on the one hand, and friendly but sceptical inquiry and accountability, on the other, it will make external intervention largely unnecessary.

## NEW STRUCTURES AND ELECTORAL REFORM

The part of the programme most obviously concerned with democratic renewal is that dealing with changing the convoluted electoral arrangements of local government and reform of executive structures.[15] The object

[14] Green Paper, para. 3.3. [15] See pp. 14–16 and 230–46 above.

of each is to increase public interest and participation in local democracy, so reversing what has been a long-term decline.

However, more is at stake here than increasing the pitifully small turnout in local elections. The two underlying issues which must be considered are the responsiveness of local authorities to the public and the creation of effective, transparent, and accountable political leadership. There may be a tension between these concerns. On the first, while more frequent elections may make councils more responsive to the electorate, they may also risk inducing voter fatigue. Annual elections should in theory produce more frequent changes in the control of councils; the possibility of this might, on the other hand, increase voter interest but it also risks undermining the second strand—the creation of effective political structures. A local council which is on perpetual election alert and whose political leadership could, as a result, in extreme cases rotate in three years out of four is unlikely to have a clear sense of direction.

Nor do these proposals address what everyone agrees is a long-standing difficulty—the substantial number of authorities for whom there is little incentive to be responsive to the public or indeed for the public to take much interest, because the electoral geography has produced decades of unbroken one-party rule. Proportional representation might address the latter point, but it would exacerbate political instability in other cases. This dilemma does much to explain the fascination for new forms of engaging the public; referendums, citizens' juries, user surveys, focus groups, 'visioning', and so on. Although a sophisticated approach needs to be developed to these practices and the differing ways in which they add to representative democracy, local government might ultimately have much to teach the public sector as a whole.

One innovation which seems an undoubted success in engaging public interest is the introduction of elected mayors. The contest in the spring of 2000 for Mayor of London produced months of news coverage of local government of a kind never seen before in the United Kingdom. It will take a much longer period, however, to assess the effectiveness and responsiveness of this type of office in a British setting.

The government has claimed that its reforms of executive structures will attract into local government a new calibre of elected member, while giving worthwhile and rewarding roles to all councillors, irrespective of whether they are members of the political executive. This may be true of very high-profile posts such as the elected mayors of major conurbations. There are, however, grounds to be sceptical in the other cases and, in particular, with what is likely to be the dominant model in practice—the leader and cabinet. It remains to be seen whether the political parties will rise to the challenge of the new environment by breaking ingrained habits of secrecy and party loyalty to make the overview and scrutiny mechanisms effective.[16] It is unclear also whether potential candidates will find the back-bench councillor roles of overview and scrutiny as appealing as the government believes.

Even if they do, it must be open to doubt whether the electorate would be equally engaged in voting not only more frequently but also for representatives whose role may seem less important than those of the present-day councillors.[17] While the backbench roles of representing a constituency and overview and scrutiny of the executive may be worthy, will they excite the voters so that turnout is increased? In terms of crude self-interest, for the majority of local electors who never visit a councillor's surgery, there may seem little point in voting at all unless there is a realistic prospect of a change in power and, hence, in policies.

There may also be a mismatch between other aspects of the political executive and electoral reforms. The inevitable result of holding more frequent local elections will be that councils change hands politically more often. It follows, too, that the political executive will need to be recomposed either when individual members lose their seats or when the majority party as a whole loses control of the council. This electoral instability is likely to act as a deterrent to the new political cadre that the government wish to attract. High-quality candidates may be unwilling to interrupt or give up their careers to take up a full-time place on the executive if there is a significant risk of being unemployed in as little as a year's time due to a change in electoral fortunes.[18] Paradoxically, the very possibility which is likely to arouse interest in the electorate may deter would-be councillors.

## NEW POWERS

As we have seen,[19] three changes are being implemented which may free councils from some of the constraints of the ultra vires rule: expanded discretionary powers to enter into partnership arrangements with other local bodies, organizations, or agencies; the new power of community initiative, enabling them to promote the economic, social, and environmental

[16] Colin Copus concludes: 'Little will change in local political decision-making unless the renewal project adequately addresses councillors' concepts of group loyalty, how councillors conduct representation, their attitudes towards those they represent, their preference for privacy in the political process, and their adherence to a Burkean approach towards representation, seeing the councillor as the final arbiter of local affairs': 'The Party Group: A Barrier to Democratic Renewal', (1999) 25 LGS 76, 89.

[17] A. Forge, 'New Political Structures for Local Government: Legal Context and Potential Implications for Representative Government', (1998) 1 JLGL 74, 75.

[18] S. Leach, 'Introducing Cabinets into British Local Government', (1999) 52(1) Parl. Affs. 77, 84.

[19] See pp. 56–66 above.

well-being of their areas; and ministerial relaxation of controls for authorities which can demonstrate that they deserved greater freedom because of their strong existing performance (Beacon Councils). The first and second of these especially are linked to the vision of the council as 'the elected leader of its local community'. However, as we have seen, while useful, the community well-being power falls short of the quasi-constitutional, overarching rationale for local government first proposed. It is doubtful if by itself it will enable councils to break free from their judicially imposed shackles under ultra vires. As with Best Value, ministerial powers and control are strong features of the Beacon Council scheme.[20] Indeed, it is likely that Beacon status may become strongly linked to the Best Value process in a sophisticated game in which ministers alternately hold out sticks and carrots to local authorities.

If the idea of community leadership is to be taken seriously, it implies more discretion than councils currently enjoy and powers which distinguish them from other agencies and actors operating on the local stage. There is, however, a potential rivalry with the strategic role and powers envisaged for devolved and regional government. There are many parallels with the seemingly similar aspirations of regional chambers and councils exercising community leadership. The approach taken to the legal powers of the Scottish Parliament, the National Assembly of Wales, and the Greater London Authority, although different in each case, contrasts completely with the traditional attitude towards local government under the ultra vires rule and the limited reforms introduced under the Local Government Act 2000. The lack of a written constitution with a clear role and a protected status for local government is a continuing deficiency.

[20] LGA 2000, s. 5 (general power to allow Secretary of State by order to remove enactments which obstruct authorities from promoting the well-being of their communities) and s. 6 (allowing the Secretary of State to suspend requirements to prepare statutory plans or strategies). Further powers are contained in LGA 1999, s. 16(1); ministers may also confer additional powers on authorities by order where it is considered to be necessary or expedient in order to permit or facilitate compliance with best value: ibid., s. 16(2).

# *Bibliography*

## BOOKS AND ARTICLES


ADLER, M., PETCH, A., and TWEEDIE, J., *Parental Choice in Education Policy* (Edinburgh, 1989).

ARDEN, A., MANNING, J., and COLLINS, S., *Local Government Constitutional and Administrative Law* (London, 1999).

ARROWSMITH, S., *Civil Liability and Public Authorities* (Winteringham, 1992).

——'Government Contracts and Public Law', (1990) 10 Legal Studies 231.

——*Government Procurement and Judicial Review* (Toronto, 1988).

——'Judicial Review and the Contractual Powers of Public Authorities', (1990) 106 LQR 277.

——*The Law of Public and Utilities Procurement* (London, 1996).

——'Protecting the Interests of Bidders for Public Contracts: The Role of the Common Law', (1994) 53 CLJ 104.

——'Public Procurement as an Instrument of Policy and the Impact of Market Liberalisation', (1995) 111 LQR 235.

ATIYAH, P., *An Introduction to the Law of Contract* (5th edn., Oxford, 1995).

BAILEY, S., *Cross on Principles of Local Government Law* (London, 1992).

BARENDT, E., 'Libel and Free Speech in English Law', [1993] PL 449.

BARRON, A., and SCOTT, C., 'The Citizen's Charter Programme', (1992) 55 MLR 526.

BATEY, E., 'The Assisted Places Scheme: Crossing the Public/Private Divide', (1996) 8 Education and Law 191.

BILLINGHAM, Z., 'Partnerships and the Legal Framework', in Local Government Information Unit, *A Framework for the Future* (London, 1997).

BIRKINSHAW, P., *Freedom of Information: The Law, the Practice and the Ideal* (2nd edn., London, 1996).

——*Government Information: Law Relating to Access, Disclosure and Regulation* (London, 1990).

——*Grievances, Remedies and the State* (2nd edn., London, 1995).

——*Open Government, Freedom of Information and Local Government* (London, 1985).

——'Open Government—Local Government Style', [1988] Public Policy and Administration 46.

——HARDEN, I., and LEWIS, N., *Government by Moonlight* (London, 1990).

——and PARRY, N., 'Every Trick in the Book', [1999] EHRLR 372.

————'The End of the Beginning? The Freedom of Information Bill 1999', (1999) 26 J. of L. and S. 538.

BRADLEY, A., 'The Role of the Ombudsman in Relation to the Protection of Citizens' Rights', [1980] CLJ 304.

BRANSON, N., *Poplarism, 1919–25: George Lansbury and the Councillors' Revolt* (London, 1979).

BRAYNE, H., 'The Local Government Mandate and the Courts', [1986] Law Society's Gazette 514.

BUCK, T., 'School Admissions Appeals', (1985) JSWL 227.

BULL, D., 'Monitoring Education Appeals: Local Ombudsmen Lead the Way', (1985) JSWL 189.

BUTLER, D., ADONIS, A., and TRAVERS, T., *Failure in British Government: The Politics of the Poll Tax* (Oxford, 1994).

BYRNE, T., *Local Government in Britain* (6th edn., Harmondsworth, 1994).

CANE, P., 'Do Banks Dare to Lend to Local Authorities?' (1994) 110 LQR 514.

CARNAGHAN, R., and BRACEWELL-MILNES, B., *Testing the Market* (Institute of Economic Affairs, Research Monograph 49) (London, 1993).

CARNWARTH, R., 'The Reasonable Limits of Local Authority Powers', [1996] PL 244.

CHILD, T., and SCHWEHR, B., 'Power to the People', (1998) 1 JLGL 71.

CIRRELL, S., and BENNETT, J., *Encyclopaedia of Competitive Tendering* (London).

CLIPSON, A., 'Bradford's 'Open Government' Experience', in R. Chapman, and M. Hunt, *Open Government* (Beckenham, 1987).

COCHRANE, A., *Whatever Happened to Local Government?* (Buckingham, 1995).

COMMISSION FOR LOCAL DEMOCRACY, *Taking Charge: The Rebirth of Local Democracy* (London, 1995).

CONSTITUTION UNIT, *Regional Government in England* (London, 1996).

——*Scotland's Parliament* (London, 1996).

——and Electoral Reform Society, *Report of the Commission on the Conduct of Referendums* (London, 1996).

COOPER, D., 'Defiance and Non-compliance: Religious Education and the Implementation Problem', (1995) 48 Current Legal Problems 253.

——*Governing Out of Order: Space, Law and the Politics of Belonging* (London, 1998).

——'Local Government Consciousness in the Shadow of Juridification', (1995) 22 J. of Law and Society 506.

COPUS, C., 'The Party Group: A Barrier to Democratic Renewal', (1999) 25 (4) Local Government Studies 76.

——'The Party Political Group: Model Standing Orders and a Disciplined Approach to Local Representation', (1999) 25 Local Government Studies 17.

CRAIG, P., *Administrative Law* (3rd edn., London, 1994).

——'Legitimate Expectations: A Conceptual Analysis', (1992) 108 LQR 79.

CRAM, I., 'Public Authorities, Political Protest and Judicial Review', (1995) 24 Scots Law Times 213.

CRAWFORD, C., 'Complaints, Codes and Ombudsmen in Local Government', [1988] PL 246.

——'European Influence on Local Self-Government', (1992) 18(1) Local Government Studies 69.

——*Local Authority Powers: The Way Forward* (London, 1998).

——'Powers for the New Vision', (1998) 1 JLGL 31.

——'Subsidiarity, Local Government and Privatisation of Services', (1997) 18 Holdsworth LR 3.

——'Trusting Experiments', (1998) 1 JLGL 8.

——'Where Judges Fear to Tread', [1982] JPL 619.

——and MOORE, V., *The Free Two Pence* (London, 1983).

CRIPPS, Y., *The Legal Implications of Disclosure in the Public Interest* (2nd edn., London, 1994).

CULLEN, H., 'Freedom of Association as a Political Right', (1999) EL Rev. HR 30.

CUMBERBATCH, J., 'The Quiet Revolution in Freedom of Speech: A Comment on *Derbyshire CC v Times Newspapers*', (1994) 45 NILQ 219.
DAINTITH, T., 'Regulation by Contract: The New Prerogative', (1979) 32 CLP 41.
——'The Techniques of Government' in J. Jowell and D. Oliver, *The Changing Constitution* (3rd edn., Oxford, 1994).
DAVEY, M., 'The Housing Act 1988', (1989) 52 MLR 661.
DAVIES, K., *Local Government Law* (London, 1983).
DE SMITH, S., WOOLF, H., and JOWELL, J., *Judicial Review of Administrative Action* (5th edn., London, 1995).
DEHN, G., and ROSE, N., 'The Case for the Public Interest Disclosure Bill', [1996] PL 235.
DISTRICT AUDITORS' SOCIETY, *Watchdogs' Tales: The District Audit Service—The First 138 Years* (London, 1986).
DOIG, A., 'Continuing Cause for Concern? Probity in Local Government', (1995) 21 (1) Local Government Studies 99.
——*Corruption and Misconduct in Contemporary British Politics* (Harmondsworth, 1984).
DREWRY, G., 'Mr. Major's Charter: Empowering the Consumer', [1993] PL 248.
ELCOCK, H., 'Leading People: Some Issues of Local Government Leadership in Britain and America', (1995) 21 (4) Local Government Studies 546.
ELIAS, P., 'Legitimate Expectation and Judicial Review', in J. Jowell and D. Oliver (eds.), *New Directions in Judicial Review* (London, 1988).
EMERY, C., *Administrative Law: Legal Challenges to Official Action* (London, 1999).
EMILIOU, N., 'Subsidiarity: An Effective Barrier against "the Enterprises of Ambition"', (1992) 17 EL Rev. 383.
ESCOTT, K., and WHITFIELD, D., *The Gender Impact of CCT in Local Government* (Manchester, 1995).
EWING, K., 'The Human Rights Act and Labour Law', (1998) 27 Ind. LJ 275.
——'Swimming with the Tide: Employment Protection and the Implementation of European Labour Law', (1993) 22 Ind. LJ 165.
FEINTUCK, M., *Accountability and Choice in Schooling* (Buckingham, 1994).
FENNELL, P., '*Roberts v Hopwood*: The Rule against Socialism', (1986) 13 J. of Law and Society 401.
FINN, P., 'Integrity in Government', (1991) 3 Public Law Review 243.
FORSYTH, C., 'The Provenance and Protection of Legitimate Expectations', [1988] CLJ 238.
FRANKLIN, B., and Murphy, D., *What's News? The Market, Politics and the Local Press* (London, 1991).
FREDMAN, S., and MORRIS, G., 'The Costs of Exclusivity: Public and Private Re-examined', [1994] PL 69.
————*The State as Employer: Labour Law in the Public Services* (London, 1989).
FREEDLAND, M., 'Government by Contract and Public Law', [1994] PL 86.
——'The Rule Against Delegation and the *Carltona* Doctrine in an Agency Context', [1996] PL 19.
GANZ, G., 'The Allocations of Functions Parts I and II', [1972] PL 215.
——'The Depoliticisation of Local Authorities: The Local Government and Housing Act 1989, Part I', [1990] PL 224.

GANZ, G., 'Legitimate Expectation', in C. Harlow (ed.), *Public Law and Politics* (London, 1986).

GEDDES, M., *Extending Democratic Practice in Local Government* (London, 1996).

GOBERT, J., and Punch, M., 'Whistleblowers, the Public Interest and the Public Interest Disclosure Act 1998', (2000) 63 MLR 25.

GRACE, C., 'Local Government Law: Components of a New Framework', in Local Government Information Unit, *A Framework for the Future* (London, 1997).

GRANT, E., and SMALL, J., '*Derbyshire CC v Times Newspapers* in the House of Lords: Molecular Rather than Molar Motion', (1994) 14 Ox. JLS 287.

GRANT, M., 'Central–local relations: The Balance of Power', in J. Jowell and D. Oliver (eds.), *The Changing Constitution* (2nd edn., Oxford, 1989).

——*Rate Capping and the Law* (2nd edn., London, 1986).

——*The Rehabilitation of Local Government: Vires or Virus* (London, 1990).

GRANTHAM, R., and RICKETT, C. (eds.), *Corporate Personality in the 20th Century* (Oxford, 1998).

GREENWOOD, J., 'Facilitating Officer/Councillor Relationships: Meeting the Post-Widdicombe Challenge', (1990) Local Government Studies 77.

——and WILSON, D., 'Towards the Contract State: CCT in Local Government', (1994) 47 Parl. Affs. 405.

GREER, A., and HOGGETT, P., 'Quangos and Local Governance', in L. Pratchett and D. Wilson (eds.), *Local Democracy and Local Government* (Basingstoke, 1996).

GRIFFITH, J., *Judicial Politics since 1920* (Oxford, 1993).

GYFORD, J., LEACH, S., and GAME, C., *The Changing Politics of Local Government* (London, 1989).

HARDEN, I., *The Contracting State* (Buckingham, 1992).

——and LEWIS, N., *The Noble Lie: The British Constitution and the Rule of Law* (London, 1986).

HARLOW, C., and RAWLINGS, R., *Law and Administration* (London, 1984).

————*Law and Administration* (2nd edn., London, 1997).

HARRIS, B., 'The "Third Source" of Authority for Government Action', (1992) 108 LQR 626.

HARRIS, N., 'Educational Choice in a Multi-Cultural Society', [1992] PL 522.

——*Law and Education: Regulation, Consumerism and the Education System* (London, 1993).

HARRISON, T., *Access to Information in Local Government* (London, 1988).

HEALEY, P., PURDUE, H., and ENNIS, F., *Gains From Planning? Dealing With the Impact of Development* (York, 1993).

HENNESSY, P., *Never Again: Britain 1945–51* (London, 1992).

HILL, D., *Democratic Theory and Local Government* (London, 1974).

HIMSWORTH, C., 'Poll Tax Capping and Judicial Review', [1991] PL 76.

HIRSCHMAN, A., *Exit, Voice and Loyalty: Responses to Decline in Firms, Organizations and States* (Cambridge, Mass., 1970).

HOGG, P., 'The Doctrine of Executive Necessity in the Law of Contract', (1970) 44 ALJ 154.

——*Liability of the Crown* (2nd edn., Toronto, 1989).

HOLDSWORTH, W., *History of English Law*, xiv (Aberdeen, 1964).

HOLLINGSWORTH, K., WHITE, F., and HARDEN, I., 'Audit, Accountability and Independence: the Role of the Audit Commission', (1998) 18 LS 78.

HOUGH, B., 'Local Authorities as Guardians of the Public Interest', [1992] PL 130.

HUTCHINSON, A., and JONES, M., 'Wheeler-Dealing: An Essay on Law, Politics and Speech', (1988) 15 (3) J. of Law and Soc. 263.

JENNINGS, SIR I., *Principles of Local Government Law* (4th edn., by J. Griffith, London, 1960).

JOHNSON, A., 'Making a Reality of Partnership', in Local Government Information Unit, *Turning Community Leadership into Reality* (London, 1999).

JONES, G., 'Herbert Morrison and Poplarism', [1973] PL 11.

JONES, M., '"Chairman's Action": The Courts, the Local Ombudsman and the Widdicombe Committee', [1987] JPL 612.

——*TECs and Local Accountability: Options for Reform* (London, 1996).

JONES, R., *The History of the Financial Control Function of the Local Government Accounting in the United Kingdom* (New York, 1992).

——*Local Government Audit Law* (2nd edn., London, 1985).

JUDGE, D., STOKER, G., and WOLMAN, H. (eds.), *Theories of Urban Politics in Political Leadership in Urban Politics* (London, 1995).

KEITH-LUCAS, B., 'Poplarism', [1962] PL 52.

KING, D., and PIERRE, J. (eds.), *Challenges to Local Government* (London, 1990).

KINGDOM, J., *Local Government and Politics in Britain* (Hemel Hempstead, 1991).

KITCHIN, H., *General Competence for Local Authorities in Britain in the Context of European Experiments* (London, 1995).

——'A Power of Community Initiative?', (1996) 3 Local Authority Law 7.

——'A Power of General Competence for Local Government', in L. Pratchett and D. Wilson (eds.), *Local Democracy and Local Government* (Basingstoke, 1996).

LABOUR PARTY, *New Leadership for London* (London, 1997).

——*Renewing Democracy, Rebuilding Communities* (London, 1995).

——*A Voice for London* (London, 1996).

LASKI, H., 'Judicial Review of Social Policy in England', (1926) 39 Harv. LR 832.

LAWS, SIR J., 'Is the High Court the Guardian of Fundamental Constitutional Rights?', [1993] PL 59.

LEACH, S., 'Introducing Cabinets into British Local Government', (1999) 52(1) Parl. Affs. 77.

——'The Strange Case of the Local Government Review', in J. Stewart and G. Stoker (eds.), *Local Government in the 1990s* (Basingstoke, 1995).

——'Strengthening Local Democracy? The Government's Response to Widdicombe', in J. Stewart and G. Stoker (eds.), *The Future of Local Government* (Basingstoke, 1989).

——and STEWART, J., *The Politics of Hung Authorities* (Basingstoke, 1992).

LEIGH, I., 'The Proposed Duty of Well-Being: Comparable Powers and Duties', in Local Government Information Unit, *Turning Community Leadership into Reality* (London, 1999).

LESTER, A., and BINDMAN, G., *Race and Law* (Harmondsworth, 1972).

LEWIS, D., 'Whistleblowers and Job Security', (1995) 58 MLR 208.

LEWIS, N., *Choice and the Legal Order: Rising Above Politics* (London, 1996).

LEWIS, N., 'Reviewing Change in Government', [1994] Public Law 105.
——and BIRKINSHAW, P., *When Citizens Complain* (Buckingham, 1993).
——, SEVERANTNE, M., and CRACKNELL, S., *Complaints Procedures in Local Government* (Sheffield, 1987).
LOCAL GOVERNMENT ASSOCIATION, *Leading the Agenda: Case Studies of New Political Management Arrangements* (London, 1999).
——*Leading the Agenda, No. 2: Further Case Studies of New Political Management Arrangements* (London, 1999).
LOUGHLIN, M., *Administrative Accountability in Local Government* (London, 1992).
——'Innovative Financing: The Limits of Legal Instrumentalism, Pt. II', [1991] PL 568.
——'Law, Ideologies and the Political-Administrative System', (1989) 16 J. of Law and Society 21.
——*Legality and Locality: The Role of Law in Central–Local Relations* (Oxford, 1996).
——*Local Government in the Modern State* (London, 1986).
——'Report of the (Widdicombe) Committee of Inquiry into the Conduct of Local Authority Business', (1987) 50 MLR 64.
——'The Restructuring of Central–Local Government Relations', in J. Jowell and D. Oliver (eds.), *The Changing Constitution* (3rd edn., Oxford, 1994).
——'Ultra Vires: Hail and Farewell', in Local Government Information Unit, *A Framework for the Future* (London, 1997).
LOVELAND, I., 'Defamation of Government: Taking Lessons from America', (1994) 14 Legal Studies 206.
LOWNDES, V., 'Citizenship and Urban Politics', in D. Judge, G. Stoker, and H. Wolman (eds.), *Theories of Urban Politics* (London, 1995).
LUSTGARTEN, L., and LEIGH, I., *In From the Cold: National Security and Parliamentary Democracy* (Oxford, 1994).
MACKENZIE, S., 'Subsidiarity: A Busted Flush?', in D. Curtin and D. O'Keefe (eds.), *Constitutional Adjudication in European Community and National Law* (Dublin, 1992).
MACPHERSON, M., 'Local Ombudsman or the Courts?', [1987] J. of Pl. and Env. Law 92.
MARR, A., *Ruling Britannia* (London, 1995).
MASON, D., *Revising the Rates System* (London, 1985).
MCAUSLAN, P., 'Administrative Law, Collective Consumption and Judicial Policy', (1983) 46 MLR 1.
——'Public Law and Public Choice', (1988) 51 MLR 681.
MEREDITH, P., *Government, Schools and the Law* (London, 1992).
——'Judicial Review and Education', in B. Hadfield (ed.), *Judicial Review: A Thematic Approach* (Dublin, 1995).
MILL, J. S., *Representative Government*, in *Three Essays* (Oxford, 1975).
MILLER, W., *Irrelevant Elections? The Quality of Local Democracy in Britain* (Oxford, 1988).
——and DICKSON, M., *Local Governance and Local Citizenship* (Glasgow, 1996).
MITCHELL, J., *The Contracts of Public Authorities* (London, 1954).
MORRIS, A., 'Equal Helpings: *Ratcliffe and others v. North Yorkshire County Council*', [1995] 4 Web JCLI.

MORRIS, G., 'The Human Rights Act and the Public/Private Divide in Employment Law', (1998) 27 Ind. LJ 293.

——'Local Government Workers and Rights of Political Participation: Time for a Change?', [1998] PL 25.

——'The Political Activities of Local Government Workers and the ECHR', [1999] PL 122.

MORRIS, P., 'Legal Regulation of Contract Compliance: An Anglo-American Comparison', (1990) 19 Anglo-American LR 87.

MUNRO, C., *Constitutional Studies* (London, 1987).

LEWIS, N., 'A New Way of Governing?', (1992) 64 Pol. Q. 316.

NAPIER, B., *CCT, Market Testing and Employment Rights: The Effect of TUPE and the Acquired Rights Directive* (London, 1993).

NARDELL, G., 'The Quantock Hounds and the Trojan Horse', [1995] PL 27.

NORTON, A., *International Handbook of Local and Regional Government* (Aldershot, 1994).

OLIVER, D., 'The Case of the Shorthand Writers', [1993] PL 214.

PAINTER, C., *Local Government and the Unelected State* (London, 1996).

PAINTER, J., 'Compulsory Competitive Tendering in Local Government', (1991) 69 Public Administration 191.

PALMER, S., 'Freedom of Information—Principles and Problems: A Comparative Analysis of the Australian Proposed UK Systems', in University of Cambridge Centre for Public Law, *Constitutional Reform in the United Kingdom: Practice and Principles* (Oxford, 1998).

PARKINSON, M., and Judd, D., *Leadership and Urban Regeneration* (London, 1990).

PERCY-SMITH, J., *Discussing Democracy: The Response to "Taking Charge: The Rebirth of Local Democracy"'* (London, 1996).

PRATCHETT, L., 'Introduction: Defining Democratic Renewal', (1999) 25(4) Local Government Studies 1.

——'New Fashions in Public Participation: Towards Greater Democracy?', (1999) 52(4) Parl. Affs. 616.

PRIOR, D., 'Citizens Charters', in J. Stewart and G. Stoker (eds.), *Local Government in the 1990s* (Basingstoke, 1995).

PUBLIC CONCERN AT WORK, *Local Government: Blowing the Whistle on Fraud and Corruption* (London, 1994).

PURDUE, M., YOUNG, E., and ROWAN-ROBERTSON, J., *Planning Law and Procedure* (London, 1989).

RADFORD, M., 'Auditing for Change: Local Government and the Audit Commission', (1991) 54 MLR 912.

——'Competition Rules: The Local Government Act 1988', (1988) 51 MLR 747.

RAJAK, H., 'Judicial Control: Corporations and the Decline of Ultra Vires', (1995) 26 Cambrian Law Review 9.

RALLINGS, C., TEMPLE, M., and THRASHER, M., *Community Identity and Participation in Local Democracy* (London 1994).

——and THRASHER, M., *Electoral Reform for Local Government* (London, 1991).

RANSON, S., 'From Reforming to Restructuring of Education', in J. Stewart and G. Stoker (eds.), *Local Government in the 1990s* (Basingstoke, 1995).

RAWLINGS, H., and WILLMORE, C., 'Local Government Act 1986', [1987] MLR 52.

RHODES, R., 'The Reform of Local Government: Revival of an Industry', 65 Public Administration 193.

RIDLEY, N., *The Local Right: Enabling Not Providing* (London, 1988).

ROGERSON, P., 'On the Fettering of Public Powers', [1971] PL 288.

ROSE, N., 'Whistleblowing: Time for a Change?', NLJ, 27 Jan. 1995, 113.

ROSEN, F., *Jeremy Bentham and Representative Democracy: A Study of the Constitutional Code* (Oxford, 1983).

SARGEANT, M., 'Transfers of Undertaking: A New Meaning?', (1999) 25 Local Government Studies 71.

SCOTT, C., 'Regulation Inside Government: Re-badging the Citizen's Charter', [1999] PL 595.

SHARPE, J., 'Theories and Values of Local Government', (1970) 18 Political Studies 153.

SHELL, D., 'The British Constitution 1991–92', (1993) 46 Parliamentary Affairs 1.

STEWART, J., 'Appointed Boards and Local Government', (1995) 48 Parliamentary Affairs, 226.

——'Recent Experience of Extending Devolution and Democracy in Local Government', in Royal Borough of Kingston-upon-Thames, *Extending Devolution and Democracy in Local Government* (Kingston-upon-Thames, 1996).

——*Reforming the Local Appointed Boards* (London, 1996).

——'Reforming the New Magistracy', in L. Pratchett and D. Wilson, *Local Democracy and Local Government* (Basingstoke, 1996).

——and STOKER, G. (eds.), *Local Government in the 1990s* (Basingstoke, 1995).

STOKER, G., *The Reform of the Institutions of Local Representative Democracy: Is There a Role for the Mayor–Council Model?* (London, 1996).

——and WOLMAN, H., 'Drawing Lessons from US Experience: An Elected Mayor For British Local Government', (1992) 70(2) Public Administration 241.

STOKES, M., 'Company Law and Legal Theory', in W. Twining (ed.), *Legal Theory and Common Law* (Oxford, 1986).

SULLIVAN, G., 'Reformulating the Corrruption Laws: The Law Commission Proposals', [1997] Crim. LR 731.

SUPPERSTONE, M., and GOUDIE, J., *Judicial Review* (London, 1992).

——and PITT-PAYNE, T., 'The Greater London Authority Bill', [1999] PL 581.

TEMPLE, M., 'Political Influence in Hung and Non-Hung Councils', *Local Government Policy Making*, July 1993.

THOMAS, R., 'Stag Hunting, Irrelevant Considerations and Judicial Review', [1996] 3 Web JCLI.

THOMPSON, H., and Game, C., 'Section 137: Propaganda on the Rates?', [1985] Local Government Studies 11.

THRASHER, M., and Rallings, C., 'An Audit of Local Democracy in Britain: The Evidence from Local Elections', (1999) 52(1) Parl. Affs. 58.

TREVELYAN, G., *English Social History from Chaucer to Queen Victoria* (London, 1978).

TURPIN, C., *Government Contracts* (Harmondsworth, 1972).

TWEEDIE, J., 'Rights in Social Programmes: The Case of Parental Choice of School', [1986] PL 407.

VICKERS, L., 'Whistleblowing in the Public Sector and the ECHR', [1997] PL 594.

VINCENT-JONES, P., 'Central–Local Relations under the Local Government Act 1999: A New Consensus', (2000) 63 MLR 84.
——'Competition and Contracting in the Transition from CCT to Best Value: Towards a More Reflexive Regulation', (1999) 77 Pub. Admin. 273.
——'The Limits of Contractual Order in Public Sector Transacting', (1994) 14 Legal Studies 364.
——'The Limits of Near-Contractual Governance: Local Authority Internal Trading Under CCT', (1994) 21 J. of Law and Society 214.
——'Responsive Law and Governance in Public Services Provision: A Future for the Local Contracting State', (1998) 61 MLR 362.
WADE, H., 'Prerogative and Procedure in Public Law', (1985) LQR 180.
WALKER, N., 'After Rates? The Community Charge in Scotland', [1987] PL 586.
WALSH, K., *Competitive Tendering for Local Authority Services: Initial Experiences* (London, 1991).
——*Public Services and Market Mechanisms: Competition, Contracting and the New Public Management* (Basingstoke, 1995).
——and DAVIES, H., *Competition and Service: The Impact of the Local Government Act 1988* (London, 1993).
WATCHMAN, P., and LOGIE, J., *The Local Ombudsman* (Edinburgh, 1990).
WEBB, S., and WEBB, B., *English Local Government* (London, 1922).
WEIR, S., and HALL, W., *EGO trip: Extra-governmental Organisations in the UK and their accountability* (Colchester, 1994).
WHITEHEAD, A., *Holding Quangos to Account* (London, 1995).
WILLETT, C. (ed.), *Public Sector Reform and the Citizen's Charter* (London, 1996).
WILLIAMS, G., *Salmond on Jurisprudence* (11th edn., London, 1957).
WILSON, M., 'Contracting Corruption', (1991) 17 (3) Local Government Studies 2.
YOUNG, K., and DAVIES, M., *The Politics of Local Government since Widdicombe* (York, 1990).
YOUNG, K., 'Party Politics in Local Government: An Historical Perspective', in *Aspects of Local Democracy, Research Volume IV: Report of the Committee of Inquiry in the Conduct of Local Authority Business* (London, 1986).

## OFFICIAL PUBLICATIONS

### Command Papers

*The Political Activities of Civil Servants*, Cmd. 8783 (1953).
*Report of the Royal Commission on Local Government in England*, Cmnd. 4040 (1969).
*Report of the Royal Commission on Local Government in Scotland*, Cmnd. 4190 (1969).
*Report of the Royal Commission on the Constitution 1969/73*, Cmnd. 5460-i (1973).
*Report of the Committee of Inquiry into Local Government Finance*, Cmnd. 6453 (1976).
*Salmon Commission, Report of the Royal Commission on Standards in Public Life 1974–76*, Cmnd. 6524 (1976).
*Local Government Finance*, Cmnd. 6813 (1977).
*Report of the Armitage Committee, Committee on the Political Activities of Civil Servants*, Cmnd. 7057 (1978).
*The Civil Service Government Observations on the Eleventh Report from the Expenditure Committee, Session 1976–1977*, HC535 Cmnd. 7117 (1978).

*Report on Non-Departmental Bodies*, Cmnd. 7797 (1980).
*Alternatives to Domestic Rates*, Cmnd. 8449 (1981).
*Department of the Environment, Streamlining the Cities. Proposals for Reorganising Local Government in London and the Metropolitan Counties*, Cmnd. 9063 (1983).
*Paying for Local Government*, Cmnd. 9714 (1985).
*Report of the Committee of Inquiry Into the Conduct of Local Authority Business*, Cmnd. 9797 (1986).
*Government Response to, The Conduct of Local Authority Business*, Cm. 433 (1988).
*The Citizen's Charter: Raising the Standard*, Cm. 1599 (1991).
*Competing For Quality*, Cm. 1730, (Nov. 1991).
Report from the Committee on Standards in Public Life (the Nolan Committee) Cm. 2850 (1995).
Government Response to Report from the Committee on Standards in Public Life (the Nolan Committee), Cm. 2931 (1995).
*Department of the Environment, Annual Report for 1996*, Cm. 3207 (1996).
Second Report from the Committee on Standards in Public Life, Spending Bodies, Cm. 3270 (1996).
*Government Response to the Report of House of Lords Select Committee on Relations Between Central and Local Government, 'Rebuilding Trust'*, Cm. 3464 (1996).
*Scotland's Parliament*, Cm. 3658 (1997).
*Excellence in Schools*, Cm. 3681 (1997).
*Third Report from the Committee on Standards in Public Life, Standards of Conduct in Local Government in England, Scotland and Wales*, Cm. 3702 (1997).
*A Voice for Wales*, Cm. 3718 (1997).
*Government White Paper: Building Partnerships for Prosperity: Sustainable growth, competitiveness and employment in the English Regions*, Cm. 3814 (1997).
*Your Right to Know*, Cm. 3818 (1997).
*A Mayor and Assembly for London*, Cm 3897 (1998).
*Modern Local Government: In Touch with the People*, Cm. 4014 (July 1998).
*Government Response to the Report of the Joint Committee on the Draft Local Government (the Organisation and Standards) Bill*, Cm. 4529 (1999).
*Local Leadership, Local Choice*, Cm. 4298 (1999).

**Parliamentary Papers**

*Select Committee on the Parliamentary Commissioner for Administration, Second Report for 1991/92: The Implications of the Citizen's Charter for the Work of the Parliamentary Commissioner*, (1991–2) HC 158.
*First Report from the House of Commons Environment Committee, Standard Spending Assessments*, (1993–4) HC 90.
*House of Lords Select Committee on Relations Between Central and Local Government, 'Rebuilding Trust'*, (1995–6) HL 97.
*Report from the Select Committee appointed to consider the draft Freedom of Information Bill*, (1998–9) HL 97.
*Report of the Joint Committee on the Draft Local Government (the Organisation and Standards) Bill*, (1998–9) HL 102-I, HC 542-I.
*Environment, Transport and Regions Select Committee, Local Government Finance*, (1998–9) HC 78–1.

Select Committee on Public Administration, Freedom of Information Draft Bill 3rd Report, (1998–9) HC 570-I.

**Series**

*Audit Commission Reports*

*Occasional Paper No. 7: Preparing for Competition* (1989).
*Passing the Bucks: The Impact of Standard Spending Assessments on Economy Efficiency and Effectiveness* (1993).
*Realising the Benefits of Competition: The Client Role for Contracted Services* (1993).
*Protecting the Public Purse* (1993).
*Making Markets: A Review of the Audits of the Client Role for Contracted Services* (1995).
*Watching Their Figures* (1994).

*Commission for Local Administration in England Reports*

*Annual Reports for 1988/9, 1989/90, 1990/1, 1991/2, 1992/3, 1993/4, 1994/5, 1995/6, 1998/9, 1999/2000.*

**Other Official Publications**

Cabinet Office, *Service First: The New Charter Programme* (1998).
Committee of Inquiry into the Conduct of Local Authority Business, *Interim Report* (1995).
Department of Education, *Report of a Committee of Enquiry: A New Partnership for our Schools* (1977).
——*The Nursery Education Scheme: The Next Steps* (1996).
Department of Education and Science, *The Admission of Pupils to Maintained Schools: Consultation Paper* (1987).
Department of the Environment, *The New Local Authorities: Management and Structure* (1972).
——*The Internal Management of Local Authorities in England* (1991).
——*The Structure of Local Government* (1991).
——and Welsh Office, *Handling of TUPE matters in Relation to CCT* (1994).
——*Report of the Financial Management and Policy Review of the Commission for Local Administration in England, Stage One: Prior Options Review* (1995).
——*Report of the Financial Management and Policy Review of the Commission for Local Administration in England, Stage Two* (1996).
Department of Environment, Transport and the Regions, *Community Leadership and Representation: Unlocking the Potential* (1993).
——*Government Response to Financial Management and Policy Review of the Commission for Local Administration in England* (1996).
——B. Walker, S. Delay, and A. Marsh, *Challenges to Local Authority Accounts* (1997).
——*Guidance on Enhancing Public Participation in Local Government* (1998).
——*Quinquennial Financial Management and Policy Review of the Audit Commission: Prior Options Assessment* (1998).
——*Modernising Local Government: The Ethical Framework* (1998).
——*Modernising Local Government: Improving Local Services through Best Value* (1998).

Department of Environment, Transport and the Regions, *Modernising Local Government: Local Democracy and Community Leadership* (1998).
——Regional Development Agencies, Guidance on the general principles of designation of voluntary regional chambers (1998).
——N. Mason, R. Turner, and Michael Dodd Consulting Ltd, *Local Authority Activity under Section 137, Local Government Act 1972* (1999).
——*The Beacon Council Scheme: Prospectus* (1999).
——*Protocol on Intervention Powers* (1999).
——*Local Government Bill: Consultative Drafts for Proposed Guidance and Regulations on New Constitutions for Council* (2000).
Law Commission, *Corruption; Consultation Paper No 145* (1997).
Lord Chancellor's Department, *Access to Justice: Interim Report* (1995).
——*Access to Justice: Final Report to the Lord Chancellor on the Civil Justice System* (1996).
Mallaby Committee, *Report of the Committee on Staffing of Local Government* (1967).
Ministry of Housing and Local Government, *Report of the Committee on the Management of Local Government* (1967).
*Report of the Committee of Management of Local Government* (London, 1967).

*Scotland*

*Report of the Commission on Local Government and the Scottish Parliament* (June 1999).
*Report of the Commission on Local Government and the Scottish Parliament: The Scottish Executive's Response* (Sept. 1999).
Scottish Executive, *An Open Scotland. Freedom of Information: A Consultation Paper* (Nov. 1999).

# Index

Lightning Source UK Ltd.
Milton Keynes UK
UKOW051609101012

200354UK00004B/2/A

9 780198 256984